BRONZE AGE MIGRATIONS IN THE AEGEAN

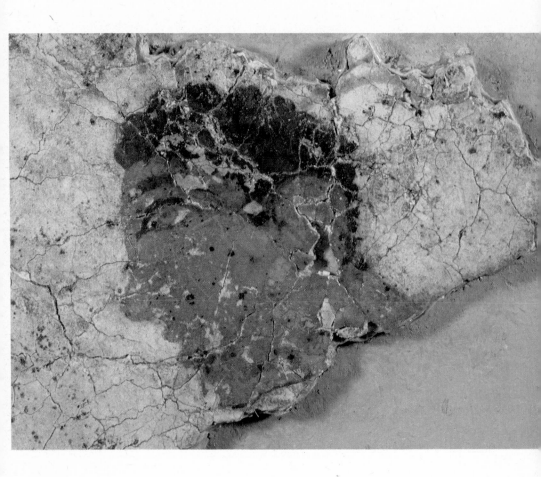

Thera. Fragment of a fresco with head of an African (?).

SP. MARINATOS

BRONZE AGE MIGRATIONS IN THE AEGEAN

Archaeological and linguistic problems in Greek prehistory

*Proceedings of the First International Colloquium
on Aegean Prehistory, Sheffield,
organized by the British Association for Mycenaean Studies
and the Departments of Greek and Ancient History
of the University of Sheffield*

Edited by

R. A. CROSSLAND
Professor of Greek in the University of Sheffield

and

ANN BIRCHALL
Assistant Keeper in the Department of Greek and Roman Antiquities, British Museum

NOYES PRESS

Published in the United States by
NOYES PRESS
Noyes Building
Park Ridge, New Jersey 07656

Contents

PART THREE: Linguistic problems

PART FOUR: Final discussion

PART FIVE: Editorial review and discussion

Preface

The Colloquium on Bronze Age Migrations in the Aegean Region, held in Sheffield, 24–26 March 1970, was proposed at the annual meeting of the British Association for Mycenaean Studies in 1969 as a successor to the first colloquium arranged by the Association, on 'The Minoans'. The subject originally suggested was the origin, distribution and significance of Minyan pottery. After the Departments of Greek and Ancient History of the University of Sheffield had accepted the Association's invitation to arrange the Colloquium, it was decided to widen its scope, in order to accommodate the unexpectedly broad range of subjects on which papers were offered. The support which the Colloquium received from abroad was most encouraging, and the participation of foreign scholars made a special contribution to its success. It was particularly gratifying to the organizers that we had with us as contributors and guests Professor Vladimir Georgiev, Vice-President of the Academy of Sciences of the Republic of Bulgaria, Professor Spyridon Marinatos, Director General of Antiquities of Greece, and Professor Ivan Pudić, delegate of the International Association for South-East European Studies. It was an honour, followed by sadness, that Mr. R. W. Hutchinson was with us, a week before his death.

Our thanks are due in the first place to the British Association for Mycenaean Studies, for sponsoring the Colloquium and informing its members of our programme; to the University of Sheffield, for financial help, entertainment and the use of lecture rooms; and to the British Council, the Great Britain—South-East Europe Centre and the International Association for South-East European Studies for grants which enabled members from abroad to take part. Next we thank Dr. Edith Johnston, the Warden of Tapton, the Hall of Residence in which the majority of members stayed, and her colleagues and staff there, for the notable pleasantness and efficiency of the hospitality arranged for them. We thank Mrs. Pauline Sykes, Mrs. E. M. Hudson, Mrs. G. E. Reed and Mrs. Doreen Spurr, secretaries in the Departments of Greek and Ancient History at Sheffield, for invaluable work in the preparation and running of the Colloquium and subsequently in the production of these Proceedings; and the staff of the Arts Tower of the University, and Mrs. Mary Blenkinsop, Miss Jacqueline Bourne, Miss Sarah Bradbeer, Miss Jeanine Hart, Mrs. Linda Haslehurst, Miss Susan Lathbury, Miss Lorraine Lightbody, Mr. Michael Monk, Mr. David Rudkin and

Miss Sally Sellars, students in the Department of Ancient History, for practical help of many kinds and the welcome which they gave to members.

For permission to reproduce figures and plates we thank the American
Schools of Oriental Research, for Plate 21; Antiquity Publications Ltd.,
for Figure 26.2; the Editors of *Athens Annals of Archaeology* for the *Frontispiece* and Plates 12, 13, 15, 14, 16 and 17; the Managing Committee of the
British School at Athens and Oxford University Press, for Figure 17.1;
the Syndics of Cambridge University Library, for Figures 7.1, 7.2, 7.3;
the Alfred Druckenmüller Verlag, for Figure 26.1; Harvard University
Press, for Plates 24 and 25; the State University of Tirana for Plates 28 and
29; and Dr. D. H. French and the University of Thessaloniki for the *End
Map*. Professor Sp. Marinatos and the Editors of *Athens Annals of Archaeology* kindly provided copies of the *Frontispiece* for insertion in this volume.
Some other acknowledgments are made in the text. Miss Valerie
Inkpen and the Cartographers of the Department of Geography at Sheffield
gave most welcome help in the drawing of maps.

Since the range of subjects covered by papers and discussions was wide,
we hope to have the indulgence of contributors and readers if we have not
presented all texts as effectively as we would have wished. Our extenuation,
if defects are severe, must be that synopsis of events in the Aegean and in
adjacent regions less well known to Classical scholars must be attempted if
Aegean prehistory is to be understood, and that juxtaposition of linguistic
and archaeological findings was a main aim of the Colloquium. Professor
M. L. Godart decided to publish his paper on 'Les tablettes du scribe 101 et
les depôts d'archives de Cnossos' in a forthcoming monograph, *Les tablettes
du personnel à Cnossos*.

Among lesser matters, transcription of Greek names proved troublesome,
as to many before us, and logic lapsed into compromise. For ancient Greek
names we took refuge in the advice of the Editors of the Annual of the
British School at Athens (*BSA* 65: 277-80) and have accepted the results of
our contributors' discretion, modestly systematized. The state of transcription of Modern Greek is vertiginous. The primarily linguistic Editor, at
least, would have preferred 'phonetic' transcription, i.e. a system which was
basically phonemic but offered some indication of the current pronunciation
of sounds of Modern Greek where needed by main groups of foreign readers.
But in the absence of an agreed system of this kind, compromise seemed best.
May we suggest that the Academy of Greece would assist Hellenic studies
abroad considerably if it would decide on an approved system in collaboration with interested societies and groups abroad, and then recommend it?
The practice which the Royal Hellenic Automobile Club has evolved for
transcribing place-names on road-signs in Greece seems to have much in its
favour.

Research in Aegean archaeology and Greek linguistics is active at present, and new thinking about prehistory in general is vigorous. So no organizer of a conference on any branch of Aegean prehistory should expect to resolve main outstanding problems to general satisfaction and produce a consensus which will last for many years. To define and draw attention to problems is a certain achievement in itself. We count it as a sign of success, as well as an honour, that Professor Marinatos and his colleagues in Greece arranged a colloquium in Athens in the spring of 1971 to continue discussion of some of the questions raised at Sheffield. At this meeting, it was decided that a continuing series of International Colloquia on Aegean Prehistory should be planned, of which the Sheffield Colloquium and that held at Athens should be the first and second. The third was held in the spring of 1973.

R. A. Crossland
Ann Birchall

August 1973

List of Members

Chairman of the Colloquium
R. J. Hopper
Professor of Ancient History in the University of Sheffield

Chairman of the British Association for Mycenaean Studies
J. Chadwick
Reader in Greek in the University of Cambridge

Organizing Secretary of the Colloquium
R. A. Crossland
Professor of Greek in the University of Sheffield

Members of the Colloquium
Professor V. I. Georgiev, Vice-President of the Academy of Sciences of
Bulgaria
Professor Sp. Marinatos, Director General of the Department of Antiquities
of Greece
Professor I. Pudić, University of Belgrade, Delegate of the International
Association for South-East European Studies

Mr. R. L. N. Barber	University of Glasgow
Dr. R. D. Barnett	British Museum
Professor A. Bartoněk	University of Brno
Dr. Dagmar Bartoňkova	University of Brno
Mrs. Marta Beér	Sheffield
Professor E. L. Bennett ·	University of Wisconsin
Mrs. E. L. Bennett	
Dr. Ann Birchall	British Museum
Mr. D. J. Blackman	University of Bristol
Dr. J. Bouzek	Charles University, Prague
Miss Jacqueline Bourne	University of Sheffield
Miss Sarah H. Bradbeer	University of Sheffield
Mr. W. C. Brice	University of Manchester
Mrs. Helen Hughes-Brock	Cambridge

Dr. H.-G. Buchholz	Universität Giessen
Mr. G. Cadogan	University of Oxford
Mr. W. Campion	British Institute of Archaeology at Ankara
Professor J. L. Caskey	University of Cincinnati
Mrs. J. L. Caskey	
Professor I. Chester Jones	University of Sheffield
Mr. J. T. Chesterman	University of Sheffield
Mr. J. N. Coldstream	University of London
Professor N. E. Collinge	University of Toronto
Professor J. M. Cook	University of Bristol
Mrs. J. M. Cook	
Dr. Anna Morpurgo Davies	University of Oxford
Professor B. C. Dietrich	Rhodes University, Grahamstown
Dr. Margaret S. Drower	University of London
Dr. G. P. Edwards	University of Aberdeen
Professor J. D. Evans	University of London
Mrs. J. D. Evans	
Mr. A. Fleming	University of Sheffield
Dr. D. H. French	British Institute of Archaeology at Ankara
Professor M. I. Garašanin	University of Belgrade
Dr. Monique Gérard-Rousseau	Liège
Mrs. Barbara Gibson	London
Professor Marija Gimbutas	University of California, Los Angeles
Dr. L. Godart	Academia Belgica, Rome
Dr. J. B. Hainsworth	University of Oxford
Professor N. G. L. Hammond	University of Bristol
Dr. D. A. Hardy	New University of Ulster, Coleraine
Dr. Gillian R. Hart	University of Durham
Miss Jeanine Hart	University of Sheffield
Mrs. Linda Haslehurst	University of Sheffield
Mr. G. S. Hathorn	King's Lynn
Professor C. F. C. Hawkes	University of Oxford
Mr. R. F. Hoddinott	London
Mrs. B. Hoddinott	
Mr. M. S. F. Hood	Oxford
Mr. J. T. Hooker	University of London
Professor Ph. H. J. Houwink ten Cate	Universiteit van Amsterdam
Mr. R. J. Howell	University of Birmingham
Dr. R. W. Hutchinson	Cambridge
Mr. R. H. Jordan	Belfast
Miss Susan E. Lathbury	University of Sheffield

Miss Susan Laycock	University of Durham
Professor M. Leroy	University of Brussels
Mr. G. D. Lewis	Sheffield City Museums
Miss Lorraine Lightbody	University of Sheffield
Dr. D. V. Luce	Trinity College, Dublin
Dr. J. H. McQueen	University of Bristol
Mr. T. Madigan	University of Sheffield
Mrs. Sp. Marinatos	
Dr. Molly Miller	Glasgow
Dr. Elpis Mitropoulou	University of Birmingham
Mr. M. Monk	University of Sheffield
Dr. Alessandra Nibbi	Oxford
Miss Mary Pearce	University of Sheffield
Professor E. D. Phillips	Queen's University, Belfast
Mrs. Gladys Pike	University of Reading
Mr. M. W. M. Pope	Oxford
Mr. N. Postlethwaite	University of Leicester
Dr. T. G. E. Powell	University of Liverpool
Mr. A. J. N. W. Prag	University of Manchester
Mrs. A. J. N. W. Prag	
Mr. A. Renfrew	Burren, Eire
Dr. A. C. Renfrew	University of Sheffield
Dr. Jane Renfrew	University of Sheffield
Professor L. J. D. Richardson	Trinity College, Dublin
Mr. N. J. Richardson	University of Oxford
Mrs. N. J. Richardson	
Professor R. J. Rodden	University of California, Berkeley
Mr. D. Rudkin	University of Sheffield
Miss Nancy K. Sandars	Little Tew, Oxfordshire
Dr. R. Schmitt-Brandt	Universität Heidelberg
Mrs. R. Schmitt-Brandt	
Miss Sally Sellars	University of Sheffield
Mr. S. J. Shennan	Fitzwilliam College, Cambridge
Mr. A. Sherratt	Peterhouse, Cambridge
Dr. A. M. Snodgrass	University of Edinburgh
Mrs. Christiane Sourvinou-Inwood	St. Hugh's College, Oxford
Professor Luigia A. Stella	University of Trieste
Mr. W. W. Stewart	London
Miss Angele Tamvakis	Lady Margaret Hall, Oxford
Dr. I. Tegyey	University of Debrecen
Professor F. J. Tritsch	University of Birmingham
Dr. A. Vraciu	Universitatea 'Alexandru Ioan Cuza', Iaşi

Note on Abbreviations, Transcriptions and Illustrations

With few exceptions, abbreviations used are as follows: for archaeological periodicals and other publications, those recommended by the Editors of the *American Journal of Archaeology* (*AJA* 65: 201-6); for linguistic literature, those adopted in *Linguistic Bibliography/Bibliographie Linguistique* 1968 (Heffer, Cambridge) and 1969 (Spectrum, Utrecht); for the names of ancient Greek and Roman authors, those used in H. G. Liddell and R. Scott, *Greek-English Lexicon* (New Edition; Oxford, 1925-40) and C. T. Lewis and C. Short, *Latin Dictionary* (Oxford; 1933). Additional and alternative abbreviations used are listed below. Classical Greek, Hellenistic and Byzantine names have been given in latinizing transcription for the most part. Phrases and vocabulary words of ancient Greek are transcribed according to the system adopted in the periodical *Word*. For Modern Greek, the practice proposed in *Annual of the British School at Athens* 44 (1949), 331-2, has been followed, except that the sequence *epsilon-iota* is transcribed as *ei*. Russian, Ukrainian and Bulgarian names are transcribed according to the 'Foreign Office' system, except that in Russian words both '*i* kratkoye' and 'hard *i*' ('yeri') are transcribed as *y*. Yugoslav Latin-alphabet orthography has been used for Serbian and Macedonian. On the transcription of Hittite and other languages written in the cuneiform of Boğazkale, see R. A. Crossland, *Transactions of the Philological Society* 1951, 122-30; E. H. Sturtevant and E. A. Hahn, *Comparative Grammar of the Hittite Language I* (1955), 12-26. Transcriptions of ancient Egyptian names are as in the revised volumes I and II of the *Cambridge Ancient History*. References to 'Linear B' texts are given in heavy type; on the classification used see M. Ventris and J. Chadwick, *Documents in Mycenaean Greek* (Cambridge, 1956) and literature cited; E. L. Bennett, *The Pylos Tablets* II (Princeton, 1958), *The Mycenae Tablets* II (*Trans. American Phil. Soc.* 48); J. Chadwick, 'The classification of the Knossos tablets', *Minos* 12: 20-50. The *Maps*, 1-5, are for general reference and to illustrate articles which are not accompanied by a map included as a *Figure*. References to *Figures* and *Plates* in the book are indicated by *Fig.*, *Figs.*, *Pl.*, *Pls.*; references to illustrations in works mentioned in the text by *fig.*, *pl.* etc.

Note on Abbreviations, Transcriptions and Illustrations

List of Abbreviations

ArchRep.	*Archaeological Reports*; supplements to *Journal of Hellenic Studies*
AthAA.	*Athens Annals of Archaeology/Arkhaiologika Analekta ex Athinon*
*Atti*ICIM	*Atti e memorie del Io Congresso Internazionale di Micenologia* 1–3 (*Incunabula Graeca* XXV, 1–3; ed. C. Gallavotti); Rome, 1968.
BUSS	*Buletin per shkencat shoqerore Tirane*; Tirana (continued as *Buletin i Universitetit shtetëror të Tiranës; Seria shkencat shoqerore*)
BUST	*Buletin i Universitetit shtetëror të Tiranës; Seria shkencat shoqerore*; Tirana.
CAH	*Cambridge Ancient History*
Cat.	E. Laroche, 'Catalogue des textes hittites.' *Révue hittite et asianique; fasc.* 58, 33–8; 59, 69–116; 60, 30–89; 62, 18–64.
Chronologies	R. W. Ehrich (ed.), *Chronologies in Old World Archaeology*. Chicago and London, 1965.
ENA	Early Neolithic Age.
GP	*Godishnik na narodniya arkheologicheski muzei.* Plovdiv.
Herod.	Herodotus
IBoT	*İstanbul Arkeoloji Müzelerinde bulunan Boğazköy Tabletleri* (*Boğazköy-Tafeln in archäologischen Museen zu Istanbul*). Istanbul.
Indo-European and Indo-Europeans	G. Cardona, H. M. Hoenigswald and A. Senn, *Indo-European and Indo-Europeans*. Philadelphia, 1970.
JdI/AA.	*Jahrbuch des deutschen archäologischen Instituts. Archäologischer Anzeiger.*
KBoT	*Keilschrifttexte aus Boghazköi.* Berlin and Osnabrück.
KritKhron.	*Kritika Khronika.* Iraklion.
KUB	*Keilschrifturkunden aus Boghazköi,* Berlin.
LNA	Late Neolithic Age
Mycenaean Studies	*Mycenaean Studies: Proceedings of the Third Inter-*

	national Colloquium for Mycenaean Studies, Wing-spread, 1961 (ed. E. L. Bennett); Madison, Wisconsin, 1964.
Nitra Baden Symposium	*Symposium on neolithic Baden cultures* (Nitra, 1969; Chairman, J. Toček; in press).
Obv.	Obverse
OR.	*Omagiu lui Alexandru Rosetti la 70 de ani* (Acad. Republicii Socialiste România); Bucharest, 1966.
Plovdiv Symposium	*L'ethnogénèse des peuples balkaniques: symposium internationale sur l'ethnogénèse des peuples balk-eaniques; Plovdiv,* 1969 (*Studia Balcanica* 5; ed. V. I. Georgiev); Sofia, 1971.
Plut.	Plutarch
Prague Symposium	J. Böhm and S. J. De Laet, *L'Europe à la fin de l'âge de la pierre: actes du symposium consacré aux problèmes du néolithique européen.* Prague, 1961.
RE(1)	Pauly-Wissowa, *Realencyclopädie der classischen Alter-tumswissenschaft.*
RE(2)	Pauly-Wissowa, *Realencyclopädie der classichen Alter-tumswissenschaft.* Reihe 2.
Rev.	Reverse
Salamanca Colloquium	*Acta Mycenaea, I, II: Proceedings of the Fifth Inter-national Colloquium on Mycenaean Studies, Salamanca,* 1970 (*Minos,* N.S. 12; ed. M. S. Ruiperez). Sala-manca, 1972.
SBoT	*Studien zu den Boğazköy-Texten.* Wiesbaden.
SCŞtB	*Studii şi cercetări stiinţifice: ştiinţe sociale* (Ministerul Invăţămîntului. Institutul Pedagogic din Bacău) Bacău.
SCŞtI	*Studii Şi cercetări ştiintifice: filologie* (Acad. R. S. R. Filiala Iaşi). Iaşi.
Ztschr.	Zeitschrift

List of maps and figures

List of plates

PART ONE
Introductory Papers

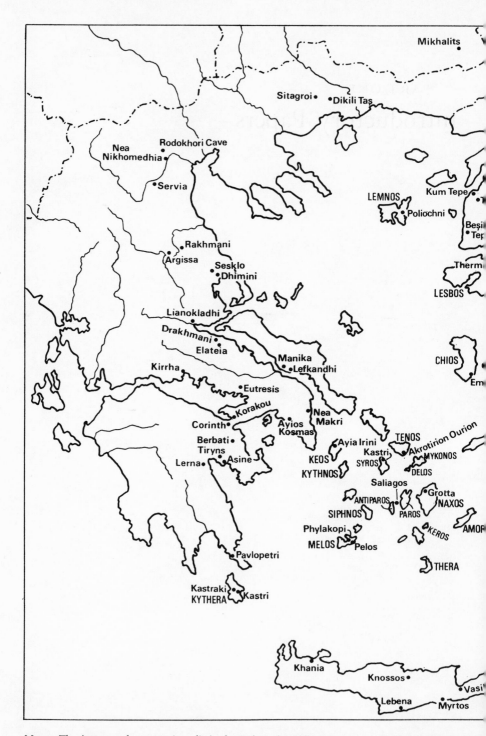

Map 1. The Aegean and western Anatolia in the Early and Middle Bronze Age, showing principal sites.

SEA OF
MARMARA

Lake İznik

•Yenişehir

İnegöl

•Tavsanlı

Kütahya•

lıkesir

•Yortan

•Akhisar

Manisa

•Beycesultan

S

ani

Linguistics and archaeology in Aegean prehistory

R. A. CROSSLAND

University of Sheffield

'PROGRESS' in science or scholarship at present often involves principally loss of confidence. Assumptions and methods that were taken for granted by pioneers or the *doyens* of the previous generation are suddenly found dubious or impracticable. Aegean prehistory is no exception. In the 1930s Sir John Myres and C. W. Blegen, for example, saw no objection to the use of both archaeological and linguistic data in reconstructing its events. Today, hardly anyone would claim to control the *corpora* of the two kinds of evidence in any branch of prehistory in which both are available, and even to try to survey or discuss both, however generally, will seem almost hybristic. All the same, it may be worth while to reconsider the problems, or perhaps one should say the possibilities, of correlating archaeological and linguistic evidence in deducing the events of a proto-historic or late prehistoric period. The attempt to do so has at least the merit, according to current tendencies in prehistory, of being itself a phenomenon of parallel evolution. The recent conference on Indo-European studies at Philadelphia and the Symposion on the Ethnogenesis of the Balkan Peoples at Plovdiv in 1969 were largely concerned with those problems, and they were prominent at the Colloquium on Hamito-Semitic Comparative Linguistics recently held by the Linguistics Association in London (Cardona 1970; Georgiev 1971; Bynon, T. and Bynon, J. 1970).

Correlation of archaeological and linguistic findings certainly does not appear to have become easier in Aegean studies during the past few years, and some may think that the chances of reaching agreed or even plausible conclusions through it are so poor that it would be best to give it up. That would mean that archaeologists and linguists would work in parallel and without liaison, and reach their own independent results without considering each other's conclusions. The more optimistic attitude is to accept that in most sciences greater sophistication in handling evidence seems to bring in at first more new problems than it solves old ones, and to decide that we ought not to be discouraged if this appears to have been the immediate result of improved methods and new theories in our own field.

Migrations

As the theme of this Colloquium contains the word 'migrations', we should perhaps consider how far these ought to be our main subject for discussion. The first circular should have indicated that the word was to be understood in a broad sense, including population changes of any kind. Presumably no one now expects to indulge in the lurid fantasies about prehistoric Indo-European migrations that used to be fashionable on the fringes of real scholarship: those visions of lusty, auburn-haired charioteers sweeping down from the North to revitalize flaccid Mediterraneans. (One wonders whether their real if subliminal purpose was not to compensate for un-colourful lives in the late second and early third millennia A.D.) More seriously, it should now be possible to take a balanced view of the 'Indo-European theory' and treat it like any other scientific hypothesis again. Reaction against its misuse in racialist theorizing, irrelevant to scientific study in any case, ought now to be over. The theory is now being questioned for a different reason. There is a strong tendency at present in prehistoric studies to minimize the importance of movement and mixture of populations in explaining cultural change. This has certainly been a keynote in recent work on Mediterranean and Near Eastern prehistory before the second millennium B.C. Here, not only has the role of migrations been questioned, but also that of cultural diffusion in contrast with independent cultural evolution and invention (Renfrew 1970: cf. Klejn 1970). This tendency is probably a healthy corrective in studies of late periods also. But it is perhaps being taken too far in their case. After all, there is a point in the history of many regions, for example the end of the Roman Imperial period in Europe, at which large-scale migration in tribes or large groups certainly did have substantial results in cultural change. Can we say that before a certain stage in the prehistory of a particular region such events or results could not have occurred? If so, where should we put the chrono-logical dividing line? The unbiased approach is presumably to see first what we can deduce about the equipment and social organization of peoples in the area and the period with which we are concerned and to draw conclusions about the kind of migration that is likely to have been feasible for them. Innovations like the domestication of the horse and the produc-tion of efficient waggons would have made a great difference. Such study should provide a frame of reference for judging what movements of population are likely to have occurred. The other key question is that of the nature and extent of the archaeological evidence which will indicate that a substantial new population has arrived in an area (see below p. 8).

The archaeologist's first task is to establish change in material culture in the region whose artefacts he is studying. He will only be able to establish, as distinct from deduce, whether such change was associated with an alteration in the genetic composition of its prehistoric population if he has sufficient skeletal remains; and some may consider it unimportant to know whether changes of the two kinds were associated or not. Similarly, the question whether change in culture was associated with linguistic change may seem to some to be of academic interest only. If so, one may defend academic interest: it may be thought natural to want first to deduce as much as one can about the characteristics of an ancient community and to decide afterwards what information about it is important according to overriding criteria. Otherwise, it may seem important to discover the physical type or language of a community only on one assumption: if it is thought that in the period or cultural phase that one is studying changes in genetic characteristics or language take place only when previously dis-similar communities have amalgamated or come into close contact. This may be particularly relevant when change of language is in question. It is now rather trite to observe that genetic type and use of a particular language or type of language are not necessarily associated. Some people suggest also that language is not an important cultural trait, relative to others, since communities will change their languages more readily than they will change other social habits. This suggestion may be another healthy correc-tive that has become an over-reaction. The myth of the racially 'pure' and culturally superior, as well as linguistically united, Indo-Europeans needed to be exploded. But the demolition may have been too indiscriminate. Much of the argument against assuming general association of language and overall culture-pattern in prehistoric communities has consisted of analogies drawn from phenomena in historical periods which are atypical: usually the ease with which Latin was adopted in south-western and western Europe, and the fact that large Negro populations in the U.S.A. speak English. These are not good analogies from which to deduce the linguistic developments that are likely to have taken place among late pre-urban and early urban communities in Greece and its vicinity in the third and second millennia B.C. In general, when one language is adopted in place of another, without actual amalgamation of communities having taken place, an unusually wide cultural difference will be found to have existed between those who have adopted the language and those from whom they have adopted it, as there was between the Gauls and the Romans; often in addition there will have been an exceptional social factor: that the adopting community has been under the political control of those whose language it has adopted. This implies that when a new language had been adopted in an area in earlier times when such factors were not present, it was most probably brought in by immigrants, even if they have left little or no trace in the archaeological record. Consequently, when linguistic evidence is available to use in study of a period like the Aegean Bronze Age, the first question that it raises is 'What may change of language imply in terms of change in population?' In prehistoric and proto-historic periods it will almost always imply *some* immigration or admixture. It will sometimes occur without being accompanied by other important cultural changes; and we do not know what factors determine whether the language of immigrants will be adopted by natives or that of natives by immigrants, in particular circumstances, when linguistically different communities have amalgamated or come to live in close contact; or indeed whether there is likely to be any regularity in human behaviour in such situations, though impressionistic conclusions about it are current.

Two other linguistic questions seem important for prehistorians. First, what may we deduce from the differentiation of a language into dialects (or of a prehistoric language into historical derivatives) about the history of the communities who speak them? Secondly, how far back in pre-literate periods can we make plausible deductions about the language that was spoken in a given area? The first question itself comprises three: (1) How is language differentiation thought generally to have taken place in pre-literate times? (2) Does linguistic differentiation imply differentiation of the speakers into distinct communities? (3) The third question is relevant mainly to deductions from place-names. Granted that we can recognize in a historical language a structure, usually of or in place-names, which is distinct from the main structures of the language and presumably retained from an ante-cedent language, how far back before the historical or literate period of the area in question should we assume this latter 'substrate' language to have been in use in it?

The second of these principal questions is concerned with a controversial development in linguistics: 'glottochronology' or 'lexico-statistics' (Lees 1953; Swadesh 1955). Its basic hypotheses are that changes in vocabulary are the most significant in the development of languages; and that the average rate of change in vocabulary is very nearly the same in all languages, at least over periods longer than a few centuries. If this is correct, it will be possible to deduce from the degree of difference in 'basic' vocabulary between genetically related languages the length of time that has elapsed since the communities that developed the dialects which were ancestral to them lost contact with each other. If such calculations are sound, they give us a method of fixing an earliest possible date for the original differentiation of the prehistoric languages which were ancestral to the various historical Indo-European language-groups and isolated languages (e.g. Armenian, Greek), and so perhaps for the separation of linguistically distinct prehistoric Indo-European communities; and they might also indicate which among them remained in contact until relatively late. Regrettably, the results of 'glottochronology' do not appear to be consistently reliable (Plath 1963; Polomé 1964; Haas 1966; Crossland 1971: 232–3). It will probably not be helpful in any case in reconstructing the development of the dialects of Greek, since these seem to have remained in close contact, and even most of those who regard 'glottochronology' as fundamentally valid admit that it may not be reliable over short periods. Another source of guidance in estimating how long prehistoric language-differentiation may have taken might be analogies in historical times. The difficulty here is that of finding processes of differentiation which can be followed over several centuries and which occurred under conditions, e.g. of material culture, which are likely to be similar to those of prehistoric periods under study. The differentiation of Latin can be traced, with some gaps, over more than a thousand years. But Latin was in an unusual 'socio-linguistic position' in the Roman Empire, and its rate and manner of differentiation may therefore not have been normal (Crossland 1971: 233).

The Aegean region in the Bronze Age and the early Iron Age

Bearing these generalities in mind, it may be useful to turn an outsider's eye on the problems of the Aegean region in the Bronze Age and the immediately following centuries, and to summarize what we may consider ourselves to know about it in that period, at the cost of repeating some matter that is obvious or well known.

1. We may consider it certain, as a minimum, that there was a well-defined Greek linguistic continuum from the first centuries of the first millennium B.C. onwards, extending over most of Greece, the Aegean islands, Crete and part of Cyprus. There was a clear difference between Greek and the languages of adjacent areas, with the possible exception of that spoken in Macedonia. Within the Indo-European family Greek seems relatively similar to Iranian, Armenian and Phrygian, as far as this last language can be reconstructed (Birwe 1955; Crossland 1971: 230–1, 235). But there is no question of its having belonged, within the family, to a group (comparable e.g. to the Germanic) which included one or more of these languages or Illyrian. The dialectal differentiation of Greek itself was well advanced by the fifth century B.C.; speakers of its most divergent dialects may have had real difficulty in understanding each other. But one of the main controversial questions in Greek dialectology at present is that of the date at which the differentiation of its principal dialect-groups began, and whether the traditional classification of its dialects into Attic-Ionic, Aeolic, Arcado-Cyprian and North-Western-Doric groups is valid. The solutions accepted for these questions will naturally affect conclusions about the grouping of Greek-speaking communities at the end of the Bronze Age and the question whether one, two or several waves of 'proto-Greeks' entered the Greek

peninsula during the Bronze Age, or at least moved from one part of Greece to another during it.

2. The second sequence of developments in Greece during the Bronze Age and the early part of the first millennium which should be examined as phenomena perhaps associated with immigration are the two successive appearances of advanced or urban civilization in it. To borrow terms from linguistics, both may be regarded as 'adstrate' or 'superstrate' phenomena to a large extent. That is to say, they were largely stimulated by influences from areas to the south or east of Greece: Crete in the case of Mycenaean civilization, Syria in the case of Hellenic. So there is no reason to expect a considerable, general difference in culture in the EBA and MBA, before Mycenaean civilization developed, between Greek-speaking areas, whatever their extent may have been in those periods, and neighbouring lands in which Illyrian or Thracian, for example, may have been in use.

3. The archaeologist will show us in the first place a 'congeries' of Neolithic cultures developing into or being replaced by Bronze Age cultures during the third millennium. He may or may not think that particular changes in culture which he observes were due to immigration; and he may or may not think them important, involving a radical change in customs and way of living such as large-scale immigration might have caused.

   The linguistic hypotheses and problems in more detail
The main questions that should be asked, and possible answers to them, would seem to be as follows.

1. Could people speaking Greek have been settled in Greece even before *c.* 2500 B.C.? The linguist will probably give the following answers:
   (*a*) A well-defined, direct ancestor of Greek could only have been in use by that time in Greece or anywhere else if the differentiation of Indo-European itself was already well advanced, and opinions differ about how early it did begin. If 'proto-Greek' had differentiated and become a distinct language by 2500 B.C., it might of course already have been introduced into Greece from elsewhere by that time. But there seems to be no way to suggest whether it was differentiated so early or not, unless one accepts 'lexico-statistical' comparison of the Indo-European languages as valid.
   (*b*) If one thinks that Greece was part of the original continuum over which Indo-European developed and then differentiated, one may naturally assume that one or more Indo-European dialects which developed into Greek were already in use in Greece about 3000 B.C. or even earlier.
   Unfortunately for those who like their frames of reference to be tidy, clearly different and mutually exclusive views are still held about the period

and region in which Indo-European evolved and then differentiated. Two hypotheses about this now seem to hold the field. One suggests that Indo-European evolved in a continuous process from the fourth millennium B.C. onwards, over most of south-eastern Europe. According to this view, Greece might have been part of the original IE-speaking continuum. The second, which I find more plausible, is that Indo-European took shape later, perhaps as late as 3000 B.C., among communities living on the western Asiatic steppes, or through linguistic amalgamation in the Pontic region (Crossland 1957:35–8; 1967: 49–52). If one accepts this, it is rather unlikely that any already differentiated prehistoric Indo-European language would have been introduced into Greece much before 2500 B.C.

2. If the problem is approached from the opposite direction, by working back from Greek as we find it in the Classical period and in the Mycenaean texts, one may ask whether there are indications that it had been adopted by a linguistically alien population, at least in central and southern Greece, as late as the second half of the second millennium B.C. No features of Greek as we know it point to such adoption. If it took place, then either the immigrants who introduced Greek were very numerous, or else the assumed preceding native population adopted Greek with unusually little change and with unusually little retention of their own previous vocabulary. Considered as an Indo-European language, Greek does not seem to have been greatly modified in line with the characteristics of a non-Indo-European language, or in line with those of another Indo-European language which had itself already undergone considerable modification, like Luwian (Crossland 1967: 28–9).

Consequently, linguistic evidence does not appear to give any clear indications about possible changes in population in Greece in the Bronze Age. For what it is worth, it seems to give one negative indication: that there was no strong non-Greek influence on prehistoric Greek during that period, either from a substrate language or from the language of non-Greek immigrants.

Hypotheses based partly on archaeological evidence
Finally, the main current hypotheses about Bronze Age Aegean prehistory which are based on both archaeological and linguistic evidence should be considered.

1. The first is a 'congeries' of theories which agree in regarding the appearance of 'Minyan' pottery in central and southern Greece *c.* 1900 B.C. as an indication of the arrival of some new ethnic element. This was first suggested clearly by J. B. Haley and C. W. Blegen (1928). Their idea that 'Minyan' pottery was introduced into Greece *c.* 1900 B.C. by a first wave of proto-Greeks, probably coming from the north, was the one most widely

accepted until about twelve years ago, though Sir Arthur Evans' firm belief that at least the aristocracies of the Mycenaean states were immigrants from Crete caused some resistance to it.

Since 1958 two new explanations have been offered of the appearance of 'Minyan' wares in Greece both of which treat it as an indication of immigration. The first was J. Mellaart's suggestion that 'Minyan' ware was developed by proto-Greeks who settled for some centuries in north-western Anatolia during the course of migrations to Greece from an area further to the north, and then moved to Greece in a major migration by sea, introducing the ware there (Mellaart 1958: 26–32; 1964: 47–50). Although this explanation was widely accepted, there seemed to be weaknesses of method in it, quite apart from questions of how the development of the 'Minyan' pottery style should be reconstructed: in particular proto-Greek migration from north-western Anatolia was deduced, and migration into Greece directly from the north was treated as excluded, while it was still left unclear whether southern Thrace (East Macedonia in current Greek usage) had been adequately explored for MBA sites or not (Crossland 1957a; 1957b: 40–1; 1967: 26–8). The explanation thus depended partly on an unjustified *argumentum e silentio*. Mellaart has now withdrawn the essential part of it, the suggestion that it was proto-Greeks who introduced 'Minyan' ware into Greece (Mellaart 1969: 172).

The second current 'Minyan-based' theory about proto-Greek migration to Greece is the one proposed by Professor L. R. Palmer and now apparently adopted by Mellaart (Palmer 1958: 93–7; Mellaart 1969: 173). Palmer's conclusion is that the 'Minyan' style of pottery was brought into Greece from north-western Anatolia, and that the people who introduced it there were 'Luwians', people closely related to the Hittites in language, whom he and Mellaart consider to have been settled in most parts of western Anatolia at the beginning of the second millennium B.C. The definition of 'Luwians' and the delimitation of the area in which they were living at that time are questions which need to be re-examined (Crossland 1968; see below p. 160). Palmer considers that his conclusion is strongly supported by the well-known occurrence of place-names in –ss– in Greece, Crete and parts of Anatolia, and he equates them with names in –assa– in Hittite texts which may be regarded as Luwian. I have pointed out elsewhere the objections to equating the formants in the Greek and Anatolian names directly (Crossland 1957a: 2; 1961; 1967: 28–9). More generally, the argument mentioned above against assuming substantial influence of a 'substrate' or other 'adstrate' language on Greek (the absence of apparent major modifications in the phonic and morphological systems of Greek) tells against the conclusion that Greece, or part of it, was Luwian-speaking in the first half, or the first six centuries, of the second millennium (Crossland 1967: 29). The lack of such apparent innovations is particularly surprising if it is assumed that Greek replaced Luwian in central and southern Greece, at least, as late as the fourteenth or thirteenth century B.C.

2. Finally, problems of the end of the Mycenaean period and the first centuries of the first millennium may need to be considered. The destruction and abandonment of almost all the main centres of Mycenaean civilization need to be explained, whether a 'Dorian Invasion' is postulated or not. Here again much recent discussion of the transition from Late Bronze Age to the early Iron Age in Greece has discounted the importance of migrations, although Greek tradition supports the idea that tribes or groups who spoke early Doric or north-western dialects of Greek moved into the Peloponnese from the north about 1100–1000 B.C., and the differences between Arcadian and the rest of the dialects of the Peloponnese in the Classical period, their relative positions, and the similarities between Arcadian and Cyprian are satisfactorily explained if the tradition is accepted. The lack of archaeological evidence for the arrival of new elements in the Peloponnese between *c.* 1200 and 1000 B.C., who might be identified with Doric-speaking immigrants, has been emphasized lately. In some recent discussions the decline of Mycenaean civilization is attributed to mass emigration from the Peloponnese, the inhabitants leaving either to escape the effects of some natural disaster, such as drought, or because raids from the north had alarmed them. It is suggested that the Peloponnese was largely depopulated for a century or more at the end of the second millennium or just after it (Desborough 1964: 4–5, 34–5, 77–82, 90, 97, 112–15, 221–57; Carpenter 1966: 34–42, 54–79: cf. Wright 1968). This explanation assumes that the Peloponnese and other areas of Mycenaean civilization were populous overall during the fourteenth and thirteenth centuries B.C.; and this assumption should be examined. On present evidence the 'urban' centres of the Mycenaean world were small in comparison even with those of Syria and central Anatolia in the same period. In fact, one might ask whether they should be regarded as 'cities' or 'urban settlements' rather than as palaces with attached quarters for people who were directly employed by them. The wealth of their rulers may have been just the fruits of effective overseas trade and perhaps also successful raiding and does not necessarily imply that the territories which were governed from them were heavily populated or generally rich. If they were not, then the 'collapse of Mycenaean civilization' may really have been a matter of the destruction of a few centres of wealth, artistic activity and specialized production for trading, which were supported by commerce and perhaps also by predation, and which did not have considerable resources of man-power, food or materials to draw on within their own territories. The theory of mass-migration from the Peloponnese at the end of the Bronze Age would certainly be more convincing if it had been demonstrated that

the number or size of settlements decreased substantially over a large part of it between *c.* 1250 and 1100 B.C. We need a new sub-discipline of 'palaeo-demography'. So far, only the work of R. J. Hope-Simpson and W. A. McDonald and the University of Minnesota expeditions in Messenia appears to have assembled evidence on which reliable conclusions about the size of populations at the end of the Bronze Age might be based. The events of that period in Greece are clearly another area of research where the provisional findings of linguistics and archaeology may at present conflict.

The purpose of this paper has been to point out certain problems of method and interpretation of evidence in Aegean Bronze Age studies that may deserve special attention, and to suggest that convincing solutions for some of them may depend on correlation, perhaps reconciliation, of the results of linguistic and archaeological research. Our studies should at least not lose vigour and impetus through lack of problems to stimulate them.

References

BIRWE, R. 1955. *Griechisch-Arische Sprachbeziehungen im Verbalsystem.* Walldorf-Hessen.

BYNON, T., and BYNON, J. 1970. *Proceedings of the Colloquium on Hamito-Semitic Comparative Linguistics.* (School of Oriental and African Studies, University of London) 1970; in press).

CARDONA, G., HOENIGSWALD, H. M. and SENN, A. 1970. *Indo-European and Indo-Europeans.* Philadelphia, Pa.

CARPENTER, R. 1966. *Discontinuity in Greek civilization.* Cambridge.

CROSSLAND, R. A. 1957a. 'Beycesultan: the preliminary historical deductions.' *Minutes of the Mycenaean Seminar* (privately distributed by the Institute of Classical Studies, London). 9 January 1957: 1–5.

——. 1957b. 'Indo-European origins: the linguistic evidence.' *Past and Present*, 12: 16–46; 13: 88.

——. 1961. 'The supposed Anatolian origin of the place-name formants in –*ss*– and –*tt*–.' *Atti VII Congr. Int. di Scienze Onomastiche* I (Florence; 1961, ed. C. Battisti and C. A. Mastrelli).

——. 1967. 'Immigrants from the North.' *CAH* (rev. ed.) I, Chap. XXVII/Fasc. 60.

——. 1968. 'Who were the Luwians?' *Proc. of the Classical Assn*, 75: 36–8.

——. 1971. 'The position in the Indo-European language-family of Thracian, and Phrygian and their possible close cognates.' *Plovdiv Symposium* (1969): 225–36.

DESBOROUGH, V. R. d'A. 1964. *The last Mycenaeans and their successors.* Oxford.

GEORGIEV, V. I. 1971. 'L'ethnogenèse de la péninsule balkanique d'après les données linguistiques.' *Plovdiv Symposium* (1969); 155–69

HAAS, M. R. 1966. 'Historical linguistics and the genetic relationship of languages'; in T. Sebeok, *Current Trends in Linguistics* 3 (The Hague): 116–52.

HOPE-SIMPSON, R. and McDONALD, W. A. 1969. 'Further explorations in south-western Peloponnese.' *AJA*, 73: 124–77.

KLEJN, L. S. 1970. 'On trade and culture process in prehistory.' *Current Anthropology*, 11: 169–71.

LEES, R. B. 1953. 'The basis of glottochronology.' *Lg*, 29: 113–27

MELLAART, J. 1958. 'The end of the Early Bronze Age in Anatolia and the Aegean.' *AJA*, 62: 9–33.

——. 1964. 'Anatolia *c.* 2300–1750 B.C.' *CAH* (rev. ed.) I, Chap. XXIV, i–vi/Fasc. 20.

——. 1969. Review of R. A. Crossland, *Immigrants from the North. JHS*, 89: 172–3.

PALMER, L. R. 1958. 'Luvian and Linear A.' *TPhS*, 1958: 75–100.

PLATH, W. 1963. 'Mathematical linguistics': in C. Mohrmann, *Trends in European and American Linguistics 1930–1960*. Utrecht, 21–57.

POLOMÉ, E. 1965. 'Considérations sur la valeur des données lexicostatistiques.' *Comm. et Rapports du Ier Congrès Int. de Dialectologie Générale* (Louvain; 1960; ed. A. J. van Windekens and S. Pop).

RENFREW, A. C. 1969. 'Trade and culture process in European prehistory.' *Current Anthropology*, 10: 151–69.

——. 1970. 'On trade and culture process in prehistory. Reply.' *Current Anthropology*, 11: 173–5.

SWADESH, M. 1955. 'Towards greater accuracy in lexicostatistic dating.' *IJAL*, 21:121–30.

WRIGHT, H. E. 1968. 'Climatic change in Mycenaean Greece.' *Antiquity*, 42: 123–71.

The archaeological evidence and its interpretation: some suggested approaches to the problems of the Aegean Bronze Age

J. D. EVANS

Institute of Archaeology, University of London

MY task in this paper is to encourage discussion by a general consideration of the archaeological evidence from the Aegean Bronze Age in relation to the theme of the present Colloquium. While not so forbidding as Professor Crossland's subject (see above, pp. 5-14), it is none the less forbidding enough, considering the bulk of the material itself and the literature concerning it. Fortunately, as this is an introductory paper, I am not so much concerned with conclusions as with setting the stage for other more detailed papers and discussions. Nevertheless, in trying to give it a manageable scope, I felt that it would be best to confine myself to the material from the Early Bronze Age and to questions of its chronology. Limitation of space is one reason; another is that Professor Marinatos has dealt with the succeeding period (see below, pp. 105-13).

My approach to my subject is necessarily that of a prehistorian who is not in any sense a Classicist or a philologist. While I hasten to say that I do not for that reason undervalue linguistic studies, my ideas about the relation that should subsist between archaeological studies and linguistic do differ some-what from those put forward by Professor Crossland. It does seem to me important that in a field in which various kinds of evidence, philological, literary and anthropological, as well as archaeological, are available, they should in one important sense be kept separate. Though comparisons of findings in each must be useful at all stages, it seems to me fatal to mix elements drawn from more than one in elaborating an argument. The kind of information provided by each of them is so distinct that when inter-mingled they inevitably weaken the reasoning. This must, in fact, be able to stand up first to judgment in terms of the strict logic of its own discipline.

Archaeology is the record of the consequences, in terms of more or less permanent modification of the environment, of human activity. It is, therefore, inevitably only a partial record, since a great deal of human activity does not lead to such changes, or at any rate not to recognizable or permanent ones. Some of the traces which do remain tell us a good deal about the people who left them. We can in fact ideally recover a relatively detailed picture of the changing pattern through time of human settlement and economy in any particular area and of changing fashion in equipment of various kinds. But the archaeological record usually does not tell us directly what the agents were that brought about the various changes. That we must try to guess as best we can, using all the available evidence, and any general principles about human behaviour and historical process which we may think fit to accept.

It is at this stage of interpretation that it is perhaps most vital for an archaeologist to have a mind unclouded by any considerations extraneous to the archaeological material itself. If it is not possible to decide a question on the basis of the available archaeological evidence, then it is better to suspend judgment than to call in other kinds of evidence to decide the matter. There are literally thousands of instances to show that to call in other kinds of evidence to decide obscure questions of archaeological interpretation is only to lay up trouble for the future.

Explanations of change in the archaeological record are essentially somewhat stylized, involving the use of such blanket conceptions as population movement, diffusion, and independent development, or some combination of them. As Professor Crossland has pointed out, the first, and to some extent the second, are out of favour at the moment. Yet no one really doubts that both played a part; and it is in fact a question of emphasis. It has been remarked that in the New World, where records of historical events are not available for pre-Colombian times, archaeologists have traditionally laid stress on the continuing process of development, whereas in Europe, where scholars were familiar with records of migration from Classical times and the European 'Dark Ages', they have in the past over-emphasized its role. Reaction has now set in, and it is on the whole a healthy one. At least it means that claims for evidence concerning migration will be carefully scrutinized, and that only a really overwhelming case will be accepted. A change in one item of equipment is no longer enough, nor is the mere evidence of destruction of sites, unsupported by something more concrete.

With this preface I now turn to the evidence for the Aegean Early Bronze Age. What sort of pattern does it now seem to show us, and how does this relate to possible population movements? First of all, I think we must take into account that the transition to the Bronze Age was a process and not an event, and part of a long continuing cultural development. In mainland Greece there is now evidence of three to four thousand years of settled life, based on an economy of mixed farming, which preceded the beginning of the Bronze Age. There is no reason to believe that this period was much, if at all, shorter in the Aegean coastal regions of Anatolia, though this remains to be demonstrated in detail. We start, therefore, with a settled population of appreciable size and long standing, which without any doubt contributed largely, and probably overwhelmingly, to the gene pool of the Early Bronze Age population. One further point may be noted before passing on. During the millennium or so occupied by the Late Neolithic (4000–3000 B.C.) there is of course archaeological evidence in Greece for contact with, and almost certainly for infiltration of people from, the lands to the north, beyond the Balkan range. This seems worth emphasizing for comparison with the situation during the Bronze Age itself. The various types of Late Neolithic black wares provide the main evidence. V. Milojčić showed that in Thessaly at least they can be associated with a people practising a different kind of animal husbandry from that of the contemporary Dhimini people, who continued the traditions of the Early and Middle Neolithic in this respect (Milojčić 1956: 182). Though the black ware tradition can ultimately be traced back to Anatolia (Weinberg 1965: 42), it seems most likely that it reached Greece by land from the north and east rather than across the Aegean. The northern connections are emphasized by the finds of Late Neolithic black-topped pottery, comparable with Vinča, at Nea Nikomedhia and the Rodhokhori cave (Rodden 1964: 115–17, 123), and by Weinberg's identification of the black ware 'legs' from Elateia and Corinth as parts of 'coal-scuttle' vases identical with those common in the Danilo-Kakanj culture (Weinberg 1962: 190–5, pls. 63, 65); though these, in conjunction with parallels between the painted pottery of the Danilo culture and some Greek Late Neolithic vases, may point to a sea route via the Adriatic rather than to a connection overland.

The Early Bronze Age occupied roughly the third millennium B.C. in the Aegean. On the Anatolian littoral the evidence all seems to indicate unbroken development of pre-existing Late Chalcolithic traditions into the first stages of the Bronze Age, as in the rest of Anatolia, though a number of localized pottery styles seem to have crystallized out of the less differentiated earlier ones. In the eastern Aegean islands this situation is reversed, and the pottery is uniformly of Troy I style, succeeding more varied Late Neolithic types. In mainland Greece, Crete and the Cycladic islands change is more evident, though the picture which now emerges is far from simple and each region seems to have had its own pattern of development. The overall impression is that the current of cultural influence was setting strongly from east to west in the Aegean at this time, but that the resulting changes in Greece and the islands were a very piecemeal affair. Though some movement of people may be involved, it was certainly not on the scale once envisaged, and seems in no sense co-ordinated.

Troy I influence is seen most markedly in Thrace and Macedonia, where it does seem to have something of the character of an extension of the Troy I culture itself, as suggested by J. Mellaart, especially in the more easterly areas (Mikhalits and Photolivos/Sitagroi; Mikov 1948: 18–20; Mellaart 1962: 11–15: Fraser 1969: 25–6). However, as work progresses it may well be that greater weight will ultimately be given to local elements (e.g. through study of the economic basis at Photolivos). Thessaly seems to have undergone a slower and less complete process of acculturation, though the relationship of the Early Bronze phases to those of the latest Neolithic remains obscure. In central Greece there is, from Eutresis at least, some evidence for continuity of occupation beyond the conventional limits of the Neolithic, though the first of the definitely EB phases there shows traces of Troy I influence again in the pottery and clay 'anchors'.

In Attica little is yet known of the earliest phases, but it seems significant that when a connected record does become available, in EH II, close contacts with the Cyclades are attested, with evidence that these had something to do with trade in obsidian and perhaps marble products, *inter alia*. It is worth remarking that the principal Neolithic site so far investigated in Attica, Nea Makri, shows that this trade was already important to the area at that time, and probably continued to be so right through (Theokharis 1956: 1–29). In the Peloponnese too the beginnings of the Bronze Age are still far from well defined, but seem likely to be varied from region to region, though it is striking that Cycladic contacts are again attested from many parts.

Crete presents a separate problem. After the controversies of the last decades it is now at last possible to rehabilitate and demonstrate beyond doubt the substantive existence of a fairly long Early Minoan period. A number of discoveries have contributed largely to this, including M. S. F. Hood's work at Knossos (the EM I well, EM III strata above EM II; Hood 1962: 295). Alexiou's Lebena tombs (Alexiou 1960), Tzedhakis' work in the west, and P. W. Warren's excavations at Myrtos (Warren 1968, 1969a). Finally my own excavations at Knossos in 1969 revealed substantial deposits of EM, including some well-preserved building remains, below the West Court and running under the Palace itself (Fraser 1970: 27).

At the first Colloquium of the British Association for Mycenaean Studies in 1968, Dr. Warren stressed the complexity of the process which led to the 'Minoanization' of Crete, whose beginnings go back into the Late Neolithic, and I would say, even earlier, into the Middle Neolithic (Warren 1969b). Various views are obviously possible of the elements in this, but it seems to me to have been a process which may be better explained largely by gradually increasing contacts with various parts of the central and eastern Aegean, than by any theory which involves large-scale movements of people. Finally, the Cycladic islands seem likely to show a similar pattern eventually, since though at present there is a chronological gap between the end of the Neolithic Saliagos culture and the earlier Bronze Age of Grotta/Pelos type, there are links between the two, and the later phases of the Saliagos culture seem to be moving in some respects in the direction of the EB forms (e.g. loss of white painted decoration, emergence of a blade industry in the obsidian).

If we turn now to the middle phases of the EB (I avoid as far as possible using the old numbered period terminology) we find a much greater uniformity developing in certain respects over large areas. In pottery, for example sauce-boats, *askoi*, the *depas amphikypellon*, *pyxides* and other shapes are very widely distributed. Much of the house-architecture, based on irregular complexes of roughly square or oblong rooms and with other details in common, which has so long been regarded as characteristic of the EB period in the Aegean, comes from deposits dating to these phases. Also, certain types of metal objects show a wide distribution in this period and may hold the key to the explanation of the other similarities. It has been forcibly pointed out recently by A. C. Renfrew, K. Branigan and others that this second phase of the EB in the Aegean displays a remarkable development of metal-using; indeed, this seems to be the first time we are really justified technologically in using the term 'Bronze Age' for the Aegean (Renfrew 1967: 14–8; Branigan 1968: 54–5). There seems to be no doubt that the demand for metal products must have had a profound effect in escalating contacts between all parts of the circum-Aegean world.

While the evidence from Greece and the islands seems to suggest that the transition to this stage was not attended by any upheavals or large-scale redistribution of population, the western Anatolian evidence leads to the opposite conclusion for that area. J. Mellaart has argued that the successive destructions of Troy I and IIa and the desertion of large numbers of Troy I sites which are not re-occupied till much later provide incontrovertible evidence of widespread violence; so does the sudden appearance of many north-west Anatolian features in the culture of Beycesultan XVI, since these seem readily attributable to the presence of refugees, probably on a large scale (Mellaart 1962: 23–6). However, Mellaart goes on to explain this as the result of an invasion from south-eastern Europe (Thrace), though the evidence is admittedly negative. Whatever the merits of this, it seems only wise to keep in mind the possibility of alternative explanations of the phenomena. Could they not have resulted from processes at work within the area itself? At all events, it seems to me that the choice of invasion as the explanation in this case may have been prompted by a desire to provide a convenient point of entry for Indo-European speakers into Anatolia rather than by anything in the archaeological evidence itself.

The final phases of the Early Bronze Age are of great importance for our present subject, because we are getting into the period which has often been associated with the first appearance of Indo-European languages in the Aegean. Anatolia again provides us with abundant evidence of violence at the beginning of this period. Not only Troy I, but a number of other sites with contemporary levels, both in Anatolia and the eastern Aegean islands, can be shown to have been destroyed and burnt at this time, which Mellaart puts about 2300 B.C. In 1964 he produced an impressive register showing the catastrophic decrease in numbers of sites from EB 2 to EB 3 in a further reinforcement of his argument (Mellaart 1964: 28–37), but it does occur to one to wonder whether all those which have not produced EB 3 material were really deserted at this time, or whether they simply escaped the violence and continued their earlier traditions. This is a suggestion which may not be substantiated but it seems worth while to look into whether it might be possible. (Mellaart also regards the introduction of a north-west Anatolian culture into Cilicia as occurring at this time, while others see it as happening contemporary with Troy II; Mellaart 1964: 30–1; Mellink 1965: 115.)

At all events north-western Troy II elements, hitherto restricted to a small area, are now found, sometimes in variant forms (e.g. the small grooved *depas*) in the south-west. Mellaart once more invokes an invasion from Thrace to account for this upheaval, though again there is no positive archaeological evidence which can be pointed to to substantiate it. He goes on to recognize in this the movement which brought the Luwians, already in the north-west as a result of the first invasion which destroyed Troy I, into the south-west. My only concern here is to emphasize that this theory is built of two elements: the archaeological evidence for upheaval itself, and the rough correspondence of the area over which it is traceable with that in which later it is shown that Luwian speakers were present. Is the link between the two really sufficient to bear the weight placed on it?

It is arguable that the backwash of these events in Anatolia was felt in Greece at the beginning of the third phase of the Early Bronze Age, but it did not affect all areas equally. The excavations by the British School of Athens at Lefkandhi have made it clear that people using largely wheel-made pottery of west Anatolian affinities established themselves in Euboea in a phase which must post-date EH II there; it is not an isolated occurrence, for similar pottery has been found at Manika, to the north of Chalcis, also, and there are traces of something similar at Ayia Irini (Agia Eirini) on Keos (see below, p. 30; Fraser 1970: 24–5). Attica seems to have suffered a setback in the last phase of the Bronze Age since objects of EH III type are rare there. Agios Kosmas, and perhaps other sites, were burnt and deserted. But it is the Argolid which at present offers the most thoroughgoing evidence of invasion and destruction. Lerna III was destroyed, the great House of the Tiles being burnt and reduced to ruins. Professor Caskey has shown convincingly that this was a disaster that affected neighbouring sites, such as Tiryns and Asine, also (Caskey 1964: 18). The argument is clinched by the evidence that in the final phase of EB Lerna was settled by people with different traditions from those of the Lerna III folk. Though it has not been possible to find exact parallels for the equipment of the Lerna IV people, there seems little doubt that its affinities are eastern. The 'small painted' *depas* cups are the equivalent of the small south-west Anatolian ones of EB 3, and tankards also occur; but the closest ties are said by Caskey to be with the painted wares in the later phases of the First Town of Phylakopi. The occurrence at Lerna of 'anchor' ornaments and a bossed bone plaque of Trojan type, however, point to the contacts with the north-east, as does an imported jar of Troy IV type (Caskey 1964: 18).

Thus it now seems clear that parts of the eastern seaboard of Greece were affected at the time indicated by widespread disruption which might well be connected with the troubles attested in western Anatolia at the end of EB 2 there. The Phylakopi I culture seems to have been introduced to Melos by the same agency, and according to Renfrew there is evidence that the older Keros/Syros culture which was dominant in the Middle phases of the EBA in the Cyclades continued in islands like Amorgos and southern Naxos in a later form (Renfrew 1967: 8–9, 14–15). The interior of the Peloponnese, on Caskey's interpretation of the rather imperfect archaeological evidence, also felt the weight of this invasion—for it seems to have been no less—some sites being re-occupied but many not (Caskey 1964: 15–20).

Further north in Greece the effects seem to have been much less severe. At Eutresis there is no sign of a catastrophe, but some features of the pottery attest change. Sauceboats die out and tankards and various other new forms appear. Contacts with the Cyclades seem to be attested by the appearance of a narrow-spouted jug shape which appears there in Phylakopi I, and a few fragments of dark-on-light ware have been found. Destruction at Eutresis came at the end of the third phase of EB and is perhaps of more local significance than the EB 2 destruction of Lerna. Further north there is little evidence of any happenings comparable to those of the Peloponnese at the end of Lerna III. To the south, again, in Crete, the events of this time made scarcely a ripple. Certainly objects of Cycladic origin, such as incised and impressed *pyxides* of clay, of types found in Phylakopi I, and developed types of figurine, become relatively common as imports in EM III; but the development of the Minoan culture was not interrupted, and the creation of the dark-on-light style of painted pottery was probably a local affair.

We certainly have evidence, then, of fairly widespread disruption and re-organization in large parts of the Aegean towards the end of the EBA, and it seems possible to argue that they are interrelated. It seems to me questionable, however, whether these happenings can be satisfactorily correlated with the appearance of new languages or peoples from outside the Aegean area at that time.

The transition to the MBA in western Anatolia is marked by continuity of cultural tradition, but a rapidly accelerated rate of progress. Only at Troy among the excavated sites is there a significant change, with the appearance of the so-called 'Grey Minyan' ware, and even this change seems now to have a very different significance from the one once attributed to it. We owe a considerable debt to J. Mellaart and D. H. French for trying to set this phenomenon in its true perspective, by illuminating the western Anatolian background of its emergence. According to Mellaart, 'Minyan' wares developed in north-western Anatolia out of the red and grey wares of Troy v tradition, the soapy quality being first developed in an area lying to the east of Troy itself in the Marmara and İznik regions. He argues that it belongs firmly in the earlier north-west Anatolian tradition, which is present also in Troy v, and that though a ware with special qualities, it belongs with the red and ordinary grey wares of that phase in other parts of the region. Even the pattern burnish of Troy v is found on wares with the true 'Minyan' feel at other sites. In the following period (Troy vi) however, pattern burnish was not used at Troy: thus it is not found on the Troy vi 'Minyan' and this has helped to confuse the issue (Mellaart 1964: 48).

Mellaart's original suggestion that Middle Helladic Grey Minyan wares might be derived from north-western Anatolia has now been abandoned both by French and himself (French 1967: 62, 64; Mellaart 1969: 172–3) but their surveys have nevertheless thrown new light on developments in Anatolia at this time, and have shown also that other features taken as diagnostic of Troy vi have a wide distribution inland behind the Aegean and Marmara as far as the western areas of the Anatolian plateau. On the opposite shores of the Aegean recent work has also illuminated the Minyan problem in quite a new way. At Lerna the first occurrence of Minyan ware is in the later levels of Lerna iv where it is used for bowls which are also known in thick-slipped red, brown or black ware. Some of these 'Minyan' type bowls are wheel-made, as are also some other pots. A parallel appearance of Minyan before what was once thought to be its due time is also now attested from Lefkandhi in Euboea. Here it is found in the phase following the one already referred to above, which itself seems to post-date the EH ii phase at Lefkandhi. Here, in Lefkandhi ii, it appears alongside a new type of coarse ware with knobs or warts on the shoulder, sometimes in pairs; a type which continues to appear throughout the MH levels of the site. The Lefkandhi ii Minyan was mostly hand-made and seems experimental. The fabric was rather coarse and grey-brown in colour, though there are a few pieces of fine grey, wheel-made ware. Bowls with everted rim were characteristic. Together with the varieties of pottery there were some which seemed to indicate some survival of the traditions of Lefkandhi i. Finally, there was dark-on-light patterned ware of the type found at Lerna iv and in the Argolid generally and at least one 'ouzo' cup of Lerna iv type. Thus

French's equation of Lefkandhi I with the earlier part of Lerna IV and Howell's of Lefkandhi II with the later seem fully justified (French and Howell 1968: 8–9). What interpretation can be put on this evidence?

It is certainly clear that in Greece, as well as Anatolia, Minyan ware was being made before the beginning of the MBA, though it appears after the beginning of EH III, as defined at Lerna. Can it therefore be taken to indicate the arrival of new people, as was long thought? The Lefkandhi evidence might suggest that it could, but there seems little to suggest a break in the continuity of Lerna IV. The production of Minyan ware could be taken as a technical innovation which was widely taken up and developed because it allowed the potter to make wares which reproduced some of the qualities of metal vessels (cf. Crossland 1967: 26–7). At a time when these must have been highly prized but rather rare this would be understandable. Minyan ware itself seems to be an Aegean phenomenon, whatever the background to its development. Obviously much about that background still remains to be discussed.

To sum up, the Bronze Age seems to have begun in Greece in a somewhat patchy way, the evidence indicating that western Anatolia was a powerful focus within the Aegean from which influence and perhaps people moved westwards. The middle phases of the EBA seem to represent a development due to quickening intercourse between the various parts of the region, and it is only at the end of this phase, and during the following, final phase, that we have evidence which must be taken to indicate serious upheavals, which may be connected with those of western Anatolia, occurring there at the end of EB 2. It is clear, at all events, that there was a temporary lowering of the standard of living in the region in the final phase of the EBA and the earlier part of the MBA.

Can these events be linked with substantial movements of people into the Aegean region from outside? I have taken the view here that they need not be, but that they could be explained in terms of an explosion within the Aegean world itself. Others present evidence for an opposite point of view. This evidence needs to be carefully weighed. Three criteria which ought to be applied are how far it is scattered, how far it makes a consistent whole, and what is the scale of movement implied.

References

ALEXIOU, S. 1960. 'New light on Minoan dating: Early Minoan tombs at Lebena.' *ILN*, 6 August 1960.
BRANIGAN, K. 1968. *Copper and Bronze working in Early Bronze Age Crete* (*Studies in Mediterranean Archaeology*, 19). Lund.

CASKEY, J. L. 1964. 'Greece, Crete and the Aegean Islands in the Early Bronze Age.' *CAH* (rev. ed.) I, Chap. XXVIa/Fasc. 24.

CROSSLAND, R. A. 1967. 'Immigrants from the North.' *CAH* (rev. ed.) I, Chap. XXVII/Fasc. 60.

FRASER, P. M. 1969. 'Archaeology in Greece, 1968–69.' *ArchRep*, 15/ *JHS*. 89: 3–39.

——. 1970. 'Archaeology in Greece, 1969–70.' *ArchRep*, 16/ *JHS*, 90: 3–31.

FRENCH, D. H. 1967. 'Prehistoric sites in north-west Anatolia I. The İznik area.' *AnatStud*, 17: 49–96.

—— and HOWELL, R. J. 1968. In M. R. Popham and L. H. Sackett, *Excavations at Lefkandi, Euboea, 1964–66*: 8–9.

HOOD, M. S. F. 1962. 'Knossos.' *Deltion* 17. *Khron.*: 294–6.

MELLAART, J. 1962. 'Anatolia *c.* 4000–2300 B.C.' *CAH* (rev. ed.) I, Chap. XVII/Fasc. 8.

——. 1964. 'Anatolia *c.* 2300–1750 B.C.' *CAH* (rev. ed.) I, Chap. XXIV, i–vi/Fasc.20.

——. 1969. Review of R. A. Crossland, *Immigrants from the North*. *JHS*, 89: 172–3.

MELLINK, M. 1965. 'Anatolian chronology' in R. W. Ehrich, *Chronologies*: 101–31.

MIKOV, V. 1948. *Razkopi i Proucvaniya* I. Sofia.

MILOJČIĆ, V. 1956. 'Bericht über Ausgrabungen in Thessalien 1958. I.' *JdI./AA*, 71 (1956): 142–83.

RENFREW, A. C. 1967. 'Cycladic metalwork and the Early Aegean Bronze Age.' *AJA*, 71: 1–20.

RODDEN, R. J. 1964. 'Recent discoveries in prehistoric Macedonia.' *Balkan Studies*, 5: 109–24.

THEOKHARIS, D. R. 1956. 'Nea Makri. Eine grosse neolithische Siedlung in der Nähe von Marathon.' *AthMitt*, 71: 1–29.

WARREN, P. M. 1968. 'A textile town—4,500 years ago?' *ILN*, 17 February 1968.

——. 1969a. 'Minoan village on Crete.' *ILN*, 8 February 1969.

——. 1969b. 'The origins of the Minoans.' *BICS*, 16: 156–7.

WEINBERG, S. S. 1962. 'Excavations at prehistoric Elateia, 1959.' *Hesperia*, 31: 190–5.

——. 1965. 'The Stone Age in the Aegean,' *CAH* (rev. ed.) I, Chap. X/Fasc. 36.

PART TWO

Archaeological problems of the Bronze Age in the Aegean and Anatolia

1
Archaeology of the Early Bronze Age

The Early Bronze Age at Ayia Irini in Keos: preliminary notes

J. L. CASKEY

University of Cincinnati

THE site of Ayia Irini is on a small promontory near the inner end of a great land-locked bay on the north-western coast of the island of Keos. One of the principal sea lanes in this part of the Aegean runs past it, and the harbour must have been used often by mariners since the earliest days of sea-faring.

Excavations conducted by the University of Cincinnati, under the auspices of the American School of Classical Studies in Athens and as authorized by the Greek Archaeological Service, have cleared large parts of the ancient town. Most of the buildings uncovered in the campaigns of 1960–9 are, necessarily, those nearest to the surface; they belong to a period of great prosperity, corresponding in date to that of the later palaces in Crete, MM III to LM IB. Many had deep basement rooms or cellars, which were used presumably for storage of goods. To build them it was necessary to dig deep into the underlying earth and debris, a process which removed most of the remains of earlier habitations. In the greater part of the site, therefore, it has been impossible to learn much about the more ancient settlements, although stray potsherds and a few miscellaneous objects showed that the place had indeed been populated from very early times.

In recent years, however, good luck has led us to some accessible and remarkably well preserved structures in the west-central part of the town: first, in 1967–8, a long stretch of early fortification wall with gateway and tower, belonging to the older phases of the Middle Bronze Age; then, in 1969, at lower levels, a series of rooms which were occupied in the Early Bronze Age (Pl. 2).

Masonry of this earliest period is of a characteristic and pleasing quality, the walls generally being straight and true, composed of small flat stones neatly laid, the doorways trim and fitted with pivot stones to hold the door-posts. Four rooms have been cleared and walls of others have been found in various soundings. Nearby, projecting outward from the main area of the houses, there was a heavier building which served some other purpose. Parts of it were destroyed by later constructions. We suppose that it was connected in one way or another with the principal supply of fresh water, since the place of a natural source, which in Mycenaean times was to be enclosed by a spring chamber, is only a few metres away.

Most of these buildings were discovered in the latest season of digging; neither they nor the objects found in them have yet been studied in detail. Our preliminary observations suggest that two main phases of occupation in the EBA are represented. The first is marked by the presence of sauceboats in abundance, along with other pottery characteristic of EH II (Pl. 1), four examples of Cycladic marble figurines, and part of an amusing theriomorphic pot (Pl.3) very similar to one found long ago in Syros (National Museum, Athens, No. 6176; Zervos 1957: 180–1, pl. 238–9). No signs of burning or sudden catastrophe are evident at the end of this phase. The succeeding occupation, however, was of a somewhat different character. Although certain of the old rooms appear to have been used again, and new ones added in the same distinctive style of masonry, the pottery now shows changes in fabric and shapes. Most notable are deep plates and shallow bowls in red-brown and black burnished ware, jugs with globular bodies and tall splaying rims, and two *depa amphikypella* of familiar Trojan type. It is to be noted that the patterned wares of EH III (e.g. the dark-on-light version which is common in the Argolid and the light-on-dark of Phocis and Boeotia) are not found at Ayia Irini.

The chronology of these settlements and their relationship to others in the Aegean area remain to be determined. Clearly at one time there were affinities with the material culture of EH III on the mainland; thereafter with another culture which was derived in part, directly or indirectly, from Anatolia. Burnished pottery of the latter phase finds very close parallels in the earliest major deposits yet tested at Lefkandhi in Euboea, and a number of the typical jugs are known to have come from Siphnos, Syros, and Naxos (e.g. National Museum Nos. 4943–4, 5026, 6127.)

References

ZERVOS, C. 1957. *L'art des Cyclades du début à la fin de l'âge du bronze, 2500–1100 avant notre ère*. Paris.

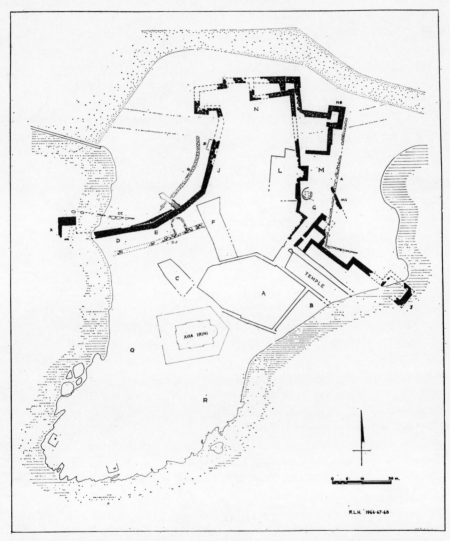

Fig. 3.1. Ayia Irini, Keos. General plan of the site. Wall DJ, fortifications of the Middle Bronze Age, early phases. Houses of the Early Bronze Age have been found chiefly between Buildings C and F.

Kythera: the change from Early Helladic to Early Minoan

J. N. COLDSTREAM

Bedford College, University of London

STUDENTS of the Early Bronze Age have given much thought to the relations between the three main cultural areas of the Aegean: the southern mainland, the Cyclades and Crete. In the view of most scholars today, it is only in the second phase that these relations were at all close. Early Bronze 2 is usually seen as a long period of peaceful progress in the civilized arts, in the skills of metalworking, and in commercial exchanges within the Aegean. On the whole it is a calm and stable period, never disturbed by invasion until the very end. On the mainland one thinks of the steady development of Lerna, where the House of Tiles represents the culmination of seven architectural phases; and in Crete, the equally steady accumulation of burials in the family vaults of the Messara. Yet at some time in the middle of this period, there is evidence of a slight ripple on an otherwise calm surface.

Between the three main cultural areas, the island of Kythera occupies a fairly central position: ten miles from the southern Peloponnese, sixty miles from western Crete, and seventy miles from Melos. The best land on the island lies in the Palaiopolis valley on the east coast; that is where most of the ancient inhabitants had the sense to live. In 1963–5, excavations were conducted by the Pennsylvania University Museum and the British School of Archaeology at Athens under the direction of Professor G. L. Huxley (preliminary report: Huxley and Coldstream 1966: 29). The main site was the promontory of Kastri, where a settlement of Minoan type goes well back into the Early Bronze Age. Under houses of the LM IB period were found many rubbish deposits representing the earlier phases. The earliest, resting on natural soil, contained a mixture of EM II, EM III and MM IA, in terms of the Cretan sequence. But the Early Minoan people were not the first settlers in the area. About a hundred metres inland is a small spur which the locals call Kastraki; there a trial trench was dug in a circular rock-cut pit three metres in diameter and five metres deep. This produced pottery of mainland type going back to the beginning of the Bronze Age, and ending somewhere in EH II. As at Kastri, no contemporary house walls were found; in fact, the only structure there was an early Byzantine building partly overlying the pit. A scatter of EH I–II sherds could be followed further inland, on the other side of the modern road; but, apart from the deep pit, Kastraki is so badly eroded that any search for EH house walls might prove a forlorn quest. So we are left with two groups of EBA pottery from neighbouring sites, each probably covering a long period of time, and yet quite distinct from one another in date and in character.

Conspicuous among the Kastraki sherds (Pl. 4) is a fine red ware, slipped and burnished, sometimes with incised decoration filled with white paste (1–2). This is EH I, the earliest known pottery from Kythera; Mr. R. Howell kindly drew our attention to the very similar ware from Eutresis in Boeotia (Caskey and Caskey 1960: 139–40, Group III). But in the same rubbish fill are some sherds equally typical of EH II (Pl. 5): mainly sauceboats (14) and saucers with incurving rims (17). The micaceous red pieces (e.g. 14, 17, 23, 24) are probably local; but some fine yellow sherds (e.g. 18, 19) may well be imports from the Argolid. There are also a few pieces of *Urfirnis* ware (e.g. 15, 16), probably also imported. On the evidence of these scraps it is hard to fix the lower terminus of this deposit with any precision. In the earlier excavations at Eutresis, high sauceboat feet like 22 seemed to be early in EH II (Goldman 1931: 94); but according to Professor Caskey's Lernaean sequence, semi-cylindrical sauceboats like 14 are of his Type III, not the earliest, and not the very latest (Caskey 1960; 290, fig. I III). Among the coarse wares, a corner of a large baking tray bears '*kerbschnitt*' ornament (impressed triangles); this feature might suggest Cycladic influence, yet it also occurs at many mainland sites, and even as far west as Lefkas (Dörpfeld 1927: *Beilage*, 61b, 68b).

The EM deposit at Kastri is of a wholly different character. Plates 5, 6 and 7 show some of the finer wares. The chief drinking vessel here is the goblet (or 'egg-cup') typical of EM II–MM IA; it is usually decorated with comb-pricks (25) or with barbotine waves (40). Neither design is common at Knossos, but both occur frequently among recent finds at two west Cretan sites: the Kastelli of Khania, and the Platyvola Cave (Tzedhakis 1967: 502, pl. 375e). The shallow bowls from Kastri can be easily matched with EM II and III forms found in the Knossos excavations of 1957–61; the type with concave walls (28, 35), as G. Cadogan kindly informs us, corresponds to Knossian EM III. The spout with metallic bosses (27) reminds us of EM II drinking jars, or 'teapots' (cf. Forsdyke 1925: pl. 6, A 424); a sherd with 'barnacle' work (34), according to Evans' classification, would come early in MM IA (Evans 1935: 102). Also present is the mottled Vasiliki ware (42,

43), which in Crete is a hallmark of EM IIB (Warren 1965: 21–3) and never, to my knowledge, found in any later context. Straight-sided jars with one or two horizontal lug handles (37, 38) are paralleled only among Y. Tzedhakis' recent finds in western Crete. (My thanks are due to Mr. Tzedhakis for permission to refer to this material.)

Nowhere else in the Greek world is Early Helladic followed by Early Minoan. Since the Kastri deposit was found immediately above natural soil, it surely indicates the arrival of new settlers from Crete who chose to live on a virgin site by the sea; and the analogies seems to suggest that they came from western Crete. It is inconceivable that the EH occupation of Kastraki continued after their coming; for the two deposits are so different in character that it would be hard to imagine two separate communities living but a stone's throw from one another in a state of peaceful co-existence, yet without any sign of mutual exchanges. There may, perhaps, have been a gap in time between the two deposits; but in that case the departure of the EH people would remain unexplained. It is more natural to suppose that the Cretan newcomers ousted the mainlanders; in which case this event would offer a useful fixed point in the relative chronology of the Early Bronze Age—well after the beginning of EH II, but well before the end of EM II. At all events, we can safely say that all the EM from Kastri is later than all the EH from Kastraki: there is no question of an overlap.

I end with two highly speculative suggestions. The first bears on the absolute date of the arrival of Cretan settlers in Kythera. A small stone bowl, No. 4578 in the National Museum of Athens (Evans 1897: 349–50; Stevenson Smith 1965: 8–9 fig. 10), is one of the most mysterious of the older finds from Kythera; but its provenance seems quite secure. It is one of the very few certain imports to the Aegean from the Old Kingdom of Egypt. The hieroglyphics inscription refers to the Sun Temple at Abusir built by the Pharaoh Userkaf, the founder of the Fifth Dynasty. How did this unimpressive little object reach Kythera? The Cretans seem to be the most likely carriers; it could, of course, have been traded in before their arrival in Kastri, but its presence in Kythera would be easier to explain if the Cretans were already established there. The current date for Userkaf is 2487–2478 B.C. Now stone vases can have a long life, and perhaps there are too many other uncertainties for the date to have any bearing on Aegean absolute chronology. Yet the very presence of this Egyptian import shows how wide were the foreign relations of the island at the time when it was beginning to pass into the Minoan sphere of influence.

My other suggestion concerns the political relations between Crete and the mainland in the Early Bronze Age. So far there is no sign of any other Cretan settlement in the vicinity of Kythera. Indeed, there is now some negative evidence from a site some ten miles to the north of Kythera. At the underwater site of Pavlopetri near Elaphonisos, explored and surveyed in

1968 by a team of divers from Cambridge, it seems that Early Helladic was succeeded by Middle Helladic as the normal ware (Harding, Cadogan and Howell 1969: 135). Thus from EM II onwards the Minoans of Kythera lived near a frontier: possibly a rather uneasy frontier in view of the rarity of commercial exchanges in either direction. A. C. Renfrew observed in 1964 that "EH II has ample links with the Cyclades and west Anatolia, but none whatever with Crete" (Renfrew 1964: 137); the more recent discovery of one possible EH II sauceboat at Khania (Tzedhakis 1968: 415, pl. 376c) hardly alters the picture. If this lack of exchange indicates political tension on the frontier between the EM and EH spheres of influence, one of the causes—or perhaps one of the symptoms—is the seizure of the best land in Kythera by Cretan settlers some time during Early Bronze 2—a small ripple on the otherwise calm surface of life in the middle of the third millennium B.C.

References

CASKEY, J. L. 1960. 'The Early Helladic Period in the Argolid.' *Hesperia*, 29: 285–303.
—— and CASKEY, E. G. 1960. 'The earliest settlements at Eutresis.' *Hesperia*, 29: 126–67.
DÖRPFELD, W. 1927. *Alt-Ithaka*. Munich.
EVANS, A. J. 1897. 'Further discoveries of Cretan and Aegean Script.' *JHS*, 17: 327–95.
——. 1935. *The Palace of Minos IV*. London.
FORSDYKE, E. J. 1925. *Catalogue of the Greek and Etruscan Vases in the British Museum I/1: Prehistoric Aegean*. London.
GOLDMAN, H. 1931. *Excavations at Eutresis in Boeotia*. Harvard.
HARDING, A., CADOGAN, G. and HOWELL, R. 1969. 'Pavlopetri: an underwater Bronze Age town in Laconia.' *BSA*, 64: 113–42.
HUXLEY, G. L. and COLDSTREAM, J. N. 1966. 'Kythera: first Minoan colony.' *ILN*, 27.8.1966: 28–9.
RENFREW, A. C. 1964. 'The Cyclades before Rhadamanthus.' *KritKhron*, 18, 107–41.
STEVENSON SMITH, W. 1965. *Interconnections in the Ancient Near East*. Yale.
TZEDHAKIS, Y. 1967. 'Arkhaiotitis kai mnimeia dhitikis Kritis.' *Deltion*, 22: Khron.: 501–6.
——. 1968. 'Arkhaiotitis kai mnimeia dhitikis Kritis.' *Deltion*, 23: Khron.: 413–20.
WARREN, P. M. 1965. 'The first Minoan stone vases and Early Minoan chronology.' *KritKhron*, 19: 7–14.

Bronze Age sites in the Troad

J. M. COOK
University of Bristol

The following information about prehistoric sites in the Troad was obtained during journeys made there between 1959 and 1969. Prehistoric sherds found during them were classified by J. Mellaart and N. Bayne. I have omitted a few sites near Troy where reports of finds of prehistoric pottery remain unconfirmed. The difficulty of distinguishing second millennium and Archaic grey wares should not be overlooked. Some of the sites yielded very small samples and there is no reason to think that occupation was necessarily confined to the periods mentioned. The paucity of sites in the interior on the map is not fortuitous. We were specially diligent in prospecting there, and only about one in ten of the ancient sites discovered yielded prehistoric pottery, whereas half of the ancient sites known to us on the coasts did so. The sites are listed in north to south order as far as possible. 'Troy mission' refers to the University of Cincinnati expedition's investigations in the 1930s.

List of sites

1. *Dardanos (Şehitlik Batarya)*: hill citadel above the sea; Troy VI pottery remarked by French (1964: 37); no prehistoric found 1959, 1966; Greek and Roman city, from eighth or seventh century B.C.

2. *Rhoiteion (Palaiokastro;* apparently called *Kukumağu Tepe* by the 'Troy mission'; now *Baba Kale)*: hill citadel above the sea; Troy VI pottery (Judeich 1898: 532), Troy VI–VII (Sperling 1936: 123); no certain prehistoric 1966; Hellenic town from eighth or seventh century.

3. *Çoban Tepe* (called thus by 'Troy mission'; *Tavolia (Ta Molia)* by F. Calvert; now *Tek Top* (?) at *Karanlık)*: promontory; prehistoric hand-polished pottery (Calvert 1880: 34–6: Calvert and Thiersch 1902: 241–2),

Troy I and VI (Blegen 1950: 15, figs. 28, 35); polished hand-made found 1969; very little Hellenic occupation, some Hellenistic.

4. *Kum Tepe:* mound (Koşay and Sperling 1936: 24–8); not accessible 1966–8.

5. *Troy:* settlement mound; wares of all Troy periods; Greek and Roman city, from eighth century.

6. *Beşika Burnu:* promontory west of *Beşik Tepe* (cf. Lamb 1932: 125); abundant Troy I and second millennium grey pottery found 1959, 1967; Hellenic site from at least sixth century.

7. *Beşik Tepe:* tumulus-mound; pre-Troy I and a little EBA and possibly MBA pottery noted by Lamb (1932: 124–9; finds in Berlin).

8. *Hanay Tepe:* mound; EBA, Troy V–VII according to Lamb (1932: 112–24; finds in Berlin); EBA, second millennium found 1959, 1968–9; Classical cemetery sixth to fourth centuries B.C.

9. *Ballı Dağ* (now *Ballı Kaya*): hill citadel; no prehistoric according to Calvert (Hellenic grave-finds; Calvert 1864; also *Collection Catalogue*, unpublished), Schliemann (1869: 141–4, 149–50; 1875: 44, 318; 1884: 264–5), Lamb (1932: 130); prehistoric stratum claimed by Koşay and Sperling (1936: 4–7); post-Troy VII by Blegen (1958: 147–8); nothing earlier than 600 B.C. found 1959, 1968; Hellenic citadel.

10. '*Tomb of Priam*'; tumulus (?) on *Ballı Kaya*: no prehistoric according to Schliemann, Winnefeld (Schliemann 1884: 262–3) but Troy VI–VII according to Lamb (1932: 111; finds in Berlin, possibly confused with material from *Paşa Tepe* near Troy, Winnefeld in Dörpfeld: 1902: 545).

11. *Han Tepe:* mound on shore; Troy I (Blegen 1050: 35): EBA, second millennium grey, red, and buff found in 1959; a few Hellenic and Roman sherds.

12. *Alexandria Troas*, site above sea to north of *Dalyan:* Troy I inverted-rim bowl, second millennium grey found 1967; Hellenic sherds (black glaze).

13. *Savran Tepe:* hillock and mound (?) by R. Scamander (Menderes); Troy VI–VIIA grey and micaceous buff 1959; Hellenistic fort (?).

14. *Çiftlik Tepe:* settlement mound; Troy I black burnished inverted-rim bowls and tubular lug, rather later red jug sherd probably EB 3, hand-made and wheel-made second millennium grey and red, LBA gold wash and grey found 1967, 1968; nothing between prehistoric and Turkish.

15. *Palaiskepsis* (?) (*İkizce*): mountain top citadel; one hand-made sherd, EB 3 (?) found 1968; one Hellenic sherd (black glaze).

16. *Colonae* (*Beşik Tepe* at *Aktaşovası*): crest above sea; Troy I–II dark

burnished, second millennium grey, with wavy line ornament found 1959; Hellenic town from eighth or seventh century.

17. *Kümbet Kocabahçe*: hillock; Troy I and MBA Troy VI (micaceous grey ridged bowls) 1959; Late Hellenistic–Roman sherds.

18. *Cebren* (*Çal Dağ*) mountain site; no prehistoric found in 1959 (cf. Lamb: 1932: 111; no prehistoric among Schliemann's sherds in Berlin); some grey ware claimed as prehistoric 1966 (ribbed goblet stem perhaps early-middle Troy VI?, 'Minyan' arched handles); Hellenic city from seventh century.

19. *Larisa* (*Liman Tepe*): crest above sea; EB 3, early-middle Troy VI bowl and other second millennium grey, red *kylix* stem found 1959; Hellenic town from eighth century.

20. *Smintheion* (shelf below *Gülpınar*): two sherds EBA, polished, found 1959; Greek and Roman sanctuary.

21. *Polymedion* (*Asarlık*): promontory; two sherds (red and grey) about Troy V period, second millennium grey ridged stem, 1959; Archaic to Hellenistic town.

22. *Assos*; hilltop above sea; Troy I–II (?) (Clarke 1902: 164); no prehistoric found 1959, 1966, 1968; Greek and Roman city from *c.* 600 B.C.

23. *Altınoluk* (*Papazlı*): adjacent site not identified 1959; Troy I and VI finds seen by Mellaart (1958: pl. 2/6).

24. *Thebe* (?) (*Mandıra Tepe*): mound site; prehistoric, especially MBA–LBA, reported by N. Bayne (1960: unpublished survey); Archaic to Roman sherds.

References

BLEGEN, C. W. 1950. *Troy I.* Princeton.
——. 1958. *Troy IV.* Princeton.
CALVERT, F. 1864. 'Contribution towards the Ancient Geography of the Troad. On the site of Gergithe.' *ArchJ*, 21: 48–53.
——. 1880. 'Ueber die asiatische Küste des Hellespont.' *Ztschr. für Ethnologie*, 12: 30–9.
—— and THIERSCH, H. 1902. 'Beiträge zur Topographie der Troas.' *AthMitt*, 27: 239–52.
CLARKE, J. T., BACON, F. H. and KOLDEWEY, R. 1902. *Investigations at Assos 1881–3* (ed. F. H. Bacon, 1902–21). London, Cambridge, Mass., Leipzig.
DÖRPFELD, W. 1902. *Troja und Ilion.* Athens.
FRENCH, D. H. 1964. 'Recent archaeological research in Turkey, III.' *AnatStud*, 14: 35–7.
JUDEICH, W. 1898. 'Bericht über eine Reise im nordwestlichen Kleinasien.' *SBBerl*, 1898: 531–55.
KOŞAY, H. Z. and SPERLING, J. 1936. *Troad'da dört yerleşme yeri.* Istanbul.
LAMB, W. 1932. 'Schliemann's prehistoric sites in the Troad.' *PZ*. 23: 111–31.

MELLAART, J. 1958. 'The end of the Early Bronze Age in Anatolia and the Aegean.' *AJA*, 62: 9–33.

SCHLIEMANN, H. 1869. *Ithaka, der Peloponnes und Troja*. Leipzig.

——. 1875. *Troy and its remains*. London.

——. 1884. *Troja*. London.

SPERLING, J. 1936. 'The site of Sigeion.' *AJA*, 40: 122–3.

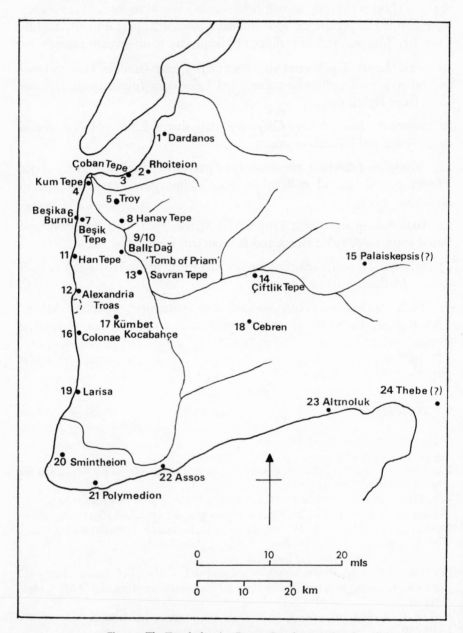

Fig. 5.1. The Troad, showing Bronze Age sites mentioned

Crete, 3000-1400 B.C.: immigration and the archaeological evidence

P. M. WARREN

University of Durham

1. The island of Crete was not populated to any extent until the Late Neolithic period (Evans J. D. 1968: 295–6; Weinberg 1965a: 59–61). In this period, the final centuries of the fourth millennium B.C. and the beginning of the third[1], some sixty-seven sites are known, while only Knossos and about four others have pre-Late Neolithic occupation[2]. It seems likely that new groups were moving into the island, albeit on a fairly small scale and over several centuries. However the possibility that the Late Neolithic population represents a slow expansion from the Early and Middle Neolithic population cannot be ruled out.

At the beginning of the Early Bronze Age around 2800 B.C. there seems to have been a more rapid expansion of population. Some eighty-three EM I sites are known and the new foundations are marked in the north-central and south-central (Messara-Asterousia) regions. For example Arkalokhori, Elenes, Krasi, Kyparissi and Pyrgos are first used now in the north, immediately preceded by the Eileithyia Cave at Amnisos and Partira, while at least nine circular tombs (implying nine occupation sites) are known from EM I in the south, where there had been very little Late Neolithic habitation. From the numerical count alone it seems less likely that this fairly rapid expansion of population and new sites, especially open settlements, arose out of the previously existing population than that the new groups came into the island. But it is when we observe that these EM I sites have a large number of ceramic links with Thermi, Troy I and the preceding north-west Anatolian cultures as seen at Poliochni (Blue Archaic phase), Kum Tepe, Beşika Tepe and Samos-Tigani that the case is strong for new groups coming in from that region at the beginning of the Bronze Age. I have listed many of the links in detail elsewhere (Warren 1965: 37–8; 1969a: 156)[3]. Particularly to be stressed are regular, formal designs in pattern burnish on the exteriors and interiors of chalices and bowls (Weinberg 1947: 178–9 and pl. XXXII/e–g; Furness 1956: 199, 208–9). To the parallels with Beşika Tepe (Lamb 1932) and Samos cited by S. S. Weinberg and A. Furness more and even closer links can now be added from Partira[4] and Platyvola, since these patterns are on the interiors of the vases as at Samos and Beşika Tepe (cf. Tzedhakis 1967: pl. 378/e; 1968: pl. 376/e and Lamb 1932: 126 fig. 13 No. 5, cf. No. 9). There are also many parallels in highly distinctive pottery shapes such as a barrel vase on little feet and vases with animal protomes, again on tiny feet, well evidenced in the Troy 1 and Yortan cultures. A particular form of chalice among the varieties in the Pyrgos cave in Crete is closely paralleled at Poliochni (Xanthoudhidhis 1918: fig. 5 No. 3; fig. 10 Nos. 74, 78. Levi 1955–6: 303 fig. 19; Brea 1959: fig. 5; 1964: 553–4, 556 and pl. IX c–d).

Two points against the west Anatolian case must not be omitted. Dark on buff painted pottery and the communal circular built tomb are quite new in EM 1 and the origin of neither can be placed in west Anatolia on present evidence. It may be, however, that the circular tomb was not introduced at all, but represents on flat, open ground the burial cave of the hillier regions as K. Branigan has suggested (1970: 201), while the light on dark EM 1 vase patterns are regularly found together with and paralleled in pattern burnish, and one of the most common in both techniques, the multiple zig-zag or chevron, is frequent in Anatolia.

The Syro-Palestinian and Egyptian regions have been proposed as possible areas of origin for the people of Early Minoan Crete (Weinberg 1954: 94–6; 1965b: 302, 307; Branigan 1970: 198–200). A rejection of the cases for these points of origin necessarily demands a detailed and somewhat lengthy discussion, out of place here (cf. fn. 3). Branigan's case for connection in the Proto-Urban period seems the strongest, but I feel the connections proposed in ceramic decoration are slight and that the Proto-Urban pottery corpus as a whole has very little in common with that of EM 1 (Branigan favours an indigenous origin in the Neolithic for EM 1, with external influences, but argues that if an external origin is to be sought the Palestinian Proto-Urban culture is the most likely; 1970: 201.)

Some cardinal features of the Early Minoan 1 assemblage such as the chalice shape, pattern burnish and scored or wiped surfaces begin earlier, in the Late and latest Neolithic. These features however should not be taken to mean that EM 1 arises out of the Neolithic tradition as a purely indigenous process. The Late Neolithic itself is largely a new phenomenon in Crete, as pointed out above, and features like the chalice, pattern burnish with formal designs and open carinated bowls with one lug on the body (Zervos 1956: pl. 74 right; Levi 1957–8; fig. 197; Heidenreich 1935–6: F42, F43, F72) are not only new in Late or latest Neolithic but have close north-west Anatolian or east Aegean parallels. In the continuous Neolithic sequence at

Knossos (Evans, J. D. 1964b; 1968) it is true there is no marked break between Middle and Late Neolithic, but major aspects of the latter (red wares, scored or wiped surfaces and the chalice) are new. J. D. Evans has made out a detailed case (1968: 273–4) for the Early Neolithic pottery of Knossos having many features in common with north-west Anatolian and east Aegean EB I and preceding wares. Evans of course accepts that there is an enormous time gap between EN Knossos and EB I north-west Anatolia. For developments in the latest Neolithic and in Early Minoan I we must stress the newness of sites and ceramic features in Crete, their many and varied links with north-west Anatolia and the contemporaneity of the Cretan and Anatolian cultures.

The position is best summarized thus: new groups seem to have reached Crete in the Late and latest Neolithic and some features in the assemblage point to north-west Anatolia and the east Aegean. The Early Minoan I assemblage has some features from the preceding period, but, taken as a whole, is remarkably distinct from it (cf. Hood 1966). Population expansion is now rapid by comparison, especially on to virgin, open sites; very many of the EM I ceramic features have explicit parallels with the Troy I, Thermi and immediately preceding cultures.

2. There is then a strong case, persuasive to me, for some movement of people into Crete from the west Anatolian region to join the Late Neolithic population at the end of the fourth millennium and beginning of the third, namely at the start of the Early Bronze Age and in the immediately preceding 'Partira' phase. After this time, throughout the whole Bronze Age down to the arrival of Mycenaeans at Knossos around 1450 B.C. there is no archaeological evidence whatever for immigrations into the island.

In the Early Minoan period we find burnt destructions at the close of EM II (*c.* 2170 B.C.) at Myrtos (Fournou Korifi) and Vasiliki, the only two EM settlements uncovered on a substantial scale. But in the next period, EM III, we find complete continuity and evolutionary development in pottery, metalwork, sealstones, stone vessels and tomb types, as also in domestic architecture, though only Mallia provides good evidence, with its buildings on the south edge of the Palace (Chapouthier, Demargne and Dessenne 1962: 14–16, 41–3 and Plan II). This building complex recalls Myrtos in both general layout of small interconnecting rooms and in individual details such as the entrance passage and benches against walls.

3. The first Palaces were founded *c.* 1900 B.C. or a little earlier, at the end of Middle Minoan IA (Mackenzie 1906; Evans 1921: 144, 146; Fiandra 1962: especially 125). But there is no evidence for new people at this time. Artefacts, tomb and cemetery types (circular communal tombs, rectangular tombs and ossuaries, pithos burials (see now Pini 1968) continue as before.

Peak sanctuaries flourish, having started in Early Minoan III on Petsofa at least. The Palaces themselves have been convincingly shown by J. W. Graham (1962: 229–33; 1964: 195–215) to owe little or nothing to contemporary palaces outside the island. They are best seen, I think, as an evolution, albeit on a grand scale, from Early Minoan architecture (cf. Branigan 1970: 48). We may compare the large single building complexes at Myrtos (Warren 1969c: fig. 2) and Vasiliki (Seager 1908: pl. XII) with the Palaces. The latter are also large single building complexes, based on a great central court. The central court system is new, but the west court of the Palaces is already found at EM II Vasiliki. Here a court over ten metres long, north-south, lies beside the western facade of the building (Alexiou 1964: pl. 522). It may in fact be much longer since it must have continued southwards besides the parts of the buildings now covered (Rooms 11–26, Alexiou 1964: 445, Seager 1908: pl. XII) and what seems to be a continuation of it in the opposite direction is exposed in the field to the north. Such a court must have been even more closely comparable with the west courts of the Palace than it now appears.

The Palaces themselves are the outcome of a long developed and increasingly strong Early Minoan economy, which finds its outward expression in the island's wide overseas contacts before and during the first Palatial period.

Before the end of this period the Linear A script had been developed, since it was evidenced in destruction deposits of the first Palace at Phaistos. A tablet was found in Room XXVIII and inscribed sealings in Room LI (Levi 1952–4: 389, 416 and fig. 43, 441; Carratelli 1957–8: 363–88, especially 386).

4. Major destructions of the Palaces of Knossos, Phaistos and probably Mallia occurred about 1700 B.C., at the end of the Middle Minoan II. But again there is no evidence for new peoples at this time or immediately following. Linear A continued into its main period of use, MM III–LM I. MM III pottery styles and shapes develop in the previous tradition. Circular communal tombs continue in the MM III period, as at Kamilari near Phaistos (Levi 1961–2) and on the Gypsadhis Hill at Knossos (Hood 1957: 22–3 and fig. 6c; 1958). The Middle Minoan III—Late Minoan I villas are a development of the large individual houses of MM I like House A and Quartier Gamma at Mallia or the two at Vasiliki (Seager 1907: fig. 8). Branigan has shown that daggers and swords evolve out of the metalwork of the first Palace period (1968). The only new features cited by Sir Arthur Evans for what he called the 'New Era' (MM III) were Linear A writing, which we now know goes back to the first Palatial period, certain architectural features like floor cists at Knossos, and new types of signet seal. New but surely not remarkable architectural features and new seal types seem insufficient evidence for 'new ethnic ingredients' as Sir Arthur Evans called them (1921: 316) though he thought the continuity too strong to suggest sub-

jection to a foreign yoke. The MM III archaeological record is essentially one of continuity and development from the first Palace period, MM I–II.

5. A major destruction next occurred throughout the island *c.* 1450 B.C., marked on very many sites by rich deposits of Late Minoan IB material. There can be little doubt that this destruction was due to the effects of the great volcanic eruption of Santorini. Knossos suffered a destruction in LM IB (Hood 1961–2: 96–7 and pl. B; 1962) but quickly recovered. Other sites, Ayia Triadha, Gournia, Mallia, Palaikastro and Phaistos, were reoccupied a little later since their earliest pottery after the LM IB destruction corresponds to the pottery in use at Knossos when it was finally destroyed as a Palace *c.* 1400–1380 B.C. (in LM IIIA 1–early 2) (Popham 1966: 27–8; Warren 1969b: 187 and n. 3 for references). The last Palace period at Knossos, *c.* 1450–1380 B.C., shows new people in the island for the first time since the beginning of the Bronze Age. They are the Mycenaeans, using Linear B writing, developing a new formalism in pottery styles, the Palace Style of LM II, and displaying a military or warrior aspect quite new to Crete, in the Warrior Graves at Knossos (Hood and De Jong 1952; Hood 1956). They also introduced a style of spiraliform stone carving of purely Mycenaean, mainland type (Warren 1967: 198–9 and notes 26–7; 1969b: 6).

6. The archaeological evidence bearing upon the question of immigration before the Mycenaeans of Late Minoan II has been discussed. If my view is accepted a final and most interesting linguistic question may be posed. If there were no major movements of people into Crete after *c.* 2800 B.C. until the Mycenaeans, and since, on the usual view, Indo-European peoples did not reach Greece or Anatolia until the late third millennium, how can Linear A be Indo-European? It is unlikely that such a major thing as the language of Crete could have been introduced without substantial new peoples to introduce it. Archaeologically therefore Linear A would be non-Indo-European, and non-Semitic, in fact a developed and written form of the third millennium Cretan language, the language, as it were of Troy I.

Notes

1. The Cretan Late Neolithic was probably late in the fourth millennium. The latest in the Knossos Neolithic series of C-14 dates gives 3730± 150 B.C. (5570 half-life) for the end of the Early Neolithic (BM–279; Evans 1968: 272). (This will give a true, calendrical date several centuries earlier when calibrated on the bristle-cone pine curve.) Then comes the Middle Neolithic period before the Late. Early Minoan I begins *c.* 2800 B.C. on the evidence

of the Troy I links both with Crete and with EH II. The calibrated C–14 dates from EH II Lerna and Eutresis indicate a start for Troy I before 2600 B.C.

2. The site totals are based on work for my *The Early Bronze Age of Crete* (in preparation).

3. The links are fully discussed in *The Early Bronze Age of Crete*.

4. The Partira vases have been photographed for publication by Dr. A. Zoes. The photographs show varied and well-developed patterns on the interiors of most of the bowls, a confirmation of the links with north-west Anatolia which was wholly unsuspected (e.g. by Renfrew 1964: 116). One of the bowls has a herring-bone design on the inside, the commonest pattern at Beşika Tepe (Lamb 1932: 126, fig. 13, nos. 1–3, 12).

References

ALEXIOU, S. 1964. 'Arkhaiotitis kai mnimeia kritis, 1963.' *Deltion*, 19: 436–47.

BRANIGAN, K. 1968. 'A transitional phase in Minoan metallurgy.' *BSA*, 63: 185–203.

——. 1970. *The Foundations of Palatial Crete*. London.

BREA, L. B. 1959. 'Poliochni.' *ILN*, 18 April 1959.

——. 1964. '*Poliochni, Città Preistorica nell' Isola di Lemnos*, I. Rome.

CARRATELLI, G. P. 1958 'Nuove epigrafi Minoiche di Festo.' *ASAtene*, 35–6: 363–88.

CHAPOUTHIER, F., DEMARGNE, P. and DESSENNE, A. 1962. 'Fouilles exécutées à Mallia. Quatrième Rapport.' *Études Crétoises* XII.

EVANS, Sir ARTHUR 1909. *Scripta Minoa I*. Oxford.

——. 1921. *The Palace of Minos at Knossos*, I. London.

EVANS, J. D. 1964a. Excavations in the Neolithic mound of Knossos 1958–60.' *Bulletin of the University of London Institute of Archaeology*, 4: 35–60.

——. 1964b. 'Excavations in the Neolithic settlement of Knossos 1957–60.' *BSA*, 59: 132–240.

——. 1968. 'Knossos Neolithic Part II.' *BSA*, 63: 267–76.

FIANDRA, E. 1962. 'I periodi struttivi del primo Palazzo di Festos.' *KritKhron*, 15/16: 112–26.

FURNESS, A. 1956. 'Some early pottery of Samos, Kalimnos and Chios.' *ProcPS*. N. S., 22: 173–212.

GRAHAM, J. W. 1962. *The Palaces of Crete*. Princeton.

——. 1964. 'The relation of the Minoan palaces to the Near Eastern palaces of the second millennium'; in *Mycenaean Studies* (ed. E. L. Bennett): 195–215.

HEIDENREICH, R. 1935. 'Vorgeschichtliches in der stadt Samos. Die Funde.' *AthMitt*, 60/61: 125–83.

HOOD, M. S. F. 1956. 'Another warrior grave at Ayios Ioannes near Knossos.' *BSA*, 51: 81–99.

——. 1957. 'Archaeology in Greece 1956.' *ArchRep*, 1956(*JHS*, 77): 3–23.

——. 1958. 'The largest ivory statuettes to be found in Greece; and an early tholos tomb; discoveries during the latest Knossos excavations.' *ILN*, 22 February 1958.

——. 1962a. 'Stratigraphic excavations at Knossos.' *KritKhron*, 15/16: 92–7.

——. 1962b. 'Sir Arthur Evans vindicated: a remarkable discovery of Late Minoan IB vases from beside the Royal Road at Knossos,' *ILN*, 17 February 1962.

——. 1966. 'The Early and Middle Minoan Periods at Knossos.' *BICS*, 13: 110–11.

—— and DE JONG, P. 1952. 'Late Minoan warrior graves from Ayios Ioannes and the new hospital site at Knossos.' *BSA*, 47: 243–77.

LAMB, W. 1932. 'Schliemann's prehistoric sites in the Troad.' *PZ*, 23: 111–31.

LEVI, D. 1954. 'La Campagna di Scavi a Festòs nel 1953.' *ASAtene*, 30–32: 389–469.

——. 1956. 'Atti della Scuola.' *ASAtene*, 33–34: 292–303.

——. 1958. 'Gli Scavi a Festòs nel 1956 e 1957.' *ASAtene*, 35–36: 193–361.

——. 1962. 'La Tomba a Tholos di Kamilari presso a Festòs.' *ASAtene*, 39/40: 7–148.

MACKENZIE, D. 1906. 'The Middle Minoan pottery of Knossos.' *JHS*, 26: 243–67.

PINI, I. 1968. *Beiträge zur minoischen Gräberkunde*. Wiesbaden.

POPE, M. W. M. 1962. 'The Date of Linear B.' *KritKhron*, 310–19.

——. 1964. 'Aegean writing and Linear A.' *Studies in Mediterranean Archaeology*, 8.

——. 1966. 'The origins of writing in the Near East.' *Antiquity*, 40: 17–23.

——. 1968. 'The first Cretan palace script.' *AttiiCIM* (1): 438–47. Rome.

POPHAM, M. R. 1966. 'The destruction of the Palace of Knossos and its pottery. *Antiquity*, 40: 24–8.

RENFREW, A. C. 1964. 'Crete and the Cyclades before Rhadamanthus.' *KritKhron*, 1964. 107–41.

SEAGER, R. B. 1907. 'Report of Excavations at Vasilike, Crete, in 1906.' *Transactions of the Department of Archaeology of the University of Pennsylvania* II, Part II: 111–32.

——. 1908. 'Excavations at Vasilike'; in H. Boyd Hawes, *Gournia* (Philadelphia): 49–50 and Pl. XII.

TZEDHAKIS, I. 1967. 'Arkhaiotitis kai mnimeia Dhitikis Kritis 1966.' *Deltion*, 22: 501–6, pls. 375–9.

——. 1968. 'Arkhaiotitis kai mnimeia Dhitikis Kritis.' *Deltion*, 23: 413–20, pls. 373–90.

VENTRIS, M. and CHADWICK, J. 1956. *Documents in Mycenaean Greek*. Cambridge.

WARREN, P. M. 1965. 'The first Minoan stone vases and Early Minoan chronology'. *KritKhron*, 19: 7–43.

——. 1967. 'A stone vase-maker's workshop in the Palace at Knossos.' *BSA*, 62: 195–201.

——. 1969a. 'The origins of the Minoans.' *BICS*, 16: 156–7.

——. 1969b. *Minoan Stone Vases*. Cambridge.

——. 1969c. 'Minoan village on Crete.' *ILN*, 8 February 1969: 26–7.

WEINBERG, S. S. 1947. 'Aegean chronology: Neolithic period and Early Bronze Age.' *AJA*, 51: 165–82.

——. 1954. 'The relative chronology of the Aegean in the Neolithic period and the Early Bronze Age'; in R. W. Ehrich (ed.), *Relative Chronologies in Old World Archaeology*, (Chicago): 86–107.

——. 1965a. 'The Stone Age in the Aegean.' *CAH* (rev. ed.) I, Chap. X/Fasc. 36.

——. 1965b. 'The relative chronology of the Aegean in the Stone and Early Bronze Ages'; in R. W. Ehrich (ed.), *Chronologies*: 285–320.

XANTHOUDHIDHIS, S. 1918. 'Megas protominoïkos taphos Pirgou.' *Deltion*, 4: 136–70.

Discussion

W. C. BRICE: I would agree with Dr. Warren that a linear script (whether called 'Proto-Linear' or 'Linear A') was in use in Crete before the generally accepted date of the arrival of Indo-European speech in the

Aegean region; further that there is no evidence of any ethnic change in Crete during MM II; and therefore that it looks very much as though the people who used the early linear script in Crete were not Indo-European speakers. I would go further and say that I do not believe that there is enough evidence of ethnic change in the middle of the second millennium to warrant the assumption that those who used the Linear B script were of a different ethnic and linguistic stock from the users of Linear A. Nor do I believe that there is sufficient difference between the two varieties of Linear script, A and B, to make it clear that they were associated with different languages. May I add this further *caveat*, that it may be misleading automatically to equate a script with a language, and a change of script with a change of language? The Cretan Hieroglyphic scripts, and I would say the Cretan linear scripts also, were in large measure concerned with the abbreviated and short-hand expression of a limited range of standard ideas rather than with the recording of languages *in extenso*. The differences between these scripts were doubtless technical rather than linguistically based, just as the records of a mathematician, an engineer, an accountant, and a heraldic official would look different today. As for the 'cause' for the beginning of writing in Crete, I would prefer to consider the economic and cultural changes in pre-Palatial times, which have been so well set out by Dr. K. Branigan in this context, rather than any assumed 'invasion'. The early linear writings were undoubtedly modelled on some Mesopotamian or Syrian style, and the hieroglyphs doubtless inspired from Egypt—but this need not of course imply anything other than peaceful cultural borrowing.

M.W. M. POPE : I hate to disturb the attractive tranquillity of Dr. Warren's thesis, but two causes of doubt occur to me. First, the Linear A script of the first Palace at Phaistos does exhibit some differences (both in signary and in the layout of the writing on the tablet) from Agia Triadha Linear A, and a change of language cannot be absolutely excluded. Secondly, Dr. Warren does not mention the so-called Pictographic script. Since this appears to have been in use concurrently with Linear A the most likely assumption is that it was used for a different language. If so, would Dr. Warren imagine a Crete that was originally bilingual?

P. M. WARREN : First, I agree that a change of language between MM II and MM III 'cannot be absolutely excluded'; but this criticism has force only when expressed at its most extreme, 'absolutely'. It is much more probable that essentially the same Linear A script was used to express essentially the same language at Phaistos, Agia Triadha and elsewhere. Secondly, the discussions of Sir Arthur Evans (1909: 245–8, accepted by Ventris and Chadwick 1956: 29) and Pope (1966: 17–23; 1968; cf. 1964: 7) are persuasive in suggesting that the Hieroglyphic or Pictographic script of Crete was 'phonetic', i.e. syllabic, though not all would agree (for example, J. J. Reich) and Pope himself (1968) lists major difficulties: on sealstones the script seems often to have been used in a purely ideographic or at any rate non-phonetic way (Pope 1968; Reich 1964, 1968; also *Atti1 CIM* (1): 446).

Nevertheless the case for regarding the First Cretan Palace script, to use Pope's name for it, as phonetic and syllabic is strong. This means that the script represented a spoken language. Linear A, which exhibits variations from site to site (cf. Pope 1961–2), evolved as a script from Hieroglyphic (so e.g. Evans 1909: 245; Chadwick 1956: 29) as early as MM II (Phaistos Linear A). Why this happened, and whether Linear A represents a different language from Hieroglyphic or was intended as a simplified script for the same language to facilitate Palace records and literacy inside and outside the Palaces, are at present quite open questions. In my paper I was concerned to put the case from the archaeological side: that there is no evidence for immigration between the beginning of the Bronze Age and the time of the Mycenaeans in LM II. I agree with Pope that if it could be shown with probability that Linear A represents a language different from that represented by Hieroglyphic, then it would look very much as though new people came in with Linear A. But *linguistically* this is quite uncertain at present, and *archaeologically* the arrival of new people in the middle of the first Palace period (MM II), one of the few Minoan periods not broken by a major destruction, and a period totally evolved out of MM I in artefactual and artistic terms, would indeed be astonishing.

R. A. CROSSLAND: Most linguists will agree that no linguistic evidence indicates that any language that was written with Linear A script was Indo-European, or Semitic. Nevertheless, Dr. Warren's own final suggestion in his paper, however tentative, that dialects of the same language were spoken in Crete and Troy in the third millennium also calls for comment from the linguistic standpoint. It shows the risk opposite to the one that he rightly criticizes (that of assuming that any change in language in an area under study must result from immigration): i.e. the risk of assuming that because there was similarity or stability of culture in an area during a given period, the languages that were in use in it are likely to have been genetically related or closely similar as a result of convergent development.

References

REICH, J. J. 1964. *A study of the distinction between the meaningful and ornamental elements in the Minoan hieroglyphic script, with special reference to the spiral sign* (M.A. dissertation for the University of Manchester; unpublished).

——. 1968. 'The rôle of the naturalistic signs in the Minoan hieroglyphic script.' *Atti1 CIM*(1): 448–60.

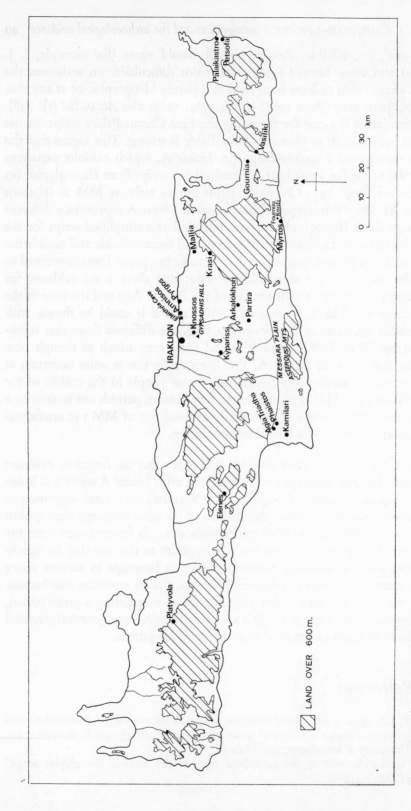

Fig. 6.1. Crete, showing sites mentioned

2
Archaeology of the Middle Bronze Age

Migrations and 'Minyan' pottery in western Anatolia and the Aegean

D. H. FRENCH

British Institute of Archaeology at Ankara

THIS paper presents conclusions and suggestions, based on my previously published discussions of the Bronze Age pottery of western Anatolia and the Aegean, which may be pertinent to the subject of the Sheffield Colloquium.

'Minyan' pottery, especially the Grey variety, was developed in central and southern Greece (i.e. Euboea, Phocis and Boeotia, Attica and the Peloponnese) and not in north-western Anatolia. There is a late third-millennium grey ware in north-western Anatolia. In shape and surface treatment it is parallel to the more widespread west Anatolian red-slipped pottery best known at Beycesultan in levels XII–VI. Its distribution is inland, especially around the modern towns of İznik, Yenişehir and İnegöl, hence the term 'İnegöl grey' ware. Its origins may perhaps be sought in the mid-third-millennium pottery of the Akhisar-Manisa and Balıkesir regions where there is found a grey-black ware which is parallel to the more common red-slipped variety. There is no indication that 'İnegöl Grey' pottery had any influence in the formation of early grey Minyan ware, though it remains an unproven hypothesis, that the *idea*, if not the technique, of 'grey' pottery may have become a fashion in north-western Anatolia before passing on to the Greek mainland. For the greater part of the second millennium, a grey ware (usually known as Troy VI grey ware) was common in the coastal regions of western Anatolia. This pottery is one of several varieties which make up pottery assemblages on western Anatolian sites. It was apparently carried as far as Cyprus, Syria and Palestine but scarcely penetrated inland, to the plateau of western Anatolia. Although there are demonstrable connections with Middle Helladic groups from the Greek mainland (e.g. Lianokladhi goblets at Troy), in shape and surface treatment it remains essentially one of the varieties of west Anatolian second-millennium pottery. Its origins may (*pace* Blegen 1953: 9) perhaps be sought in the grey ware of north-western Anatolia at the end of the third millennium. (For a more complete account see French 1967a and 1969 and for a more full discussion of the late third millennium, French 1968. Descriptions, drawings and maps are to be found in French 1967a and 1969. Mellaart (1969: 172–3) has retracted his earlier views on the origin of Greek Minyan ware (1958: 15–16 and 1964: 49). For second-millennium Grey ware, see Blegen 1953; drawings and distribution map in French 1969: 68–98 and fig. 6; for the transition, Troy v to Troy vi, see French 1967a: 62–3; quoting Bittel 1956, 241.)

The ancestors of 'Minyan' pottery, therefore, are to be sought in central and southern Greece at the end of the third millennium. I suggest that early forms of the Lianokladhi goblets and two-handled bowls (two of the most characteristic features of 'Minyan' pottery) may be seen in the EH iii painted and unpainted wares of central and southern Greece; the implication is clear. (See French 1967a: 64 for EH iii–MH transitional forms).

A wheel-made non-'Minyan' pottery has been found in late third-millennium contexts in Euboea, the Cyclades and the offshore islands of western Anatolia. This group is closely related to west Anatolian red-slipped pottery. There may, perhaps, be connections in the development of 'Minyan' pottery between this 'west Anatolian' group and the earliest 'Grey Minyan' wares (on the Anatolian pottery of Lefkandhi phase i, see French in Popham and Sackett 1968: 8). 'Anatolian' pottery of the late third millennium (possibly EC 3; perhaps to be called the 'Kastri' phase) occurs in the Cyclades at the following sites:

Delos—Kythnos: (1. pottery in collection of British School of Archaeology at Athens, unnumbered; 2. Plassart 1928).

Keos—Ayia Irini: (Caskey 1969: 436; chronology revised later, according to information from the excavator).

Syros—Kastri: (Bossert 1967).

Tenos—Akrotirion Ourion: (1. pottery in collection of British School at Athens, unnumbered; 2. French 1966a: 50, fig. 7/2).

Regarding Bronze Age sites and finds in Macedonia and Thrace, the only intensive survey has been my own of central Macedonia. For such Grey Minyan as has been found there, see my site-map (French 1966b: fig. 3); on finds of local MB wares there, see French 1967b. Evidence for occupation in Turkish Thrace *c.* 2300–1100 B.C. hardly exists (see French 1961: 100, 103; 1964; 1965: 34–5, fig. 13; 1966a: 49, figs. 5/1–48, 6/1–31.)

My conclusions are as follows. First, I suggest that the question of the 'coming' of the Greeks should be separated from the problem of the origin of 'Minyan ware' (French 1966b: 109; Renfrew 1964: 135–41). At the same time, I would add that a 'Luwian' invasion of Greece at the end of 'EH II' cannot be supported on the evidence of pottery. The pottery which followed the *Urfirnis* groups of 'EH II' is different in central Greece, in southern Greece, in Euboea (together with the Cyclades) and in Crete. If there was a 'Luwian invasion', the immigrants brought differing pottery styles to each region (see Mellaart 1964: 50, on 'Luwian' invasions). For good measure, let me also indicate that I do not believe in an 'Anatolian' invasion at the beginning of EH I. I see a straightforward ceramic development in central and southern Greece from 'Neolithic' through to Mycenaean. It seems to me more profitable to develop hypotheses based on 'culture-process' (as A. C. Renfrew would have it) than to suggest historical conclusions based on distinctions between pottery groups. On continuity between 'Late Neolithic' and EH I, see French 1971; on 'culture-process' in the Aegean, Renfrew 1969: 153: on the persistence of conservative shibboleths, Renfrew 1969: 166–7, (*contra* Weinberg). I tend to agree with Renfrew on a second point: why not think of the Greeks as 'autochthonous', present in Greece perhaps since the late Pleistocene? Are we not all too fond of using the idea of 'migration' as a *deus ex machina* to solve our problems?

References

BITTEL, K. 1956. Review of C. W. Blegen and others, *Troy III*; *Gnomon*, 28: 241.

BLEGEN C. W. and others 1953. *Troy III*. Princeton.

BOSSERT, E. M. 1967. 'Kastri auf Syros.' *Deltion*. 22: 53–76.

CASKEY, J. L. 1969. 'Crises in the Minoan-Mycenaean world.' *ProcAmPhilSoc*, 113: 433–49.

FRENCH, D. H. 1961. 'Late Chalcolithic pottery in north-west Turkey and the Aegean.' *AnatSt*, 11: 99–142.

——. 1964. 'Prehistoric pottery from Macedonia and Thrace.' *PZ*, 42: 30–48.

——. 1965. 'Recent archaeological research in Turkey. Surface finds at various sites.' *AnatSt*, 15: 34–9.

——. 1966a. 'Recent archaeological research in Turkey. Surface finds from various sites. Anatolian pottery in the Aegean area.' *AnatSt*, 16: 49–53.

——. 1966b. 'Some problems in Macedonian prehistory.' *Balkan Studies*, 7: 103–110.

——. 1967a. 'Prehistoric sites in north-west Anatolia I. The İznik area.' *AnatSt*, 17: 49–96.

——. 1967b. *Index of Prehistoric Sites in Central Macedonia* (privately distributed; copies in libraries of University of Thessaloniki and University of Sheffield).

——. 1968. 'Anatolia and the Aegean in the third millennium B.C. (University of Cambridge doctoral dissertation, unpublished; copies in University Library, Cambridge and at Institute of Archaeology, London).

——. 1969. 'Prehistoric Sites in north-west Anatolia II. The Balıkesir and Akhisar-Manisa Areas.' *AnatSt*, 19: 41–98.

——. 1972. *Prehistoric Pottery Groups from Central Greece* (privately distributed).

MELLAART, J. 1958. 'The end of the Early Bronze Age in Anatolia and the Aegean.' *AJA*, 62: 9–33.

——. 1962. 'Anatolia *c.* 4000–2300 B.C.'. *CAH* (rev. ed.), I., Chap. XVIII/Fasc. 8.

——. 1964. 'Anatolia before *c.* 4000 B.C. and *c.* 2300–1750 B.C.' *CAH* (rev. ed.), I, Chap. VII, xi-xiv and XXIV, i-vi/Fasc. 20.

——. 1969. Review of R. A. Crossland, *Immigrants from the North. JHS*, 89: 172–3.

PLASSART, A. 1928. *Delos XI*. Paris.

POPHAM, M. R. and SACKETT, L. H. 1968. *Excavations at Lefkandi, Euboea 1964–66*. London.

RENFREW, A. C. 1964. 'Crete and the Cyclades before Rhadamanthus.' *KritKhron*, 18: 107–37.

——. 1969. 'Trade and culture process in European prehistory.' *Current Anthropology*, 10: 151–69.

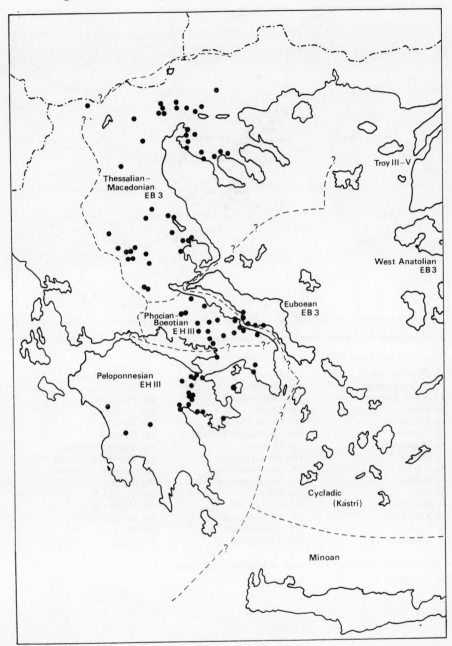

Fig. 7.1. Pottery zones in Greece in EH III/EB 3 (after French 1968: fig. 77)

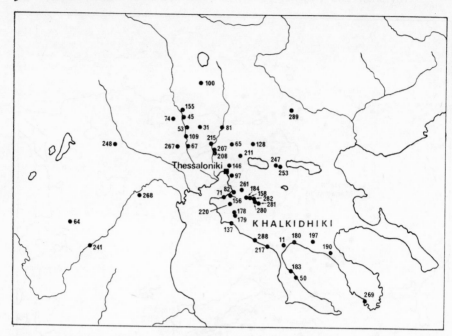

Fig. 7.2. Central Macedonia: distribution of Macedonian EB 2 pottery (after French 1968: fig. 76)

1. *Sites in central Macedonia with Macedonian EB2 pottery*

11 Agios Mamas	137 Kritsana	215 Philadelphiana
31 Anthophytos A	146 Lembet	217 Phlogita
45 Aspros Toumba	155 Limnotopos	220 Plagiari II
50 Athytos	156 Livadhi	247 Skholarion
53 Axiokhori	158 Loutra Thermis	248 Skydhra
65 Dhrymos	178 Mesimeriani Toumba	253 Stivos B
67 Dourmousli	179 Mesimeri	261 Thermi Toumba
71 Epivatai	180 Molyvopyrgos	267 Toumba Kouphalia
74 Evropos	183 Nea Phokaia	268 Toumba Verginas
81 Galliko	184 Nea Raidhestos	269 Torone
82 Gona	190 Nikita	280 Vasilika A
97 Kalamaria	197 Ormylia 2	281 Vasilika B
100 Kalindhria	207 Pentalophos A	282 Vasilika C II
109 Kastania	208 Pentalophos B	288 Veria
128 Khrysavgi	211 Perivolakion	289 Vergi

2. *Sites in western Macedonia with imports of Macedonian EB2 pottery*

  64 Dhrepanon II   241 Servia

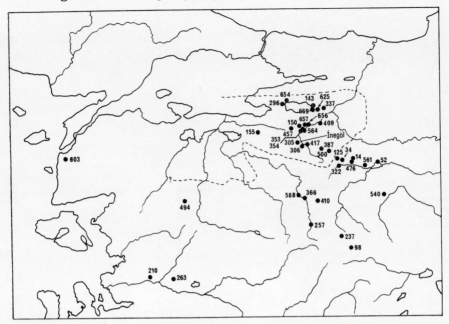

Fig. 7.3. North-western Anatolia: distribution of İnegöl Grey Ware (after French 1968: fig. 48 b4)

1. *Find-places in the İnegöl area*

143 Çakırca	353 Karası I	564 Söylemiş
150 Çardak	354 Karası II	603 Troy
155 Çayırköy	387 Kınık (Pazaryeri)	625 Üyücek
296 İlicapınar	409 Köprühisar	654 Yeniköy
305 İnegöl I	417 Kurşunlu	656 Yenişehir I
306 İnegöl II	457 Marmaracık	657 Yenişehir II
337 Karadın	500 Pazaryeri II	669 Yügücek

2. *Find-places of imports of İnegöl grey ware in other areas of north-western Anatolia*

(a) *Akhisar-Manisa area*
   210 Eğriköy
   263 Halitpaşa II
(b) *Altıntaş area*
   98 Beşkarısı
   237 Gecek
   257 Hacikebir
(c) *Balıkesir area*
   494 Pamukcu

(d) *Eskişehir area*
   14 Aharköy
   34 Akpınar
   52 Alyamak Hüyük
   125 Bozüyük
   322 Kandilli
   476 Oluklu

   540 Seyitgazı
   561 Söğütönü I
(e) *Kütahya area*
   366 Kayı
   410 Köprüören
   588 Tavşanlı

Northern penetration of Greece at the end of the Early Helladic period and contemporary Balkan chronology

SINCLAIR HOOD
Oxford

THERE seems to be a certain amount of evidence for movements of people from the north into Greece at the end of the Early Helladic period. These movements may have been complex, with some groups moving over longer, some over shorter distances; some perhaps coming as raiders who returned, others as permanent settlers, whether as invaders or refugees. Among these groups, as M. Gimbutas has emphasized, there may have been elements of 'Kurgan' or 'Mound' (alternatively known as 'Yamna' or 'Pit-grave') people originating from the steppes of southern Russia. A few bits of pottery decorated with cord impressions characteristic of the Kurgan culture have been found in central Greece and assigned to the end of Early Helladic III there. Cord-ornamented pottery seems to appear for the first time in northern Greece, in Thessaly and Macedonia, in the local Early Bronze Ages, which are usually assumed to have begun in Early Helladic I or II, but which I believe began much later, at a time contemporary with the end of Early Helladic III or with an early phase of Middle Helladic in southern Greece.

Fragments of corded ware of northern origin have been reported from two sites in central Greece, Eutresis and Ayia Marina. The fragments from Ayia Marina, whose context appears to be unknown, were first noted by H. Frankfort (1927: 44 note 1, pl. IV/6), and he illustrated one of them. Four scraps of corded ware were found at Eutresis (Pl. 8), but only one of them in a stratified context. This scrap (it is not clear which of the four illustrated in the report it was) is said to have come from a definite context of the end of EH III (Goldman 1931: 123 fig. 169/1–4). M. Gimbutas (1965: 489 fig. 4/3) has assigned the fragments of corded ware from Eutresis and Ayia Marina to the last of the four phases (IV) into which N. Merpert (1961) has divided the Kurgan culture. The four sherds drawn by Gimbutas (1965: 489 fig. 4/3) appear to be all from Ayia Marina (Milojčić 1955: 151 fig. 1). That at the top left might be the same as the one from Ayia Marina illustrated by Frankfort (1927: pl. IV/6). The grounds for assigning the fragments of corded ware from Eutresis and Ayia Marina to phase IV of the Kurgan culture are therefore not entirely clear. Indeed the rather distinctive design on one of the fragments from Eutresis (Pl.8/3; Goldman 1931: fig. 169/3; a triangle with fringes and horizontal hatching) seems identical with that on a vase from the 'Neolithic' grave pit at Berezhnovka on the lower Volga (Pl.8/4; Gimbutas 1956: pl. 13 bottom left), which Merpert (1961: 183) assigns to Kurgan phase I. It is interesting to note in this connection that layer 1 of the settlement of Mikhailovka (Mykhailivka) is assigned to Kurgan phase I by Gimbutas (1965: 478–9, 492 Table 3). But according to T. Sulimirski (1970: 415 Table 10) Mikhailovka layer 1 is of the period of Tripolye B2, which is the equivalent of Cucuteni A–B, and therefore contemporary with the end of EH III or the beginning of Middle Helladic on the chronology which I would like to suggest here (Fig. 8.3), According to Gimbutas, however, Kurgan I overlaps with Tripolye A (pre-Cucuteni III), and Kurgan II with Cucuteni A.

The settlement at Eutresis was destroyed by fire at the end of EH III. Possibly the scraps of corded ware found there came from vases brought by the people who destroyed the settlement. But there is nothing to suggest that makers of corded ware afterwards settled in the area. Another settlement which appears to have been destroyed at the end of EH III is Korakou near Corinth (Caskey 1960). These destructions in southern and central Greece at the end of EH III might have been connected in some way with movements of people southwards into Thessaly about this time. These movements may have begun at the end of the Thessalian Neolithic, which is usually equated with the end of the Neolithic in southern Greece, but which I believe ought to be placed much later, contemporary perhaps with the end of EH II there.

The Thessalian Larissa horizon (Milojčić 1959b), with pottery very different from that of the preceding Dhimini horizon but comparable in many respects with that of the Late Neolithic of western Macedonia as found at Servia (Heurtley 1939), could reflect one such movement of people into Thessaly from the region immediately to the north. The pottery of the Thessalian Early Bronze Age closely resembles that of the Macedonian Early Bronze Age, and might reflect a subsequent movement of this kind. On stronger grounds perhaps the Middle Bronze Age of Thessaly is thought to have been inaugurated by a movement of people southwards from Macedonia (Milojčić 1959b). These three stages reflecting possible movements of people into Thessaly from the north may not have been separated by very long intervals of time. Successive movements of this kind could have been side-effects of the penetration of the Balkans by Kurgan or related peoples whose raids might have caused the destruction of sites like Eutresis and Korakou in central and southern Greece at the end of EH III.

It has been suggested that groups of Kurgan people were also responsible for the great horizon of destruction in southern Greece at the end of the preceding period, EH II. M. Sakellariou (1968: 296) has indeed implied that fragments of pottery characteristic of Kurgan phase III were found at Lerna in the Peloponnese in a context of the end of EH II there, and this would be in harmony with the views of Gimbutas (1965). But the evidence for this does not appear to have been published as yet, and until it is published it is impossible to comment. On the other hand there is a good deal of evidence accumulating for large-scale movements of people westwards across the Aegean from Anatolia at the end of EH II or in EH III (e.g. French 1968: 8). These movements may have been due to pressure from other peoples who were entering Anatolia from the north at this time, either from Thrace or across the Caucasus. And the entry of these peoples into Anatolia may well have been connected in some way with the expansion of the Kurgan people from southern Russia into the Balkans.

Pottery with corded decoration is first attested in northern Greece, in Macedonia and Thessaly, at the beginning of the Early Bronze Age there (Heurtley 1939: 83; Milojčić 1959b: 27 fig. 21/1–2 cf. Milojčić 1956: 157 fig. 13). In Thessaly at any rate corded decoration seems to occur on vases of local EB shapes. In contrast to this the fragments of corded ware found at Eutresis appear to come from vases of actual Kurgan type, which must have been imported if they were not brought with them by invaders (Gimbutas 1965: 490 fig. 4/3). There is a widespread belief at the moment that the Early Bronze Age of northern Greece (Thessaly and Macedonia) spans roughly the same period of time as Early Helladic I–III in southern Greece (Milojčić 1959b: 19 Chart; Caskey 1964: 5–6). On this view the appearance of cord-ornamented pottery in Thessaly and Macedonia at the beginning of the local Early Bronze Ages will precede by some centuries the end of the EH III period in central Greece. But as I have already suggested, there are some grounds for thinking that the Early Bronze Ages of Thessaly and Macedonia may have begun a good deal later, towards the end of EH III or at the beginning of Middle Helladic times.

The Early Bronze Age pottery of northern Greece (Thessaly and Macedonia) is admittedly very different in character from that of the Early Helladic phases in southern Greece, and it is therefore difficult to find points of resemblance that might be significant for chronological correlations. None of the comparisons made by V. Milojčić (1959b) for instance between Thessalian EB pottery and that of the Early Helladic phases appear very convincing. On the other hand there are obvious affinities between the EB pottery of northern Greece and that of the Trojan area. The North Greek EB pottery has often been compared with that of Troy I. But the carinated bowls (e.g. Blegen 1950: pls. 258–261, Shape A 12; see Pl. 9/1), which are common in the horizon of Troy I, appear to be as rare in the Early Bronze Ages of Thessaly and Macedonia as they are in later periods at Troy. At the, same time the incurved (Pl. 9/2, top row) and T-shaped rims (Pl. 9/2 bottom row), characteristic of bowls of the North Greek Early Bronze Age, are comparable with those found on bowls of Troy III and IV, and more especially perhaps with those on bowls on Troy V. Compare for example some of the rims in Blegen 1951: pl. 60 (from Troy III), pls. 176–84 (from Troy IV), and pls. 251–57 (from Troy V), with those in Milojčić 1959b: 26–7, fig. 22 (from Thessaly) and Heurtley 1939: 166 fig. 36 (from Kritsana in Macedonia; see Pl. 9/2–3). There seem to me to be strong reasons for thinking, as R. J. Howell has independently suggested, that Troy II is roughly contemporary with EH III in southern Greece. If Troy II is contemporary with EH III, Troy III–V must overlap with an early phase of the succeeding Middle Helladic period. In that case the Early Bronze Ages of Thessaly and Macedonia with T-rim bowls akin to those of Troy III–V should also coincide with an early phase of Middle Helladic.

There are certain difficulties, however, in the way of these suggested correlations. Distinctive clay 'anchor ornaments' (Pl.10) are common in the Early Bronze Ages of Thessaly and Macedonia (Milojčić 1959b: 28; cf. Milojčić 1956: 150 fig. 8; Heurtley 1939: 87), and they are also found in the EH III horizon at Lerna (Caskey 1956: 162 pl. 47/l–p), and earlier still it seems, in EH I–II contexts, at Eutresis (Goldman 1931: 196 fig. 269/1, 3) and at a site near Galaxidhi (Vatin 1964: 566) which is also in central Greece. But these curious objects have a way of appearing at widely different times in different places. Further west in Italy, Sicily and Malta, for instance, they occur in the Middle to Late Bronze Ages, and even into the Early Iron Age (Evans 1956: 99–101; 1958: 187; Trump 1960: 295). In spite of their very much later date these anchor ornaments and related clay hooks of the Italian peninsula appear to be connected in some way with the similar ones of the Aegean area and the Troad (Evans 1956: 100). An horizon with anchor ornaments in northern Greece contemporary with the early part of the Middle Helladic period makes a plausible stage in the spread of these objects from the Aegean and the Troad to the Italian peninsula.

A more serious objection against correlating the Early Bronze Age of northern Greece with an early phase of Middle Helladic in southern Greece is a fragment of what appears to be imported EH III patterned ware from the top level of the key EB site of Kritsana on the coast of Chalcidice in Macedonia (Heurtley 1939: 22, 121, 170 fig. 43). This sherd was only published in a drawing, and it now appears to be lost. A similar type of painted decoration is found on a variety of patterned ware characteristic of the earliest phase of Late Neolithic at Akropotamos in eastern Macedonia (Mylonas 1941: 558 fig. 3/1–4, variety E). But it is difficult to believe that this horizon of Late Neolithic in eastern Macedonia was contemporary with the end of the Early Bronze Age in western Macedonia.

Other evidence for an infiltration of Greece by groups connected with the Kurgan people of southern Russia may be provided by the burial mounds, which are mostly to be found in the western parts of the Peloponnese, but which are also attested in central Greece and in Attica (Hammond 1967). The majority of these mounds in Greece appear to date from the Middle Helladic period or later. But some of the so-called R-graves under circular cairns on the island of Leucas (Dörpfeld 1927) contained vases of types characteristic of the EH II period in the eastern part of the Peloponnese. It is always possible that the EH II culture survived for a time in some parts of western Greece after it had been extinguished in the eastern coastal areas. But even if people from the north did reach Greece at the end of the Early Helladic period bringing with them a custom of burial under circular mounds, there is no reason why a native tradition of burial under mounds should not have flourished in some parts of Greece before then. In Egypt, for instance, the mass of ordinary people were buried in pits under low circular mounds during the early part of the Dynastic period (Emery 1961: 139 fig. 82, 147 fig. 88), which should overlap with the beginning of Early Helladic in southern Greece.

Hammer-headed pins seem characteristic of phase IV of the Kurgan culture, and some copper pins which appear to be early versions of hammer-headed pins were found in the royal tombs at Alaca Hüyük in central Anatolia (Gimbutas 1961: 197; 1965: 487). The Alaca tombs are thought to belong to the period of Troy II (Mellink 1965: 126 Chart), and they would therefore be contemporary with EH III in southern Greece on the system of correlations which I have suggested. This is in harmony with the fact that bone hammer-headed pins, imported from the north or copied from northern types, have been recovered from contexts of the succeeding Middle Helladic period at Lerna on the eastern coast of the Peloponnese (Pl. 8/6) and at Asea in Arcadia (Holmberg 1944: 130 fig. 121 No. 16).

Pottery made in Greece may have been travelling as far as Rumania by this time. The ringed stem of a pedestal bowl (Pl. 8/9), wheel-made and with a grey burnished surface was found in 1910 at Cucuteni in eastern Rumania, and was identified by the excavator, H. Schmidt (1924: 351–2, figs. 1–2; 1932: 45, 87–8, pl. 36/1 a, b) as Minyan ware imported from Greece. This fragment is said to have come from an undisturbed level, immediately above the burnt destruction which ended Cucuteni A and in a firm association with material assignable to an early phase of Cucuteni B. Cucuteni B is thought to have overlapped with phase IV of the Kurgan culture (Gimbutas 1965: 492 Table 3). Bowls of Grey Minyan ware with ringed stems like the fragment from Cucuteni are especially at home in central Greece (Pl.8/7–8) where they occur from the beginning of the Middle Helladic period but not earlier. Southwards they are found in the Peloponnese, and northwards at some coastal sites in Macedonia like Molyvopyrgo (Heurtley 1939: 210–11, figs. 78–9). They are not uncommon at Troy, and it has been suggested (e.g. Wace, 1934: 130) that the Cucuteni fragment belonged to a vase imported from the Troad. But, as Schmidt noted, ring-stemmed bowls of Grey Minyan ware appear earlier in Greece than they do at Troy, where they are not attested until the time of Troy vi. It now seems clear that the beginning of Troy vi must be set later, and on the system of correlations which I have suggested a good deal later, than the beginning of the Middle Helladic period in southern and central Greece. It is true that at Beycesultan in the interior of Anatolia bowls of grey burnished ware with ringed stems were found as early as level xvi, which was equated by the excavators with the opening phases of Troy ii (Lloyd and Mellaart 1962: 147 fig. P 24 No. 20, and 112 Chart). But these bowls were made by hand, not on the fast wheel, which is not attested at Beycesultan until the Early Bronze 3 period (level xii and later) contemporary with Troy iii–v (Lloyd and Mellaart 1962: 199).

Another fragment of what was taken to be Minyan ware was recovered in a settlement at Fedeleşeni in Rumania dating from the end of Cucuteni A (Cucuteni A4) (Gimbutas 1965: 462 Table 1). This fragment, from the body of a wheel-made vase of grey ware (Nestor 1932: 45, 51 fn. 180), was apparently found in the ruins of a house destroyed by fire that may have belonged to the local chieftain. In a corner of the same building was a stone horse-head sceptre of Kurgan origin (Pl. 8/5; Nestor 1932: pl. 2/2). Such distinctive sceptres are thought to date from the period of Kurgan expansion in Kurgan phase iii (Gimbutas 1965: 484). Vases of Grey Minyan ware (although not ring-stemmed bowls) were already being made on the fast wheel in southern Greece in Early Helladic iii (Caskey 1960: 295). The fragment of wheel-made grey ware from Fedeleşeni, which does not appear to have been published, might therefore prove assignable to EH iii rather than to Middle Helladic times, if it were really Minyan ware.

Rumanian archaeologists, however, are now inclined to believe that these two fragments of wheel-made grey ware from Cucuteni and Fedeleşeni are not contemporary imports from Greece, but local pottery of much later date (La Tène period; Dumitrescu 1959: 40). One common form among the La Tène pottery of Rumania is a ring-stemmed bowl (Vulpe 1932: 298, 309 fig. 85). Many later objects, including some of La Tène character, were admittedly recovered at Cucuteni, and Schmidt (1911: 594) noted that some of these later objects were found mixed with material of the upper level of the Cucuteni culture. At the same time he insisted that the fragment of supposed Minyan ware came from a pure context assignable to an early phase of Cucuteni B. Moreover this ringed stem from Cucuteni (Schmidt 1932: pl. 36/1a, b) closely resembles one from the second or third building level of Middle Helladic at Eutresis in central Greece (Pl. 8/8; Goldman 1931: 136 fig. 183/10), while as far as I can see it is only comparable in a general way with ringed bowl-stems of La Tène date from Rumania.

A ribbed pedestal foot resembling those of some Minyan vases, found at Poieneşti in Rumania, seems to be assigned to Cucuteni A by Vulpe (1953: 269, fig. 44/5). But a large amount of later material, some of it La Tène, was evidently recovered from this site.

The occurrence of imported Grey Minyan ware assignable to the Early Helladic III or Middle Helladic periods of southern Greece in contexts of the end of Cucuteni A or the beginning of Cucuteni B would imply that Cucuteni B began *c.* 2000 B.C. at the earliest. This seems to me right, although it is in complete defiance of the Carbon–14 dates for the Neolithic sequences of the Balkans, according to which the beginning of Cucuteni B should fall a thousand years or more earlier, in the region of *c.* 3000 B.C., reckoning with the 'conventional' half-life of 5568 years (Quitta 1967: 269, 265 fig. 1). The date for the beginning of Cucuteni B comes seven or eight hundred years earlier still if these dates are calibrated with those obtained from tree rings of the long-lived bristle-cone pine (Renfrew 1968: 279–80; Selkirk 1970: 180–1).

V. Dumitrescu (1959) has emphasized the Bronze Age character of the later phases of the Cucuteni culture, and has in the past argued on independent grounds that the end of Cucuteni A should be dated *c.* 1950/ 1900 B.C., that is to say, about the time of the transition from Early Helladic III to Middle Helladic in southern Greece. It must be emphasized that in reaching this conclusion Dumitrescu did not use the evidence of the supposed Minyan sherds from Cucuteni and Fedeleşeni, which he took to be strays of the La Tène period. But on this chronology it would be quite in order for wheel-made Grey Minyan ware from Greece to be reaching Rumania at the end of Cucuteni A and the beginning of Cucuteni B[1].

Nor is there any reason why clay vases of Early Helladic III or Middle Helladic date should not have travelled from Greece as far north as Rumania. Pottery made in Rumania appears to have been finding its way to northern Greece about this time or earlier. Fragments of vases of Cucuteni A or Gumelniţa I type that may have come from Rumania are reported by Milojčić from contexts assignable, it seems, to the horizon of the post-Dhimini Larissa culture at Otzaki-magula in Thessaly (Milojčić 1959a: 46–7, figs. 3, 4). If, as I have suggested, the Early Bronze Age of Thessaly is contemporary with an early phase of the Middle Helladic period in southern Greece, the Larissa horizon should overlap with Early Helladic II.

These fragments from Otzaki-magula and the corded ware from a context of the end of EH III at Eutresis may not be the only evidence we have for clay vases reaching Greece from the north about this time. Some little flasks recovered from the earliest level of Middle Helladic at Lerna in the Peloponnese appear to be imports brought from a distance. (Pl. 11/1–2; Caskey 1957: 150 pl. 40/d, f; 1956: 160 pl. 43/b). A similar flask, also apparently of foreign fabric, was found in a context of the same date at Kirrha on the bay of Itea below Delphi (Dor 1960: 87–8 pl. xliv/34). The horizon from which this flask came is called in the report of the excavations Middle Helladic Ib; but according to J. L. Caskey (1962: 211) what is termed Middle Helladic Ib at Kirrha corresponds to the earliest Middle Helladic at Lerna. A flask of this shape from Eutresis, however, may have been made locally in a variety of Grey Minyan ware (Goldman 1931: 141 fig. 193). M. Garašanin has noted some resemblances between the Lerna flasks and certain pots from Bubanj near Niš in Yugoslavia assignable to period IA there (Caskey 1957: 150; Garašanin 1958: 57 fn. 316). Period IA at Bubanj appears to be contemporary with the last phase (D) of the Vinča culture. Some vases from Vinča itself (Pl. 11/3), belonging to the later Vinča (Vinča-Plocnik or Vinča C–D) horizon, are not altogether unlike the Lerna flasks in shape, and like some of the Lerna flasks they have channelled decoration including bold spirals (Vasić 1936a: 101 pl. liv/193; 112 pl. lxv/222; 1936b: 78 pl. xlvii/109a, b, c; Milojčić 1949a: 123 fn. 12, pl. 33/11; 1949b: 281 fig. 7/11).

Most of these imported flasks at Lerna were found in a long apse-ended house and in outbuildings on the other side of an open court from it (Caskey 1957: 149–50, fig. 4). O. Dickinson has suggested to me that this compound might have belonged to a chieftain who ruled Lerna at the beginning of the Middle Helladic period. The fragment of supposed Minyan ware from Fedeleşeni in Rumania was similarly recovered from what appears to have been a chieftain's house. Perhaps some rudimentary form of long-distance trade in the shape of gift-exchanges between chieftains was already taking place in this part of Europe by the beginning of the second millennium B.C. But in that case exchanges were surely not confined to clay vases. Vases of precious metal, for instance, may have been travelling long distances in some such way by this time. Thus the mysterious treasure of massy gold found at Vălchitrăn in Bulgaria has been regarded as an import from the south and assigned to a horizon of *c.* 2000 B.C. or earlier (Popović 1959; Seyrig 1954: 222–3). But it may in fact be very much later in date, if not of local manufacture. Sandars (1968: 213) places it in the first millennium and suggests that it is Phrygian, while Mikov (1958) argues that it is a product of the Balkans dating from the eighth century B.C.

But there is other and more cogent evidence for the existence of gold vases in the Balkans by *c.* 2000 B.C. or earlier. Traces of gilding have been noted on some clay vases assignable to the variant of the Rumanian

Gumelniţa culture found in southern Bulgaria, and on others belonging to the Bubanj-Hum culture of Yugoslavia (Popović 1959: 110). Gilt clay vases like these were evidently meant to imitate gold ones. It is interesting to note that a fragment of a clay vase with traces of where gilding had been applied was actually found during the early excavations at Bubanj in a level corresponding to Bubanj-Hum 1A, the horizon in which vases comparable with the Lerna flasks are said to have been recovered (Orsić-Slavetić 1943: 17, 34, pl. IX. 1).

Note

1. Professor Dumitrescu tells me that he would now suggest a date between *c.* 3000 and 2500 B.C. for the end of Cucuteni A and the beginning of Cucuteni B (in letter dated 2 June 1970).

References

BLEGEN, C. W. 1950. *Troy I*. Princeton.

——. 1952. *Troy II*. Princeton.

CASKEY, J. L. 1956. 'Excavations at Lerna, 1955.' *Hesperia*, 25: 147–74.

——. 1957. 'Excavations at Lerna, 1956.' *Hesperia*, 26: 142–62.

——. 1960. 'The Early Helladic period in the Argolid.' *Hesperia*, 29: 285–303.

——. 1962. Review of L. Dor, J. Jannoray, H. and M. van Effenterre, *Kirrha: étude de préhistoire phocidienne*. *AJA*, 66: 211.

——. 1964. 'Greece, Crete and the Aegean Islands in the Early Bronze Age.' *CAH* (rev. ed.) I, Chap. XXVI (a) Fasc. 60.

DÖRPFELD, W. 1927. *Alt-Ithaka*. Munich.

DOR, L. and others 1960. *Kirrha: étude de préhistoire phocidienne*. Paris.

DUMITRESCU, V. 1959. 'La civilisation de Cucuteni.' *Berichte van der rijksdienst*, 9: 7–48.

EMERY, W. B. 1961. *Archaic Egypt*. Harmondsworth.

EVANS, J. D. 1956. 'The "Dolmens" of Malta and the origins of the Tarxien Cemetery culture.' *ProcPS*, 22: 85–101.

EVANS, J. D. 1959. *Malta*. London.

FRANKFORT, H. 1927. *Studies in the Early Pottery of the Near East. II. Asia, Europe and the Aegean, and their Earliest Interrelations*. London.

FRENCH, D. H. 1968. In R. Popham and L. H. Sackett, *Excavations at Lefkandi, Euboea, 1964–66*. London: 8.

GARAŠANIN, M. 1958. 'Neolithikum und Bronzezeit in Serbien und Makedonien.' *RGKomm*, 39: 1–130.

GIMBUTAS, M. 1956. *The Prehistory of Eastern Europe Part I. Mesolithic, Neolithic and Copper Age Cultures in Russia and the Baltic Area*. Cambridge, Mass.

——. 1961. 'Notes on the chronology and expansion of the Pit-grave culture.' *Prague Symposium*: 193–200.

——. 1965. 'The relative chronology of Neolithic and Chalcolithic cultures in Eastern Europe north of the Balkan Peninsula and the Black Sea'; in R. W. Ehrich, *Chronologies*: 459–502.

GOLDMAN, H. 1931. *Excavations at Eutresis in Boeotia*. Cambridge, Mass.

HAMMOND, N. G. L. 1967. 'Tumulus-burial in Albania, the grave circles of Mycenae, and the Indo-Europeans.' *BSA*, 62: 77–105.

HEURTLEY, W. A. 1939. *Prehistoric Macedonia*. Cambridge.

HOLMBERG, E. J. 1944. *The Swedish Excavations at Asea in Arcadia*, Lund and Leipzig.

LLOYD, S. and MELLAART, J. 1962. *Beycesultan I*. London.

MELLINK, M. 1965. 'Anatolian Chronology'; in R. W. Ehrich, *Chronologies*: 101–31.

MERPERT, N. I. 1961. 'Eneolit stepnoy polosy evropoyskoy chasti SSSR.'/'L'énéolithique de la partie européenne de l'U.R.S.S.' *Prague Symposium*: 161–75; 176–92.

MIKOV, V. 1958. *Le trésor d'or de Vâlcitrân*. Sofia.

MILOJČIĆ, V. 1949a. *Chronologie der jüngeren Steinzeit Mittel und Sudosteuropas*. Berlin.

——. 1949b. 'South-eastern elements in the prehistoric civilisation of Serbia.' *BSA*, 44: 285–306.

——. 1949c. 'Zur Zeitstellung der ältesten Siedlung von Troja.' *JdI/AA*, 63/64 (1948/49) *Beiblatt*: 2–11.

——. 1949d. 'Die dorische Wanderung im Lichte der vorgeschichtlichen Funde.' *JdI/AA*, 63/64 (1948/49) *Beiblatt*: 11–30.

——. 1955. 'Zur Frage der Schnurkeramik in Griechenland.' *Germania*, 33: 151–4.

——. 1956. 'Bericht über Ausgrabungen auf der Gremnos-Magula.' *JdI/AA*, 71 (1956): 142–83.

——. 1959a. 'Bericht über Ausgrabungen in Thessalien 1958. I. Die Ausgrabungen im Gebiet der Gremnos-, Otzaki- und Soufli–Magula bei Larissa.' *JdI/AA*, 74 (1959): 36–56.

——. 1959b. 'Ergebnisse der deutschen Ausgrabungen in Thessalien 1953–1958.' *RGZM*, 6: 1–56.

MYLONAS, G. 1941. 'The site of Akropotamos and the Neolithic period of Macedonia.' *AJA*, 45: 557–76.

NESTOR, J. 1932. 'Der Stand der Vorgeschichtsforschung in Rumänien.' *RGKomm*, 22: 11–181.

ORSIĆ SLAVETIĆ, A. 1943. 'Bubanj, eine vorgeschichtliche Ansiedlung bei Niš.' *Mitt. der Prähistorischen Kommission der Akademie der Wissenschaften*, 4 (Vienna): 1–46.

POPOVIĆ, V. 1959. 'Encore le trésor d' orfévrerie de Vâlcitrân.' *RA*, 1959/II: 106–10.

QUITTA, H. 1967. 'The C-14 chronology of the central and SE European Neolithic.' *Antiquity*, 41: 263–75.

RENFREW, A. C. 1968. 'Wessex without Mycenae.' *BSA*, 63: 277–85.

——. 1970. 'New configurations in Old World archaeology.' *World Archaeology*, 2: 199–209.

SAKELLARIOU, M. 1968. Comment on Sp. Marinatos, 'Mycenaean culture within the frame of Mediterranean anthropology and archaeology.' *Atti 1 CIM* (1): 295–6.

SANDARS, N. K. 1968. *Prehistoric Art in Europe*. Harmondsworth.

SCHMIDT, H. 1911. 'Vorläufiger Bericht über die Ausgrabungen 1909/10 in Cucuteni bei Jassy (Rumänien).' *Ztschr. für Ethnologie*, 1911: 582–601.

——. 1924. 'Die Ausgrabungen von Cucuteni und Sarata-Monteoru (Rumänien) im Lichte der ägäischen Vorgeschichte.' *JdI/AA*, 39 (1923–4): 348–56.

——. 1932. *Cucuteni in der Oberen Moldau, Rumänien*. Berlin.

SELKIRK, A. and SELKIRK, W. 1970. 'The radio-carbon revolution.' *Current Archaeology*, 18: 180–4.

SEYRIG, A. 1954. 'Note sur le trésor de Tôd.' *Syria*, 31: 218–24.

SULIMIRSKI, T. 1970. *Prehistoric Russia*. London.

TRUMP, D. 1960. 'Pottery "anchors".' *Antiquity*, 34: 295.

VASIĆ, M. M. 1936a. *Preistoriska Vinča*, II. Belgrade.

VASIĆ, M. N. 1936b. *Preistoriska Vinča*, IV. Belgrade.

VATIN, C. 1964. 'Un site helladique ancien à Galaxidi.' *BCH*, 1964: 559–68.

VULPE, R. 1953. 'Săpăturile dela Poieneşti din 1949.' *Materiale Arheologice*, 1: 213–506.

———— and VULPE, E. 1932. 'Les fouilles de Poiana: campagne de 1927.' *Dacia*, 3/4: 253–351.

WACE, A. J. B. 1934. 'Thessaly and Tripolje.' *Eurasia Septentrionalis Antiqua*, 9 (Minns Memorial Volume): 123–34.

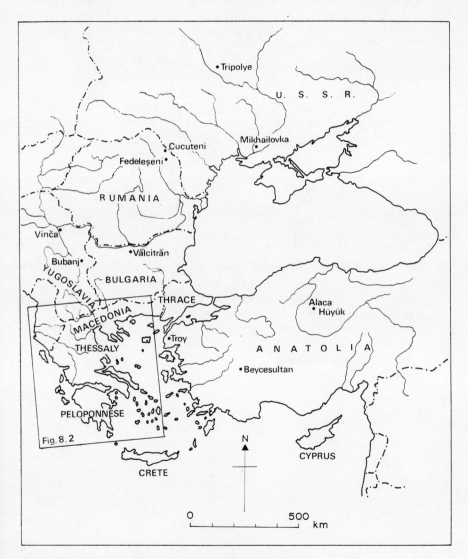

Fig. 8.1. Eastern Europe and Anatolia, showing sites mentioned

Fig. 8.2. Greece, showing sites mentioned

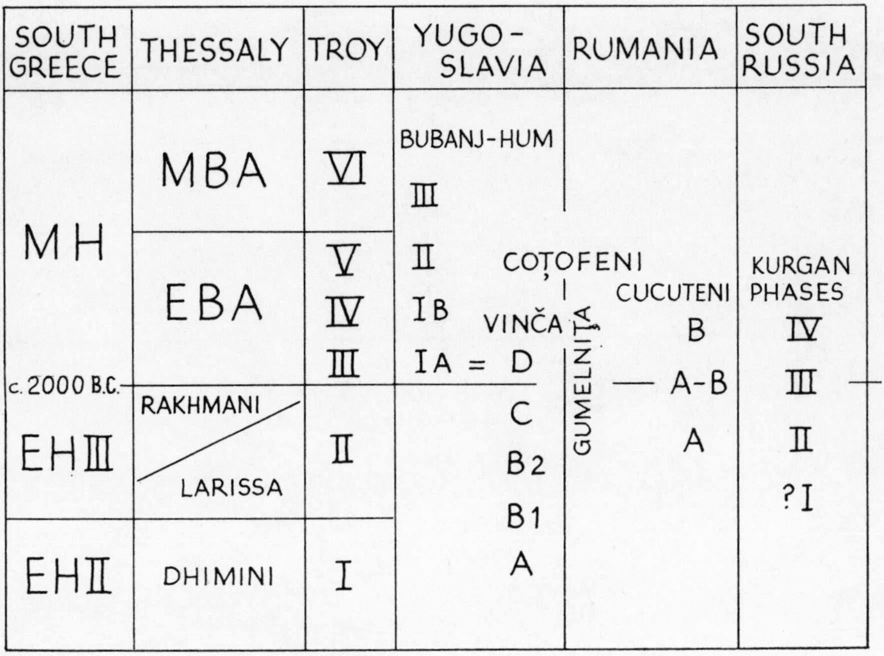

SOUTH GREECE	THESSALY	TROY	YUGO-SLAVIA	RUMANIA	SOUTH RUSSIA
MH	MBA	VI	BUBANJ-HUM III		
	EBA	V	II COTOFENI		KURGAN PHASES
		IV	IB VINČA CUCUTENI B		IV
		III	IA = D GUMELNIŢA A-B		III
c. 2000 B.C.	RAKHMANI		C A		II
EH III	LARISSA	II	B2		?I
			B1		
EH II	DHIMINI	I	A		

Fig. 8.3. Scheme of suggested correlations

The origins of the Middle Helladic culture

R. J. HOWELL

University of Birmingham

A. J. B. WACE and C. W. Blegen advocated the division of the Greek Bronze Age into what were termed Early, Middle and Late Helladic periods in an article published in 1918 (Wace and Blegen 1918). The periods were defined on the basis of pottery styles, and it was noted that while there appeared to be a break in the ceramic tradition between the Early and Middle Helladic periods, there were signs of continuity between the Middle and Late Helladic. Some scholars already felt at that time that the Late Helladic culture, or Mycenaean as it was otherwise known, must have been the creation of Greek-speaking peoples since it reflected in many ways the heroic world of the Homeric poems. The continuity between Middle and Late Helladic noted by Wace and Blegen seemed to indicate that the Greeks must already have been in Greece in Middle Helladic times also. The break between Early Helladic and Middle Helladic, on the other hand, provided a possible indication of their arrival. In this way a special interest was created in the material culture of the Middle Helladic period and the problem of its origins.

As we have mentioned, Wace and Blegen's definition of the Middle Helladic period was based on pottery styles, and perhaps as a result pottery has always tended to dominate any investigation of the origins of the period. Even before 1918, there had been speculation on the origin of the type of pottery that came to be seen as most typically characteristic of the period, the so-called Grey Minyan ware. H. Schliemann had first come across a 'dull black' ware, as he described it, in his excavations at Troy in 1871–1873, and assuming it to belong to the historical period, he called it Lydian (Schliemann 1880: 587–97). He then found a very similar ware at Mycenae in 1874–76, (Schliemann 1878: 137, 154) and again at Orchomenos in 1880 and 1887 (Schliemann 1881: 40–5). It was so abundant at the latter site that he later re-christened it 'Minyan' in honour of the legendary king of Orchomenos, *Minyas*, and his subjects the *Minyai*. Two schools of thought soon developed about the place of origin of Grey Minyan, one preferring Greece, the other Anatolia. Wace and M. S. Thompson, in the publication of their investigations in Thessaly, favoured Orchomenos (Wace and Thompson 1912: 21, 251–2), whereas E. J. Forsdyke preferred Troy (Forsdyke 1914). Forsdyke's arguments were rejected the following year by V. G. Childe, who thought that the ware probably originated somewhere in the Boeotia—Phocis area (Childe 1915).

Linguistic considerations turned the attention of archaeologists to possible connections with the north, especially after the publication of J. B. Haley and C. W. Blegen's article suggesting an Early Helladic association for the pre-Greek place-names (Haley and Blegen 1928). This necessitated an examination of evidence other than ceramic, for neither of the two principal Middle Helladic wares, Grey Minyan and Matt Painted, could be convincingly shown to originate in the Balkans or further north. S. Fuchs, however, thought that certain pot shapes and decorative elements betrayed influences from central and northern Europe. He envisaged a gradual penetration of these 'Indo-European' influences beginning already in the EH II period and ending with an invasion at the end of EH III. His main non-ceramic evidence was the large increase in perforated stone axes, the so-called battle-axes, after EH III (Fuchs 1937: 95–144). A. W. Persson saw a north Balkan origin for certain Middle Helladic artefacts such as perforated stone axes, antler hafts and picks, and clay seals, but suggested that they could have entered Greece via Anatolia together with Grey Minyan pottery. A later movement from Anatolia would have introduced *pithos* burials, Matt Painted pottery and certain types of bronze pins at the beginning of MH II; and in MH III another movement, this time from the north, would have brought a coarse kind of pottery with knobbed decoration, which he called 'Achaean' ware, and possibly the horse and as well (Frödin and Persson 1938: 433–4). At about the same time W. A. Heurtley claimed to have found a 'Proto-Minyan' ware in Macedonia in levels of the Early Bronze Age, but he thought that its development was interrupted there and that it subsequently developed in southern Greece, to be reintroduced in Macedonia at a later stage (Heurtley 1939: 82, 123, 128). In 1958 J. Mellaart re-stated the case for the invasion of Greece from north-west Anatolia at the beginning of the Middle Helladic period, but again his argument was based mainly on the evidence of Grey Minyan pottery (Mellaart 1958).

In most of the investigations into the origins of the Middle Helladic culture that have so far appeared, little trouble has been taken to analyse its constituent elements in detail. Often parallels for one or two salient Middle Helladic features only have been used in order to demonstrate the place of origin of the whole culture. A serious analysis of the characteristic features of Middle Helladic should include an examination of settlement and house types, burial customs, ceramic traditions and stone, bone, metal and terra-cotta artefacts. Most of the relevant material has recently been usefully assembled by K. Syriopoulos (Syriopoulos 1964: 1968). After establishing the most characteristic features which justify setting up 'Middle Helladic' as a cultural period, the next step should be an examination of the immediately preceding period, to see if there is any evidence that the Middle Helladic culture was the product of a natural evolutionary process. If certain MH features seem to be quite different from anything found in the preceding period then possible proto-types may be looked for elsewhere; and if the culture as a whole seems to be intrusive, its place of origin should obviously be sought in that region where the greatest possible number of similarities can be shown to have existed in or from a slightly earlier period.

Middle Helladic settlements and architecture

On the whole Middle Helladic peoples seem to have chosen for their settlements rocky hills, or eminences of a type that could be easily defended. Only one such site, Malthi in Messenia, has been excavated in anything like its entirety as yet (Valmin 1938); most have had only very small areas exposed. It would be unwise to say much about the general layout of MH settlements in view of this. A fortification wall was found surrounding the main part of the settlement at Malthi, and traces of similar walls have been found on a number of other sites, though in some cases only a short extent has been uncovered and it is not possible to tell whether it really belongs to a fortification wall, rather than just a terrace wall; e.g. Brauron (Papadhimitriou 1957: 24); Thorikos (Stais 1893: 16, pl. B3); Lerna (Caskey 1956: 160); Mycenae (Rowe 1954: 248–53). More certain fortification walls are those from Molyvopyrgos (Heurtley 1938: 14), Plasi near Marathon (Marinatos 1970: 154) and Argos (Vollgraff 1907: 141, 143), though the date of the latter two is not certain. Fortification walls are to be inferred from the stratigraphy at Tiryns (Müller 1930: 16, 18, 62, 93–4, 204) and Lefkandhi (Megaw 1965: 17). The typical Middle Helladic house seems to have been either oblong or apsidal in plan, the apsidal plan being basically the same as the oblong, with an additional apsidal room at one end. Some of the houses were divided into two or three rooms by cross walls, and the walls were of mud brick resting on stone socles two or three courses high. The manner of roofing is not certain, but in some cases reeds plastered with clay may have been one of the materials used (Caskey 1966a: 19).

Middle Helladic burial customs

In most of the Middle Helladic sites that have been excavated burials have been found within the settlement, either beneath the floors of houses or against walls. Regular cemeteries also existed, however, outside some settlements, as is clear from the excavations at Sesklo, Eleusis, Old Corinth,

Zygouries, Mycenae and Prosymna (Caskey 1966a: 19–20). Tumulus burials are also found in Middle Helladic times, and they usually consist of a central burial covered by a pile of stones, over which an earthen mound was heaped up, with a retaining wall round its base. Secondary burials were often made in the mound subsequently (Hammond 1967: 91–6). Tumuli have been found at Elateia in Phocis, Aphidna, Vrana (Marinatos 1970: 158–64), Athens (on the north slope of the Acropolis), Nidhri in Lefkas, Lopesi—Katarrakhtis in Achaea, Samikon in Triphylia, and Peristeria and Papoulia in Messenia. (Marinatos reports at least twenty-four other tumuli in western Messenia, but some of these are Late Helladic; Marinatos 1954: 315.) The dead were usually laid in a crouched position in simple pits of stone-lined rectangular cists with slab covers, but sometimes placed in a *pithos*. Single burial was the rule, though occasionally two or three burials were made in one grave; more often than not no grave goods accompanied the dead (Syriopoulos 1964: 330–53; 1968: 305–23).

Middle Helladic pottery

With regard to the pottery, it is important to take into account the changes that had been brought about by the use of the potter's wheel, which is well attested in Middle Helladic times. The potter's trade became a more specialized concern, though individual householders probably continued to make the coarse vessels used in preparing food themselves, since they are always hand-made. The specialist potter using the wheel could achieve a much greater output than was possible before, and this favoured experimentation with shapes and styles of decoration, which in turn led to a faster rate of evolution. Local styles tended to emerge, but some potting centres may have grown up which were able to export their products over a wider area. The appearance of a new type of pottery under such conditions does not necessarily indicate the arrival of new people and we should perhaps restrict ourselves to using only general features that are common to several different varieties of MH ware in our search for the origins of the ceramic traditions. Such features include everted rims and vertical, flattened, strap or ribbon handles, and an interest in polished surfaces. We can perhaps add to this an interest also in firing vessels under reducing conditions, that is, in a closed kiln, from which the air could be excluded to prevent iron particles in the clay from oxidizing and producing a light coloured fabric. The coarse household or kitchen ware displays a much more conservative spirit on the part of the potter than the fine wares, and for this reason can be used as a safer criterion when dealing with the question of its origins. The principal characteristics of this domestic ware are the abundant use of stone chips for tempering and frequently smoothed or polished, greyish brown to black, often patchy surfaces. The interiors of vessels are sometimes black whilst the exteriors are variegated. Everted rims are common, and sometimes the lips have finger-impressed or slashed decoration. The handles are generally vertical and flattened, but tongue-shaped, forked and horsehoe-shaped lugs also appear. A common feature is the use of plastic knobs or warts, usually arranged in pairs on the shoulders of vessels, as decorative elements (Frödin and Persson 1938: 280–4; Goldman 1931: 175–8).

Middle Helladic stone artefacts

Characteristic of the Middle Helladic stone industry are the shaft-hole hammer-axes, which are perhaps related to the battle-axe, though simpler in outline. In horizontal section they are roughly the shape of a flat-iron, though sometimes they have a rounded butt end, and in vertical section they are a straightforward rectangle (Goldman 1931: 206–7). The shaft-holes were either drilled straight through from one side only, or else two separate drillings were made from opposite sides. Also characteristic are spherical mace heads. Other typical stone objects include the so-called arrow-straighteners, usually of sandstone (Buchholz 1962: 4–20), whetstones, and stones of a roughly cubic shape with slightly rounded edges, variously described as pounders, grinders or weights. Although obsidian was known and used, chert and flint are perhaps commoner. Typical objects in these materials include leaf-shaped arrow-heads (Buchholz 1962: 20–7) and saw-toothed blades, which may have been used as sickle insets (Syriopoulos 1964: 390–404; 1968: 343–53).

Middle Helladic bone and horn artefacts

Bone and horn were commonly used for tools and ornament: bone was sharpened to form awls and punches, and frequently carved into fine ornamental pins with knobbed and grooved heads. Worked boar's tusks are often found on Middle Helladic sites, sometimes split longitudinally; antler was used for hammers, for hafting stone celts and probably for pickaxes too (Goldman 1931: 215; Frödin and Persson 1938: 253–4).

Middle Helladic metal artefacts

Copper and bronze were certainly known and used in MH times; both were used for tools—knives, chisels and flat axes; weapons—daggers, spearheads and arrow-heads; and toilet articles—tweezers and articles of adornment—ear-rings, hair coils, bracelets, rings, pins and beads (Syriopoulos 1964: 390–404; 1968: 343–53). Gold, silver and electrum are less frequently found and were used mainly for jewellery. Lead was used for mending pots.

Middle Helladic terracotta artefacts

Typical terracotta objects include spools or 'cotton reels' with flaring ends, pierced down the centre (Miss J. Carington Smith has suggested to me that they might have been used in preparing warp threads for a loom (as in Khadzizogidhis 1898: 541–55; illustration of *dhiastra*), and spindle whorls many of which were biconical in shape and sometimes decorated with incised patterns. We might add a cup-shaped vessel with pierced sides which is usually known as a strainer, but is sometimes called a brazier or incense burner. It generally has a short pedestal foot with its sides irregularly punctured in the form of 'T' shaped slits (Goldman 1931: 181, fig. 250; Dor, Jannoray and Van Effenterre 1960: 84, pl. XLVIII/14).

This concludes the list of the most characteristic features of the material culture of the Middle Helladic period as known at present. Future excavations will certainly add to it, particularly research in the field of environmental studies, which should eventually allow us to reconstruct the characteristic features of Middle Helladic man's exploitation of his environment. At present the internal divisions of the period are not well established; in particular our knowledge of the early phase is weak; in the case of subsequent phases it is not always possible to say whether a certain object which has been listed as typical occurs from the very beginning of the period or was introduced later on.

Early Helladic III

Having established a list of characteristic features for the Middle Helladic, we must now examine the preceding Early Helladic III period, to see how many of them, if any, can be said to originate there. Caskey's careful excavations at Lerna in the 1950s led him to observe that, contrary to previously held opinions, there appeared to be a marked cultural break between EH II and EH III, and that some sites seem to have been destroyed at the end of EH II (1960: 299–303). Distinct new features in EH III noted by Caskey include apsidal houses, a profusion of *bothroi* or rubbish pits, small terracotta anchor-shaped objects, and above all a striking new range of ceramic wares and shapes (1960: 293–7). He points out that a crude version of the potter's wheel was now in use, and that the new wares include the first Grey Minyan as well as a coarse ware with shapes including cups and open jars, almost always with knobs on the shoulder, and goblets sometimes pierced like strainers, all generally with an uneven, slightly burnished surface. He also observed that the change from EH III to MH was far less abrupt than had previously been supposed. There was no general break in the sequence at Lerna, no layer of burnt debris, nor any signs of catastrophe. In fact on closer examination, only two sites seemed to show a destruction layer between EH III and MH: Eutresis in Boeotia and Korakou near Corinth. Nevertheless, Caskey thought that significant changes could be observed, most obviously in certain classes of pottery. Matt Painted ware begins suddenly at Lerna, and so does Argive Minyan with its decoration of fluting and incised festoons. There was also a sudden widespread appearance of intramural burials (Caskey 1960: 298–9). However, the potter's wheel, certain pot shapes, Grey Minyan ware, apsidal and rectangular house plans, and bored-stone hammer-axes all provided definite links between EH III and MH (Caskey 1966a: 11).

The excavations of Popham and Sackett at Lefkandhi in Euboea in the 1960s have confirmed Caskey's observations (Popham and Sackett 1968: 8–9). It is particularly important to note that Grey Minyan now seems to develop in Greece within the EH III period. It first occurs in the later stages of the fourth settlement at Lerna, in simple shapes which imitate those of other fabrics. It appears at the beginning of the EH III level at Lefkandhi, though there is reason to believe that that level represents a late stage in the development of EH III. Some of the sherds are difficult to distinguish from MH Grey Minyan, though others are less successful and much cruder. It would seem from this that the ware was in a formative stage.

In making a closer comparison between EH III and MH we are hampered by the fact that so little EH III material has been excavated yet. Only at Lerna has a fairly wide area with good stratigraphy been exposed. Before Caskey's re-definition of the two periods, there was some confusion over what exactly was EH II and what was EH III. One factor contributing to this confusion was undoubtedly the widespread occurrence of *bothroi* in EH III settlements, for even such a careful and experienced excavator as Caskey admits that they are often extremely difficult to detect (Caskey 1960: 294). It is more than probable then, that unobserved *bothroi* have led to some EH III material being reported as EH II and *vice versa*.

Early Helladic III settlements and architecture

Practically all the known EH III sites were occupied in the Middle Helladic period as well. As far as we can tell at present, the same type of site was preferred in both periods. We have already noted similarities in house plans, and although *bothroi* are much commoner in EH III levels, they are also found in the MH period (Goldman 1931: 37, 234).

Early Helladic III burial customs

It is difficult to tell how far there were any similarities in burial practices, since hardly any EH III burials have so far been found. Those said to be of EH III date at Asine (Frödin and Persson 1938: 42, 212, 336–41) and Argos (Courbin 1954: 176) appear from the associated finds to be rather of EH II date, and the one from Berbati (Säflund 1965: 110–11, 123–4) could also be earlier. Two intramural infant burials were found at Lerna in the EH III level (Caskey 1955: 37 note 20). N. G. L. Hammond suggests that the mound heaped over the house of tiles at Lerna after its destruction is possibly related in some way to the MH tumuli (Hammond 1967:90).

Early Helladic III stone artefacts

We have already noted ceramic similarities between the two periods. As regards stone, bone, metal and terracotta objects, however, there is generally not enough clearly stratified material to enable us to say what is characteristic of EH III. For the time being we can only make a list of typical MH features which occur in EH III levels. Stone shaft-hole hammer-axes were found in EH III levels at Lerna, and in pure late EH (EH III?) levels at Asea (Holmberg 1944: 122); they are said to occur in all levels at Kirrha, where excavation stopped at the top of the EH II level. Perforated stone mace-heads were also found in all levels at Kirrha (Dor, Jannoray and Van Effenterre 1960: 105); another was found in an EH level at Agios Kosmas (Mylonas 1959: 28, 30). Two arrow-straighteners were found at Asea in late EH levels (Holmberg 1944: 126), and two barbed arrow-heads were found by Goldman at Eutresis, (Goldman 1931: 206). Caskey found another in the area of the 'chasm', which seems to have been dug down through the EH II level from above, although it was mostly filled with EH II material (Caskey 1960:150). Similar obsidian arrow-heads were found in EH levels at Agios Kosmas (Mylonas 1959: 144, fig. 166/17, 18), Zygouries (Blegen 1928:199) and Asine (Frödin and Persson 1938: 243). Hexagonal stone grinders or weights were found in all levels at Kirrha (Dor, Jannoray, and Van Effenterre 1960: 105–6), and in EH levels at Eutresis (Goldman 1931: 204, fig. 275), Zygouries (Blegen 1928: 200), Prosymna (Blegen 1937: 257–8) and Asea (Holmberg 1944: 124). Flints or cherts with saw-toothed edges were found in EH III levels at Eutresis (Goldman 1931: 204–6), and in EH levels at Zygouries (Blegen 1928: 199). They are said to come from all levels at Asea (Holmberg 1944: 128), and in the report on Asine they are listed under the section on EH III but no specific date is given to them (Frödin and Persson 1938: 243).

Early Helladic III bone artefacts

The typical MH bone pin with fairly short, well-polished, rounded stem and knobbed or grooved head, has not definitely been proved to occur in EH III levels, but two examples are reported from EH levels at Eutresis (Goldman 1931: 212, fig. 283/4, 6). An antler pickaxe was found in a level bordering between EH and MH at Asine (Frödin and Persson 1938: 253), and others are reported from EH levels at Zygouries, though they are said not to be common (Blegen 1928: 193–4). Boar's tusk was found in EH levels at Eutresis (Goldman 1931: 220), and was plentiful at Zygouries, though unworked (Blegen 1928: 194). At Asea is is said to be all of MH date (Holmberg/1944: 130).

Early Helladic III metal artefacts

EH III copper or bronze weapons, tools and ornaments include a knife from

Eutresis (Goldman 1931: 218), a dagger, nail and pin from Lerna (Caskey 1955: 43, pl. 23a, 1956: 168), and a hoard from Thebes consisting of a hammer-axe, two flat axes and two chisels (Platon and Stasinopoulou-Touloupa 1964: 896). The dagger, chisels and flat axes are very similar in type to those found in MH levels.

Early Helladic III terracotta artefacts

Terracotta strainers were found by Caskey at Lerna in EH III levels (Caskey 1956: 161, pl. 43d; 1960: 296), and examples from Zygouries (Blegen 1928: 124–5) and Asea (Holmberg 1944: 63) are possibly also EH III. It should be noted that the fragments of strainers from Malthi (Valmin 1938: 284), said to be of EH date, should be classed with the MH examples, since it is now clear that all of the so-called Neolithic and EH material there really belongs to the MH period. This is clear from the field-work of W. A. Macdonald and R. Hope-Simpson, who have discovered several typical EH II sites in Messenia: there is even one less than a kilometre from the Malthi acropolis itself (MacDonald and Hope-Simpson: 1969: 141, 172). The sherds found at these sites are very similar to those from other EH II sites in Greece, and quite unlike anything found at Malthi. Valmin was obviously uneasy about the primitive quality of much of the Malthi material, and tried to explain it by deriving the material in question from Neolithic antecedents in a direct line of development; but the discovery of typical EH II material in Messenia now makes this impossible.

Although not all the objects listed above were found in definite EH III levels, it is perhaps significant that most of them cannot be said to be typical of EH II, and in all cases they were found at sites which have some trace of EH III occupation. As we have seen, Caskey emphasizes the differences between the EH III and MH periods, but these could be no more than the results of a natural process of change, such as might occur in any culture over a certain period of time. The evidence from Lefkandhi suggests that the early part of MH is one of the least known periods, and this could explain the apparent suddenness of some of the changes (Popham and Sackett 1968: 9).

Although there are still many points to be cleared up, there is perhaps already enough evidence to warrant the assumption of a genetic relationship between MH and EH III. In other words, EH III can be thought of as the first manifestation of the MH period in Greece. It would be confusing however, to start calling EH III 'Middle Helladic' at this point, and I would prefer therefore, to use the generic term 'Minyan' to cover the period from EH III to MH III, in the same way as the term 'Mycenaean' is used for the Late Helladic period. The EH III phase might then be labelled 'Proto-minyan', MH I 'Early Minyan', MH II 'Classical Minyan' and MH III 'Late Minyan'.

Early Helladic II settlements and architecure

We must now examine the EH II period, to see how far EH III can be said to develop out of it, if at all. Caskey strongly contrasted the two periods in his work on the Early Helladic in the Argolid (1960a: 293–7). EH II sites were often settled in our 'Minyan' period as well, but a fair proportion of EH II settlements is on low hillocks or barely perceptible mounds, which were not on the whole favoured in the 'Minyan' period. In some areas it seems as though small hamlets, and perhaps even single farmsteads, were not uncommon in EH II times (Hope-Simpson 1961: 146–8; Howell 1970: 111). This may help to explain why, in areas that have been more intensely explored, such as Attica, the north-eastern Peloponnese, the plain of Tripolis, the Helos plain and Elaphonisi, EH II sites appear to be more numerous than MH. In the 'Minyan' period people were perhaps more defence-conscious. There is a difference too, in the layout of settlements. In EH II times the houses tended to be rectilinear and conglomerative, new rooms being added as needed until several houses were joined together in a single complex. The 'Minyan' houses, on the other hand, were independent free-standing structures. The apsidal house does not occur in EH II, and flat terracotta and schist tiles, which have been found in association with several EH II buildings, have not been found in 'Minyan' levels.

Early Helladic II burial customs

EH II burial practices, in so far as they are known at present, differ from MH practices, though we do not know whether they differ from those of EH III. The evidence from Agios Kosmas and Zygouries, the only sites where EH II cemeteries have been widely excavated, suggests that multiple burial in hollow pits or stone-constructed chambers may have been a common practice (Syriopoulos 1964: 231–40; 1968: 220–5).

Early Helladic II pottery

On the whole the ceramic traditions of the two periods are different, and there is little in the EH III tradition that can be directly related to that of EH II. An exception is perhaps the rather streaky dark brown wash that forms the background of the light-on-dark or 'Ayia Marina' style in Phocis and Boeotia, which may be related to the dull *Urfirnis* of the late phases of EH II (French 1968: 60–1). It may be that there was a stronger survival of EH II traditions in the Phocis-Boeotia area than in the Peloponnese.

Early Helladic stone, bone and terracotta artefacts

Whereas obsidian was extensively used in the microlithic industry in EH II, there was a swing to chert in the 'Minyan' period. Some objects that are typical of EH II are not found in 'Minyan' contexts. These include well-shaped stone pestles (Blegen 1928: fig. 186) and marble 'Cycladic' figurines, as well as polished, lozenge-shaped, bone objects (Blegen 1928: fig. 181/5–8), terracotta 'fire dogs' (Müller 1938: 65, fig. 51), spoons and ladles (Blegen 1928: fig. 84, 94; Frödin and Persson 1938: 224–5, fig. 164/3, 4; Caskey 1955: 45, pl. 23c), *phalloi* (Blegen 1928: 186–7, fig. 177), and animal figurines (Goldman 1931: 196, fig. 269/2, 4: Walker Kosmopoulos 1948: 60, figs. 42, 43). One object that may have been inherited by EH III from EH II is the terracotta 'anchor' though the evidence is hardly conclusive as yet. An example from Kheliotomylos near Corinth (Waage 1949: 421) does seem to come from an EH II context, and another very similar one was found at Corinth itself, where evidence for EH III occupation is not positively demonstrated (Walker Kosmopoulos 1948: fig. 41 a–b). Five others are said to come from EH I or II levels at Eutresis (Goldman 1931: 196, fig. 269/1, 3). 'Anchors' cannot be said to be frequent on most EH II sites, however.

Early Helladic II metal artefacts

Very few copper or bronze objects have been found in EH II levels but it should be noted that examples of knives, flat axes, daggers and tweezers of typical 'Minyan' shapes have been attributed to this period (Blegen 1928: 182–4, pl. XX/12, 25; Goldman 1931: 215–16, fig. 287; Caskey 1955: 46, pl. 23b; 1956: 168; Mylonas 1959: 28–9, 74, 78, 101, 137, fig. 163).

Crete

Taking into account the destruction levels at some sites at the end of the EH II period, and the abandonment of others (Caskey 1960a: 299–303), the suggestion that there may have been an invasion of a new population element at this time is perhaps not unreasonable. In favour of such an hypothesis are the differences mentioned above in settlement and house types between EH II and EH III, the cessation of certain typical EH II objects and the introduction of others that become typical of the 'Minyan' period. In any case it is clear that many of the most typical features of the 'Minyan' period do not originate in EH II, and their origins must be sought elsewhere.

To the south of the Peloponnese, Crete seems to have led an independent existence until the Late Bronze Age. On the basis of Cretan imports from Lerna, it would seem that the following synchronisms can be made: 'Early Minyan' (MH I)—Early Lerna v = MM Ia; 'Classical Minyan' (MH II)—Middle Lerna v = MM II; 'Late Minyan' (MH III)—Late Lerna v = MM III (Caskey 1966a: 22–3). R. W. Hutchinson suggested that EM III and MM Ia patterns were being imitated in the first city at Phylakopi on Melos, which, as we shall see, was contemporary with the 'Early Minyan' (MH I) period (Hutchinson 1968: 111–12). EM III as well as MM Ia may therefore be contemporary with 'Early Minyan' (MH I). The evidence from Lefkandhi suggests that the latter was a fairly long period, and the two former seem to have been closely related anyway (Branigan 1970: 33). 'Protominyan' would seem then to be contemporary with EM II. Evidence from Kastri on Kythera supports this equation, for the earliest material from the Minoan colony there seems to belong to EM II. Close by, however, a homogeneous deposit of EH II sherds was found; they are quite distinct from the EM II sherds from the colony, and this leads us to the conclusion that EM II is probably later than EH II there (Huxley and Coldstream 1966: 28–9, fig. 3; Coldstream, see above, p. 35). We may note also that EM II Agios Onouphrios ware sometimes approaches in technique the dark-on-light ware of 'Protominyan' (EH III), with its slightly dull paint on a polished surface.

If any of the typical 'Minyan' features originated in Crete we would expect to find them then, in the EM I And sub-Neolithic periods, but unfortunately these are amongst the least known periods there. Pierced-stone mace heads have been found but they are not very similar to the typical spherical 'Minyan' ones, and are rather more closely related to the Egyptian examples (Branigan 1970: 180, 197). Parallels can be found for some of the 'Minyan' copper or bronze objects such as knives, daggers and tweezers, but they are hardly earlier than EM II (Branigan 1970: 79–84).

The Cyclades

The excavations at Lefkandhi have thrown valuable new light on the relative chronologies of southern Greece, the Cyclades and the eastern Aegean during the 'Minyan' period. From the material found in the first major settlement there, the picture of a new cultural assemblage is gradually emerging. For the moment, not much more than the pottery is known, but it is already clear that it has a distinct character of its own and cannot be classed as either EH II or EH III. Characteristic pot shapes are plates and shallow dishes, some of which are clearly wheel-made, and one-handled cups; red, black and brown polished slips, often scribble-burnished, are not uncommon in fine or slightly coarse wares (Popham and Sackett 1968: 6–8). The material is obviously related to that from the well-known tombs at Manika (French 1966: 49–53; 1968: 61–2), on the basis of which we can add beak-spouted jugs to the repertoire of shapes (Papavasileiou 1910: pl. Θ/[1]) It can now be seen that individual features of this group have long been known in the Cyclades, in particular the typical 'Trojan' cup shape, which has been found on Siphnos, Syros, Naxos, Delos etc. (Refrew 1964: 117, pls. Z/3, 4; French 1968: figs. 51, 56). Until recently, there was no stratigraphical evidence that these objects belonged to a separate chronological horizon; consequently they have been classed as Early Cycladic II (Keros-Syros culture). Now a new deposit of this group has been discovered in the Cyclades at Kea (Caskey 1968a: 393; 1968b: 18; Irwin 1970: 283; pl. 351c). The chronological position of the Lefkandhi I group is illustrated by the stratigraphy at Lefkandhi. It would seem to be later than EH II, as the use of the potter's wheel indicates; only a few isolated sherds that might possibly be attributed to EH II were found there, although we know from Sackett's survey of Euboea that EH II was a flourishing period in the island, with several sites in the immediate neighbourhood of Lefkandhi (Sackett and others 1966: 52–68). It does not seem possible, then, that Lefkandhi I could have been contemporary with EH II as there would surely have been much more evidence of mutual contact if such had been the case. Lefkandhi I was overlain by a thin level of the 'Protominyan' (EH III) phase, in which Grey Minyan ware appears from the beginning. This can be taken to indicate that it was in a fairly late stage of its development that EH III succeeded Lefkandhi I; the earlier stages of the 'Protominyan' period should be at least in part contemporary with Lefkandhi I. This is borne out by an obvious Lefkandhi I type import which was found at Korakou (Blegen 1921: 137, fig. 17), in the highest layer of the first stratum which Blegen assigns to the end of the EH period. Typical EH III dark-on-light and light-on-dark wares are similarly described (Blegen 1921: 11); and, fortunately, associated sherds are still preserved in the Museum at Corinth, which confirm his attribution.

With the new evidence from Kea, it seems that the Lefkandhi I group may in fact eventually prove to be the characteristic aspect of Early Cycladic III. Some of the material from the Khalandhriani cemetery on Syros is contemporary (Tsountas 1899: 77–115), but the settlement at Kastri appears to be slightly later (Bossert 1967: 73–4) and should be contemporary rather with the 'Early Minyan' (MH I) period. Slightly later than Kastri but also contemporary with the 'Early Minyan' period is the First City at Phylakopi.

The following synchronism is suggested:

'Protominyan' (EH III)   = EC III (Lefkandhi I: Khalandhriani cem-
                               etery-Syros)
'Early Minyan' (MH I)   = MC I (Khalandhriani-Kastri settlement:
                               Phylakopi First City)
'Classical Minyan' (MH II) = MC II (Phylakopi Second City)
'Late Minyan' (MH III)   = MC III (late Phylakopi Second City and
                               possibly beginning of Third City?).

Early Cycladic II, or the Keros-Syros culture, as it is sometimes called, was closely related to EH II (Caskey 1964: 28), so we should not expect to find much in common with the 'Minyan' culture in it. In view of the fact that Lefkandhi I elements have previously been attributed to EC II, it would be perhaps unwise to make too much of any similarities that may exist, until the whole Cycladic material has been re-worked, and objects belonging to different stages have been separated. The adoption of the potter's wheel in the 'Minyan' period is possibly due to contact with the Lefkandhi I culture, and typical Lefkandhi I shapes have been found on the mainland opposite Euboea; 'Trojan' cups were found at Ayia Marina (Kunze 1934: 55–6), Orchomenos (Kunze 1934: 54–6, fig. 15, pl. XXII/2–4), Eutresis (Goldman 1931: 105, fig. 138), and Raphina (Theokharis 1952: 145, fig. 12); and the two-handled vessel called by Schliemann 'depas amphikypellon', which was also found at Orchomenos (Kunze 1934: 56, 89, pl. XXX/5d, pl. XXIII/1), may be another feature that was introduced under the influence of Lefkandhi I. In view of the fact that several settlements of Lefkandhi I type are known on the coast of Euboea opposite the mainland, it may well be that settlements of this type will also be found on the mainland coast eventually (French 1968: 129–35). It should be noted that copper or bronze chisels, flat axes, daggers and tweezers very similar to typical 'Minyan' examples have been attributed to the Keros-Syros culture (Renfrew 1967).

The Eastern Aegean and Anatolia

In the eastern Aegean ceramic similarities with Lefkandhi I and Manika are found in Troy II. They include almost identical wheel-made plates and shallow dishes as well as 'Trojan' one-handled cups. Schliemann's *depas amphikypellon* is found in the late stages of Troy II, and beaked jugs similar to those found at Manika are found at Troy and elsewhere in western Anatolia (French 1968: 129–35; Blegen 1950: pls. 370a, 414). Related material has also been found in the fourth settlement at Poliochni on Lemnos (Red Phase) (Bernabo-Brea 1964: pls. CXLIII–CXLIX). French has noted other related material at Emporio on Chios (Hood 1965: 224–5), and the Heraion on Samos (Milojčić 1961: 38–52; French 1968: 129–35, figs. 49–51). A few vessels belonging to the same complex were found at Beycesultan, in level XIIIa, where they are said to be imports (Lloyd and Mellaart 1962: 190, 192–3, fig. 46 nos. 1–6). One wonders, however, whether they might not form a separate level which was thinly represented at that site for some reason or other. M. Mellink has shown that pottery from Karataş in Lycia, and even Tarsus in Cilicia, belongs to the same complex, which can be dated to the EB III period (Mellink 1965: 115–16). It would seem from this that the origins of the ceramic traditions of Lefkandhi I at least should be sought in southern or western Anatolia. The following synchronisms are suggested between 'Minyan' Greece and Troy, on the basis of the evidence from Lefkandhi:

> 'Protominyan' (EH III)   = Troy II
>
> 'Early Minyan' (MH I)   = Troy III-v
>
> 'Classical Minyan' (MH II) ⎱
> 'Late Minyan' (MH III)   ⎰ = Troy VI (early)

Fortunately there is other material, apart from the ceramic, from Troy, which can be used for making comparisons with 'Minyan' Greece. The site itself was on a hill with a stone fortification wall. Houses were generally free-standing rectangular structures (Blegen 1963: 91–2, 99–101, 105–7, 124–38). No cemeteries have been found as yet, and only a few intramural burials are known, mostly of infants. Perforated stone tools and weapons such as hammer-axes, mace-heads and battle-axes are known from Troy II–v (Blegen 1950: pl. 361; Dörpfeld 1902: 373–77). Of these, the mace-heads and one or two of the shorter type of hammer-axes are very similar to the 'Minyan' types. Very few true battle-axes have been found in 'Minyan' Greece as yet, however. In the same levels were also found arrow-straighteners (Dörpfeld 1902: figs. 340, 368), and saw-toothed flints and obsidians, though they were not so deeply or regularly serrated as the typical 'Minyan' examples (Blegen 1950: fig. 362; Dörpfeld 1902: figs. 360–63). Some copper and bronze objects such as chisels and flat axes (Blegen 1950: fig. 358 nos. 36.430, 35.551; Dörpfeld 1902 figs. 267, 275), coiled hair-rings (Blegen 1950: fig. 358 No. 36.432) and pins with knobbed heads (Blegen 1950: pl. 358: 1951: pls. 47, 147, 234; 1953: pl. 297) are very similar to those found in 'Minyan' Greece, and bone pins with carved heads are likewise comparable with Minyan examples (Blegen 1950: pl. 364; 1951: pls. 51, 235; 1953, pl. 303). It seems possible that some of these objects were introduced into Greece from Anatolia by way of Euboea in the Lefkandhi I period. It is now very clear, thanks to Lerna and Lefkandhi, that Grey Minyan pottery could not have been introduced into Greece from north-western Anatolia, since it begins earlier in Greece. True Grey Minyan occurs at Troy only in the sixth settlement, which is contemporary with the 'Classical Minyan' phase in Greece, as is shown by the appearance of the ring-stemmed pedestal goblet in both these contexts. In Greece it occurs two stages before this, and is probably even earlier than the İnegöl Grey ware, which Mellaart saw as a possible ancestor of the Grey Minyan at Troy (Mellaart 1958: 26–32).

It is interesting to observe that stone shaft-hole hammer-axes, battle-axes and mace-heads, serrated flints and obsidians, coiled metal hair-rings and knobbed pins are found in Troy I (Dörpfeld 1902: 321–5; Blegen 1950: pls. 215, 217, 222). Similar objects were found in Poliochni II and III (Blue and Green phases) (Bernabo Brea 1964: pls. LXXXVI, LXXXVII, LXXXIX, C, CI, CII, CV, CLXXVII, CLXXXIII, CLXXXIV) and Thermi I–v (Lamb 1936: 166, 182–185, pls. XXV, XXVI, XXVII), as well as in EB 2 levels at Beycesultan (Lloyd and Mellaart 1962: 276, 289) and Tarsus (Goldmann 1956: 273, 294–5, 298, 313–4, pls. 417, 430, 432, 438). Part of what may have been an apsidal house was also found in Troy I (Blegen 1950: 37, 82, 83, pls. 103, 133–8, 425, 427). Troy I is probably contemporary with EH II in Greece, since the only recognizable sauceboat fragments found at Troy came from that level (Blegen 1950: 40, 54, 186, 193, pls.

252/5, 12, 17). A sauceboat fragment was also found in level v at Thermi (Lamb 1936: 91 fig. 32). It would seem then, that the objects mentioned above have a greater antiquity in the eastern Aegean and Anatolia than in Greece.

Thessaly

The situation in the regions immediately to the north of the 'Minyan' area in Greece is somewhat obscure, owing to the lack of published material from well stratified sites. As we have seen, the 'Protominyan' phase appears at Lefkandhi only towards the end of its development; in other words there was an expansion into Euboea. We have also noted that there may have been a stronger survival of EH II elements in Phocis and Boeotia, and the same areas seem to have been more heavily influenced by Lefkandhi I than the Peloponnese was. It would seem from this that the 'Protominyan' culture developed first in the Peloponnese and then gradually spread northwards into eastern Rumeli (i.e. eastern Greece, between southern Thessaly and the Isthmus of Corinth). It may have taken even longer to reach Thessaly, which was not fully drawn into the 'Minyan' orbit until the 'Classical Minyan' phase (Milojčić 1960: 30–1). It was in this period too, that 'Minyan' influence was felt in Chalcidice and the north-eastern Aegean. Before this Thessaly seems to have enjoyed a more independent existence (Milojčić 1960: 28–9). There may have been some influence from the Phocis-Boeotia area in Milojčić's Early Thessalian II period (Milojčić 1960: 27–8; French 1968: 67–8), spreading perhaps via Lianokladhi and Tsani (levels IV and V) in southern Thessaly (Wace and Thomson 1912: 143–4, 177–8). It is possible that most of Milojčić's EBA sequence for Thessaly is contemporary with the 'Protominyan' phase, if the typical corded ware vessel found in an Early Thessalian Ib context at Argissa is contemporary with the corded ware sherd said to come from the end of the EH III period at Eutresis (Milojčić 1960: 27; Goldman 1931: 123). The following synchronism might be suggested on this basis:

$$\begin{array}{ll} \text{'Protominyan' (EH III)} & = \text{ETh Ib – III} \\ \text{'Early Minyan' (MH I)} & = \text{MTh I – IV} \\ \text{'Classical Minyan' (MH II)} & = \text{MTh V – VII} \end{array}$$

The Thessalian sequence between the Dhimini stage of the Late Neolithic and Milojčić's ETh Ib is still somewhat obscure, and it is difficult to see what was contemporary with EH II. For this reason we should perhaps reserve judgment on the possibility of influence from that direction in the formation of the 'Minyan' culture until more stratified material is forthcoming.

North-western Greece

Even less clear is the situation in north-western Greece, for comparatively little excavation of prehistoric sites of the periods concerned has taken place. Provincial styles of Minyan wares, including some Grey Minyan, have been found as far north as Lefkas, from several sites around the plain of Nidhri (Dörpfeld 1927: 279, 312–14, 316–18). Similar material has been found at Pelikata and Polis on Ithaca (Heurtley 1939: 30–1; Benton 1938: 52). Grey Minyan pottery is reported from four different sites in Cephallenia (Benton 1934: 220, 222, 224, 225), and Middle Helladic at Grabes in Acarnania (Benton 1934: 243–4; 1938: 52) and at Thermon in Aetolia (Romaios 1915: 256–70; 1916: 184–5). As far as it is possible to tell most of these sherds belong to the 'Classical Minyan' or 'Late Minyan' phases, though some of the Pelikata material seems to be 'Protominyan' (Heurtley 1939: 22–8). Typical Minyan objects such as stone shaft-hole hammer-axes have been found at Pelikata (Heurtley 1939: 37–8), an arrow-straightener, flint arrow-heads and bronze chisels, knives and flat axes from the S graves at Skaros in the Nidhri plain (Dörpfeld 1927: 209, 311, pls. 69, 70, 71). Terracotta reels were found at Pelikata (Heurtley 1939: fig. 30), and EH III type 'anchors' at Pelikata (Heurtley 1939: fig. 31, pl. 9/154. EH II material occurs also as far north as Lefkas, and is found on Ithaca and at Grabes in Acarnania.

No EH II or Grey Minyan has yet been found north of Lefkas, and a great many prehistoric sites in Epirus have been distinguished only by coarse wares which are difficult to date accurately (Hammond 1967: 291–314). Some of this material is probably contemporary with the Mycenaean sherds that were found with it at Dodona (Dhakaris 1968: 56–7, pl. 40), Kastritsa (Dhakaris 1951: 182, fig. 7; 1952: 347, fig. 3) and at the Nekyomanteion at Mesopotamos (Dhakaris 1963: 91). On the basis of his excavations at Kastritsa, Dhakaris has distinguished a coarse ware with plastic decoration and a dark brown or black monochrome ware, called K–2 and K–3 respectively by Hammond (Dhakaris 1951: 177–8; Hammond 1967: 292). An interesting feature of the K–2 ware is that it resembles typical 'Minyan' coarse household ware both in fabric and in certain decorative elements. Everted rims, sometimes nicked or bearing finger-tip impressions and strap handles from the rim or base of the neck to the shoulder are characteristic, and knobs or warts, often arranged in pairs on the shoulder, tongue-shaped or forked lugs, and horse-shoe shaped moulded grips are frequently found. Bases are normally flat and thickened, but sometimes pointed (Evangelidhis 1935: 195–C, pls. 2–9). All these features are found not infrequently in coarse Minyan ware, though one feature that is very common in the Epirote ware, finger-tip impressed plastic band decoration, is not. Similar wares have been found at several sites in Korfu (Sordhinas 1965: 144–5; 1968: 80–3; 1969: 410–14). Apart from the coarse ware, the only other features that suggest contemporaneity with the 'Minyan' period are stone shaft-hole hammer-axes from Dodona, Aphiona and Spartilas, chert arrow-heads from Aphiona, and terracotta reels from Dodona, Aphiona and Kephali (Evangelidhis 1935: pls. 7a, 9b/2, 4, 10, 10a; Bulle 1934: 165 fig. 4/1, 166 fig. 4–7, 167 fig. 4/20).

The Balkans and central Europe

Coarse ware very similar to the K–2 ware of Epirus has recently been found in level IIIa at Maliq near Korcë in south-east Albania (Prendi 1966: 262–3). In the same level, which is dated to the Early Bronze Age, were found stone shaft-hole hammer-axes. Almost exactly the same kind of coarse ware is said to be typical of the EBA of southern Bosnia, central and southern Dalmatia and Montenegro, and to continue in use in the Middle and Late Bronze Age as well (Čović 1969: 259). Certain Baden elements were found together with the coarse ware at Maliq. They also occur in the preceding level, level IIb (Prendi 1966: 260–2). So-called Baden features which are widespread in the Balkans and central Europe serve to relate chronologically several cultural groups which seem to vary widely in some respects but are surprisingly similar in others (Ehrich 1965: 430–2; de Laet 1967: 78–9; E. and J. Neustupný, 1961: 67–9; Banner 1956: Kalicz 1963: 67–9; Trbuhović 1968: 37–42; Berciu 1961: 131–48). The area in which these features have been found stretches from southern Germany, Czechoslovakia and southern Poland in the north, to Albania, Macedonia, Thrace and north-western Anatolia in the south. The northern groups have been known the longest and are therefore the best studied. Separate stages in the development as a whole have been discerned, though the exact sequence has not yet been finally worked out (Simeonova 1970: 87–8). Only in the last decade or so has it been realized that Baden features are also found much further south (Neustupný 1968: 24). Kalicz has pointed out the similarities between Baden-Pecel and Troy I, and he attributes an important role to Anatolia in the development of the Baden complex. His attempts to show that the Baden area was also influenced by later developments at Troy are less convincing (Kalicz 1963: 19). Mainly on the basis of field surveys, French has been able to distinguish four other variants of the Troy I culture; one of these is located in Turkish Thrace, another in the İznik region, a third in the regions of Balıkesir and Akhisar-Manisa, and a fourth in the southern Sporades (French 1968: 19–26). Periods II and III at Poliochni (Blue and Green periods) are related to Troy I and also show links with the Cotofeni culture of western Rumania and with other Baden groups in the Carpathian region (Neustupný 1968: 25–8). Certain similarities with Troy I pottery can also be seen in material from the first two settlements at Kritsana in Chalcidice (Heurtley 1939: 17–22, 79–89, 166–71), as well as in that from the fortified settlement at Mikhalits in south-east Bulgaria (Mikov 1948: 7–25). The recent excavations of A. C. Renfrew and M. Gimbutas at

Sitagroi-Photolivos in East Macedonia (Greek Thrace), have produced important new stratigraphical evidence for the ceramic sequence between the Aeneolithic Gumelniṭa culture and the Early Bronze Age (Renfrew 1970: 131–4). Typical Baden features were found in level IV, and links with Troy I could be seen in level vb. The evidence from Sitagroi suggests that there may be a phase missing in the Bulgarian sequence as known from Karanovo and Ezero-Dipsiska Mogila (Georgiev 1961: 87–9; Georgiev and Merpert 1965; 1966). In south-eastern Rumania, the Cernavoda I and II phases have recently been linked with the Baden complex (Morintz and Roman 1968: 45–106, 119–28) and Baden material has been found in southern Yugoslavia at Bubanj-Hum (level Ib), Hisar (Level II) and Gladnica (Garašanin 1958: 226–44; Todorović 1963: 26–9).

It should be pointed out that most of the Baden features that have been noted in the Balkans are ceramic ones, and that a great deal of work remains to be done in defining individual cultural groups and analysing their content. Even in central Europe, the problem of the origins of the various Baden groups and their degree of relationship is still very much a matter for debate, as the papers presented at the international symposium on the Baden culture recently held in Czechoslovakia clearly show (Simeonova 1970: 87–8). The chronological position of Baden cultures with regard to 'Minyan' Greece is shown by Troy. From the evidence of Sitagroi it would seem that the Troy I group belongs to a late stage of the Baden horizon, and Troy I, as we have noted above, is contemporary with EH II in Greece. An EH II sauceboat fragment is said to have been found at Zlotska Pečina in Serbia, together with Cotofeni and Baden-Kostolac pottery (Neustupný 1968: 24). The later part of the Baden horizon at least would thus seem to be contemporary with EH II. This is substantiated by the occurrence of corded ware in the 'Protominyan' (EH III) levels at Eutresis (Goldman 1931: 123, fig. 169). In central Europe the corded ware horizon follows that of Baden (Ehrich 1965: 432–6). Sherds of corded ware were also found at Agios Mamas and Kritsana in Macedonia and serve to date the Macedonian Early Bronze Age as represented in the third to sixth settlements at Kritsana to the 'Protominyan' period. A piece of dark-on-light ware, obviously an import from the 'Protominyan' area, was found in the sixth settlement. (Heurtley 1939: 83, 172). We have noted above the occurrence of corded ware in Milojčić's Early Thessalian Ib phase in Thessaly (Milojčić 1960: 26–7).

The Baden horizon precedes the 'Minyan' period, if these chronological observations are correct. Nevertheless certain interesting parallels between the two can be clearly seen at Vučedol near Belgrade, for example. The settlement there was on a barely accessible hill top and seems to have had a wooden palisade for defence (Schmidt 1945: 48–52; de Laet 1967: 78). The houses appear to have had a wooden framework with walls of wattle and daub, and two houses had apsidal ends (Schmidt 1945: 15–30). Another apsidal house of wooden construction was found in level va at Sitagroi (Renfrew 1970) and others are known from EBA levels at Karanovo, Razkopanitsa and Ezero in Bulgaria, which though perhaps slightly later in date, obviously stem from the same traditions (Mikov 1959: 94–5; Georgiev 1961: 87–9). We have noted above the apsidal house in Troy 1, which however had a stone socle foundation. It is interesting to note that in 'Minyan' Greece, where the apsidal house was a common feature, some of the earliest houses of the type appear to have been wooden constructions. One of the first houses to be built after the destruction of the third settlement at Lerna, for example, was just such a construction (Caskey 1966: 145–6). At Eutresis too, there is some evidence for wooden post-hole buildings in the EH III levels (Goldman 1931: 28, fig. 32), and at Pheneus in Arcadia Mrs. Protonotariou–Dheilaki found traces of similar building techniques in the earliest Middle Helladic levels (Protonotariou–Dheilaki 1965: 159). In north-western Greece wooden framework houses may have continued in use much later than in southern Greece; an example from Thermon may date from 'Late Minyan' times (Romaios 1915: 235–7, 255) and others from Kastritsa and Dodona belong to the Late Bronze Age (Dhakaris 1967: 39–40).

Distinct features of the settlement at Vučedol are the large number of *bothroi* (Schmidt 1945: 31–46) and intramural burials. Baden burial customs seem to have varied widely from area to area, and both inhumation and cremation were practised (Kalicz 1963: 14–18). At Vučedol crouched inhumation burials were found in chambers entered from the base of a shaft (Garašanin, M. 1967). The extent to which tumulus burials occurred in the Baden period is not yet clear. Čović reports very late Baden sherds from some tumuli at Glasinac, and ochre burials in tumuli are said to be found in Rumania and to belong to the Cotofeni and Cernavoda III groups (Berciu 1961: 148; Morintz and Roman 1968: 118). Long barrows are found in the Ohrozim group of northern Moravia, which was basically a late Funnel Beaker group which underwent Baden influences (Neustupný 1961: 66).

Much of the Baden pottery was fired under reducing conditions, so that the predominant colours are dark grey and black. Surfaces were sometimes well polished and strap handles are a characteristic feature. Stone shaft-hole hammer-axes, battle-axes and mace-heads were found at Vučedol (Schmidt 1945: 69–70) and are commonly found in all Baden groups. Flint was used at Vučedol for knife blades (Schmidt 1945: 70–1), and bone and horn industries are well in evidence (Schmidt 1945: 70–1, pl. 27). Copper was certainly known and used in Baden times, and moulds for weapons and tools show that smelting techniques were being used (Jovanović 1966: 27–8). Exploitation of the copper sources of central Europe and the Balkans may have been an economic factor behind the expansion of Baden features over this area.

Some of the features mentioned above have a venerable ancestry in central Europe and the Balkans, going back well into Neolithic times. Apsidal houses were found in the Vinča-Plocnik levels at Vinča (Milojčić 1949: 280) and a possible proto-type can be seen at Bylany in Slovakia (Müller-Karpe 1968: 235, pl. 194/H). Crouched burials are found as early as the *Bandkeramik* period (Müller-Karpe 1968: 363–5), and so are bored stone axes, mace-heads and arrow-heads (Müller-Karpe 1968: 124–25, 128, 129, 131, 132). Arrow-straighteners occur from *Stichbandkeramik* levels onwards (Müller-Karpe 1968: 128, pls. 201/B10, 201/C1, 220/A7), and antlers were not infrequently used for tools throughout the Neolithic period (Müller-Karpe 1968: 123).

Italy

We should perhaps look at one other region for possible connections with 'Minyan' Greece, that of southern Italy and Sicily, to the west. There seems to have been a strong break between the Late Neolithic period and the Aeneolithic in this region, with distinct changes in ceramic styles, tomb types, weapons and tools (Bernabo-Brea 1968–9: 27). The subsequent Aeneolithic and Early Bronze Age sequence is complex and not exactly clear in places, probably owing to gaps in our knowledge (Trump 1966: 63–109; Peroni 1967: 78–92; Bernabo-Brea 1968–9: 20–58). The beginning of the Middle Bronze Age in Apulia and the end of the Early Bronze Age in the Aeolian Islands are firmly linked chronologically to the beginning of the Late Bronze Age in Greece by the imports of LH I pottery in an early phase of the Middle Apennine period at Porto Peroni near Leporano, and of LH I and II in a late phase of the Capo Graziano period on Lipari and Filicudi (Bernabo-Brea 1968–9: 56; Lo Porto 1963b: 333–4). Further links between Apulia and Greece are suggested by the presence of Grey Minyan and Matt Painted sherds in levels of the 'Early Apennine' period at Porto Peroni, though the chronology of this period is disputed (Peroni 1967: 88–99). For the earlier periods correlations with the 'Minyan' sequence are difficult to demonstrate as yet. It is interesting to note, however, that from the Aeneolithic period onwards certain tools and weapons occur, which are very similar to typical 'Minyan' weapons and tools. These include stone shaft-hole hammer-axes (Trump 1966: 85, 96, fig. 24; Bernabo-Brea 1966: 99, 107), mace-heads (Trump 1966: 79, 94, pl. 37; Peroni 1967: 81; Bernabo-Brea 1968–9: 31, 34, 39) and hollow-based arrow-heads (Trump 1966: 93). A stone arrow-straightener was found in a tomb at Cellino San Marco in Apulia (Franco 1952: 234–46). Copper flat axes and triangular daggers are other characteristic features for which parallels can be found in 'Minyan' Greece (Trump 1966: 74, 75, 82, pl. 37; Peroni 1967: 81). Another possibly significant feature is a tendency to produce dark-surfaced vessels in the initial stages of the Aeneolithic period. Some of these features are perhaps due to the influence of the Late Neolithic Lagozza culture of north Italy (Trump 1966: 67), and they may ultimately be derived from the central European and Balkan traditions of the Baden area. The type of tomb 'a forno e pozzetto' which was introduced in the Aeneolithic period is surely closer to the shaft and chamber tombs found at Vučedol in the Baden-Kostolac levels than to the Cypriot and Aegean tombs that Bernabo-Brea sees as their proto-types (Bernabo-Brea 1968–9: 27; Garašanin, M. 1967). The use of red ochre in burials, which becomes widespread in Italy in the Aeneolithic period. (Peroni 1967: 81) is also found in the Baden area (Berciu 1961: 148).

Conclusions

Following this brief examination of the material of the Middle Helladic and preceding periods in Greece, and the comparison between it and that of contemporary and earlier periods in neighbouring regions, what conclusions can be drawn? One of the most obvious is that in spite of a century or more of excavation in many cases, there are still enormous gaps in our source material, and that much more excavation will have to take place before the origins of the Middle Helladic or 'Minyan' culture can be defined conclusively. It is to be hoped that anthropological and environmental studies, which are still in their infancy in many of the regions with which we are concerned, will eventually place additional information at our disposal. On the existing evidence a few tentative suggestions may be made, which should not be regarded, however, as much more than hypotheses. The EH III ('Protominyan') period should be considered the first expression of what is regarded as the Middle Helladic tradition in Greece. It has little in common with the period that precedes it. Indeed the break at its beginning is strong enough to suggest the arrival of new people with new traditions. Some of the new features that were introduced can be paralleled in western Anatolia, though there are sometimes slight differences. At the same time as the 'Protominyan' culture appeared on the mainland of Greece, a contemporary but different culture was established in the Cyclades and Euboea, whose pottery at least derived from Anatolia. The 'Protominyan' (EH III) ceramic traditions are different, and it seems that, though there may have been some influence from the eastern Aegean, a more direct source of origin for the 'Minyan culture' should be looked for elsewhere. The typical 'Protominyan' stage may well have evolved in the Peloponnese, whence it spread northwards. In eastern central Greece there was perhaps a stronger survival of EH II traditions, and the same area was more heavily influenced by the Cycladic-Euboean culture represented by Lefkandhi I (Early Cycladic III?). A similar situation is found in Thessaly, where the 'Minyan' traditions arrived even later. This would seem to preclude the north-east from having played an important role in the establishment of the 'Minyan' culture. Although little material is available yet, one or two features found in the north-west are very close to typical 'Minyan' features, and in view of the fact that these and other 'Minyan' features are found generally in the areas of central Europe and the Balkans occupied by the Baden group of cultures, which chronologically belong to an earlier horizon, it may be that the 'Minyan' traditions generally, can be ultimately traced back to this region via north-western Greece. It is not impossible that similar features which have been noted in Italy and Anatolia might have derived from the same area. It is tempting to speculate on the implications of this for the Indo-European question, but a vast amount of excavation, publication and analysis will be needed before we shall be in anything like a position to answer any of these questions authoritively.

References

BANNER, J. 1956. *Die Peceler Kultur* (*Archaeologia Hungarica: Dissertationes Archaeologicae Musei Nationalis Hungarici N.S. 35*). Budapest.

BENTON, S. 1932. 'The Ionian Islands.' *BSA*, 32: 213–46.

——. 1935. 'Excavations in Ithaca III.' *BSA*, 35: 45–73.

BERCIU, D. 1961. *Contributii la Problemele Neoliticului in Rominia in Lumina Noilor Cercetari*. Bucharest.

BERNABO-BREA, L. 1964. *Poliochni I*. Rome.

——. 1966. *Sicily before the Greeks*. London.

——. 1968–9. 'Considerazioni sull' Eneolitico e sulla Prima Età del Bronzo della Sicilia e della Magna Grecia.' *Kokalos*, 14–15: 20–58.

BLEGEN, C. W. 1921. *Korakou, a Prehistoric Settlement near Corinth*. Boston and New York.

——. 1928. *Zygouries, a Prehistoric Settlement in the Valley of Cleonae*. Cambridge, Mass.

——. 1937. *Prosymna, the Helladic Settlement Preceding the Argive Heraeum*. Cambridge.

——. 1950. *Troy I*. Princeton.

——. 1951. *Troy II*. Princeton.

——. 1953. *Troy III*. Princeton.

——. 1958. *Troy IV*. Princeton.

——. 1963. *Troy and the Trojans*. London.

BRANIGAN, K. 1970. *The Foundations of Palatial Crete*. London.

BOSSERT, E. M. 1967. 'Kastri auf Syros.' *Deltion*, 22: 53–75.

BUCHHOLZ, H.-G. 1962. 'Der Pfeilglätter aus dem VI Schachtgrab von Mykene und die Helladischen Pfeilspitzen.' *JdI*, 77: 1–58.

BULLE, H. 1934. 'Ausgrabungenbei Aphiona auf Korfu.' *AthMitt*, 59: 147–240.

CASKEY, J. L. 1955. 'Excavations at Lerna 1954.' *Hesperia*, 24: 25–49.

——. 1956. 'Excavations at Lerna 1955.' *Hesperia*, 25: 147–73.

——. 1960. 'The Early Helladic Period in the Argolid.' *Hesperia*, 29: 283–303.

——. 1964. 'Greece, Crete and the Aegean Islands in the Early Bronze Age.' *CAH* (rev. ed.), I, Chap. XXVIa/Fasc. 24.

——. 1966a. 'Greece and the Aegean Islands in the Middle Bronze Age.' *CAH* (rev. ed.), II, Chap. IVa/Fasc. 45.

——. 1966b. 'Houses of the Fourth Settlement at Lerna.' *Kharistirion eis Anastasion K. Orlandhon* III (*Bibliothiki tis en Athinais Arkhailogikis Etaireias* 58): 144–52.

——. 1968. 'Excavations in Kea.' *Deltion*, 23 Khron.: 389–93.

—— and CASKEY, E. G. 1960. 'The earliest settlement at Eutresis, supplementary excavations, 1958.' *Hesperia*, 29: 126–67.

CHILDE, V. G. 1915. 'On the date and origin of Minyan ware.' *JHS*, 35: 196–207.

COURBIN, P. 1954. 'Chroniques des fouilles en 1953, Seconde Partie; Travaux de l'École Francaise: Argos IV, Nécropole et Céramique.' *BCH*, 78: 175–83.

ČOVIĆ, B. 1969. 'Bronze Age of the "Central Illyrian Area".' *Actes du Premier Congrés International des Études Balkaniques et Sud-Est Européennes II*. (1966: ed. V. I. Georgiev, N. Todorov, V. Tăpkova-Zaimova; Sofia): 255–71.

DHAKARIS, S. I. 1951. 'Anaskafi eis Kastritsan Ioanninon.' *Praktika*, 1951: 173–83.

——. 1952. 'Anaskafi eis Kastritsan Ioanninon.' *Praktika*, 1952: 362–86.

——. 1963. 'Anaskafi eis to Nekyomanteion tou Akherontos.' *Praktika*, 1963: 89–92.

——. 1967. 'Anaskafi tou Ierou tis Dhodhonis.' *Praktika*, 1967: 33–54.

——. 1968. 'Anaskafi tou Ierou tis Dhodhonis.' *Praktika*, 1968: 42–59.

DOR, L., JANNORAY, J., VAN EFFENTERRE, H. and VAN EFFENTERRE, M. 1960. *Kirrha: étude de préhistoire phocidienne*. Paris.

DÖRPFELD, W. 1902. *Troja und Ilion*. Athens.

——. 1927. *Alt Ithaka. Ein Beitrag zur Homer-Frage*, I. Munich.

EHRICH, R. W. 1965. 'Geographical and chronological patterns in East and Central Europe'; in R. W. Ehrich, *Chronologies*: 403–58.

EVANGELIDHIS, D. 1935. 'I Anaskafi tis Dhodhonis 1935.' *Ipeirotika Khronika*, 10: 192–260.

FORSDYKE, E. J. 1914. 'The pottery called Minyan ware.' *JHS*, 34: 126–56.

FRANCO, A. 1952. 'La tomba a forno di Cellino S. Marco nel quadro della civiltà sicula del Salento.' *Atti Io Congr. Int. di Preistoria e Protostoria Mediterranea* (1950; ed. P. Graziosi, A. Micheli, M. Pallottino; Florence): 224–55.

FRENCH, D. H. 1966. 'Recent archaeological research in Turkey.' *AnatSt*, 16: 25–53.

——. 1968. '*Anatolia and the Aegean in the third millennium B.C.*' (Ph.D. dissertation, University of Cambridge; unpublished).

FRÖDIN, O. and PERSSON, A. W. 1938. *Asine—Results of the Swedish Excavations 1922–1930*. Stockholm.

FUCHS, S. 1937. *Die Griechischen Fundgruppen der Frühen Bronzezeit und ihre auswärtigen Beziehungen*. Berlin.

GARAŠANIN, M. V. 1958. 'Kontrollgrabung in Bubanj bei Niš.' *PZ*, 36: 223–44.

——. 1967. 'Die Bestattungen des Vučedoler "Berghungels".' *Archaeologia Iugoslavica*, 8: 27–33.

GEORGIEV, G. I. 1961. 'Kulturgruppen der Jungstein- und der Kupferzeit in der Ebene von Thrazien (Sudbulgariens).' *Prague Symposium*: 45–100.

—— and MERPERT, N. J. 1965. 'Razkopki Mnogosloynovo Poselenia u S. Ezero.' *Izvestia* (*Bulgaria*), 28: 129–59.

1966. 'The Ezero Mound in south-east Bulgaria.' *Antiquity*, 40: 33–7.

GOLDMAN, H. 1931. *Excavations at Eutresis in Boeotia*. Cambridge, Mass.

——. 1956. *Excavations at Gozlu Kale, Tarsus: II*. Princeton.

HALEY, J. B. and BLEGEN, C. W. 1928. 'The coming of the Greeks.' *AJA*, 32: 141–54.

HAMMOND, N. G. L. 1967a. 'Tumulus burial in Albania, the grave circles of Mycenae, and the Indo-Europeans.' *BSA*, 62: 77–105.

——. 1967b. *Epirus*. Oxford.

HEURTLEY, W. A. 1934–35. 'Excavations in Ithaka II.' *BSA*, 35: 1–44.

——. 1939. *Prehistoric Macedonia*. Cambridge.

HOLMBERG, E. J. 1944. *The Swedish Excavations at Asea in Arcadia*. Goteborg.

HOOD, M. S. F. 1965. 'Excavations at Emporio, Chios 1952–55.' *Atti del VI Congresso Internazionale delle Scienze Preistoriche e Protostoriche 2* (1962; ed. M. Pallottino, R. Peroni, M. Corona; Florence): 224–30.

HOWELL, R. J. 1970. 'A survey of eastern Arcadia in prehistory.' *BSA*, 65: 79–127.

HUTCHINSON, R. W. 1968. *Prehistoric Crete*. London.

HUXLEY, G. L. and COLDSTREAM, J. N. 1966. 'Kythera, first Minoan colony.' *ILN*, 27 August 1966: 28–9.

IRWIN, M. 1970. 'News letter from Greece.' *AJA*, 74: 261–84.

JOVANOVIĆ, B. 1966. 'Apparition et histoire sommaire de la métallurgie du cuivre dans l'Eneolithique Balkano-Danubien.' *Starinar*, N.S., 17: 1–14.

KALICZ, N. 1963. *Die Peceler (Badener) Kultur und Anatolien*. Budapest.

KHADZIZOGIDHIS, N. G. 1898. 'Thessalika Zitimata.' *Athina*, 10: 541–55.

KUNZE, E. 1934. *Orchomenos III*. Munich.

LAMB, W. 1936. *Excavations at Thermi in Lesbos*. Cambridge.

LAET, S. J. DE, 1967. *La préhistoire de l'Europe*. Brussels.

LLOYD, S. and MELLAART, J. 1962. *Beycesultan I*. London.

LO PORTO, F. G. 1963a. 'La Tomba di Cellino S. Marco e l'inizio della civiltà del Bronzo in Puglia.' *Bolletino de Paletnologia Italiana*, N.S., 11: 71–225.

——. 1963b. 'Leporano (Taranto): La stazione protostorica di Porto Peroni.' *Notizie Degli Scavi*, 17: 280–380.

MARINATOS, SP. 1954. 'Anaskafe en Pylo.' *Praktika*, 1954: 299–316.

——. 1970. 'Further news from Marathon.' *AthAA*, 3: 155–66.

McDONALD, W. A. and HOPE SIMPSON, R. 1969. 'Further explorations in south-western Peloponnese.' *AJA*, 73: 123–77.

MEGAW, A. H. S. 1965. 'Archaeology in Greece 1964–65.' *ArchRep*, 1965 (*JHS*, 86): 3–24.

MELLAART, J. 1958. 'The end of the Early Bronze Age in Anatolia and the Aegean.' *AJA*, 62: 9–33.

MELLINK, M. J. 1965. 'Anatolian Chronology'; R. W. Ehrich, *Chronologies*: 101–31. Chicago.

MIKOV, V. 1948. 'Fouilles du site préhistorique près de Mikhalitch.' *Fouilles et recherches*, 1 (Sofia): 7–25.

——. 1959. 'The prehistoric mound of Karanovo. *Archaeology*, 12: 88–97.

MILOJČIĆ, V. 1949. 'South-eastern elements in the prehistoric civilization of Serbia.' *BSA*, 44: 258–306.

——. 1960. *Hauptegebnisse der deutschen Ausgrabungen in Thessalien 1953–58*. Bonn.

——. 1961. *Samos I. Die prähistorische Siedlung unter dem Heraion: Grabung 1953 und 1958*. Bonn.

MORINTZ, S. and ROMAN, P. 1968. 'Aspekte des Ausgangs des Äneolithikums und der Übergangsstufe zur Bronzezeit in Raum der Niederdonau.' *Dacia*, N.S., 12: 45–128.

MÜLLER, K. 1930. *Tiryns III. Die Ergebnisse der Ausgrabungen des Instituts*. Augsburg.

——. 1938. *Tiryns IV. Die Ergebnisse der Ausgrabungen des Instituts*. Augsburg and Munich.

MÜLLER-KARPE, H. 1968. *Handbuch der Vorgeschichte, II*. Munich.

MYLONAS, G. 1959. *Aghios Kosmas: an Early Bronze Age Settlement and Cemetery in Attica*. Princeton.

NEUSTUPNÝ, E. F. 1968. 'Absolute chronology of the Neolithic and Aeneolithic periods in central and south-eastern Europe.' *Slovenská Archeologia*, 16: 19–60.

——. and NEUSTUPNÝ, J. 1961. *Czechoslovakia before the Slavs*. London.

PAPADHIMITRIOU, I. 1957. 'Vravron kai Alai Aradinidhis.' *Ergon*, 1957: 20–5.

PAPAVASILEIOU, G. A. 1910. *Peri ton en Evvoia arkhaion taphon.* Athens.

PERONI, R. 1967. *Archeologia della Puglia Preistorica.* Rome.

PLATON, N. and STASSINOPOULOU-TOULOUPA, E. 'Ivories and Linear B from Thebes.' *ILN*, 5 December 1964: 896–7.

POPHAM, M. R. AND SACKETT, L. H. 1968. *Excavations at Lefkandi, Euboea 1964–66.* London.

PRENDI, F. 1966. 'La civilisation préhistorique de Maliq.' *Studia Albanica*, 3: 255–80.

PROTONOTARIOU-DHEILAKI, E. 1965. 'Anaskafai Feneou.' *Deltion*, 20 Khron.: 158–59.

RENFREW, A. C. 1964. 'Crete and the Cyclades before Rhadamanthus.' *KritKhron*, 18: 107–41.

—— 1969. 'Cycladic metallurgy and the Aegean Early Bronze Age.' *AJA*, 71: 1–20.

——. 1970. 'The Burnt House at Sitagroi.' *Antiquity*, 44: 131–34.

ROMAIOS, K. A. 1915. 'Ek tou Proistorikou Thermou.' *Deltion*, 1: 225–79.

——. 1916. 'Erevnai en Thermo.' *Deltion*, 2: 179–86.

ROWE, K. R. 1954. 'Mycenae 1939–1953: Part III. A possible Middle Helladic fortification wall.' *BSA*, 49: 248–53.

SAFLUND, G. 1965. *Excavations at Berbati 1936–37.* Uppsala.

SACKETT, L. H. 1966. 'Prehistoric Euboea: contributions towards a survey.' *BSA*, 61: 33–112.

SCHLIEMANN, H. 1878. *Mycenae: A Narrative of Researches and Discoveries at Mycenae and Tiryns.* London.

——. 1880. *Ilios, the City and Country of the Trojans.* London.

——. 1880. *Orchomenos. Bericht über meine Ausgrabungen in Böotischen Orchomenos.* Leipzig.

SCHMIDT, R. R. 1945. *Die Burg Vučedol.* Zagreb.

SIMEONOVA, H. 1970. 'Medunaroden Simpozium Vurhu Problemite na Proižoda i Hronologiata na Kulturata Baden.' *Archeologia* (Warsaw), 21: 87–8.

SORDHINAS, A. 1965. 'Proïstoriki Erevna stin Kerkyra kata to 1965.' *Kerkyraïka Khronika*, 11: 141–8.

——. 1968. 'Proïstoriki Erevna stin Kerkyra to 1966.' *Kerkyraïka Khronika*, 14: 77–83.

——. 1969. 'Investigations of the prehistory of Corfu during 1964–1966.' *Balkan Studies*, 10: 393–424.

STAIS, V. 1893. 'Anaskafai en Thoriko.' *Praktika*, 1893: 12–17.

SYRIOPOULOS, K. T. 1964. *Proistoria tis Peloponnisou.* Athens.

——. 1968. *Proistoria tis Stereas Elladhos.* Athens.

THEOKHARIS, D. 1952. 'Anaskafi en Arafini.' *Praktika*, 1952: 129–51.

——. 1956. 'Anaskafai en Iolko.' *Praktika*, 1956: 119–30.

——. 1957. 'Anaskafai en Iolko.' *Praktika*, 1957: 54–9.

TODOROVIĆ, J. 1963. 'Die Grabung Hissar, und ihre Verhältinisse zum Äneolithikum und der Fruhen Bronzezeit.' *Archaeologia Iugoslavica*, 4: 25–9.

TASIĆ, N. 1967. *Badenski i Vučedolski Kulturni Komplex u Jugoslaviji.* Belgrade.

TRBUHOVIC, V. B. 1968. *Problemi porekla i Datovanja Bronzanog Doba u Srbiji.* Belgrade.

TRUMP, D. 1966. *Central and Southern Italy before Rome.* London.

TSOUNTAS, C. 1899. 'Kykladhika II.' *ArchEph*, 1899: 74–134.

VALMIN, N. N. 1938. *The Swedish Messenia Expedition.* Lund.

VOLLGRAFF, W. 1907. 'Fouilles d'Argos.' *BCH*, 31: 137–84.

WAAGE, F. O. 1949. 'An Early Helladic well near Old Corinth.' *Hesperia: Supplement VIII*: 415–22.

WACE, A. J. B. and BLEGEN, C. W. 1918, 'The Pre-Mycenaean pottery of the mainland.' *BSA*, 22: 175–9.

—— and THOMPSON, M. S. 1912. *Prehistoric Thessaly*. Cambridge.
WALKER KOSMOPOULOS, L. 1948. *The Prehistoric Inhabitation of Corinth*. Munich.
WATERHOUSE, H. and HOPE-SIMPSON, R. 1961. 'Prehistoric Laconia: Part II.' *BSA*,
56: 114–75.

Discussion

J. L. CASKEY: Evidence from Lerna has been cited several times at this
Colloquium. Since full reports of the excavation of that site have not yet
been published (*mea culpa*), let me add a few comments. Mr. R. J. Howell in
his thoughtful paper emphasizes the "cultural continuum" from EH III
through MH. Ten years ago this was a new idea. My colleague Mrs.
Wiencke was, I think, the first to accept, simply and directly, the implications of the stratigraphy at Lerna. Encouraged, I tried to present the main
facts and some possible explanations (*Hesperia*, 1960). There, of course, I put
emphasis on continuity, not on the remaining obstacles to assuming it,
though these were mentioned. Lerna IV (EH III), though it had Grey
Minyan bowls and apsidal houses, was not the same as Lerna V (MH).
Matt Painted and Argive Minyan wares appeared suddenly and abundantly
at the very beginning of the latter period, when also there came notable
though sporadic examples of other wares imported for the first time from
abroad. Much more important, however, is the new practice of intramural
burial which began in VA. Pottery, as we have been reminded (almost too
often), does not furnish conclusive evidence of invasions, migrations, or
basic changes in ways of life. But new burial customs almost always do
reflect new conditions: religious, political-military, economic, possibly climatic. They should not be overlooked in our estimates. The sequence of
events at Lerna can scarcely have been unique. I continue to think that it
was similar in general at Asine, Tiryns, and Zygouries. Apparently it was
somewhat different at Berbati and Korakou; possibly similar to Kirrha;
surely different at Eutresis. Results of further study are awaited from
Lefkandhi and from Ayia Irini in Keos. Nobody expects to find uniformity
(witness the good remarks by Professor J. D. Evans (see above, p. 25). For
these reasons, and with thought of the professional studies of forty years
already in print, we rejected in 1960 the obvious step of revising Helladic
terminology. Like most jargon it is imperfect, but it is established, logical,
correct in its chronological sequence, and readily intelligible. Let us have
pity on our successors who will have to read old and many new books, and
may have even less time for them than we have.

I should oppose the adoption of terms like 'Minyan culture'. ('Minyan',
by the way, has worked hard enough; Thucydides might have called it

kekmekós; it meant vaguely a people of legend, then not very precisely some classes of pots; let it rest.) 'Culture' is a feeble and unhappy word, to be used sparingly. Let us remember that the study of cultures—in the sense so vigorously advocated by Dr. A. C. Renfrew—is, in fact, by no means new in Aegean archaeology. Our failures to reach valid conclusions today come not from illiteracy or false method, but chiefly from a paucity of firmly attested facts, accurately reported. What we need most is a patient and modest assembling of the data, not a new vocabulary.

A. SHERRATT: *Cultural changes at the beginning of the Bronze Age: a note.* The question of population movements in south-eastern Europe is crucial to the problem of the origin of Indo-European languages in Mediterranean areas, and the Early Bronze Age has often been seen as a time of widespread migrations during which new elements may have reached the Aegean. The immediately preceding Aeneolithic period of south-eastern Europe is characterized by a series of striking cultures, the richness of whose painted pottery with elaborate spiral ornament, and sophisticated plastic art, has long been celebrated. These stretch from the western Ukraine to the Aegean and include the Tripolye, Cucuteni, Gumelniţa and Salcuţa cultures, and also the related West Macedonian group represented at Dikili Taş and Sitagroi-Photolivos. With these groups is associated a flourishing metal industry. A collateral (western) group, without the painted style, but with an even richer metal industry, occupies the Carpathian basin where it is represented by the Tiszapolgar-Bodrogkeresztúr and Vinča-Plocnik cultures. In the succeeding Early Bronze Age, these groups of sophisticated pottery styles are replaced by a much less pleasing series of styles, less finely finished and with a simpler series of shapes, and metal finds associated with them are much scarcer. The cultures of the eastern group (Folteşti, Cernavoda, Ezero and the Macedonian EBA) cover an area comparable to that of the eastern Aeneolithic group, and show close relations with the EBA cultures of the Carpathian ring, the Baden-Cotofeni group. Where formerly painted designs had been used to decorate pottery, a system of decoration based on white-filled impressions now became dominant. Various different methods of making these impressions were used by different groups: e.g. the so-called *Furchenstich* technique, or the use of cord. This latter was especially fashionable in the Lower Danube and Maritsa basins, but was widespread within the eastern culture-group. There is no reason to regard these changes as the result of a complete replacement of the Aeneolithic groups by a tribal group of alien origin. The EBA groups were not nomadic pastoralists, and there is no suggestion of a radical break in settlement over the whole area at this time, many EBA settlements continuing on top of Aeneolithic ones and representing a continuation of village-based mixed farming. The paucity of metal-work is probably due to technical reasons; analyses of Aeneolithic metal artefacts show that a high proportion of them was made of natural copper, which by Early Bronze Age times seems to have run out. Similarly, cord-decoration is not a single "intrusive" feature, but is part of a new style and represents part of a common response to the problems of decorating pottery other than by painting. There is no widespread common phase among the EBA cultures which might represent an undifferentiated early substratum, and instead, the series of regional styles gives a picture precisely analogous to the situation among the painted pottery cultures of the Aeneolithic period. Economic developments such as changes in the emphasis on different types of livestock do seem to have taken place at the beginning of the EBA, and no doubt new cultural features did spread from culture to culture within the continuum, but changes occurring within the major culture groups involved would seem to be a more likely explanation of the genesis of EBA cultures in these areas. In summary, then, the connections between northern Greece and the rest of south-eastern Europe at the beginning of the Early Bronze Age can be interpreted as representing a continuation rather than a break in the pattern of relations which existed during the Aeneolithic ('Late Neolithic' in Greece) with developments in the Lower Danube and Maritsa valleys being paralleled or reflected in northern Greece.

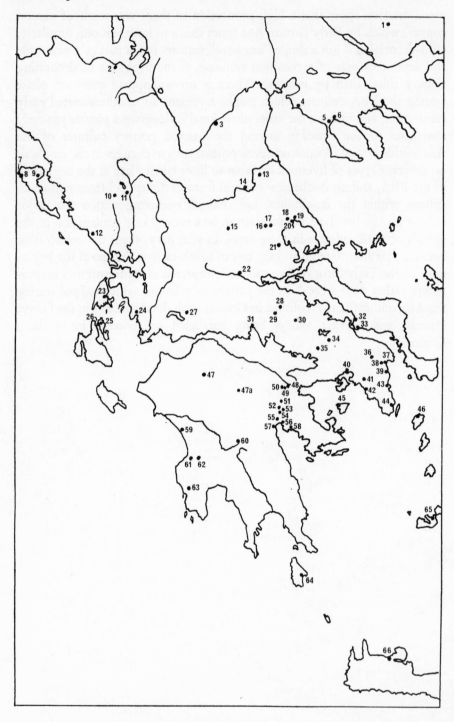

Fig. 9.1. Greece, showing sites mentioned

1. Sitagroi.	23. Nidhri.	45. Aigina.
2. Maliq.	24. Grabes.	46. Keos: Ayia Irini.
3. Servia.	25. Pelikata.	47. Lopesi-Katarrhaktis.
4. Kritsana.	26. Polis.	48. Korakou.
5. Ayios Mamas.	27. Thermon.	49. Old Corinth.
6. Molyvopyrgos.	28. Elateia.	50. Kheliotomylos.
7. Kefali.	29. Ayia Marina.	51. Zygouries.
8. Aphiona.	30. Orchomenos.	52. Mycenae.
9. Spartillas.	31. Kirrha.	53. Berbati.
10. Dodona.	32. Manika.	54. Prosymna.
11. Kastritsa.	33. Lefkandhi.	55. Argos.
12. Mesopotamos.	34. Thebes.	56. Tiryns.
13. Rakhmani.	35. Eutresis.	57. Lerna.
14. Argissa.	36. Aphidna.	58. Asine.
15. Tsani.	37. Marathon—Rasi.	59. Samikon.
16. Tsangli.	38. Marathon—Vrana.	60. Asea.
17. Rini.	39. Raphina.	61. Peristeria.
18. Sesklo.	40. Eleusis.	62. Malthi.
19. Volos.	41. Athens.	63. Papoulia.
20. Pefkakia.	42. Ayios Kosmas.	64. Kastri.
21. Zerelia.	43. Brauron.	65. Phylakopi.
22. Lianokladhi.	44. Thorikos.	66. Khania.

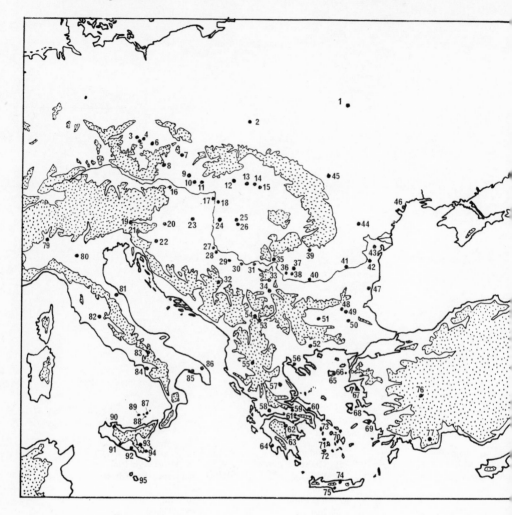

Fig. 9.2. The Mediterranean region and southern central Europe, showing sites mentioned

1. Gorodsk.
2. Złota.
3. Kamyk.
4. Vysočany.
5. Prague-Bubenec.
6. Bylany.
7. Ohrozim.
8. Jevisovice.
9. Boleraz.
10. Bošáca.
11. Stary Zamek.
12. Center.
13. Bodrogkeresztúr.
14. Székely.
15. Viss.
16. Baden.
17. Budakalász.
18. Reczel.
19. Kanzianberg.
20. Ptuj.
21. Drulovka.
22. Ajdovska jama.
23. Fonyód.
24. Kiskőrös.
25. Szentes.
26. Hódmezővásárhely.
27. Sarvaš.
28. Vučedol.
29. Gomolova.
30. Vinča.
31. Kostolac.
32. Glasinac.

33. Zlotska Pecina.
34. Bubanj Hum.
35. Peştera Hotilor.
36. Verbicioara.
37. Cotofeni.
38. Sălcuţa.
39. Retevoeşti.
40. Celei.
41. Olteniţa.
42. Cernavodă.
43. Casimcea.
44. Folteşti.
45. Horodiştea.
46. Usatovo.
47. Varna–Strashimirovo.
48. Karanovo.
49. Ezero.
50. Mikhalits.
51. Razkopanitsa.
52. Sitagroi.
53. Hisar.
54. Gladnice.
55. Maliq.
56. Kritsana.
57. Argissa.
58. Thermon.
59. Orchomenos.
60. Lefkandhi.
61. Eutresis.
62. Pheneus.
63. Lerna.
64. Malthi.

65. Poliochni.
66. Troy.
67. Thermi.
68. Emporio.
69. Heraion.
70. Khalandhriani.
71. Siphnos.
72. Phylakopi.
73. Keos.
74. Knossos.
75. Ayios Onouphrios.
76. Beycesultan.
77. Karataş.
78. Tarsus.
79. Lagozza.
80. Remedello.
81. Conelle.
82. Rinaldone.
83. La Starza.
84. Gaudo.
85. Porto Peroni.
86. Cellino San Marco.
87. Piano Quartara.
88. Piano Conte.
89. Capo Graziano.
90. Moarda.
91. Serraferlicchio.
92. Piano Notaro.
93. San Cono.
94. Castelluccio.
95. Malta.

Region	2600	2300	2000	1700	1580
ITALY	LATE NEOLITHIC	EARLY AENEOLITHIC	LATE AENEOLITHIC	EBA	EBA
CARPATHIAN BASIN	BADEN-KOSTOLAC, PÉCEL, VISS, UNY, LASINJ	VUČEDOL MAKÓ-ČAKÓ NIYERSEG CORDED WARE BEAKERS	PANČEVO-OMOLJICA HATVÁN NAGYRÉV PERJÁMOS-MÓKRIN LJUBLJANA EARLY ÚNĚTICE SCHNECKENBERG	ÚNĚTICE OTOMANI PANNONIAN INCRUSTED VATYA WIETENBERG VATTINA	EARLY TUMULUS?
LOWER DANUBE	COTOFENI I, II CERNAVODĂ I, III	CERNAVODĂ III COTOFENI III GLINA II	PROTO-MONTEORU I C4-3 GLINA III	TEI MONTEORU I C2-I4 GÎRLA MARE VERBICIOARA	TEI MONTEORU I C2-I4 GÎRLA MARE VERBICIOARA
THRACE	SITAGROI IV, Va MIKHALITS	SITAGROI Vb EZERO KARANOVO VII MIKHALITS	SITAGROI Vb KAZKOPANITSA		
AXIUS-MORAVA	BUBANJ HUM Ib HISAR II KRITSANA I, II	BUBANJ HUM II KRITSANA III-VI	BUBANJ HUM III ARMENOKHORI	VATTINA DUBOVAC ŽUTO BRDO MACEDONIAN MBA	VATTINA DUBOVAC ŽUTO BRDO MACEDONIAN MBA
ALBANIA	MALIQ IIb	MALIQ IIIa	MALIQ IIIb	MALIQ IIIc	MALIQ IIId
THESSALY	ETh Ia	ETh Ib-III	MTh I-IV	M.Th. V-VII MH II	MH III
W. ANATOLIA	TROY I POLIOCHNI II, III	TROY II POLIOCHNI IV	TROY III-V	TROY VI	TROY VI
CYCLADES	GROTTA-PELOS (EC I) KEROS-SYROS (EC II)	EC III LEFKANDHI I	MC I KASTRI PHYLAKOPI I	MC III PHYLAKOPI II	MC II PHYLAKOPI II
CRETE	SUB-NEOLITHIC EM I	EM II	EM III MM IA	MM IB MM II MM IIIA	MM IIIB
S. GREECE	EH I, II	PROTOMINYAN (EH III)	EARLY MINYAN (MH I)	CLASSICAL MINYAN (MH II)	LATE MINYAN (MH III)

Fig. 9.3. Relative chronology for the Aegean area and central and south-eastern Europe in the third and second millennia B.C.

The first 'Mycenaeans' in Greece

Sp. MARINATOS

Directorate of Antiquities of Greece, Athens

THE term 'Mycenaeans' is meant here to designate the people who were the first to organize military and political power throughout a large part of Greece during the second millennium B.C.; who first built urban capitals or developed existing settlements into strong centres; whose rulers became the first petty kings and eventually great monarchs of Greece; who created the first royal dynasties and thus gave birth to the Greek heroic legends. It is an open question whether these same people were the first to speak the Greek language in Greece. It seems probable that tribes speaking Greek, or at least a kind of Greek, were already present there some centuries before. They must have lived, however, scattered as labourers or herdsmen, without any considerable social and state organization. What the 'Mycenaeans' achieved was the organization of the population under powerful rulers. It is highly probable that these chieftains entered Greece from abroad, bringing with them immigrants who were not, however, very numerous and may not have differed much ethnically from the pre-existing population. The Albanian invasions of Greece provide a parallel to the supposed kind and scale of immigration. This is of course not a new idea. I must repeat Nilsson's words on the subject: "The fundamental fact is that the Mycenaean Age was a period of very extensive movements and migrations of the Greek tribes." (Nilsson 1932: 239).

There are two main approaches to the question of the 'origin of the Mycenaeans', the archaeological and the linguistic. The first is already old, but it has been treated most recently and most completely by Professor F. Schachermeyr and by myself three years ago (Schachermeyr 1968: 297–8; Marinatos 1968: 277–8). Much new material from recent excavations throughout Greece, Anatolia and the Balkan regions has given ample opportunity to scholars to modify older opinions and to express some new ones about the very early appearance of Indo-European tribes in Greece.

Professor Schachermeyr formulates the evidence thus: already in Early Helladic II proto-Indo-European elements may have infiltrated into Greece. Such infiltration becomes evident during the last EH phase (about 2200–1900 B.C.) when some 'Proto-Hellenic' elements can already be recognized.

The period, Middle Helladic, (1900–1600 B.C.), is of great unity and very homogeneous in character. Cist-graves, contracted skeletons, poor grave-goods (if any) with the dead, and the apsidal house-form are the typical characteristics of MH. The opinion is widespread that the first appearance of the Greeks comes in this period and that 'Minyan' pottery is their character-istic product. We know now that all these characteristics existed already during the last phases of the EH period; that Minyan pottery is widespread then and that it may reflect a technical innovation which extended widely without any ethnic change. Meanwhile, the MH period is characterized by all the features just described which last for three centuries almost without change. Until 1700 or 1650 B.C. conditions remain static.

Then, and suddenly, we have change. We have evidence of chieftains or families with power and prosperity; the tombs become larger, often reach-ing the dimensions of a small room. The dead are no longer exclusively buried contracted; we meet extended skeletons. The gifts are abundant, metal becomes commoner and, what is very characteristic, isolated burials cease. We have spectacular contacts with the Minoan culture of Crete, and also with Egypt and with countries as far north as central Europe and England.

Material possessions become richer and more varied. New weapons appear, especially the sword and the body-shield. Works of art are abundant and through them we have an insight into the life and customs of the people of this new era. They are mighty warriors, mighty hunters and mighty sea-farers. Their most surprising possession is an improved chariot (possibly invented by Indo-Iranian tribes), from which they shoot deer and with which they pursue their adversaries with spear and sword. All these phenomena constitute the triumphal inception of the civilization which we call 'Mycenaean', about 1600 B.C.

My thesis, already presented at the First Congress of Mycenology (Marinatos 1968: 278–94), is that all these radical innovations can be explained only by external causes: just before 1600 B.C. a few well-organized groups of professional warriors invaded Greece. They possessed a new weapon which had a tremendous effect upon the simple agricultural people of Greece: the chariot and the horse. There were no organized forces to oppose them, although there are reasons to believe that in some cases the invaders met heroic resistance. Labourers, when roused by some strong personality to protect their liberty, fight heroically with sickles and spades and even with ploughs. World history offers more than one example of this. But, in spite of such opposition, the professional warriors installed themselves easily in Greece. It was not difficult for them then to progress hand in hand with the native population, as they were apparently similar ethnically. After one or two generations they developed into rich and powerful dynasties. The identity of blood between the invaders and the settlers is proved by the continuity of culture which is quite apparent. Professor Schachermeyr has adduced strong evidence for it (1968: 305) and new research daily brings corroboration. It seems as if in some cases an indigenous family rose to power. In other instances, marriages with local women may have strengthened the fusion of old and new ethnic elements.

For some scholars this does not seem probable. They prefer to take the invaders, that is the early Mycenaeans around 1600 B.C., as the first Greeks, or people closely akin to Greeks, who came into Greece. Professor L. R. Palmer, for instance, holds this view (1954: 93–7; 1961: 211–15). But the archaeological facts, though by no means absolutely decisive, do not favour this opinion. In any case the evidence is certainly against opinions like that of Professor F. Hampl that the first Greeks entered Greece only as late as 1200 B.C. (Hampl 1960). This contradicts not only the full unity of the Mycenaean culture, but also the historical tradition of Greek legend, which constitutes a trustworthy proto-historical source.

The second approach to the problem, the linguistic one, is partly in accordance with Hampl's ideas. E. Risch, W. Porzig and J. Chadwick favour, though cautiously, the idea of a late appearance of the Greeks. The fundamental reason is that the historical Greek dialects are so akin that no more than a few centuries are allowed for their differentiation. Therefore, they may have become distinct only after the Dorian invasion. A Dorian, says Dr. Chadwick characteristically would have been more easily understood when speaking to a Mycenaean, than a Spartan of the fifth century B.C. when speaking to contemporary Athenians (Chadwick 1956; 1969; 6–7).

For my part I can, and must, just stress the fact that Professor Schachermeyr and many others have already stated: namely that the archaeological evidence is so strong, homogeneous and consistent, and extends over so many centuries, that it is impossible to ignore or neglect it. Only when linguistic arguments do not contradict the archaeological evidence may they be adduced as a welcome help towards the solution of the problem. I personally accept two breaks during the whole development of the Minoan-Mycenaean civilisation: the first is the Cretan *diaspora* around 1500 B.C., the result of the tremendous explosion of the volcano of Thera; the second is the Mycenaean *diaspora* around 1200 B.C. There must have been many minor disruptions, like possible quarrels between the dynasties of Mycenae or the Mycenaean 'Peloponnesian War' known to saga as the war of the 'Seven against Thebes'. But there is not the least sign of a break in the development of the civilization itself. The architectural history of the towns, tomb architecture and burial customs, art development, legends and saga form a single, solid unity. Even after the twelfth century the break comes only in material culture. Intellectual and historical continuity remained in oral tradition. Down to the Classical period the Greek people did not doubt for a moment that everything, good or bad, in its culture derived directly from the Mycenaean tradition. The new chapter in literature—drama—is concerned almost exclusively with the Greek traditional past. It is incomprehensible without the Mycenaean background. Is it possible that the first Greeks came into Greece only when this past was already over?

New evidence for a continuous tradition throughout the Mycenaean period comes almost every year. Nilsson's observation that the oldest and most famous sanctuaries of the Greeks were established in the Mycenaean period remains a most significant fact (Nilsson 1932: 27–8, 38, 76, 148). Now we have more evidence. Mycenaean remains appeared in the earliest strata at Olympia, Epidaurus (Maleatas) and Dodona. In Keos the classical Greek gods and sanctuaries take the places of the Minoan-Mycenaean ones. In Pylos more than half of the Mycenaean *tholos* and chamber-tombs were frequented by the Greeks of the Geometric, Archaic, Classical and Roman periods for cult purposes. We know from literary tradition that the Dorians in Messenia did not disturb the Achaean population; and we see now that people there offered sacrifices to forefathers of the heroic period. It may be that the same families persisted down to the Classical period. There is a break between the sixth century and the Hellenistic period only, to be ascribed to the conquest of Messenia by Sparta (Marinatos 1955).

From the reports of G. Sotiriadhis one concludes that the chamber of the Mycenaean tholos tomb at Marathon contained a thick layer of charcoal and remains of sacrifices, which surely are to be ascribed to the cult of the dead Mycenaean king or kings (Sotiriadhis 1936). During 1969 and the first months of 1970 I tried to find the corresponding second tomb at Marathon, as my experience from Pylos persuaded me that tholos-tombs appear most usually in pairs. Instead, the plain of Marathon yielded still more abundant and valuable new archaeological and historical material. Most important for our purpose here are four broad, low prehistoric tumuli of the class known as 'kurgans'. They add precious evidence for both questions, that of the first 'Mycenaeans' in Greece as well as that of the continuity of tradition (Marinatos 1970a; 1970b; 1970c).

These peculiar burial monuments lie at the westernmost part of the little valley of the Marathon plain known under the Byzantine name of Vrana. They are mentioned by Leake and Grote and by Frazer in his commentary to Pausanias (Leake 1829: 162–7; Grote 1906: 59, fn. 1; Frazer 1898: 431–44).

The tholos-tomb lies about 400 metres to the south-east. Two of the tumuli are like twins. They lie one beside the other and are the same size, some 17 metres in diameter. The third tumulus is much smaller. The fourth comes between the first two and the third in size. The third and fourth tumuli are both badly preserved. All four show the same construction. They are circular, the circumference being made of small slabs carefully built up to a height of 50–60 centimetres. The interior is filled with earth, upon which a covering of loose stones was laid. A superficial layer of earth, 10–20 centimetres thick, may be original or may have accumulated during the centuries. The original height in the centre of the tumuli was no more than 2 metres.

Tumulus I, the most prominent, has another smaller circle inside it; but the two circles are not concentric (Pl. 12). The second circle is slightly later than the original larger one. It contained a single grave with a skeleton poorly preserved. A matt-painted jug and a goblet were the only grave-goods. The form of the grave is something between a cist-grave and a shaft grave. It is rectangular, the walls are carefully lined with stone slabs and two large but thin slabs covered it. An extended corpse, or even two, could have been accommodated within it, yet the skeleton found was contracted. Exceptionally, this grave was found not filled, while all the others were filled with earth. When opened, it gave the impression that it was empty. Perhaps it was originally filled with clothes, food and other perishable material. The two vases found date the tomb to the end of the MH period, about 1600 B.C. or slightly later.

The rest of the tumulus revealed (not to mention traces of one or two older burials under the walls of the smaller circle) no less than seven tombs. One of them (the only one with an extended skeleton) was superficial and intrusive. It had two little vases by the head of the dead and a Roman bronze coin found near the mouth (surely a *danake*) dates it to the time of Licinius, A.D. 307–24. Of the rest of the tombs, two were larger, almost monumental, each one having two small pits just in front of the entrance. The shape of these larger tombs is reminiscent of older, Early Helladic and Middle Helladic tradition. The tomb proper is a small built, rectangular chamber, but through projections of the side walls a kind of vestibule is formed, while the chamber is supplied with a walled entrance. The whole was roofed with large thin slabs. The first of the tombs, although spacious enough for one or more extended corpses, contained the remains of a single not fully contracted skeleton. Eleven vases and some spindle whorls of clay were the property of the dead (Pl. 15). We have called it the 'Tomb of the Queen'. The two smaller tombs (one near each side of the vestibule) contained remains of one contracted skeleton each and no grave-goods.

The other monumental tomb, the huge lintel of which is still *in situ*, contained the wonderfully preserved skeleton of a horse of the Przewalski type (Pls. 13, 14), about eight years old, according to Dr. Melentis of the Palaeontological Museum of the University of Athens. This burial shows the curious feature that the hind legs and a few other parts of the skeleton are missing. Apparently the horse was partly sacrificed and partly buried. Even later, heroes exceptionally received sacrifices of horses. Of the two tombs near the entrance one was badly preserved; the other contained two superimposed contracted skeletons and two small vases.

All the pottery is MH, either matt-painted or of the Grey Minyan type; the examples of the latter seem to be a local imitation; they are poorly made and there is no trace of goblets with grooved foot. This pottery must be dated to the last quarter of the seventeenth century B.C. possibly extending into the first quarter of the sixteenth. The tombs surely belong to a group of invaders who entered Greece about this time and had left other tumuli behind them. Such tumuli are especially abundant along the western coast of the Peloponnese. In eastern Greece they are rather rare. Therefore, the finds at Marathon (possibly there are one or two further examples hidden under the modern hamlet of Vrana) are of particular interest. The invaders had brought with them the hairy and ugly little Przewalski horses, already known to us from the *stelai* and the gold rings of Mycenae.

The interest of the Marathon discovery is increased by the fact that in almost all the tumuli there are traces of Mycenaean art, which indicates continuity of tradition. Tumulus I yielded only some surface sherds of Mycenaean date, which may be disregarded. But Tumulus II, containing a single long tomb, with vestibule and two rooms, the last of which ends in apsidal form, is a real imitation of a megaron (Pl. 16). It was disturbed, but some fragments of long bones indicated that there had been contracted skeletons. No vase was found intact but there were Mycenaean sherds and about a dozen flint arrow-heads of the improved form of the Middle Mycenaean period.

Tumulus III yielded almost nothing. Only half of it is preserved and this shows some partly destroyed cist-graves. But Tumulus IV (situated among the houses of the village) presented interesting results. The western part of this tumulus, which contained the biggest tombs, was destroyed by the construction of a machine-gun emplacement on it during World War II. The eastern part fortunately escaped destruction. It contained a series of rectangular pits, all of them preserving burials that were *exclusively* of Mycenaean date. The skeletons were contracted and each grave contained many burials. A number of little vases and other minor finds proved that the burials are Mycenaean and date as late as the fourteenth century B.C. (Pl. 17). The tholos-tomb found a little further away by Sotiriadhis is simply the successor of these tumuli.

The value of all these facts for our problems is clear. One thing must be added: when one sees that the circular form of the stone 'kurgans' of

Marathon with the actual tomb inside them clearly represents an imitation of a house of the living, one gets a new idea about the much discussed question of the origin of the Mycenaean tholos-tombs.

References

CHADWICK, J. 1956. 'The Greek dialects and Greek pre-history.' *Greece and Rome*. N.S., 3: 38–50.

——. 1969. 'Aegean history 1500–1200 B.C.' *Studii Classice*, 11: 6–11.

FRAZER, J. G. 1898. *Pausanias's Description of Greece* II. London.

GROTE, G. 1906. *History of Greece* V (Everyman's Library edition). London and New York.

HAMPL, F. 1960. 'Die Chronologie der Einwanderung der griechischen Stämme und das Problem der Nationalität der Träger der mykenischen Kultur.' *MH*, 17: 57–86.

LEAKE, W. M. 1829. 'The Demi of Attica.' *Trans. of the Royal Society of Literature*, 1; 114–281.

MARINATOS, Sp. 1955. 'Palaipylos.' *Das Altertum*, 1: 140–63.

——. 1968. 'Mycenaean culture within the frame of Mediterranean anthropology and archaeology.' *AttiICIM*(1): 277–94.

——. 1970a. 'From the silent earth.' *AthAA*, 3: 61–8.

——. 1970b. 'Further news from Marathon.' *AthAA*, 3: 153–66.

——. 1970c. 'Further discoveries at Marathon.' *AthAA*, 3: 349–66.

NILSSON, M. 1932. *The Mycenaean Origin of Greek Mythology*. Cambridge.

PALMER, L. R. 1954. 'Luvian and Linear A.' *TPhS*, 1954: 75–100.

——. 1961. *Mycenaeans and Minoans*. London.

SCHACHERMEYR, F. 1968. 'Zum Problem der griechischen Einwanderung.' *AttiICIM* (1): 297–312.

SOTIRIADHIS, G. 1936. 'Erevnai kai anaskaphai en Marathoni.' *Praktika*, 1935: 84–158.

3

The Balkans and the Kurgan peoples

Ethnographic problems of the Bronze Age in the central Balkan peninsula and neighbouring regions

M. GARAŠANIN

University of Belgrade

ARCHAEOLOGICAL research undertaken during the last twenty years in the central Balkan peninsula and neighbouring regions makes it possible for us today to determine more precisely the general character of the Bronze Age culture of this area of south-eastern Europe. From the geographical point of view, we are concerned in the first place with the valleys of the rivers Morava and Vardar and with those of their tributaries. Here lay the old important natural route of communications which from Neolithic times onwards linked the Aegean area with Pannonia and the Carpathians. Here too, as we shall see, the Bronze Age culture was close to that of the Balkan–Carpathian complex (Garašanin, M. and Nestor 1970: 19–30; in 1966 it was still impossible to suggest more precise attributions for Bronze Age groups in the Morava valley). Further to the west, western Serbia and the regions of Montenegro and Albania appear to have belonged already to a different geographical entity: the mountainous Dinaric zone where later we know of the existence of Illyrian peoples (the areas in question have still not been adequately studied; on Montenegro: see Garašanin, M. and Garašanin, D. 1967: 54–75; on Albania: Anamali and Korkuti 1969: 115–49; on the Bronze Age of the territory of Macedonia see Garašanin, M. 1958: 120–5; 1968: especially 161–80). This geographical separation also played an important role in the formation of the Bronze Age cultures of these lands. The specific character of these cultures also implies a specific chronological development. Thus we distinguish here an Early Bronze Age period (corresponding more or less to 'Phase A' of Reinecke's

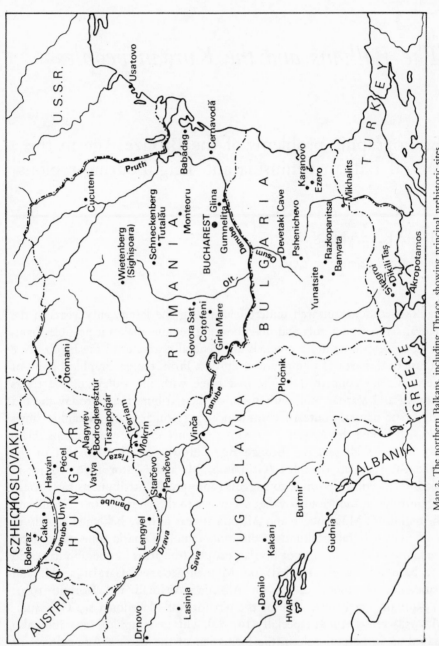

Map 2. The northern Balkans, including Thrace, showing principal prehistoric sites

chronological system), a Middle Bronze Age (Reinecke A2–C) and then a final phase, coinciding in part at least with the beginning of the period of transition to the Iron Age (the end of Reinecke C and Reinecke D). This last period corresponded, from the historical point of view, with the beginning of the period of the great ethnic movements known by the name of Aegean migrations or migrations of the 'Sea Peoples'.

It is in the Middle Bronze Age that a specific culture in fact develops in the central Balkan area, and prepares the way for the later cultural development in the Iron Age, which can be connected with sufficiently well-determined ethnic groups (Benac 1964: Garašanin, M. 1964).

This MBA culture was based, nevertheless, on a larger complex which belonged to the beginning of the Bronze Age and represented the effects of stabilization following the upheavals and movements of populations which marked the transition from the Neolithic to the metal-using ages at the beginning of the third millennium B.C. The problem of this period has already been dealt with by the present writer on several occasions (Garašanin, M. 1961a; 1961b; 1969). May it suffice then to recall the most important conclusions. The upheavals and movements of populations in the transitional period must be explained in the main as caused by successive waves of pastoral peoples from the steppes who at different times spread towards the lower Danube and south-eastern Europe. These successive influxes of invaders, which we can identify only in part, led to fusions and contacts between different populations, let us say between the pre-existing inhabitants of the regions in question and newcomers who certainly belonged to peoples of Indo-European speech. All this is easily recognized in different groups of cultures of the period; for example (1) in the Tiszapolgar and Bodrogkereztur groups in Pannonia (large flint knives, inhumation rites); (2) in the Baden group and its different regional variants (knowledge of the chariot, domestication of the horse, types of metal dagger, catacomb graves characteristic of the Baden group found at Vučedol); as well as (3) in the Vučedol group itself (pottery vessels with excised decoration set on a cruciform foot, catacomb graves; Garašanin, M. 1967). The first waves which can really be recognized appear more to the east, in Moldavia, in a relatively early period (phase Cucuteni A–B of the Cucuteni group, pottery of type Cucuteni C or Gorodsk-Usatovo), and they continue up to the Early Bronze Age period proper. Thanks to the recent research carried out by Rumanian scholars, a particularly important role is to be attributed to the Cernavoda group in its different forms (Cernavoda I–III and local variants; Morintz and Roman 1968). These different groups were also associated with very characteristic forms of burials, although they differ in detail, both from the chronological point of view and from that of the inhumation burials properly so called, burials which in *ensemble* are designated by the name 'ochre-graves'. Thus it was in these areas and on these foundations that the culture of the Early Bronze Age evolved. It was primarily characterized by the development of stock-breeding and by the emergence of groups of new local cultures, with relatively crude pottery decorated in a primitive manner with bands in relief, finger or thumb impressions; and, in particular, by globular-bodied pots with tall neck and one or two handles set between lip and body. The different varieties are represented notably in the Glina III and Schneckenberg groups in Muntenia and Transylvania, and by Verbicioara I in Oltenia and Bubanj-Hum III in the centre of the Balkan peninsula (Berciu 1961: 123–61, figs. 6, 7, on Verbicioara I; Bichir 1962, Garašanin, M. 1958: 65–6, pls. 13/2–4, 14/1, on Schneckenberg; Prox 1941, pl. XXIV/2, 4–6). One might also add other groups or variants which are still only partly known: the new Vinkovci group in Slavonia (Dimitrijević 1966: 28–36 and plates), the Pitvaros variant in the northern Banat on the Maros and the Zlatica (Aranka), with its one- or two-handled pots (similar to those of Bubanj-Hum III); the Somogyvar group with its barrow graves and variants of the same type of the one-handled pot, specialized forms of which recur in the Kosihi-Caka group in Slovakia (Bona 1964: 17–65, pls. I/6–7, II/9–11, 14, III/7). The Early Bronze Age group of Belotić-Bela Crkva in western Serbia (Garašanin, M. 1958: 90–5; Garašanin M. and Garašanin, D. 1958a; 1962) may also be placed in the same framework. The barrow graves of this last group, with interment of skeletons in family burials, are paralleled by different types of graves on the steppes, as well as by mound burials (unfortunately not well enough known to us) in Transylvania and Slovakia (Budinsky-Kricka 1947; Kalicz 1968: 22–35). The cist-graves, the presence of a stone-built enclosure round the periphery of the mounds, as well as paving with stone slabs, also connect up with the graves in the Pontic regions (Gorodsk-Usatovo) and the steppes (Garašanin, M. and Garašanin, D. 1958a, on Belotić tumuli 10, 12 and Bela Crkva tumuli 1, 2; 1962: 54–5, 61–2, on Belotić tumulus 15; Garašanin, M. 1961a: 12–13, with bibliography; Klein 1960; 1962; Leskov and Merpert 1967: 15–19 and *passim;* Morintz and Roman 1968: 118; Zirra 1960).

The analogies with the burials of the Somogyvar groups have been drawn in part correctly by Bona (Bona 1964: 44–7). The tombs with cremations constitute an equally characteristic feature, the grave-goods being set out actually on the ashes of the pyre. As for the pottery, the one-handled vessels from Bela Crkva, barrow 1, as well as those with one or two handles from Belotić, barrow 12, are related to the Schneckenberg and Verbicioara I groups and to the barrow-graves of Verbiţa in Oltenia (Berciu 1961: 147, fig. 17/1; 1966: 137–8). Thus throughout the region of the lower Danube, the central Balkans and even in Pannonia, we have a great complex of Early Bronze Age civilization; it is characterized by its pot shapes, by its economy, and to a large extent by its funerary customs. The regional differences must surely be explained by the different basic autochthonous populations on which were superimposed new foreign elements which certainly had ultimate connections with the Indo-European stock-breeders of the steppes. These elements, moreover, also spread towards the south. Thus we find them again in the Armenokhori group in Macedonia, in the elements of 'prehistoric' character of Early Thessalian III and perhaps also in the appearance of those pseudo-Minyan features which are typical of the Bubanj-Hum II group but which are also to be found in Bubanj-Hum III and appear at Lerna and other sites after the destruction at the end of Early Helladic II. Let us note, however, that these elements could equally well have a different origin, perhaps Anatolian (Heurtley, 1939: 192, figs. 320–49; Milojčić 1959: 26–8, figs. 22, 23; Caskey 1960).

The Middle Bronze Age culture in the central Balkan area in fact represents the development of this culture of the autochthonous peoples who had become Indo-Europeanized through the arrival of newcomers from the steppes. It is already differentiated into more clearly determined regional forms whose genetic relationships with the cultures of the neighbouring areas are certainly interesting from the ethnographic point of view also. A relatively early phase is represented by the Slatina group (still incompletely known) on the southern Morava (Leskovac areas) and around Niš (Garašanin, D. 1959a: 257–61; Garašanin, M. 1958: 66–7). Besides certain elements which in appearance go with Cernavoda III (pots with 'rippled' decoration; Garašanin, M. 1958: pl. 14/8; Stalio 1962: 69–74, pl. II/11, 12 on Gradac; Morintz and Roman, 1968: 94, fig. 37/1, 2, 5, 10, 12, 13) the group includes some pots with one handle rising above the rim and with a button-like or even fan-shaped appendage; some pots of large size with horizontally everted rim, and finally some handles with vertical channelling (Garašanin M. 1958: pl. 14/3–6, 8–10; on 'rippled' decoration see Heurtley 1939: 69, 74). (The parallelism with the Slatina group whose relative chronology we have discussed briefly here brings in also the problem of the date of the relevant features in the Cernavoda III aspect.) From the chronological viewpoint this group that has just been discussed must be attributed to the beginning of the Middle Bronze Age (Reinecke, A2–B1). This attribution seems to be supported by certain finds in the Early Bronze Age level at the Devetaki cave in northern Bulgaria where the pot forms just described were found associated with those of the Verbicioara II phase of Oltenia (Mikov and Džambazov 1960: 106–15, fig. 81b, Verbicioara II vase, fig. 84d; cf. also fig. 83). As we shall see later the succeeding phases of Verbicioara (III–IV) could not be earlier than a relatively developed phase of the Middle Bronze Age (Reinecke B2). As to its origin, the group may certainly be connected in part with Bubanj-Hum I–II (Salcuţa II–IV) cultures as is shown by the technique of the pots and their channelled decoration. On the other hand the similarity with Cernavoda III also indicates closer ties with the Carpatho-Balkan area. The same applies to the one-handled pots referred to, whose shape is typical of the Vattina group in the Vojvodina. Similarities with southern Bulgaria are on the contrary more difficult to recognize (Garašanin, M. 1958: 66; Čičikova 1968: 15–27, figs. 3, 4, on vases from Byukovtsi and Orakhovo in Bulgaria; Detev 1950a: 20, fig. 39; third vase from the left, from Banyata, Kapitan Dimitriyevo). The Paraćin group is in the same position. It is now well defined on the basis of an already quite sizeable number of cemeteries of flat graves with urns, located on the lower course of the Morava and extending up as far as the Timok valley (Garašanin, D. 1958: 297–309; Garašanin, M. 1958: 68–70, fig. 10; Garašanin, M., Garašanin, D. 1958b: pl. Y 14–6). The type of these burials, as well as the arrangement of the grave furniture (urns covered with a lid, small pots set at the height of the shoulder of the urn) is closely related to the funerary practice of southern Pannonia and southern Oltenia (the Vattina group and especially Dubovac-Žuto Brdo-Gîrla Mare; Dumitrescu, V. 1961; *passim;* Garašanin, M. 1958: 75–90). The pot shapes, however, are in part noticeably different; for example, the dishes with slightly everted rim, the pear-shaped urns with horizontal channelling and tongue-shaped handles. The conical, one-handled pots, as well as the shapes of handles with buttons and vertical channelling, are closely linked with the Slatina group (Garašanin, M. 1958: fig. 10/3–5). The two-handled pots belong to the large family of such pots which is well known in the Morava region and in southern Pannonia from the EBA, but which recurs in the later periods also. The surest comparisons may be made for vases of this type of the Verbicioara III and IV phases (Govora Sat: Berciu 1961: 135, fig. 5/1–5, 138–9, fig. 8/1, 5–6; Garašanin, M. 1958: figs. 10, 1, 3). The pin of *Petschaftkopfnadel* type belongs to the type of Reinecke B2–C (Garašanin, M. 1958: 69 and fig. 11/2). In view of its funerary customs, an especially important feature for ethnic interpretation, and certain of its pottery shapes, the Paraćin group is more closely connected with the Balkano-Carpathian complex, although a local origin cannot confidently be questioned.

A group which has a regional character and appears to be of special importance,but which is still not well-defined, is that of Mediana (Brzi Brod near Niš). Its distribution seems to coincide with that of the Slatina group. The two levels of the Mediana site, which were characterized by the presence of dwellings of 'zolniki' type (simple huts built partly below ground level) provided very characteristic pottery (Pls. 18–20): dishes within curved rims, as found also in the Paraćin group but distinguished by horizontal channelling on the rim and, in the latest phase, by oblique channelling, recalling the shape of the 'turban dish'; also large pots with horizontal rim decorated with concentric channelling. A pot of the Vattina-Vršac type from the upper level of the Mediana site allows that level to be dated to the end of the MBA. The handle forms belong to types known from the Slatina and Paraćin groups (Garašanin, M. 1962a; Garašanin, D. 1959b: 262–5, figs.

3, 4). The urn types represented in the graves at Lapotince near Leskovac and Ljusta are probably connected with the cemeteries in our group, as a local variant of it in Kosovo represented by the sites of Ljusta itself, Gladnice and in part Hisar in Metohija (Garašanin, M. 1958: 70–2 and pl. 15/4, on Lapotince; 1960: 62–6 and pl. VIII/1, on Ljusta; Glišić and Jovanović 1957: 225–32 and pl. I/5, 11–2, on Gladnice; Todorović 1963: pl. V, objects illustrated in centre and bottom right, on Hisar; the dating suggested is unacceptable). In its ensemble the Mediana group follows closely the development of the Bronze Age in the Morava region. Certain points, however, raise new historical questions. Thus, in the first place, the typical shapes of the Mediana pots cannot be dissociated from those of the urnfield period in Pannonia, more particularly from those of the south of that region. The Pannonian material, however, is certainly later (Tasić 1962: 127–44; 1966). Do we see the result of migratory movements whose origins must be sought in the Morava valley; of cultural influences that we are still far from understanding; or finally, the least likely possibility, of local developments whose parallelism can only be explained as resulting from the sharing of the common bases of the later cultural evolution? Here is a problem which cannot be solved at the present stage of our knowledge. On the other hand the shapes of the Mediana pottery are closely associated with the material from the LBA destruction levels at sites in Macedonia, and so, let us say, with cultural changes caused by the migrations of the 'Sea Peoples' in that region (Heurtley 1939: 98, 217, Nos. 415–19, on Macedonia; Kimmig 1964: 260; Kimmig treats the Paraćin evidence as particularly important; the Mediana group was still unknown to him). These latter peoples must be clearly distinguished from those who destroyed Troy VII 2b, of whom we find conspicuous traces in the Pshenichevo group in Thrace (besides other more or less related elements there is the incised and stamped pottery) and also in the Babadag group in the Dobrogea (Dimitrov 1968: 10–11 and figs. 3, 4; Morintz 1964, on Babadag). The same is the case with the people who transmitted cultural features of the Dubovac-Žuto-Brdo-Gîrla Mare group, some traits of which recur both in the Bronze Age levels at Dikili Taş (a statuette; Daux 1961: 931 and fig. 25) and also, at a later stage, in the pottery and objects of plastic art in some graves in the Kerameikos cemetery in Athens (Garašanin, M. 1953: 1962b; Milojčić 1949). The routes of the Aegean migrations, as well as the ethnic appurtenance of the peoples involved in these great movements of the period of transition to the Iron Age, seem to have been quite varied.

One no less important feature of the development of the Bronze Age in the Morava region is that of its cultural continuity. This has already appeared in the relations between the culture of the Mediana group and the slightly later regional groups of the period of transition to the Iron Age in

Pannonia. In its ensemble this period in the central regions of the Balkan peninsula, that is, in the Morava valley, is still far from being understood. Certain groups of cultures in that zone (Gornja Stražava) and in the area of Kosovo (Donja Brnjica), which belong to the end of the period (Reinecke Hallstatt B3), are closely linked with the Paraćin and Mediana groups by typical characteristics of their pottery (Krstić 1962, on Gornja Stražava; Srejović 1960: pls. I/2, 5, II/4, III/5, on Donja Brnjica). It follows from this that there was a continuous internal development from the Bronze Age into the Iron Age proper (Hallstatt period). This continuity is confirmed particularly by a very characteristic urn from the Paraćin cemetery, designated by D. Garašanin by the number of the grave in which it was found, 1962–2 (Garašanin, D. in press). Besides the shapes whose origins should be sought in the MBA Paraćin group (dish-lid of the Paraćin type for the urn, conical one-handled pot, channelled two-handled pot, dish with channelled, inturned rim) we have here an urn with cylindrical neck horizontally channelled, bulging body decorated with vertical channellings and lugs in the shape of tongues on the shoulder and the lower half of the body. The origin of this type of urn is to be sought in the characteristic pottery shapes of the urn graves of the Vattina group, notably those of the Ilandža cemetery (Marjanska 1957: pl. II/1, 4, III/1, on Ilandža; pls. IV/3, V/1, 4, VI/1, on evolved forms). The well-proportioned form, such as we find it at Paraćin, is known also from urn-grave No. 13 of the cemetery of Rospi Ćuprija at Belgrade, there with a dish-lid corresponding to the types of the Paraćin group and the barrow of Dobrača, similarly dated to the end of the Bronze Age (Todorović 1956: 42, figs. 19, 20; Garašanin, M. 1958: pl. 21/4–6, on Dobrača and its analogies).

It is thus possible to establish that the Bronze Age culture of the Morava valley developed continuously and without interruption right up to the period of transition to the Iron Age and in all probability during the true Iron Age itself. Although it was based on locally characterized cultures, this Bronze Age culture nevertheless has close relations with that of the Balkano-Carpathian complex. On the other hand, the features which could be associated with the culture of the Thracian regions proper, in the south of the Balkans, are found only to a limited extent. The principal question is that of incised and incrusted decoration of Bubanj-Hum II type, which is also connected with the Bronze Age of Macedonia and Thrace, and of the pots with pointed bases of Yunatsite type, which are adequately known and stratified at the site of Razkopanitsa (Garašanin, M. 1958: 63, fn. 343; Heurtley 1939: 172, No. 181, 204, fig. 68/a, b, EBA according to Heurtley; Rey 1921: 216, fig. 2, pl. XIX/1, 4–6, without precise chronological data; all on the Macedonian material; Garašanin, M. 1958: pl. 12/5, on Velika Humska Čuka; Mikov 1939: 76–83, figs. 24, 25, on Yunatsite; Detev 1950b, Popović 1965 on the chronology and stratigraphy). The ensemble of the

Bronze Age material in the areas in question cannot be related more closely than this to the Bronze Age of Thrace proper.

In the western part of the regions in which we are interested the development of the Bronze Age is appreciably different. Western Serbia, like the regions more or less adjacent to it, is characterized at this time by a regional *facies* designated as a variant of the Vattina group in western Serbia (Garašanin, M. 1958: 95–103; Garašanin, M. and Garašanin, D. 1958a; 1962). This attribution is based in the first place on the character of the pottery, which in its types and shapes is closely connected with the Vattina group. Let us note, nevertheless, the cruder technique and the heavier, thicker shapes of this pottery, as well as certain other differences in detail. There is thus no question of importation or of immigration of foreign elements from the Banat, but much rather of a transmission of elements of foreign culture (*'Kulturübertragung'*), of close contacts and influence. This is confirmed, moreover, by the funerary customs of the West Serbia group, which are characterized by the presence of funerary mounds, which are not found in the Vattina (Banat) group, and by numerous features which, taken together, demonstrate an undoubted continuity with the EBA group of Belotić-Bela Crkva: these include the presence of inhumation and cremation graves (in this case with use of urns) and of cist-graves with a central cell formed by a heap of stones set over the urn, corresponding in principle to the cell or kernel of red earth covered with stones which was found in barrow 15 at Belotić; and also family graves with both inhumation and cremation (Garašanin, M. 1958: 95–103; Garašanin, M. and Garašanin, D. 1958a: 24–30, Belotić tumulus 12, Bela Crkva tumulus 1: 1962: 51, fig. I, tumulus 7; 53–4, fig. III, Belotić tumulus 14; Belotić tumulus 7 has remains of a pyre over which the earth had been piled, which corresponds *inter alia* to what was observed in Belotić tumulus 12, burial without urn; and in Bela Crkva tumulus 1, graves with skeletons). Cremation graves containing the calcined remains of several individuals were found at Bukovac, near Valjevo, and especially at Dobrača (on the 'family graves' see especially Garašanin, M. 1958: 97, fn. 112, on graves at Dobrača; Jovanović 1892: 49). Here again the metal-work found in the graves shows that they cover the different phases of the Middle Bronze Age. Certain graves, e.g. at Dobrača, and Belotić tumulus 19, are undoubtedly to be attributed to the Late Bronze Age (Reinecke D; Garašanin, M. and Garašanin, D. 1962: 56–57, 72–63, on Belotić Tumulus 19; Garašanin, M. 1958: pl. 21–3; Garašanin, M. and Garašanin, D. 1958b: pl. Y 17/A, B, with dating of objects illustrated). So we find ourselves faced with a continuity which can be followed through, above all through its funerary customs and forms of burial, into the Iron Age proper, that is to say, to the period when the existence of the Illyrian element in these regions cannot be in doubt (Garašanin, D. 1966: 1967).

Now the phenomenon of continuity which we have just discussed is characteristic also of the development of the Bronze Age in southern Pannonia, which belongs to the Balkano-Carpathian complex. Thus it is possible to establish both the existence of relatively late graves of the Vattina group in certain cemeteries, and an uninterrupted continuity between the final phase of that group and the earliest graves of 'urnfield' type (using 'urnfield' in the sense in which German scholars use *Urnenfelder*) notably in the cemetery of Stojica Gumno at Belegiš near Zemun (Tasić 1966; the author of the present article has discussed the graves of the Vattina group in *Preistorija Srbije*, Belgrade, in press).

The observations made in this article thus allow us to establish first of all the formation in the Middle Bronze Age (from Reinecke A2 onwards) of local cultural groups which are more or less confined to the Morava region. In their origins and by their contacts with neighbouring cultures these groups are linked first of all with those of the Balkano-Carpathian complex, in particular with those of the area of the Lower Danube, situated in southern Pannonia and between the Balkan massif and the Carpathians. Though based on more or less similar foundations in the Early Bronze Age, the culture of western Serbia belongs in fact to a different complex which becomes increasingly differentiated during the course of the Bronze Age. In the two regions in question it seems possible to establish an uninterrupted cultural continuity up to the Iron Age, when the presence of clearly differentiated ethnic groups is also confirmed, at least in part, by our written sources. We cannot associate Bronze Age cultural groups and complexes with differentiated ethnic groups. On the contrary, it seems to me that definitive ethnic differentiation in our region only took place during the period of transition from the Bronze Age to the Iron Age, at the time of the Aegean migrations or those of the 'Sea Peoples'. Thus it will be only after the Hallstatt period that it may be possible, in my opinion, really to speak of large palaeo-Balkanic ethnic groups. The Bronze Age thus represents only an introductory period, previous to the formation of these groups, who nevertheless had undergone their Indo-Europeanization during the upheavals of the transitional period between the Neolithic and Metal Ages (Garašanin, M. 1961a; 1961b; 1969). Nevertheless, one fact seems to me to be beyond dispute, from the Bronze Age onwards: the formation of large, distinct cultural complexes in south-eastern Europe: (1) the south-eastern complex in the regions later inhabited by the Thracian element; (2) the western Balkan complex in the Illyrian zone; (3) to the north of the Balkan massif and as far as the Carpathians, a sharply distinct culture to be called the 'Balkano-Carpathian'. To this last complex, in its ensemble during the Bronze Age and up to the Iron Age, should be linked the region formed by the centre of the Balkan peninsula, the valley of the Morava and those of its tributaries. It was only later, during the Iron Age, that some foreign elements coming from the west, from the Illyrian area, asserted their superiority in certain parts of the region, notably in Kosovo (at Suva Reka) and in Macedonia (for example at Radanje and at Vergina in the extreme south; Djurić-Slavković 1964, on Suva Reka and funerary customs of the Illyrian group there; Garašanin, M. and Garašanin, D. 1959, on Radanje and Macedonia in general; Andhronikos 1969, on southern Macedonia). Taking account of the linguistic data, much discussed as they are, it seems to be possible that a pre-Daco-Mysian element was present in the Morava and Kosovo regions and probably also in Macedonia in the Bronze Age. This element, moreover, had links with the Bronze Age Balkano-Carpathian complex and was sharply distinguished from the pre-Thracian element in the south-east of the peninsula, and from the Illyrian element. With this last should be associated the variant of the Vattina group in western Serbia. This group had clearly differentiated culture and funerary customs, and its continuity may be traced into the Iron Age and to the historical period of the Illyrian peoples (on the linguistic data see especially: Georgiev 1969; cf. the critical remarks of Papazoglu 1969: 61–4; Garašanin, M. 1969).

References

ANAMALI, S. and KORKUTI, M. 1969. 'Problemi ilir de gjenezës së shquitarëve në dritën e kërkimeve arkeologjike shqiptare.' *Studime Historike*, 23: 115–49.

ANDHRONIKOS, M. 1969. *Vergina* I. Athens.

BENAC, A. 1964. 'Prdeiliri, Protoiliri, Prailiri.' *Simpozijum o Teritorijalnom i Hronološkom Razgraničenju Ilira u Praistorisko Doba* (Sarajevo; ed. A Benac): 59–93.

BERCIU, D. 1961. 'Die Verbicioara Kultur.' *Dacia*, N.S., 5: 123–61.

——. 1966. *Zorile istoriei în Carpaţi şi la Dunăre*. Bucharest.

BICHIR, G. 1962. 'Beitrag zur Kenntniss der frühen Bronzezeit im südöstlichen Transilvanien und in der Moldau.' *Dacia*, N.S., 6: 87–119.

BONA, I. 1964. 'The peoples of southern origin in the Early Bronze Age in Hungary.' *Alba Regia*, 4/5: 17–65.

BUDINSKY-KRICKA, V. 1947. *Slovenske Dejiny* I. Bratislava.

CASKEY, J. 1960. 'The Early Helladic Period in the Argolid.' *Hesperia*, 29: 285–303.

ČIČIKOVA, M. 1968. 'Keramika ot starata zelezna epoha v Trakia.' *Arkheologiya*, 10: 15–27.

DAUX, G. 1961. 'Chronique des fouilles archéologiques en Grèce.' *BCH*, 1961: 629–975.

DETEV, P. 1950a. 'Selishnata mogila Baniata pri Kapitan Dimitrievo.' *Godishnik na Narodniya arkheologicheski muzei*, 2: 1–23.

——. 1950b. 'Selishnata mogila Razkopanitsa.' *Izvestiya na bălgarski arkheologicheski institut*, 16–17: 171–90.

DIMITRIJEVIC, S. 1966. *Arheološka iskopavanja na području Vincovačkog muzeja*. Vinkovci.

DIMITROV, D. 1968. 'Troia VIIb2 i balkanskite trakiiski i miziiski plemena.' *Arkheologiya*, 10: 1–15.

DUMITRESCU, V. 1961. *Necropola de incineratie din epoca bronzului de la Cîrna*. Bucharest.

Djurić Slavković, N. 1964. 'Ilirski tumuli kod Suve Reke.' *Glasnik muzeja Kosova i Metohije*, 9: 537–55.

Garašanin, D. 1958. 'Ka problemu polja sa urnama u Srbiji.' *Zbornik radova Narodnog muzeja u Beogradu*, 1: 297–309.

——. 1959a. 'Iskopavanja na Gumništu u Donjoj Slatini.' *Starinar*, N.S., 9/10: 257–61.

——. 1959b. 'Iskopavanja tumula u Medvedji kod Lebana.' *Starinar*, N.S., 9/10: 263–5.

——. 1966. 'La Serbie à l'époque de Hallstatt.' *Atti del VI Congresso internazionale delle scienze preistoriche e protoistoriche* 3 (1962; ed. M. Pallottino and others; Florence): 120–5.

——. 1967. 'Miscellanea illyrica II: Iliri u halštatu Srbije.' *Zbornik radova Narodnog muzeja u Beogradu*, 5: 31–40.

Garasanin, M. 1953. 'Banat-srpsko Podunavlje-Kerameikos.' *Rad vojvodjanskih muzeja*, 2: 67–73.

——. 1958. 'Neolithikum und Bronzezeit in Serbien und Makedonien.' *RGKomm*, 39: 1–130.

——. 1960. 'Ljusta, Kosovska Mitrovica.' *Arheološki pregled*, 2: 62–6.

——. 1961a. 'Pontski i stepski uticaji u Donjem Podunavlju i na Balkanu na prelazu iz neolitskog u metalno doba.' *Glasnik Zemaljskog muzeja*, N.S., 15/16: 5–26.

——. 1961b. 'Der Ubergang vom Neolithikum zur frühen Bronze-zeit auf dem Balkan und auf der unteren Donau.' *Prague Symposium*: 15–43.

——. 1962a. 'Brzi Brod—Niš.' *Arheološki pregled*, 4: 57–61.

——. 1962b. 'Arheološki prilizi problemu velike egejske seobe.' *Diadora*, 2: 117–34.

——. 1964. 'Istočna granica Ilira prema arheološkim spomenicima.' *Simpozijum o teritorijalnom i hronološkom razgraničenju Ilira u praistorisko doba* (Sarajevo; ed. A. Benac): 135–75.

——. 1967. 'Die Bestattungen des Vučedoler Burghügels.' *Archaeologia Iugoslavica*, 8: 27–33.

——. 1968. 'Eden osvrt na preistorijata na Makedonija.' *Glasnik na institutot na Nacionalna Istorija* (Skopje), 12: 147–80.

——. 1971. 'Nomades des steppes et autochtones dans le Sud-est européen à l'époque de transition du néolithique à l'âge du bronze.' *Plovdiv Symposium* (1969): 9–14.

Garašanin, M. and Garašanin, D. 1958a. 'Iskopavanja tumula u Belotiću i Beloj Crkvi.' *Zbornik radova Narodnog muzeja u Beogradu*, 1: 17–50.

——. 1958b. 'Sépultures de l'âge des métaux en Serbie.' *Inventaria Archaeologica Jugoslavia*, Fasc. 2.

——. 1959. 'Arheološka iskopavanja u selu Radanju na lokalitetu Krivi Dol.' *Zbornik na Štipskiot Naroden muzej*, 1: 9–60.

——. 1962. 'Iskopavanja tumula u kompleksu Belotić-Bela Crkva 1959–1960 godine.' *Zbornik radova Narodnog muzeja u Beogradu*, 3: 47–68.

——. 1967. *Istorija Crne Gore* I. (Titograd): Chaps. II–IV.

Garašanin, M. and Nestor I. 1970. 'Les peuples de L'Europe du sud-est à l'époque préromaine.' *Actes du premier congrès des études balkaniques et sud-est européennes* (1966; ed. V. I. Georgiev and others; Sofia): 19–30.

Georgiev, V. I. 1971. 'L'ethnogenèse de la péninsule balkanique d'après les données linguistiques.' *Plovdiv Symposium* (1969): 155–77.

Glišić, J. and Jovanović, B. 1957. 'Praistorisko naselje Gladnice kod Gračanice.' *Glasnik muzeja Kosova i Metohije*, 1: 223–33.

Heurtley, W. A. 1939. *Prehistoric Macedonia*. Cambridge.

Jovanović, D. 1892. 'Table tumuli i gomile Bukovačkog polja Celijska pećina.' *Starinar*, 9: 46–55.

Kalicz, N. 1968. *Die frühe Bronzezeit in Nord-ost Ungarn*. Budapest.

Kimmig, W. 1964. 'Seevölkerbewegung und Urnenfelderkultur'; in R. von Uslar and K. J. Narr, *Studien aus Alteuropa* I: 220–83.

KLEIN, L. S. 1960. 'Novie dannie o khronologiseskih vzaimootnoseniykh yamnoi i katakombnoi kultur.' *Vestnik Leningradskogo universiteta: 20. Seriya istorii, yazika i literaturi*, 4: 144–8.

——. 1962. 'Katakombnie pamyatniki epokhi bronzi i problema videleniya arkheologitseskikh kultur.' *Sovyetskaya Arkheologiya*, 1962: 26–37.

KRSTIĆ, D. 1962. 'Gornja Stražava-Prokuplje.' *Arheološki pregled*, 4: 73–6.

LESKOV, A. M. and MERPERT, N. 1967. *Pamyatniki epokhi bronzy yuga evropeiskoi chasti SSSR*. Kiev.

MARJANSKA, M. 1957. 'Groblje urni kod Ilandže.' *Rad vojvodjanskih muzeja*, 6: 5–24.

MIKOV, V. 1939. 'Selishnata mogila pri Yunatsite (Pazardzhisko).' *Godishnik na Plovdivskata narodna biblioteka i muzei, 1937–1939*: 56–83.

—— and DŽAMBAZOV, N. 1960. *Devetashkata Pestera*. Sofia.

MILOJČIĆ, V. 1949. 'Die dorische Wanderung im Lichte der vorgeschichtlichen Funde.' *JdI/AA*, 63/64 (1948/49). Beiblatt: 11–30.

——. 1959. 'Ergebnisse der deutschen Ausgrabungen in Thessalien (1953–58).' *Jahrbuch des Römisch germanischen Zentralmuseums*, 6: 1–56.

MORINTZ, S. 1964. 'Quelques problèmes concernant la période ancienne du Hallstatt au Bas-Danube à la lumière des fouilles de Babadag.' *Dacia*, N.S., 8: 101–19.

—— and ROMAN, P. 1968. 'Apsekte des Ausgangs des Neolithikums und der Übergangsperiode im Raum der Niederdonau.' *Dacia*, N.S., 12: 45–128.

PAPAZOGLU, R. 1969. *Srednje-balkanska plemena u predrimsko doba*. Sarajevo.

POPOVIĆ, V. 1965. 'Sur la chronologie de l'âge du bronze en Serbie et en Bulgarie.' *Archaeologia Iugoslavica*, 6: 37–54.

PROX, A. 1941. *Die Schneckenbergkultur*. Kronstadt (Brasov).

REY, L. 1921. *Observations sur les premiers habitants de la Macédonie I-II*. Paris.

SREJOVIĆ, D. 1960. 'Praistoriska nekropola u Donjoj Brnjici.' *Glasnik muzeja Kosova i Methohije*, 4/5: 83–135.

STALIO, B. 1962. 'Bronzanodobski sloj na Gradcu kod Zlokućana.' *Zbornik radova Narodnog muzeja*, 3: 69–74.

TASIĆ, N. 1962. 'Naselja i nekropole polja sa urnama u istočnom Sremu.' *Rad vojvodjanskih muzeja*, 11: 50–121.

——. 1966. 'Problem kulture ravnih polja sa urnama u Vojvodini.' *Starinar*, N.S., 17: 15–26.

TODOROVIĆ, J. 1956. 'Praistoriska nekropola na Rospi Ćupriji kod Beograda.' *Godišnjak muzeja grada Beograda*, 3: 27–62.

——. 1963. 'Die Grabung Hissar und ihre Verhältnisse zum Neolithikum und zur frühen Bronzezeit.' *Archaeologia Iugoslavica*, 4: 25–29.

ZIRRA, V. 1960. 'Kultura pogrebenii s okhroi v zakarpatskikh oblast R.N.R.' in E. V. Konduraki (Condurachi), *Materialy i issledovaniya po arkheologii yugozapada SSSR i Rumynskoy Narodnoy Respubliki*. Kishinev.

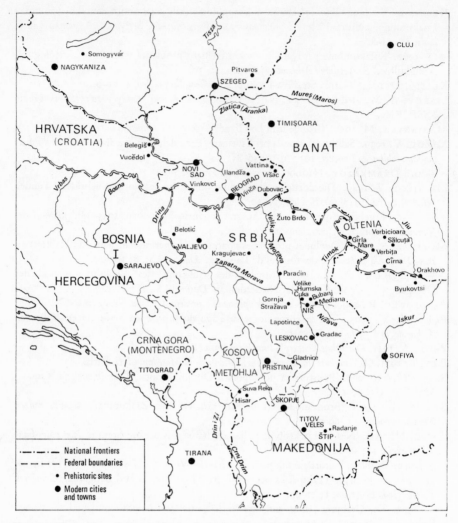

Fig. 11.1. The northern Balkan peninsula, showing sites mentioned

The destruction of Aegean and East Mediterranean urban civilization around 2300 B.C.

MARIJA GIMBUTAS

University of California, Los Angeles

THE hypothesis briefly outlined in this paper is that the destroyers of third millennium B.C. Mediterranean civilization were Indo-Europeans, 'the terrifying giants from the north'; non-urban peoples, pastoralists and horseriders who in the fourth and third millennia B.C. also developed the skills of sea-farer and charioteer. Traces of their ubiquitous presence have survived in a number of sites in the coastal regions of the Aegean, Ionian, Adriatic and East Mediterranean Seas, evidenced by cultural elements that find clear analogy in the North Pontic area and the north-western Caucasus. There, in the second half of the third millennium B.C., there existed a homogeneous, geographically definable culture characterized by an advanced metallurgy and by use of the horse, and horse-drawn vehicles, for human transportation. This is the so-called Pontic Pit- and Catacomb-grave culture, placed by the author at the end of the proto-Indo-European 'Kurgan Culture' series, and so labelled 'Kurgan IV'. Its Caucasian branch is known as the Early and Middle Kuban Bronze Age, and its early stage includes the famous Maikop and Tsarskaya (Novosvobodnaya) royal tombs. The archaeological record of Bronze Age development during the post-Catacomb-grave period in the coastal region between the lower Dniester and the Caucasus range suggests cultural continuity extending down through time until the existence of the historically recorded Cimmerians, at the end of the eighth century B.C. The group occupying the region in the third millennium B.C. may indeed have been culturally ancestral to the Cimmerians; alternatively they might have been another nuclear Indo-European group akin to the Indo-Iranian family.

The widespread violent destruction that occurred *c.* 2300 B.C. in the Aegean and East Mediterranean must be distinguished from the initial and gradual Indo-European infiltration of Europe and Anatolia one thousand five hundred years or more earlier. That process was a long one, divisible into the several chronological stages outlined below.

The first expansion of the semi-nomadic pastoralists of the south Russian (lower Volga) steppes resulted in their settlement and 'Kurganization' of the Black Sea region in the fifth millennium B.C., within the Kurgan I and II periods. (This high chronology has been established through correction of radiocarbon dates by tree-ring calibration; Movsha 1961.)[1] During the first half of the fourth millennium B.C. a massive infiltration of the Kurgan people can be discerned in eastern central Europe and the Balkan peninsula as far south as Macedonia, effecting the disintegration of the great European proto-civilizations: the *Cucuteni-Tripolye, Gumelniţa, Vinča, Butmir, Hvar, Lengyel* and *Tiszapolgár-Bodrogkeresztúr*. The presence of the infiltrating pastoralists from the east is shown by nearly five hundred Kurgan graves, dating from the fourth and early third millennia B.C., distributed over the steppe and forest steppe areas of the western Ukraine, Moldavia, the Dobrudja, the lower Danube plain and north-eastern Hungary[2]. Subsequently, in the second half of the fourth millennium B.C., in the Kurgan III period, there emerged a new Balkano-Danubian culture drastically different in its cultural characteristics, notably in art, religion and economy, from its fifth millennium predecessors. It is known by regional names: *Gorodsk* in the western Ukraine, *Cernavoda* in Dobrudja on the lower Danube and in the coastal strip along the Black Sea, *Ezero* in Bulgaria, *Cotofeni* in Transylvania and *Boleraz* in the Middle Danube area, succeeded by the *Baden* and *Kostolac* cultures. In Greek Macedonia the complex is well represented in the uppermost levels (Periods IV and V) of the Photolivos/Sitagroi mound in the plain of Drama (excavated by a joint UCLA-Sheffield University expedition in 1968 and 1969; for preliminary reports see Fraser 1970: 22; Renfrew 1970.)[3] This same cultural change was documented in the nearby mound of Dikili Taş, near Philippi, excavated since 1960 by J. Deshayes and Dh. Theokaris, sponsored by the Institute of Art and Archaeology of the University of Paris; see Daux 1962, 1968; Romiopoulou 1968; additional information has been provided by Dr. Deshayes). Cernavoda I type pottery (Kurgan III) was found there in the uppermost Gumelniţa level just before the final disappearance of the Gumelniţa culture. The proto-Indo-Europeans must have reached Macedonia through the eastern part of the Balkan Peninsula. This first infiltration was succeeded by a millennium of cultural development, well evidenced stratigraphically; it saw the formation of regional variants, their material culture reflecting the influence of the pre-Indo-European cultural substrate (Gimbutas 1970).

The Chalcolithic or Early Bronze Age I assemblages of central Anatolia include pottery significantly similar to that of Ezero-Cernavoda-Cotofeni in the Balkans, Danubian Europe and the western Ukraine. It falls within the

Kurgan III period. It is crude but usually burnished, hand-made; black, dark grey, or brownish. The ornamental technique of stabbing and incision, forming sun motifs around the vessel mouth, is typically Kurgan. The appearance of this type of pottery in the earliest layers at Büyük Güllücek and Alaca Hüyük, and in other less well-documented sites (Orthmann 1963: 52–3; pls. 41–8), has been considered by some Anatolian archaeologists to indicate the arrival of a new population element, since the ware has no local correlates or predecessors (Orthmann 1963: 78–9). Other sites further east, such as Alişar and Horoztepe, contained later variants of similar pottery (Orthmann 1963: pls. 11–14; 71). In north-western Anatolia the Troy I complex and related groups are contemporary with late phases of the Cernavoda-Ezero culture, represented, for instance, in the Sitagroi period V; and with the classical Baden culture of east central Europe. At the time in question cross-cultural contact between east central Europe and north-western Anatolia was marked; and on the basis of present knowledge it can be surmised that the north-western and central parts of Anatolia were infiltrated by proto-Indo-European speakers, either from the Balkans, through Thrace and Macedonia; or directly by sea from the north-west coast of the Black Sea (the territory between the mouth of the Danube and Odessa), a route which would have brought them into central Anatolia. In this case north-western Anatolia might have been invaded at a slightly later time, perhaps from Thrace.

As early as the fourth millennium B.C. the Indo-Europeans (more correctly, the proto-Indo-Europeans) must have been sea-farers: Indo-European evidently had words for 'oar' and 'boat', represented e.g. by Latin *remus* and Greek *naûs* (see Pokorny 1968: 338, *s.v.* 1. *erə-, re-, er(e)-* (1950), 755, *s.v.* 1. *naus-* (1954); Meillet 1943: 385 403). Like the Vikings in the Baltic and North Seas, the Kurgan III people must have ventured into the Black Sea, the Aegean and the Mediterranean, and it is not unlikely that the Indo-European tribes inhabiting the western Black Sea coast were responsible for the abrupt end of the Ghassulian culture of Palestine. According to Lapp's chronology at the site of Bâb edh-Dhrâ on the eastern side of the Dead Sea (1968a; 1968b), the Ghassulian culture was terminated by Early Bronze I newcomers in about the thirty-second century B.C. This cultural disjuncture marks a radical ethnic change. Large shaft-tombs contrast sharply with previous local burial practice, and some of the new tombs included among their contents disarticulated skeletons in baskets, a feature which may indicate lengthy warrior-burial ceremonies prior to interment, peculiarly a Kurgan and later Indo-European trait. Tomb A 76 from Bâb edh-Dhrâ (Pl. 21) included two very richly furnished oven (or ('catacomb') shaped shaft-graves, their chamber entrances secured with stones. A peculiar decorative technique administered to the burnished surface of bowls and handled vases was the application and slashed incision of a raised band, a technique for which close analogies exist in Rumania and Bulgaria in the later stage of the Cernavoda-Ezero culture which precedes the Troy I horizon (for example in the ceramic assemblages of the Folteşti II, Tirpeşti and Bogdaneşti sites in Moldavia, stored in the archaeological museums of Iaşi, Bucharest, Bacau and Celei in the district of Olt; and in those of Cernavoda II–III sites in Dobrudja, stored in the museum of the Institute of Archaeology in Bucharest; Marinescu-Bilcu 1964: 245; Marin 1968; Morintz and Roman 1968). Pear-shaped mace-heads of semi-precious stone found in Bâb edh-Dhrâ also have parallels in Rumania and the western Ukraine (Telegin 1968: 149–51)[4]. A distinction of physical type has been demonstrated between the local Ghassulians, massive and broad-headed, and their more gracile dolichocephalic successors. This first phase of disturbance in the Near East was short-lived; a period of urban development followed and persisted until the twenty-third century B.C. However, these same sea-farers, the Vikings of the fourth millennium B.C., seem to have threatened not only the East Mediterranean coasts. Cultural elements similar to those found in Bâb edh-Dhrâ are also known from western and central Italy, from the Gaudo complex, near Paestum, and the Rinaldone near Viterbo, north-west of Rome (Sestieri 1949; Lo Porto 1957; Puglisi 1959: 21–8).

The extension of proto-Indo-European influence over large areas of Europe in the fourth millennium B.C. did not affect Greece south of Macedonia and Thessaly, except at several points along the eastern seaboard of Greece, nor Crete or the Cycladic Islands where the Early Helladic, Minoan and Cycladic cultures continued to develop into urban civilizations through most of the third millennium B.C. They are the epigones of the Old European and definitely non-Indo-European civilization. Their urban culture persisted until about 2300–2200 B.C. when it was shaken by mysterious destroyers.

A number of sites in Greece, western and southern Anatolia and Syro-Palestine contain destruction levels which are roughly synchronous (Evans; see above, pp. 21–3). An overall decline in material culture followed this widespread destruction and some later sites indicate successive disturbances. The destruction of the Early Helladic II town at Lerna in the eastern Pelopennese and subsequent developments there, provide the classic example (Caskey 1960; Weinberg 1965: 311). An analogous devastation, involving the whole East Mediterranean region, afflicted these areas in the early twelfth century B.C.; it was brought by the so-called 'Peoples of the Sea' and we might consequently judge that the destruction of the third millennium was similarly inflicted from the sea. That these people were Indo-European warriors is implied by the surprising similarity of elements of their culture to those of the Kurgan IV branch north and north-east of the Black Sea (Gimbutas 1956: 56–89). Archaeological materials indicate their presence in the Mediterranean, Ionian, Adriatic, Aegean and Black Sea areas, which suggests the sea-borne passage of newly migrating Indo-European groups through the Black Sea and the Aegean and thence into the Mediterranean.

The period termed Kurgan IV belongs to the third millennium B.C. and was in its earlier part contemporary with Early Helladic II, in its later part with the destruction and post-destruction phases in Greece. The type assemblage north of the Black Sea is layer III of the Mikhailovka (Mykhailivka) hill-fort, in the district of Kherson in the lower Dnieper region, a settlement heavily fortified with massive stone walls and ditches; the assemblage included cord-decorated pottery and tanged copper daggers (Lagodovska, Shaposhnikova and Makarevich 1962). The royal burials of Maikop and Tsarskaya (Novosvobodnaya) in the northern Caucasus, representative of both the Early and Middle Kuban periods, also belong to this same Kurgan IV period (Gimbutas 1956: 58–65). In Greece and on the Ionian Islands Kurgan IV elements appeared at the latest before or around the middle of the third millennium B.C. Several instances can be mentioned: Kurgan IV corded and stabbed pottery was found in the settlement at Eutresis in Boeotia (Frankfort 1927: 44, pl. IV, No. 6). A similar ware was discovered by Dörpfeld during his excavation of tumuli on the Island of Lefkas in the Ionian Sea; the tumuli overlay pit-graves dug into virgin soil and secured by a large slab, a layer of earth and a cairn of stones (Dörpfeld 1927: 244, fig. 18; Hammond 1967: 92). The graves are dated by the presence of sauce-boat fragments of the Early Helladic II period (middle of the third millennium B.C.). This grave form is strikingly similar to that found in burials of the mid-third millennium B.C. and later in the Black Sea coastal region between Odessa in the west and the north-western Caucasus in the east (Pl. 22). It most notably resembles the graves in the tumuli at Ul' in the district of Maikop, where among the grave-goods of the central burial there was the clay model of a war-chariot, copper pins with the upper part bent over (also known from the 'I' layer of Amuq in Syria), and female figurines of clay and of marble or alabaster (Pl. 23; Veselovskiy 1910; Dobrovolskiy 1930: figs. 1, 2; Hančar 1937: 253–5, fig. 21, pl. LI/1a, 1b, 2a, 2b). The Marathon Kurgans published in this volume by Professor Marinatos are very similar to those known in the Caucasus (Plate 24, Marinatos 1970; see above pp. 111–2).

The pit-caves, called 'catacombs', appeared in the lower Don and Manych areas during the latter part of the Kurgan IV period, while regular pit-graves with remains of timber or stone mortuary houses continued to be used in other North Pontic areas. Calibrated radiocarbon dates indicate a period of about 2450–2250 B.C. [5]. This grave form consisted of a deep shaft sunk into virgin soil, with a side niche to accommodate the burial. Rites remained typically 'Kurgan', with burial accompaniments of sacrificed animals, food and drink offerings, red ochre, braziers, and pots decorated with solar motifs. The grave imitated a house; the floor was laid out with pebbles or white chalk and the entrance was secured with stones. The warrior graves are distinguished by their peculiar equipment: copper or flint daggers, flint points or arrow-heads, arrow-straighteners, battle-axes and particular ornaments, including bone, copper or faience beads interspersed with perforated animal teeth. People of higher class had deformed skulls, apparently a sign of social status. The occurrence of marble, alabaster and Mediterranean shells with burials of the Catacomb-grave periods around the Sea of Azov and the Caucasus indicates contacts with the Aegean and East Mediterranean coasts. The introduction of niched shaft-graves in the lower Don–River Manych area can perhaps be interpreted as a result of tribal homecoming after campaigns in the south. Analogous niched shaft-graves, containing similar offerings and equipment, or just pot-sherds of the Catacomb-grave phase, are known from northern Greece (e.g. Agios Mamas and several other sites in Khalkidhiki; finds are in the Thessaloniki Museum), Sicily, Apulia, and from Palestine. There is a similarity between the North Pontic catacomb graves and those of the Conca d'Oro culture of north-western Sicily, around Palermo. They have a shaft and chamber and are termed 'oven-shaped tombs'. Moreover, the manner of burial and the type of grave-goods are closely similar to their North Pontic counterparts. Included are red ochre, small copper daggers, rings and bracelets, and pots decorated with cord impressions and lines of incisions with dots below them, typical of the Kurgan IV period (Bernabo-Brea 1957: 90–94; pl. 25). Around Taranto, Brindisi and Foggia in Apulia a number of sites have yielded pottery, flint and bone tools of related character. The Laterza catacomb-graves near Taranto contained, among other things, stone arrow-straighteners and necklaces of perforated animal teeth, finds diagnostic of the Kurgan family (Biancofiore 1967). Along the Yugoslav coast, north of Dubrovnik, the stratified cave site of Gudnia yielded a stratum with typical Kurgan IV ware, including bowls and amphorae decorated with rows of cord impressions bordered by a row of stabbed triangles, similar to those from Eutresis. This stratum was above a painted pottery Hvar layer and was overlaid by Vučedol-Ljubljana (Laibach) red and yellow ware, richly decorated with white encrustation[6]. Voyages across the Adriatic are indicated by evidence of contacts between the Vučedol culture in the Middle Danube region (famous for the Vučedol hill-fort near Vukovar, in north-western Yugoslavia) and Early or Early Middle Minoan Crete. Among the finds of the Vučedol layer of the Vučedol hill-fort are Minoan horns of consecration and dove sculptures with incised double-axe motifs (Schmidt 1945). This indicates that the northern Adriatic shores were accessible to the Indo-European tribes of east central Europe.

At the end of the Early Bronze Age in Syro-Palestine there is a complete break in which the town-dwellers were succeeded by semi-nomadic pastoralists who had no interest in walled towns. Barrows of Kurgan appearance are known from the Levant as far south as the Negev desert in Israel. At the destroyed town of Bâb edh-Dhrâ there was a cemetery of cist-graves of Kurgan appearance which included single burials equipped with copper daggers and stone battle-axes (Lapp 1968a; 1968b). In Jericho Miss Kenyon has excavated 177 catacomb-graves, and similar tombs are known at the Ajjul, Duweir and Megiddo tells (Kenyon 1965: 52-3, 79, 182-9, 301). The people buried in them are considered to have been pastoralists rather than town-dwellers. Many of the catacomb-graves of Jericho and other sites duplicate the characteristic Kurgan IV burials found north of the Black Sea, both in the position of the dead and the content and placement of grave equipment. The dagger was the most usual weapon. Examination of skeletal remains from Jericho has indicated that these inhabitants were distinctly different from the earlier Mediterranean populations: they were tall-statured and dolichocephalic, with moderately high heads, mesoprosopic faces and mesorphine noses. Until the present century the mound of Bâb edh-Dhrâ was remembered as 'Tell-el-'Alawiyîn', 'Tell of the Giants'; Emim, the name of a Biblical people considered by Moabites to be their predecessors, meant 'Terrifying Giants' (Lapp 1968b: 1, 3, 24). It is not impossible for memories to endure through four thousand years. The intruding Indo-European warriors must have impressed the local populations by their tall 'gigantic' stature around 2300 B.C. just as did the tall Philistines, also apparently Indo-Europeans, in the twelfth century B.C.

Conclusions

The destruction of urban civilization in the Aegean and East Meditarranean area at around 2300 B.C. seems to have been caused by the Kurgan IV peoples from north and north-east of the Black Sea. It represents a second major wave of Indo-European attacks upon the sites of higher civilization, more violent than the first, which occurred in the last quarter of the fourth millennium B.C., initiated by the Indo-European tribes living west of the Black Sea. The North Pontic Indo-Europeans of the Kurgan IV period must have been sea-farers, frequenting or plundering the Aegean, East Mediterranean, Ionian and Adriatic Sea coasts. The waterways of the Black Sea and the Aegean offered incomparably easier access to the civilized world than did the Caucasus Mountains, although direct contact between the Caucasus and Mesopotamia and Anatolia also existed. These nomadic intrusions continued during at least several centuries and ended in the destruction of Mediterranean cities at about 2300 B.C. It is very possible that some of the Indo-European settlement of Greece was effected by Kurgan IV people coming from the coastal regions north of the Black Sea and from the north-western Caucasus, at the time of the destruction of the Early

Helladic II culture. This second wave of Indo-Europeanization, affecting Mediterranean Europe, is distinctly separate from the earlier infiltration of the Balkan peninsula, Anatolia and Italy, which was a gradual movement from areas in the Balkans with Kurgan III culture, going southward from Macedonia and Thessaly into peninsular Greece. It is impossible at present to suggest whether either of the two processes introduced 'proto-Greek' (i.e. the prehistoric Indo-European language which Greek effectively reflects and continues) into Greece. Perhaps both waves contributed immigrants and influences which formed the basis of the population and culture of Greece in Middle Helladic and Mycenaean times.

Notes

1. The earliest finds of Kurgan appearance have been shown to be contemporary with the Tripolye A and B phases in settlements in the western Ukraine, and so with the pre-Cucuteni III and Cucuteni A phases in Rumania (Movsha 1961: 186–99). Radiocarbon dates for Cucuteni A (Tripolye B) settlements (Polivanov Jar and Hăbăşeşti) are *c.* 3400 B.C.; the corresponding true age dendrochronologically calibrated is *c.* 4350 B.C. In the terminology used by Soviet archaeologists the Kurgan I complex is referred to as 'Sredniy Stog II culture'. Relevant material is in the museum of the Archaeological Institute of the Ukrainian Academy of Sciences in Kiev, largely unpublished. (These dates are based on the half-life of 5568 years).

2. The phase of second and massive infiltration into the area of the Cucuteni civilization is indicated by contemporaneity of Kurgan II and Cucuteni AB (Tripolye BII) material (Movsha 1961: 186–99). In the Tiszapolgár region of north-eastern Hungary and Transylvania the same infiltration is witnessed by the Decea cemetery (in the county of Torda-Aranyos in the Mureş valley) and by the appearance of kurgans and horse bones; and in the Balkan Gumelniţa and Vinča areas by the spread of Kurgan II graves, pottery and horse-head figurines used as sceptres (Gimbutas 1970: 158, 178–9, fn. 6, 24, 25). Two radiocarbon dates were obtained at the UCLA Laboratory of Geophysics for bones of domesticated horses from the Kurgan II settlement of Dereivka in the lower Dnieper region: UCLA No. 1466A 5515 ± 90 BP, which if calibrated by dendrochronology is 4350 B.C.; and UCLA No. 1617A 4900 ± 100 BP, 3670 B.C. if calibrated. The second date will indicate contemporaneity with Cucuteni AB, late Gumelniţa and late Vinča cultures.

3. A monograph on the excavations at Sitagroi, edited by A. C. Renfrew and M. Gimbutas, is in press. Tree-ring calibrated dates for Period IV at the site are: *c.* 3300–3000 B.C. (radiocarbon dates obtained from the Berlin Laboratory were: 2440 and 2360 ± 100 B.C.).

4. Mace-heads are known from the Mariupol and Mikolskiy cemeteries in the lower Dnieper region and other sites of the final phase of the Dnieper-Donets complex (Telegin 1968: 149–51, fig. 51). Very probably mace-heads were brought to Transylvania by the Kurgan II people; cf. finds in the Decea cemetery (Gimbutas 1965: 476). They continue to appear in Kurgan assemblages down to the Catacomb-grave (Kurgan IV) period.

5. For a catacomb-grave (grave no. 6) in barrow no. 2 at Kudinov in the county of Bagaevo in the lower Don valley (Berger and Libby 1968; Melentev 1964: 53–7) with dendrochronological calibration.

6. Excavated by S. Petrak 1964 to 1966. The finds are in the Dubrovnik City Museum.

References

BERGER, R. and LIBBY, W. F. 1968. 'UCLA radiocarbon dates VII.' *Radiocarbon*, 10: 149–60.

BERNABO-BREA, L. 1957. *Sicily before the Greeks*. London.

BIANCOFIORE, F. 1967. 'La necropoli eneolitica de Laterza; origini e sviluppe dei gruppi protoappeninici in Apulia.' *Origini*, 1: 195–300.

CASKEY, J. L. 1960. 'The Early Helladic Period in the Argolid.' *Hesperia*, 29: 285–303.

DAUX, D. 1962. 'Chronique des fouilles 1961. Dikili-Tach.' *BCH*, 86: 912–33.

——. 1968. 'Chronique des fouilles 1967. Dikili-Tach.' *BCH*, 92: 1062–77.

DOBROVOLSKIY, A. 1930. *Ètudy z nadporiz'kogo neolitu* (*Antropologiya zbirsnik kabinetu antropologii im. F. Vovka* 1929: III): 161–9, pls. 1, 2.

DÖRPFELD, W. 1927. *Alt-Ithaka*. Munich.

FRANKFORT, H. 1927. *Studies in the Early Pottery of the Near East*, II: *Asia, Europe and the Aegean, and their Earliest Interrelations*. London.

FRASER, P. M. 1970. 'Archaeology in Greece, 1969–70.' *ArchRep*, 16(*JHS*, 90): 3–31.

GIMBUTAS, M. 1956. *The Prehistory of Eastern Europe Part I*. Cambridge, Mass.

——. 1965. 'The relative chronology of Neolithic and Chalcolithic cultures in eastern Europe north of the Balkan peninsula and the Black Sea'; in R. W. Ehrich, *Chronologies*: 459–502.

——. 1970. 'Proto-Indo-European culture: the Kurgan culture during the fifth, fourth and third millennia.' *Indo-European and Indo Europeans*: 158–79.

HAMMOND, N. G. L. 1967. *Epirus*. Oxford.

HANČAR, F. 1937. *Urgeschichte Kaukasiens von den Anfangen seiner Besiedlung bis in die Zeit seiner frühen Metallurgie* (*Bücher zur Ur- und Frühgeschichte*, 6; ed. O. Menghin). Vienna and Leipzig.

KENYON, K. M. 1965. *Excavations at Jericho*, I–II. London.

LAGODOVSKA, O. F., SHAPOSHNIKOVA, O. G. and MAKAREVICH, M. L. 1962. *Mikhailivske poseleniya*. Kiev.

LAPP, P. W. 1968a. 'Bâb edh-Dhrâ Tomb A76 and Early Bronze 1 in Palestine.' *BASOR*, 189: 12–141.

——. 1968b. 'Bâb edh-Dhrâ, Perizzites and Emim.' *Jerusalem through the Ages* (Israel Exploration Society; 25th Archaeological Convention, Jerusalem): 1–25.

LO PORTO, F. G. 1957. 'La Tomba di Cellino S. Marco e l'inizio della civiltà del bronzo in Puglia.' *Bolletino Prehist. Ital.* N.S., 11: 153–70.

MARIN, D. 1968. 'Quelques considérations sur la periode de transition du néolitique à l'âge du bronze sur le territoire de la Moldavie.' *Dacia*, N.S., 12: 129–39.

MARINATOS, Sp. 1970. 'Further discoveries at Marathon.' *AthAA*, 1970: 351–7.

MARINESCU-BÎLCU, S. 1964. 'Unele probleme ale perioadei de tranzizie de la neolitic la epoca bronzului din Moldova in lumina a trei morminte plane de inhumatic descoperiet la Tirpeşti.' *Studii şi Cercetări Istorie Veche*, 2: 245.

MEILLET, A. 1937. *Introduction à l'étude comparative des langues indo-européennes*. Paris (reprinted by University of Alabama, 1965).

MELENTEV, A. N. 1964. 'Kurgany epokhi bronzy v nizhnem Podone.' *Kratkie Soobshcheniya Instituta Arkeologii* 103. Moscow.

MORINTZ, S. and PETRE, R. 1968. 'Aspecte des Ausgangs des Äneolithikums und der Übergangstufe zur Bronzezeit im Raum der Niederdonau.' *Dacia*, N.S., 12: 45–128.

MOVSHA, T. G. 1961. 'O svyasyakh plemen Tripol'skoi kul'tury so stepnymi plemenami medogo veka.' *Sovetskaya Arkheologiya*, 2: 186–99.

ORTHMANN, W. 1963. *Die Keramik der Frühen Bronzezeit aus Inner-Anatolien*. Berlin.

POKORNY, J. 1968. *Indogermanisches Etymologisches Wörterbuch*. Bern and Munich (1948–68).

PUGLISI, S. 1959. *La civiltà appenninica*. Florence.

RENFREW, A. C. 1970. 'The Burnt House at Sitagroi.' *Antiquity*, 44: 131–4.

ROMIOPOULOU, C. 1968. 'Excavation at the prehistoric site of Dikili Taş.' *AthAA*, 1: 48–50.

SCHMIDT, R. R. 1945. *Die Burg Vučedol*. Berlin.

SESTIERI, C. P. 1949. 'Primi risultati dello scavo della necropoli preistorica di Paestum.' *RendNap*, 23: 251–308.

TELEGIN, D. Y. 1968. *Dnipro-Donetska Kultura*. Kiev.

VESELOVSKIY, N. I. 1910. 'Untersuchungen einiger prähistorischer und skythischer Grabhügel in der Nähe des Weilers Ul im Maikopschen Bezirk, Kubangebiet.' *Archäologisches Jahrbuch*, 1910: 195–210.

WEINBERG, S. 1965. 'The Aegean in the Stone and Early Bronze Ages'; in R. W. Ehrich, *Chronologies*: 303–35.

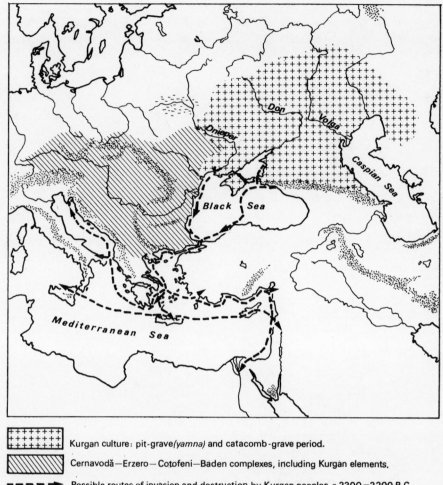

Kurgan culture: pit-grave*(yamna)* and catacomb-grave period.

Cernavodă—Erzero—Cotofeni—Baden complexes, including Kurgan elements.

Possible routes of invasion and destruction by Kurgan peoples *c.* 2300–2200 B.C.

Fig. 12.1. Expansion of Kurgan culture in the mid-third millennium B.C.

4

Contact between the Aegean region and Anatolia in the second millenium B.C.

Anatolian evidence for relations with the West in the Late Bronze Age

---

Ph. H. J. HOUWINK TEN CATE

University of Amsterdam

I. The historical and philological evidence

Some preliminary remarks are necessary on the subject of this paper. It will not deal with the archaeological evidence for relations between the Hittites and the West and it will put special emphasis on the historical data rather than on considerations of a more strictly linguistic nature. An alternative choice for the title might have been 'Some Anatolian glosses on the history of the Mycenaean Period', recalling the heading of a still valuable article by W. F. Albright, 'Some Oriental glosses on the Homeric problem' (Albright 1950). This year 1950 offers a good point for a summary of the history of research on my subject during the preceding decades. M. Ventris had not yet announced his decipherment of the Minoan Linear B script and 'believers' and 'unbelievers' in the *Ahhiyawa-Akhaioi* equation held their opinions more or less intuitively on general historical grounds. I do not wish to find fault with such an attitude. Before the actual decipherment of Linear B by Ventris and Chadwick, A. J. B. Wace and C. W. Blegen favoured the hypothesis that the main language of the Knossos, Pylos and Mycenae tablets was essentially Greek, and they did so on similar, general historical grounds. Apparently a vague historical intuition may prove more fruitful, at least in the historical field, than hundreds of pages of sceptical and in its own right impeccable philological investigation. F. Sommer's *Die Ahhijavā-Urkunden* (1932) was a philological masterpiece, but it may still

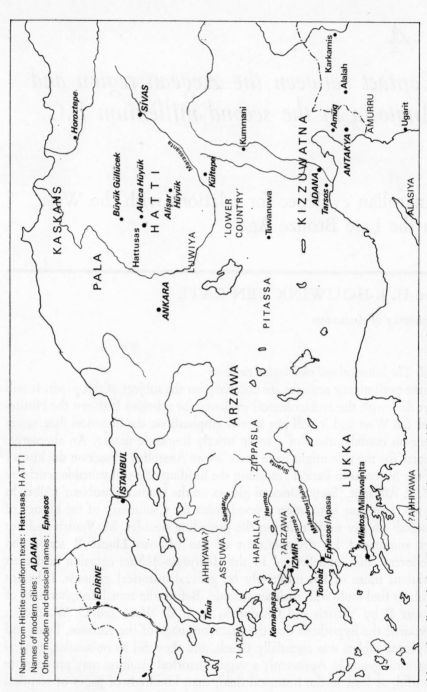

Map 3. Anatolia in the Late Bronze Age, with some Middle Bronze Age sites shown

have been misguided in its complete condemnation of E. Forrer's thesis as first presented (Forrer 1924a). In the years before 1939 personal antagonism between the main opponents, Forrer, Hrozný, Kretschmer and Schachermeyr on the one hand and Sommer, Goetze and Friedrich on the other, was largely to blame for the bitter ardour displayed in the endless discussions, on which the title of Sommer's last major contribution to the debate, 'Ahhijava und kein Ende?', may seem to have passed appropriate comment (Sommer 1937).

But before I try to deal once more with the thorny problems connected with the ethnikon *Ahhiyawa*[1] of the Hittite cuneiform texts, it may be worth while to evaluate the 'Eastern' loan-words in Mycenaean Greek. Two Greek words have been claimed to show Anatolian connections: *kuanos* and *elephas* equated respectively by Goetze (1947) and Laroche (1965a) with Hittite *kuwanna(n)*- and *lahpa*-. Both Greek words are traditionally connected with the East and they have also been explained on the basis of Semitic material. In the case of *kuanos* there is good reason to be very cautious indeed, since Laroche has recently shown (Laroche 1966b) that the Hittite word means either 'copper' or, with the determinative NA$_4$, 'precious stone'. The meaning 'azurite' (*Kupferblau*) has not been proved and it is precisely this meaning on which the equation with *kuanos* is based. In 1965 Laroche proposed to connect *elephas*, 'ivory', with Hittite *lahpa*- which occurs in the Hittite column of a trilingual text from Ugarit; but Laroche himself is now doubtful (1968) whether the Greek is directly dependent upon the Hittite (functioning as an intermediary) or whether both words should be ascribed to a common, e.g. Syrian, source (on *kuanos* see Halleux 1969).

In comparison with the Semitic loan-words in Mycenaean texts this possible maximum of two is rather low. In a recent book Emilia Masson (1967) gives an up-to-date appraisal of the early Semitic loan-words in Greek. The following are already satisfactorily attested in the Mycenaean documents, *khiton, khrusos, kuminon* and *sesamon* (Morpurgo 1963).

I will now return to the highly controversial *Ahhiyawa* problem. At the beginning of this paper I selected 1950 as the starting-point for my survey. This was the year of publication of the study in which Albright suggested identification with Ionia and Caria (1950: 167). In the same year G. P. Carratelli argued that Rhodes should be taken as the main centre of a Mycenaean *Ahhiyawa*. Rhodes had first been proposed by B. Hrozný (1929), although in that same year he also published a map, accompanying his contribution on 'The Hittites' to the *Encyclopaedia Britannica* in which *Ahhiya(wa)* is located in the north-west of Anatolia. During the past twenty years identification of at least the main area of *Ahhiyawa* with Rhodes has found growing support among those scholars who favour the identification of its people with the Mycenaean 'Achaeans': V. L. Laurenzi in 1940; K.

Völkl in 1952; R. A. Crossland on numerous occasions (1953, 1954 and 1967); A. Heubeck in 1955; D. L. Page in his eloquent book *History and the Homeric Iliad* (1959: 15–17, 35–7, notes 53–5) two archaeologists also: K. Bittel (1950: 69–72) suggesting location in Ionia and northern Caria and the isles of Samos and Rhodes; and J. Mellaart identification with the partly Mycenaean town of Miletus and the group of islands off the south-west coast of Anatolia (1955: 83).

P. Kretschmer who had earlier argued for Cilicia (1933) now proposed Cyprus (1954), elaborating on an idea expressed by C. F. A. Schaeffer (1952: 1–10, and 350–7). E. Cavaignac and O. R. Gurney preferred Crete (Cavaignac 1946; Gurney 1952: 55–6) or the Greek mainland (Cavaignac 1950: 38; Gurney 1959: 127, and *passim*). R. Dussaud (1953: 75–6, 78, 83) concluded that the 'Ahhiyawans' had their homeland on the mainland of Greece but were masters of Rhodes, Lesbos and the west coast of Anatolia (including Troy). Schachermeyr, one of the protagonists in the pre-war controversy with his book *Hethiter und Achäer* (1935), returned to the subject in 1958. He seems still to favour location of *Ahhiyawa* on the mainland of Greece, but notes the growing support for Rhodes and the possibility that Cyprus should be considered. F. Cornelius spoke for Pamphylia in 1955. In 1960 G. Huxley published a synopsis covering the whole problem in which he stated his own preference for location on the Greek mainland.

From the linguistic standpoint attention was focused on reconstruction of the Greek name which was presumably transcribed into Hittite as *Ahhiya(wa)*, irregularly as it was generally thought, the apparent change of *-ai-* to *-iya-* being a stumbling-block. In 1955 P. B. S. Andrews suggested that *Ahhiya(wa)* was based on the bare stem of the ethnikon *Akhaiwo-*, while positing *Akhaiwia* as the Mycenaean name for Greece. J. M. Aitchison opted for *Akhaiwia* (1964). J. Harmatta wavered between *Akhaiwoi* and *Akhaiwa/Akhaiwia* (1968a). In 1962 F. Cornelius proposed that Anatolian *Ahhiya(wa)* was meant to represent *Argeioi*. O. Carruba reversed the whole problem in 1964 by deriving Greek *Aiolees* by way of **Ahhiyawailes* from an indigenous Anatolian *Ahhiya(wa)-*, and similarly *Iaones* by way of **Ahhiya(w)a-wanni-* from the same *Ahhiya(wa)*. Perhaps the best solution is that proposed by B. Čop (1955: 61–2) who suggested that a Luwian diphthong (also present according to him in Luwian *wiyana-*, 'wine'; cf. Gk. *woinos*, Semitic **wainu-*) was an intermediary between the original Greek form of the ethnikon and the form or forms represented by the Hittite cuneiform orthographies. The new chronological order of the *Ahhiyawa* texts, which will shortly be discussed, shows an important caesura between the older texts mentioning *A-aḫ-ḫi-ya-a/Aḫ-ḫi-ya* and the younger ones giving the variants of the longer form *Aḫ-ḫi-ya-wa-a*. Regarding the longer form of the name, typical for Hittite texts from the time of Mursilis ɪɪ (1344–1320 B.C.) onwards, my preference is for identification with *Akhaiwoi*.

One may doubt whether the older form *A-aḫ-ḫi-ya-a* would ever have been connected with the name of the 'Achaeans', if the longer form had not turned up in other texts. Does it represent *Akhaiwia*? In that case the cuneiform rendering went far astray! Both lines of research, the attempts to localize the homeland of the enigmatic 'Ahhiyawans' and the endeavours to reconstruct the underlying Greek form of their name, are essentially based on the assumption that the original onomastic equation is correct and on the notion that the *Ahhiyawa* represent the Mycenaean 'Achaeans'. Let us now turn to those scholars who at least in a general sense continued to work along the lines of Sommer's ideas that *Ahhiya(wa)-* was an indigenous Anatolian country and that the similarity to Greek *Akhaiwoi* and *Akhaiwia* is entirely accidental. Foremost is G. Steiner who in 1964 published an excellent article under the title 'Die Ahhijawa-Frage heute'. Steiner rightly stressed that the obligation to prove their case rests with those who interpret *Ahhiya(wa)* as denoting the country of the 'Achaeans' and think that its population consisted, totally or partly, of Mycenaean Greeks. Steiner gives weighty arguments for the thesis that the historical data favour a localization on the mainland of Anatolia. When he turns to archaeological data, Steiner sticks to the usual hypothesis that the activities of Mycenaean 'Ahhiyawans' there should be indicated by the presence of Mycenaean pottery. The data on this Mycenaean pottery have recently been re-assessed by eminent authorities like Bittel (1967), Mellaart (1968) and D. H. French (1969). This part of Steiner's study has thus been superseded by later investigations. With imposing argumentation Steiner tries to dispose of all the proposals for localization outside of Anatolia (on the Greek mainland, Cyprus, Crete, Rhodes) and on the southern coast of Anatolia (Cilicia and Pamphylia). Finally he denies the identity of *Ahhiyawa* and 'Achaeans'.

I tend to agree with Steiner that a number of texts seem to indicate that *Ahhiya(wa)* was a continental Anatolian power, and as far as these texts are concerned an identification with *Mycenaean* 'Achaeans' is relatively unlikely. But perhaps these texts could refer to an *Anatolian* Greek population. This is essentially the thesis developed by J. G. MacQueen and J. Mellaart in their articles of 1968. MacQueen who is the most explicit of the two does in fact elaborate on an idea expressed by Goetze as early as 1933: "Es bliebe noch die Möglichkeit, dass im Nordwesten Kleinasiens schon sehr früh Achäer— Vorgänger der späteren Äoler—heimisch geworden sind, vielleicht geradezu von Troja aus beherrscht, und dass es dieses Staatswesen ist, das den Hethitern unter dem Namen *Ahhijawa* bekannt geworden ist. Aber auch das zu beweisen reichen die Angaben der Texte nicht aus".* (Goetze 1933: 172;

* "There remains the possibility that Achaeans, predecessors of the later Aeolians, were already settled in north-western Anatolia very early, perhaps actually governed from Troy, and that they formed the state which was known to the Hittites as *Ahhijawa*. But the statements in the texts are insufficient to prove that conclusion either".

1957: 183 fn. 5). Between 1933 and 1968 Goetze's idea found a certain response in studies by Schmidt (1956), Mellaart (1958) and Carruba (1964: 40, 45). MacQueen returns to Goetze's position when he states his preferred localization of *Ahhiy(wa)*: "And if we look with eyes that are not dimmed by the brilliance of the Homeric poems, we shall find such a country—the area known in later times as the Troad, with as its principal citadel the mound known as Hissarlik and identified with Troy". (MacQueen 1968: 179).

At this point I will insert some personal conclusions. I believe that it is possible to reconcile both basic positions and to combine the best elements of both schools of thought. Some points should be stressed: (1) A number of texts, particularly the one that now seems to be the oldest in the series (*KUB* XIV 1; the 'Indictment of Madduwattas') depicts *Ahhiya(wa)* as a continental Anatolian power situated on the sea coast. (2) Other, later, texts show that in the beginning of the thirteenth century B.C., if not already earlier during the reign of Mursilis II, *Milawata/Millawanda*, usually equated with *Milētos*, belonged to the sphere of influence of *Ahhiya(wa)*, but that it later was governed by a vassal prince of the Hittite king. (3) During the second half of the thirteenth century ships of *Ahhiya(wa)* were engaged in commerce with the Syrian coast, and at that time a scribe who prepared a draft for an important treaty relevant to that region considered at least for a moment (because he did change his mind) that *Ahhiya(wa)* a major political power on a par with Egypt, Babylon and Assur (Sommer 1932: 320–7; 1937: 283–5; Page 1959: 6, 31–2, fn. 37; see also below, p. 152).

I believe that one should seriously reckon with the possibility that the term *Ahhiya(wa)* widened considerably in its application during the fourteenth and thirteenth centuries and that it does not refer to one and the same geographical entity at the three times just indicated. The inevitable and unattractive alternative would be to assume that somewhere on the west coast of Anatolia (or, less probably, on one of the offshore islands, and in that case preferably on Rhodes) a small local power of this name developed into a major political factor in the international world of the thirteenth century B.C. For such an assumption there are no reliable historical indications at all. It is precisely the fact that the equation *Ahhiya(wa)*–'Achaeans' is reasonably consistent with the hypothesis that a term originally of restricted application acquired extended significance that makes the identification attractive, in my opinion, from a general historical point of view. There is no evidence for a considerable degree of political unity in the Mycenaean world and certainly not in the Greek world of the Bronze Age as a whole. If one is willing to operate on the assumption that some Greek tribes found their way into the north-west of Anatolia already in the second millennium B.C., the name of these groups might indeed have developed into the overall term for Greeks of later centuries, comprising also

Mycenaean Greeks at least by the time of the 'Sausgamuwa Treaty' (Sommer 1932: 320–7).

The elusive character of the people designated by it agrees very well with a hypothesis that the name widened in meaning and is consistent with the idea that it ended up as a general designation for people of Greek descent. In view of the difference between *A-aḫ-ḫi-ya-a/Aḫ-ḫi-ya* in the older texts and *Aḫ-ḫi-ya-wa-a* in the younger, it is not unlikely that the name reached the Hittites twice by different channels. But it should be conceded that *A-aḫ-ḫi-ya-a* is by no means easier to explain as a first approximation in cuneiform script than the later longer form (cf. Steiner 1964: 384–97).

Let us now turn to the Hittite texts themselves. Recent Hittitological research, inaugurated by H. G. Güterbock, H. Otten, Annelies Kammenhuber and O. R. Gurney and continued by O. Carruba, E. Neu, Otten and myself, is giving shape to an 'historical grammar' of Hittite which tries to distinguish between the various diachronic strata of the language. One of the primary results, first advocated by Carruba (1969) and then also by Otten (1969), involves a major re-ordering of Hittite historical texts. An important group of them have been re-dated from the last decades of the Hittite Empire to an earlier period between 1450 and 1380 B.C. (on the basis of the so-called 'middle chronology'; see Gurney 1966: 16, 28, 30: Houwink ten Cate 1970: 1–2), while from a linguistic point of view they have now been aptly characterized as 'Middle Hittite'. It should be added, however, that this proposed re-arrangement is still under discussion[2].

One of the texts concerned, the so-called 'Indictment of Madduwattas', is of great importance for the *Ahhiyawa* problem. But there is more: thanks to Laroche's work on Hittite onomastics (Laroche 1965c: 1966a), it is possible to be more explicit in matters of Hittite prosopography. Finally, it has recently become possible to speak with somewhat greater confidence about the political geography of western Anatolia during the middle part of the second millennium. Güterbock now suggests the following reconstruction: "Apasa, die Hafen-und Residenzstadt des Teilkönigtums Arzawa (im engen Sinne) [war] gleich Ephesos; Milawata, ebenfalls Hafen, zur Sphäre des Königs von Ahhijawa gehörig, gleich Milet mit seiner befestigten mykenischen Siedlung;" and then, with new proposals, although the first was already hinted at by Mellaart in 1955; "das Seha-Flussland, durch das man Milawata erreicht, [war] gleich der Mäander-Ebene. Der Pass an der Strasse von Torbalı nach Kemalpaşa würde dann die Grenze bilden zwischen Klein-Arzawa, also dem Kaystros-Tal mit Ephesos, im Süden und dem nördlich gelegenen Hapalla, das demnach die Hermos-Ebene umfassen würde. All das ist vorläufig hypothetisch, ergibt aber wenigstens ein in sich plausibles Bild"* (Guterbock 1967: 70).

---

* "Apasa, the port and capital of the principality of Arzawa (in the strict sense) may be equated with Ephesus; Milawata, likewise a port, belonging to the sphere of influence of the

These new developments: (1) the increasing possibility of dating texts on grammatical and lexicographical indications; (2) the growing importance of Hittite prosopography; (3) the new picture of the geography of the west coast, all affect the *Ahhiyawa* problem. To begin with the last, in view of the fact that *Ahhiya(wa)* necessarily belonged to the littoral, the only remaining possibilities for its localization are either in Caria or Lycia, often identified with *Lukka*, or in the extreme north-west, the Troad, since the *Seha*-River Land, *Arzawa*, *Hapalla*, and *Assuwa* have to be provided for (see Houwink ten Cate 1970: map). By elimination I am led to prefer the Troad (originally proposed by Goetze). Before I turn to the other two new developments some remarks should be made about the general historical situation on the west coast in the thirteenth century.

It seems that during the reign of Muwatallis the status of the *Seha*-River Land underwent an important change. This can be concluded from the fact that in Muwatallis' treaty with Alaksandus the *Seha*-River Land is omitted from the list of *Arzawa* lands, consisting at that time of lesser *Arzawa*, *Mira-Kuwaliya*, *Hapalla* and *Wilusa*. It is possible that the country received preferential treatment, since we know that one of its kings received Mursilis' daughter in marriage. The poorly preserved Annals of Hattusilis III seem to imply that a dangerous enemy overran great parts of the south-west of Anatolia in his reign. After the *Lukka* lands have twice been mentioned in *KUB XXI 6 Rev.* 3, 4, the text continues after a paragraph-divider with a long list of towns which seem to have been conquered by the enemy. Some of these towns have been located plausibly in Pisidia or in Cilicia. I am inclined to think that during the reign of Hattusilis III the term *Lukka*-lands had a wider connotation than before. Moreover, in the early years of Hattusilis' reign the king of *Mira* did not hesitate to intervene in Egypt in favour of Urhi-Tesub, the deposed predecessor on the Hittite throne. This also implies that the Hittite hold on the west coast considerably weakened during the reign of Hattusilis III. I mention these data, because this is the background against which some of the most important *Ahhiyawa*-texts should be viewed; a continued vigilance during the early reign of Muwatallis and afterwards an apparent loss of Hittite preponderance.

The date of some of the Hittite tablets which are relevant to the *Ahhiyawa* problem should now be discussed.

(a) As already mentioned, the 'Indictment of Madduwattas' has now

---

King of Ahhijawa, may be equated with Miletus, with its fortified Mycenaean settlement ... the Seha-River country, through which one reached Milawata, with the plain of the Maeander. The pass on the road from Torbalı to Kemalpaşa would then form the frontier between Lesser Arzawa, i.e. the valley of the Cayster with Ephesus, in the south and Hapalla, lying to the north, which would accordingly include the plain of the Hermus. Provisionally, all this is hypothetical, but it gives us at least a plausible reconstruction."

been re-assigned to the reign of Arnuwandas I. This re-dates the historical material given in Chapter XIX of Sommer's *Aḫḫijavā-Urkunden* to before 1400 B.C.

(*b*) A date in the early Empire also holds good for the oracle text referred to by Sommer (1934: 74) and Schachermeyr (1935: 42), now published in full as *KBo* XVI 97. Both the 'Indictment of Madduwattas' and this text (*Rev* 5, 16, 20) show the form *Ahhiya*, and grammatical features and prosopographical references date the latter to the early Empire period (Otten 1969: 35 fn. 2). Moreover, this oracle text belongs to a small group which is characterized by consistent syllabic writing of technical terms which are elsewhere abbreviated. These texts appear to belong to the very oldest of their genre.

In the 'Indictment of Madduwattas', the place name is spelled *A-aḫ-ḫi-ya-a*; it is used primarily as the name of a town, although the text does state that *Attarissiyas*, 'Man of Ahhiya' (*Obv.* 1, 60) 'went away to his own country' (*Obv.* 65). It is rather striking that *Attarissiyas* is active rather far inland but also able to take part, together with the man of *Piggaya* and the conspirator Madduwattas himself, in a naval raid on *Alasiya*, presumably the isle of Cyprus. This event (cf. *Rev.* 84 ff.; re-edited by Sommer 1932: 337–8) has already been compared by both MacQueen (1968: 178 fr. 74) and Otten (1969: 34) to the attacks by the 'Lycians' mentioned in an Amarna letter to Egypt (Knudtzon 1915: 292–3, Nr. 38, 10–2).

(*c*) As was clear from the beginning, a group of the texts stems from the reign of Mursilis II. They are: (1) the oracle text which mentions together the god of *Ahhiyawa* and the god of *Lazpa* (Lesbos) whose statues have been brought to Hattusas in order to succour the sick king (Sommer 1932: 275–94). (2) The text which at one time was thought to imply that a Hittite queen had been banished to *Ahhiyawa*; the whole banishment is dubious, and, if the text really refers to such an event, it could also be moved to the reign of Muwatallis on the assumption that the queen concerned would be Tanuhepas (cf. *KUB* XXXI 66; Sommer 1932: 300–3; Güterbock 1940: 14–15 and especially 60). (3) The text of the end of the second or the beginning of the third year of the reign of Mursilis II in which *Arzawa*, *Millawanda* and *Ahhiyawa* are mentioned in a broken context, from which Sommer (differently from Goetze) concluded that at this time Millawanda 'belonged' to the king of Ahhiyawa (Sommer 1932: 307–9). (4) Part of the 'Ten Year Annals' of Mursilis II, referring to events of his fourth year; a son of *Uhhazitis*, the king of *Arzawa*, *Ahhiyawa* and the sending of someone by ship, are mentioned in a broken context (Sommer 1932: 310–13).

(*d*) A third group of texts belongs to the time of Hattusilis III. This is certain for the text published by Güterbock (1936: 326). On account of the formula with the name Istar of Samuha it is to be compared with e.g. *KBo* XVI 36 (Riemschneider 1962: 111–14). Güterbock's text mentions Piyamaradus in a broken context. A similar date is very likely for the text *KBo* XVI 22 (Güterbock 1936: 323–4). It refers to events connected with the accession of Hattusilis III. A number of other texts probably belong to this group: a letter to a foreign king from which it appears that diplomatic relations with *Ahhiyawa* were good at the time and that products of the country were generally appreciated in the Near East; the letter refers to a journey to Egypt; it is still doubtful whether Hattusilis III actually went or not (Sommer 1932: 242–8); *KUB* XXVI 76, a text first used by Schachermeyr (1935: 41); this fragment mentions *Ahhi[yawa]*, *Kargamis*, Egypt and *Piyamaradus*. The recent historical fragment *KBo* XVI 35 mentions Piyamaradus (lines 3, 7) and '[H[attusilis, m[y] grandfather (possibly 'forefather'; line 11); other recently published fragments appear to refer to the same events: *KBo* XIX 78 (mentioning *Kupanta-*^{D}*KAL*, king of *Mira*, and *Piyamaradus*); *KBo* XIX 79 (referring to *Piyamaradus* and *Atpas*); and *KBo* XIX 80 (mentioning *Zumarra*, a place referred to as *Zumarri* in the 'Indictment of Madduwattas', *Piyamaradus* and the sons of *Kupanta-*^{D}*KAL*).

(e) At this point I should recall Güterbock's suggestion that the 'Tawagalawas Letter', the most important document in the whole dossier (Sommer 1932: 2–194), should perhaps also be dated to the reign of Hattusilis III (Güterbock 1936: 327). Sommer had left the question open (1932: 36 and fn. 1). Güterbock seems to prefer Hattusilis III as the king involved but reckons with the possibility of Muwatallis. Muwatallis was proposed by Cavaignac (1933) on good historical grounds. His reasoning was based on the fact that the treaty with *Alaksandus* does not refer to the battles around *Wilusa*, perhaps alluded to in the 'Tawagalawas Letter' (IV: 7–10) and certainly referred to in *KUB* XIX 5 (a letter of *Manapa-*^{D}*U*, king of the *Seha*-River Land and a contemporary of Mursilis II and Muwatallis). In this latter text *Piyamaradus* and *Atpas* play a major role. Cavaignac rightly concluded that the 'Tawagalawas Letter' as well as the later 'Milawata Letter' (Sommer 1932: 2–194, 198–240) should be dated *after* the treaty, but this reasoning does not preclude a still later date, e.g. under the reign of Hattusilis III, as proposed by Güterbock. In view of the fact that the activities of *Piyamaradus* presumably continued into the reign of Hattusilis III, there can be no doubt that the ^{D}*KAL-as* referred to in the 'Tawagalawas Letter' must have been the second person of that name known from Hittite prosopography and not the general from Mursilis' time (cf. Laroche 1966a: 223 No. 1747). In all probability this second ^{D}*KAL-as* was a son of Muwatallis (cf. Forrer's text-restoration for the 'Apology of Hattusilis III' (IV: 62) as accepted by both Goetze and E. H. Sturtevant and as supported by Hieroglyphic evidence; Güterbock 1942:

10–12). I am convinced that this ^DKAL-*as* is identical with *Kuruntas* (Laroche 1966a: 101 No. 652; Houwink ten Cate: 1961: 130). *Kuruntas* is perfectly possible as a phonic orthography for ^DKAL-*as* and we know that both orthographies were used for the name of the king of *Tarhuntassa* during the reign of Hattusilis III. The name of *Sahurunuwas*, another official mentioned in the 'Tawagalawas Letter', is well attested for this general period (cf. Laroche 1966a: 153 No. 1076). A few linguistic indications, all of them duly noted by Sommer in his matchless comment-ary, support an attribution to either Muwatallis or Hattusilis III. In this historical survey it is certainly of importance to note that the geographical designation 'Lukka lands' is only known from two texts; the fragmentary 'Annals of Hattusilis III' and the 'Tawagalawas Letter' (the term is implied in I: 1–5; see Sommer 1932: 36 fn. 1). Personally I feel convinced by R. Ranoszek that the writer of the 'Tawagalawas Letter' twice addresses the king of *Ahhiyawa* in an overpolite manner as a 'great king' and as his 'equal' (Ranoszek 1938: 38–9: 1950: 242; on *II*, 11ff, *IV* 53 ff.). The Hittite king tries to flatter him by the indirect use of these titles which carried great weight and prestige in the world of the ancient Near East (Sommer 1932: 7–12). At the time when the 'Tawagalawas Letter' was written *Millawanda/Milawata* clearly was reckoned to belong to the sphere of influence of the king of *Ahhiyawa*. By the time of the later 'Milawata Letter' the situation had changed: *Milawata* was governed, it seems, by a vassal prince of the Hittite king.

(*f*) *KUB* XXVI 92 was interpreted differently by Forrer (1928: 57) and by Sommer (1932: 268–74). MacQueen has already remarked that Forrer's interpretation deserves renewed consideration because it might harmonize with our new picture of the early Empire period (MacQueen 1968: 178 fn. 78). According to Forrer, this text—in his opinion a letter written by Mursilis II—recalls that the great-grandfather of the addressee was an ally of the Hittite king at a time when the king of *Assuwa* was fighting a war against the Hittites. The words which Forrer interpreted as designating this great-grandfather as an ally do perhaps in fact mean that he obstructed the Hittite king (Sommer: 'band vor', 'sperrte ab', 'hin-derte'). But the fact remains that Forrer may be right in assuming here a reminiscence of much earlier events, from the time of a king Tudhaliyas I (or II)[3] in the beginning of the Empire period. It is possible that the conflict with *Assuwa* known from two of the re-dated texts (*Cat.* 85 and 86), is alluded to here. The real uncertainty lies in the fact that we do not know whether Mursilis II was in fact the writer of these lines. In line 1 the 'lord of the country *Ahhiyawa*' is mentioned.

(*g*) *KUB* XXIII 13 (Sommer 1932: 314–19) offers many problems. This is the historical fragment in which it is said that "the king of *Seha*-River Land sinned again in two respects" (both against the Hittite king and against the king of *Ahhiyawa*?) and according to which "the great king marched on after the king of the land Ahhiyawa drew back" (but perhaps 'retreated', 'withdrew support'; the translation is a well-known enigma). The chronological clue is hidden in a remark attributed to the local inhabitants who are quoted as saying that at the time when the grand-father of His Majesty conquered the *Arzawa* lands, he did not conquer them. Both Forrer and Goetze concluded that the text alludes here to Mursilis II and that the reigning king should be identified with Tudhaliyas III (IV). Theoretically it would now be possible to equate the 'grandfather' with Tudhaliyas I (II) and to ascribe the text itself to Tudhaliyas II (III), but I hesitate to do so.

It is now time to formulate some cautious conclusions. Before I give a final personal evaluation I wish to stress that even now, almost fifty years after the first equations were proposed, any statement on the *Ahhiyawa* problem is of dubious value, being more of an 'act of faith' than a scientific proposition. But since so many Hittitologists at one time or another have expressed their personal preference for one of the various possibilities, there is no reason to abstain from judgment. I would now opt for Goetze's solution of 1933 as reviewed by MacQueen in 1968. At this point it should be mentioned that already in 1924 (independently, it seems, from Forrer) Goetze commented on the similarity between *Ahhiyawa* and Greek *Akhaiwoi* (Goetze 1924: 26 fn. 5). It is not impossible that *Ahhiya(wa)* originally denoted a Greek state in the north-west of Anatolia itself. But the term apparently widened in meaning and came to include 'Mycenaean' Greeks, especially in the thirteenth century. This is exactly what happened to the name of Ionia and the Ionians in the first millennium B.C., and much later again to the name of the Franks in Arabic sources. It is an idle hope that we will ever be able to deduce exactly what lies behind the use of the term in every passage where we meet it, because we can be fairly sure that the Hittites themselves were not completely familiar with the background of the contemporary people or peoples to whom they referred.

In view of the archaeological evidence it is tempting to suggest that the 'Ahhiyawans' of *Millawanda* (Miletus) in Mursilis' reign were Mycenaean Greeks. The same holds good for those 'Ahhiyawans' who are mentioned in the treaty concluded by Tudhaliyas III (IV) with Sausgamuwa in the famous passage where the king of the land *Ahhiyawa* is named next to recognized important kings of that period (afterwards *Ahhiyawa* was erased again, presumably by the scribe himself). Still more striking is the other passage in the same treaty where Sommer (ironically enough Sommer and not Forrer) restored "N[o] ship may go to him (i.e. to the king of Assur) [from (literally 'of') the land of Ahh] iyawa" (*KUB* XXIII 1; Sommer 1932: 320–7).

However, I doubt whether even one of the personal names which have been claimed as Greek can stand the test of more detailed criticism. In this respect the critical attitude of Friedrich and Sommer was fully justified (Harmatta's arguments against their views are not convincing; 1968b: 401–9). There may be one exception, but in that case the bearer of the name is not classified as a man of *Ahhiyawa*! I am alluding to *Alaksandus* of *Wilusa*. Here one may quote Laroche in support: 'Ce nom n'est probablement qu'une transcription maladroite du grec *Alexandros* et n'a rien à voir avec les langues asianiques' (Laroche 1966a: 26 no. 21). I am well aware of Sommer's objections to this identification, but here he was hypercritical. It now appears that *Alexandros* may occur as a Greek name in Mycenaean texts. It was first compared with *Alaksandus* by D. D. Luckenbill (1911) and the idea was taken up by Kretschmer in his article 'Alaksantus, König von Vilusa' (1924). In the same year Goetze also noted the similarity between *Wilusa* and Greek *Ilios* (Goetze 1924: 26 fn. 6). However the Anatolian place-name *Tarwisa* also needs to be accounted for in view of its similarity to Greek *Troia* (Forrer 1924: 6–7). *Tarwisa* occurs in only one passage, where it is found together with *Wilusa* in its lengthened form *Wilusiya* (Ranoszek 1934: 55). But it seems fairly certain that all these vague resemblances should not be attributed to mere chance. One personal name, two place-names and one ethnikon are perhaps not much to go by. The whole structure of historical identifications depends on four equations: *Ahhiyawa*: 'Achaeans'; *Alaksandus*: *Alexandros*; *Wilusa/Wilusiya*: *Ilios*; *Tarwisa*: *Troia*. Each of them in isolation presents a linguistic problem. It is also doubtful whether any contacts that occurred between Hittites and Greeks led to any important cultural changes. Nevertheless I see no reason to doubt that the contacts did take place[4].

II. *An Anatolian particle* -an

In a number of passages in the Hittite text *Cat.* 324 (Otten and Souček 1969) a particle *-an* may be identified which had not been recognized before the text was published. It may be equated with Greek *án* and this equation may be relevant to problems of Greek dialectology of the Mycenaean period.

Some years ago H. Pedersen analysed the Hittite particle *man* (*ma-an*) which forms optative and potential sentences into *ma+an* (Goetze and Pedersen 1934: 59). The latter of these two components Pedersen compared with Greek *án*, while pointing out that Lycian *me*, accentuated and autonomous, might provide parallel for such a use of *ma* (in Hittite normally enclitic). One might add that Lycian seems to preserve a particle *-e* (< -an) which may be adduced in support of Pedersen's etymology (Houwink ten Cate 1961: 76–7).

The total number of occurrences (nine examples in *Cat.* 324 and perhaps about seven in other texts) is insufficient for a strict delimitation of the function and meaning of this new particle. However, the following remarks on its use can be made. (1) It occurs both in main and in subordinate sentences. (2) In the usual concatenation of particles and enclitic pronouns at the beginning of a Hittite sentence it follows the enclitic pronouns -a- (-as, -an etc.) and -si, while preceding -za and kan (cf. in this last respect the 'Proclamation of Telipinus' II: 45 ḫa-aš-ša-an-na-ša-an-za-kán le-e ku-in-ki ku-en-ti, 'Do not kill any member of the (royal) family': hassanas-an-z-kan le kuinki kuenti; Sturtevant and Bechtel 1935: 190; Friedrich 1967: 60). This would seem to preclude the idea that -an was the equivalent of -kan in all its functions, since both can occur together. But I am inclined to agree with Otten and Souček that the connection in Cat. 324, between the verb peda- (with the preverbs anda and appan(-)anda) and either the particle -an (four examples; II: 45 is invalid) or the particle -kan (I: 26) does prove that -an may function in a similar way (Otten and Souček 1969: 81–2). Otten and Souček also point to KBo VI 2 (Cat. 181 A) para. 78 IV 10 where nu-uš-še-an should be compared to nu-uš-ši-kán in the younger manuscript B (Otten and Souček 1969: 82). It appears from their examples that -an does occur in alternation with -kan, both presumably functioning in an aspectual system, and that -an sometimes is replaced by -kan in a later recension. This last conclusion also follows from XVII 10 IV 17 (Cat. 258 IA; Friedrich 1967: 54; the 'Telipinus Myth'): an-da-da-an ḫar-ak-zi where an-da-da-an (anda-at-an) corresponds to [an]-da-at-ša-an (IBoT III 141 IV 13), an-da-at-kán (XXXIII 54: 7) and an-da-pát-kán (XXXIII 8 III 10) in younger versions (Laroche 1965b: 97, 104, 139).

However, its uses in a conditional sentence introduced by takku (again KBo VI 2 = Cat. 181 A, par. 44 II: 35, ták-ku-wa-ta-an (takku-at-an) pár-na-ma ku-e-el-ka pé-eš-ši-iz-zi) and in an iterative sentence governed by the relative adverb kuwatta (again in the 'Proclamation of Telipinus' II: 3–4 according to manuscript B, XI 1 II 9–10, la-aḫ-ḫa-an (lahha-an) ku-wa-at-ta EREM.MEŠ-uš pa-iz-zi; Sturtevant and Bechtel 1935: 186) vaguely recall Greek án and suggest an additional non-aspectual usage, perhaps generally emphatic. The later replacement an-da-pát-kán, quoted above, should also be noted.

Two important points strongly support Pedersen's analysis of man as ma+an: (1) the fact that the particle man excludes the sentence connective nu; this is perfectly understandable if man contains (-)ma; (2) the hitherto unrecognized fact that the place of man in the concatenation of particles and other enclitics is identical with that of -ma alone (if used enclitically -man likewise precedes -wa(r)-). In combination with (-)ma, -an apparently acquired a modal function.

I realize that this resuscitation of Pedersen's etymology can only be reconciled with the usual position of -an after the enclitic pronouns on the assumption that (-)ma and -an became an indivisible unit in an early period, long before our earliest texts (cf. eán in Greek). This might have happened before the pronoun -*a*- became restricted to enclitic position. Remnants of such a non-enclitic use are still present in forms like *a-ši* and *u-ni* as explained by Pedersen (1938: 59–61). The latter should be compared to -*un*, now attested as accusative of the enclitic pronoun (Kammenhuber 1962: 377). It is likely, in my opinion, that the enclitic pronoun originally had an accusative in -*un* and that -*an* was a later development. Such a change is a certainty for the demonstrative pronoun, where *a-pa-a-an* and *ka-a-an* are later alternatives for *a-pu-u-un* and *ku-u-un* (see Benveniste 1962: 66–71 on the accusative singular forms of the Hittite pronouns).

The enclitic use of -*an* would appear to have made the accusative of the enclitic pronoun unacceptably homonymic with the particle -*an* and to have led to the eventual disappearance of the latter from Hittite in its isolated form, but not in its combination with (-)*ma*, in *ma+an*. It is attractive to trace *anku* back to the same particle -*an* (cf. *takku*, *apiyakku* and *immakku*. Güterbock once translated *anku* with 'en particulier' (1943: 103 fn. 3).

This newly discovered Old Hittite particle, which in some cases was replaced by -*kan* in later revisions, offers an interesting parallel for Greek and in my opinion disproves the explanation first put forward by K. Forbes, that Attic-Ionian and Arcadian *án* was an innovation, replacing *kan*, which came about through false division of *ou kan* as *ouk an* (Forbes 1958)[5].

Notes

1. Cuneiform orthographies of names in Hittite texts which are transcribed with final -*a* may represent only the stems of the names. The spoken forms seem normally to have been inflected, and in some cases to have contained a formant following the stem which was not represented in writing.

2. Recent discussions at the XVIII and XIX Rencontres Assyriologiques Internationales (Munich, July 1970, and Paris, 1971) will be published in their *Comptes Rendus*. For further recent literature see the *Keilschriftbibliographien* (*Kleinasiatische Sprachen* usw.) in *Orientalia* 38 (1969), 39 (1970) and subsequent volumes.

3. The numbers in brackets are those which were given to Hittite kings named Tuthaliyas until recently in the belief that a first king of that name ruled at the beginning of the Hittite Old Kingdom or *c.* 1450 B.C.; cf. Gurney 1952: 216–17; 1966: 30; Houwink ten Cate 1970: 1.

4. I have not attempted to include references to all discussions of the Ahhiyawa problem by Classical scholars. The best summaries of previous work, with more extensive bibliographies, will be found in the studies by K. Völkl (1952), F. Schachermeyer (1958), D. L. Page (1959) and G. Steiner (1964). Additional texts relevant to the problem found after the main earlier studies are enumerated by Schachermeyr (1958: 365, fn. 1, 2). I have not been able to consult V. G. Boruchovič, 'Die Achäer in Kleinasien' (*Vestnik Drevnei Istorii* 89, 1964:

91–106) and M. Kishimoto, 'Mycenae, Arzawa, Hatti' (*Journal of Classical Studies*, Classical Society of Japan, 11: 1963: 62–74).

5. For discussions of the question published after the completion of this article, in 1970, see: O. Carruba, 'Di nuove e vecchie particelle anatoliche', *Studi micenei ed egeo-anatolici*, 12 (*IncGraec.* 45): 68–87; E. Neu, *Ein althethitisches Gewitterritual* (*SBoT*. 12): 62; V. Souček, *AO*, 38: 275–6.

References

AITCHISON, J. M. 1964. 'The Achaean homeland: *Akhaiwia* or *Akhaiwis*?' *Glotta*, 42: 19–28.

ALBRIGHT, W. F. 1950. 'Some Oriental glosses on the Homeric problem.' *AJA*, 54: 162–76.

ANDREWS, P. B. S. 1955. 'The Mycenaean name of the land of the Achaians.' *RHA*, 13: 1–19.

BENVENISTE, E. 1962. *Hittite et Indo-Européen*. Paris.

BITTEL, K. 1950. *Grundzüge der Vor- und Frühgeschichte Kleinasiens* (2nd ed.). Tübingen.

——. 1950. 'Karabel.' *MDOG*, 98: 5–23.

CAMMERER, R. 1967. 'Über den 'emphatischen Grundwert' der Partikel *án*.' *Glotta*, 46: 106–17.

CARRATELLI, G. P. 1950. 'Ahhijavā, Lazpa et leurs divinités dans *KUB* V 6.' *JKF*, 1: 156–63.

CARRUBA, O. 1964a. 'Wo lag Ahhijawa?' *Compte rendu de l'onzième rencontre assyriologique internationale* (1962). Leiden: 38–46.

——. 1964b. 'Ahhijawa e altri nomi di popoli e di paesi dell' Anatolia occidentale.' *Athenaeum*, 42: 269–98.

——. 1969. 'Die Chronologie der hethitischen Texte und die hethitische Geschichte der Grossreichszeit.' *ZDMG. Suppl.* I: 226–49.

CAVAIGNAC, E. 1933. 'La lettre Tavagalava.' *RHA*, 3: 100–4.

——. 1946. 'La question hittite-achéenne d'après les dernières publications.' *BCH*, 70: 58–66.

——. 1950. *Les Hittites*. Paris.

CHADWICK, J. and BAUMBACH, L. 1963. 'The Mycenaean vocabulary.' *Glotta*, 41: 157–271.

ČOP, B. 1955. 'Notes d'étymologie et de grammaire hittites II.' *Slavisticna Revija* (*Linguistica*), 8: 59–66.

CORNELIUS, F. 1955. 'Eine Episode der hethitischen Geschichte, geographisch beleuchtet.' *MSS*, 6: 30–4.

——. 1962. 'Zur Ahhijawa-Problem.' *Historia*, 11: 112–13.

CROSSLAND, R. A. 1953. Review of O. R. Gurney, *The Hittites*. *BiOr*, 10: 120–2.

——. 1954. 'Archaic forms in the "Mattuwattas Text".' *Compte rendu de la troisième rencontre assyriologique internationale* (1952). Leiden: 158–61.

——. 1967. 'Immigrants from the North.' *CAH* (rev. ed.) I. Chap. XXVII/Fasc. 60.

DUSSAUD, R. 1953. *Prélydiens, Hittites et Achéens*. Paris.

FORBES, K. 1958. 'The relations of the particle *án* with *ke(n) ka, kan*.' *Glotta*, 37: 179–82.

FORRER, E. 1924a. 'Vorhomerische Griechen in den Keilschrifttexten von Boghazköi.' *MDOG*, 63: 1–22.

——. 1924b. 'Die Griechen in den Boghazköi-Texten.' *OLZ*, 27: 113–18.

——. 1926. *Forschungen*, 1, 2, Berlin.

——. 1928. 'Ahhiyava', in E. Ebeling and B. Meissner, *Reallexikon der Assyriologie* (Berlin): 53–7.

——. 1929. 'Fur die Griechen in den Boghazköi-Inschriften'; in F. Sommer and H. Ehelolf, *Kleinasiatische Forschungen*, I. Weimar.

——. 1930. 'La découverte de la Grèce mycénienne dans les textes cunéiformes de l'empire hittite'. *REG*, 43: 279–94.

FRENCH, D. H. 1969. 'Prehistoric sites in Northwest Anatolia, II. The Balıkesir and Akhisar/Manisa areas.' *AnatSt*, 19: 41–98.

FRIEDRICH, J. 1967. *Hethitisches Elementarbuch*, II (2nd ed.). Heidelberg.

GOETZE, A. 1924. *Kleinasien zur Hethiterzeit*. Heidelberg.

——. 1947. 'Contributions to Hittite lexicography.' *JCS*, 1: 307–20.

——. 1957. *Kleinasien* (2nd ed.). Munich.

—— and PEDERSEN, H. 1934. 'Muršilis Sprachlähmung.' (*Danske Vid. Selsk. Hist.-fil. Medd.* 21), Copenhagen.

GURNEY, O. R. 1952. *The Hittites*. Harmondsworth.

——. 1959. *The Geography of the Hittite Empire*. London.

——. 1966. 'Anatolia c. 1600–1380 B.C.' *CAH* (rev. ed.) II, Chap. xv (a)/Fasc. 44.

GÜTERBOCK, H. G. 1936. 'Neue Ahhijavā-Texte.' *ZA*. NF 9: 321–7.

——. 1940. *Siegel aus Bogazköy I*. (*AfO, Beiheft* 5) Berlin.

——. 1942. *Siegel aus Bogazköy II*. (*AfO, Beiheft* 7) Berlin.

——. 1943. 'Le mot hittite *hartaggaš* 'serpent''.' *RHA*, 6: 102–9.

——. 1967. 'Das dritte Monument am Karabez.' *IstMitt*, 17: 63–71.

HALLEUX, R. 1969. 'Lapis-lazuli, azurite ou pâte de verre?' *Studi Micenei ed Egeo-Anatolici* 9 (*IncGraec*. 39; Rome): 47–66.

HARMATTA, J. 1968a. 'Zur Ahhiyawa-Frage'; in *Studia Mycenaea* (ed. A. Bartonek; Brno): 117–24.

——. 1968b. 'Ahhiyawa names—Mycenaean names.' *AttiICIM*(1): 401–9.

HEUBECK, A. 1955. Review of R. Dussaud, *Prélydiens, Hittites et Achéens* (Paris, 1953). *OLZ*, 50: 131–4.

HOUWINK TEN CATE, PH. H. J. 1961. *The Luwian Population Groups of Lycia and Cilicia Aspera during the Hellenistic Period*. Leiden.

——. 1970. *The Records of the Early Hittite Empire*. Leiden.

HROZNÝ, F. 1929. 'Hethiter und Griechen.' *AO*, 1: 323–43.

HUXLEY, G. L. 1960. *Achaeans and Hittites*. Oxford.

KAMMENHUBER, A. 1962. Review of J. Friedrich, *Hethitisches Wörterbuch*. *Or*, N.S., 31: 367–80.

KNUDTZON, J. A. 1915. *Die El-Amarna-Tafeln*, I. Leipzig (reprinted Aalen, 1964).

KRETSCHMER, P. 1924. 'Alaksandus, Konig von Vilusa.' *Glotta*, 13: 205–13.

——. 1933. 'Die Hypachäer. Alaksandus und andere umstrittene Namen der hethitischen Texte.' *Glotta*, 21: 213–57.

——. 1954. 'Achäer in Kleinasien zur Hethiterzeit.' *Glotta*, 33: 1–25.

LAROCHE, E. 1965a. 'Sur le nom grec de l'ivoire.' *RPh*, 56–9.

——. 1965b. 'Études de linguistique anatolienne I.' *RHA*, 23: 33–54.

——. 1965c. 'Textes hittites en transcription: mythologie anatolienne.' *RHA*, 23: 63–178.

——. 1966a. *Les noms des Hittites*. Paris.

——. 1966b. Études de linguistique anatolienne II.' *RHA*, 24: 160–84.

—— Schaeffer, C. F. A., Nougayrol, J. and Virolleaud, C. 1968. *Ugaritica* V. Paris.

Laurenzi, V. 1940. 'Rodi e l'Asia degli Ittiti.' *Nuova Antologia*, 75/Fasc. 1630: 372–80.

Lee, D. J. N. 1967. 'The modal particles *án, ke(n), ka.*' *AJPh*, 88: 45–6.

Lloyd, S. and Mellaart, J. 1955. 'Beycesultan excavations: first preliminary report.' *AnatSt*, 5: 39–92.

Luckenbill, D. D. 1911. 'A possible occurrence of the name Alexander in the Boghaz-Keui tablets.' *CPh*, 6: 85–6.

MacQueen, J. G. 1968. 'Geography and history in western Asia Minor in the second millennium B.C.', *AnatSt*, 18: 169–85.

Masson, E. 1967. *Recherches sur les plus anciens emprunts sémitiques en grec.* Paris.

Mellaart, J. 1958. 'The end of the Early Bronze Age in Anatolia and the Aegean.' *AJA*, 62: 9–33.

——. 1968. 'Anatolian trade with Europe and Anatolian geography and culture provinces in the Late Bronze Age.' *AnatSt*, 18: 187–202.

Morpurgo, A. 1963. *Mycenaeae Graecitatis Lexicon* (*Inc Graec.* 3). Rome.

Otten, H. 1968. 'Die hethitischen historischen Quellen und die altorientalische Chronologie.' *Abhandlungen der Akad. der Wissenschaften, Geistes-/Soz. Klasse*, 1968/3. Mainz.

——. 1969. *Sprachliche Stellung und Datierung des Madduwatta-Textes* (*SBoT* 11). Wiesbaden.

—— and Souček, V. 1969. *Ein althethitisches Ritual für das Konigspaar* (*SBoT* 8). Wiesbaden.

Page, D. L. 1959. *History and the Homeric Iliad.* Berkeley-Los Angeles.

Pedersen, H. 1938. *Hittitisch und die anderen Indoeuropaischen Sprachen* (*Danske Vid. selsk. Hist.-fil Medd.* 25/2). Copenhagen.

Ranoszek, R. 1934. 'Kronika króla hetyckiego Tudhaljasa IV.' *RO*, 9: 43–112.

——. 1938. Reviews of F. Sommer, *Die Ahhijava-Urkunden* and *Ahhijava-Frage und Sprachwissenschaft*. *IF*, 56: 38–41.

——. 1950. 'A propos de KUB XXIII 1.' *AO*, 18: 236–42.

Riemschneider, K. 1962. 'Hethitische Fragmente historischen Inhalts aus der Zeit Hattusilis III.' *JCS*, 16: 110–21.

Schachermeyr, F. 1935. *Hethiter und Achäer* (*Mitt. der Altorientalischen Gesellschaft.*) 9/1–2. Leipzig.

——. 1958. 'Zur Frage der Lokalisierung von Achiawa.'; in E. Grumach, *Minoica*: 365–80.

Schaeffer, C. F. A. 1952. *Enkomi-Alasia*, I. Paris.

Schmidt, W. 1956. 'Die Aḫḫiyawa-Unkunden.' *Das Altertum*, 2: 195–200.

Sommer, F. 1932. *Die Aḫḫijavā-Urkunden* (*AbhBAW Phil.-hist. Abt. NF.* 6). Munich.

——. 1934. *Aḫḫijava-Frage und Sprachwissenschaft* (*AbhBAW Phil.-hist. Abt. NF.* 9). Munich.

——. 1937. 'Ahhijava und kein Ende?' *IF*, 55: 169–297.

Steiner, G. 1964. 'Die Ahhijawa-Frage heute.' *Saeculum*, 15: 365–92.

Sturtevant, E. H. and Bechtel, G. 1935. *A. Hittite Chrestomathy.* Philadelphia, Pa.

Völkl, K. 1952. 'Achchijawa.' *La Nouvelle Clio*, 4: 329–59.

Discussion

R. A. Crossland. (1) Certain of Professor Houwink ten Cate's provisional conclusions at the end of the first section of his paper will be of special interest to those primarily concerned with Aegean prehistory and 'Greek origins', even beyond their value as part of his reappraisal of the 'Ahhiyawa problem' in the context of Hittite history. They invite us to consider afresh the idea put forward by J. Mellaart in 1958 (Mellaart 1958: 15–21, 28; withdrawn more recently: *JHS*. 89: 172–3) that the inhabitants of north-western Anatolia in the period of the Hittite Empire (at least until the first quarter of the thirteenth century) were Greeks or 'para-Greeks': people who spoke a dialect of late prehistoric Greek or a language which diverged from 'pre-Greek' as late as *c.* 2000 B.C. It would be inappropriate to state here in detail the arguments for identifying 'Ahhiyawans' as Mycenaean Greeks, if they are to be identified as Greeks at all. But they may be summarized as follows. (*a*) The relevant Hittite texts indicate that *Ahhiyawa* was a 'contin-ental Anatolian power' only in a limited sense: men alleged by Hittite kings to be under the sovereignty of the 'King of Ahhiyawa', in some cases clearly operating from *Millawa(n)ta*, whose name may be equated satisfactorily with *Milētos*, were capable of causing the Hittites trouble by raiding and securing allies in parts of western Anatolia over which the Hittites, until *c.* 1300 B.C., appear to have wished to maintain indirect political control only; (*b*) 'Ahhiyawans' were evidently competent soldiers and sea-farers by contemporary Aegeo-Anatolian standards; (*c*) They were able to trade with rulers or other individuals in Syrian countries and apparently across these with Assyria; (*d*) The Hittites regarded the 'King of Ahhiyawa' as the ruler of a state which was 'civilized' according to their concepts: they expected him to be able to understand their own diplomatic practice and, presumably, to cope with correspondence in cuneiform (they seem to have had clear ideas about the difference between an organized state and a people living under tribal social conditions). Within western Anatolia and regions just beyond it from the Hittites' standpoint, a Mycenaean community or group of communities would seem to satisfy those criteria best. A native Anatolian state might have had characteristics (*b*) and (*d*). But one should not argue from (*a*) that *Ahhiyawa* was a state of some size on the Anatolian mainland. Men as competent at war and sea-faring as the Mycenaeans appear to have been could have caused the Hittites the kind of trouble which their texts describe if operating from Rhodes and one or more advanced settlements on the Anatolian coast, like Miletus, without having occupied a large adjacent territory on the mainland. And men settled in Rhodes or south-eastern Greece would have been better situated for trading with Syria than a people of north-western Anatolia. Finally, the most important contacts between Hittites and 'Ahhiyawans', from the political point of view, seem to have been across '*Lukka*-lands', and the balance of evidence locates these in south-western Anatolia (references to raids on *Alasiya* by 'Lukkans' suggest that they lived in the south-west of Anatolia rather than the north-west; Knudtzon 1915: 292–3). If people speaking a form of Greek (or a closely similar collateral language) and calling themselves *Akhaiwoi* were living in north-western Anatolia when the Hittites first got to know that area, it is conceivable that other Hittites might subsequently have recognized that Mycenaean Greeks were linguistically akin to them and have extended the name *Ahhiya(wa)*- (< *Akhaiwo-*) to the Mycenaeans too. But *Akhaiwo-* and *Akhaiwiyo-* appear to have been used by Mycenaean Greeks of themselves and their own lands and cities; the latter stem occurs in Linear B texts; it seems reasonable to regard the Homeric use of *Akhaioi* as traditional, preserving Mycenaean usage; and settlements likely to have been founded by Mycenaean colonists have the name *Akhaia* (Carratelli 1950: 159; Morpurgo 1963: 9). Would the Mycenaeans of the Greek mainland have adopted one of their main names for themselves from a community in north-western Anatolia with which, on the evidence, they would have had very little contact, even if it spoke Greek? (2). 'Luwians' have appeared rather frequently in recent discussions of Aegean prehistory. This may be a convenient point, without special reference to Professor Houwink ten Cate's paper, to consider what is in fact known about them. The term 'Luwian' is based on names known from Hittite sources. So it might be best to reserve it, when used as a name for peoples, for the populations which on the evidence of Hittite texts spoke the language which is defined as 'Luwian' (*luwili*) by Hittite scribes; on direct philological evidence, it was spoken in part of *Hatti* proper (probably the south-western part, including the Konya plain), *Kizzuwatna* (later Cilicia), and *Arzawa*, a region lying to the west of *Hatti* but whose northern, western and southern limits are hard to deduce. There is no such direct evidence that Luwian (as just defined) was spoken in the areas known later as the Troad, Caria and Lycia, although it is probable that the 'Lukkans' of Hittite times spoke a dialect of Luwian or a language which was very closely related to it, since Lycian has such clear similarities to Luwian (Crossland 1968: Tritsch 1950; Laroche 1958; 1960; Neumann 1969). Lydian, however, which appears to belong to the same 'Anatolian' group of IE languages as Hittite and Luwian, and which may well already have been present as a distinct language in some part of western Anatolia in the second millennium, does not seem to stand specially close to Luwian within the group (Heubeck 1969). *Prima facie*, there is no good reason for referring to the peoples of north-western Anatolia, or its western sea-board as far south as later Caria, as 'Luwians', if the term is to be used accurately. It is not certain that place-names in -*ss*- were confined to Luwian, as defined here, and so indicate the presence of Luwian-speaking peoples or groups.

References

CROSSLAND, R. A. 1968. 'Who were the Luwians?' *Proc. of the Classical Association*, 75: 36–8.
HEUBECK, A. 1969. 'Lydisch', in J. Friedrich and others, *Altkleinasiatische Sprachen* (*Handbuch der Orientalistik* II, i/ii, 2; ed. B. Spuler; Leiden): 397–427.
LAROCHE, E. 1958. 'Comparaison du louvite et du lycien.' *BSL*, 53: 159–67.
——. 1960. 'Comparaison du louvite et du lycien (suite).' *BSL*, 55: 54–88.
NEUMANN, G. 1969. 'Lykisch'; in J. Friedrich and others, *Altkleinasiatische Sprachen*: 359–96.
TRITSCH, F. J. 1950. 'Lycian, Luwian and Hittite.' *AO*, 18: 494–502.

PH. H. J. HOUWINK TEN CATE: Regarding Professor Crossland's comment that it seems unlikely that Greek-speaking 'Mycenaeans' living in mainland Greece would have acquired one of their names for themselves from a people of north-western Anatolia, I would suggest that *Akhaiwoi (or an ethnikon immediately ancestral to it) was used as a name both by people of Greek descent living in that latter area, and by cognate Greek-speaking people who developed Mycenaean civilization (or acquired it in Greece). The Hittites would have come into contact first with *Akhaiwoi living in north-western Anatolia, and then have encountered members of the mainland *Akhaiwoi somewhat later as colonists or émigrés, the 'Ahhiyawans' with whom they were in contact in the central and southern parts of western Anatolia in the fourteenth and thirteenth centuries.

Connections in religion between the Mycenaean world and Anatolia

MONIQUE GÉRARD-ROUSSEAU

Liège

IN my book *Les mentions réligieuses dans les tablettes mycéniennes* (1968) I sketched in the main outlines of Mycenaean religion which we get from the study of Linear B texts. However, this work presents only the negative part of the research which I have undertaken. It has made it possible for me to dispose of a number of hypotheses which seemed to me ill founded. The research on which I am now engaged should enable me gradually to complete the picture of Mycenaean religion which has so far eluded our investigations.

It would have been agreeable to make this Colloquium an occasion for discussing some particular points in which comparison of Mycenaean and Anatolian data is enlightening. But instead of offering good examples of Anatolian influence on Mycenaean Greece, or at least of parallel development between the Anatolian and Mycenaean civilizations, I am actually going to increase the number of unsolved problems.

Before considering particular questions it is useful to remind oneself that the documentary sources available in Greece and Anatolia are essentially different and of unequal value. (I deliberately ignore at this point the archaeological material, whose interpretation is often most dubious.) The Linear B tablets are economic documents. For that reason, gods, priests or offerings are rarely mentioned, because the writers were not immediately interested in them. For them, it was much more important to note allocations and receipts. Consequently, one is continually tempted to find more in the texts than they say. Besides, these inventories are technically so complex that they require such specialization that anyone who studies them tends to work in one small sub-discipline and to develop a whole system of impressionistic ideas that he tries to prove afterwards. But though the texts do not amount to a large corpus, and they are so difficult to interpret, they are still the only documents which take us back to the twelfth or thirteenth century B.C. in the history of Greece.

The corpus of Anatolian documents, on the other hand, is large and includes many categories of material, even if we confine our attention to religious writings in cuneiform. For Hittite mythology, for instance, we have as evidence literary compositions, mainly epics, which give versions of foreign myths, mostly Hurrian; and rituals which allude constantly to Anatolian myths (Güterbock 1961; Laroche 1965: 3–4). For some time oriental origin has been claimed for many religious phenomena or divinities of Greece. Many are thought to have come from Anatolia through what was, in a certain period, Asianic Hellas. The new documentation which the Linear B texts provide now makes it possible to assign some such borrowings to a period much earlier than the sixth or seventh century B.C., which was as a rule the earliest time that students of the question could formerly trace them back to. This is the case, for example, with the 'Great Mother' whose Asianic origin has been accepted for a long time, though it has been recognized that she was a deity who evolved, and in whom various elements had amalgamated (Rapp 1886: col. 1638–72; Farnell 1907: 289–306). Greek literary evidence made it certain that the figure which would be the classical *mḗtēr theṓn* was taking shape in the sixth century B.C. and that it had come from Asia (Will 1960; Laroche 1960). This goddess, who was honoured under many names in antiquity, was for the Greeks essentially the 'Mother of the Gods'. Now, one Pylian tablet, No. 1202 in the **Fr** series, which lists quantities of oil, mentions in the dative case a recipient *ma-te-re te-i-ja (matrei theiai)*, 'divine mother' (**Fr** 1202: *pa-ko-we* CT 4 *me-tu-wo-ne-wo/ma-te-re te-i-ja* OLEUM + *PA* 5 CSL 1). The name certainly indicates a goddess and this interpretation is confirmed by the fact that many of the tablets in question mention gods and goddesses as recipients (Bennett 1958). Such attestation of a *mā̆ter theia* does not of course prove borrowing from Anatolia or from the Orient in general. Such a title existed in almost every ancient religion with an organized pantheon. What is more interesting is the fact that the Greek title of the 'Great Mother', *mḗtēr theṓn*, which is not found in alphabetic Greek texts before the sixth century B.C., had a direct ancestor in Linear B Greek texts in the *ma-te-re te-i-ja* for whom offerings of perfumed oil were provided. This will enable us to re-examine the question of the origins of the goddess, in Greece itself, in the light of the archaeological evidence, and it will be possible to trace her history on the Greek mainland from the thirteenth century B.C. to the sixth. (A Hittite goddess who would correspond to the *mā̆ter theia* would be *Hannahannas*, ideographically written NIN.TU or MAḪ, Goetze 1938: 58; or *Siwanzannis*, SA.AMA. DINGIR-*lim*, Palmer 1963: 257; or even *Hepat*.)

We also find in the Pylian tablets several mentions of a goddess *di-wi-ja* or *di-u-ja* of whom classical Greek tradition did not keep many traces. This goddess appears in tablet **PY Tn** 316, which also reveals that she had her own sanctuary, the *di-u-ja-jo* (**PY Tn** 316: v. 4); her name is also found twice in the genitive case, indicating the appurtenance of slaves (*do-e-ro/do-e-ra:* **PY Cn** 1287: 6; **An** 607: 5; the context is lost in the Knossos tablet **KN X** 97; the only trace of the goddess's name in later Greek seems to be in that of the nymph *Dione*, mother of Aphrodite; e.g. *Iliad V*, 370; or possibly *Diwia* in a Pamphylian inscription of Sillyon; see Gérard-Rousseau 1968: 68 and fn. 3).

It is certain that the divine name *di-wi-ja/di-u-ja* contains the stem **diw-* which occurs in case-forms of the name *Zeus*. However our goddess is not paired with Zeus as his *paredros*, as her name would induce us to believe, because the tablet which mentions her sanctuary, the *di-u-ja-jo*, also mentions a *di-u-jo* for Zeus, Hera and *di-ri-mi-jo*, son of Zeus (**Tn** 316: 8–10). Much has been said about this apparent triad; but while the couple Zeus–Hera came to hold a very high position in the Greek pantheon, *di-ri-mi-jo* disappeared (Gerard-Rousseau 1968: 65–66). We may find in that development exactly the opposite to what happened to Tesub, Hebat and Sarruma. That group of deities, which is one of the most firmly established in the whole Hittite imperial pantheon, came to include relatively late the 'son' Sarruma who belonged to the ancient Anatolian background (Laroche 1963: 277–302). It would thus be very useful to re-examine the 'triad-theories' in general because those two examples are a good proof that the label 'triad' has been given too quickly without supporting explanation to groups which are far more complex than was believed.

Another of the numerous problems which the text **Tn** 316 presents is that of the existence of diversified sanctuaries in Pylos. I will only indicate briefly some of the riddles which face us. In that tablet alone are found, besides the *di-u-ja-jo* and *di-u-jo* already mentioned, at least three other sanctuaries which are all located at *pu-ro*, Pylos (i.e. v. 1, 4: *po-si-da-i-jo; pe-re-82-jo; i-pe-me-de·ja-<jo>*). Now the archaeologists have not identified any true Mycenaean temple so far. They have generally found traces of cult-chapels inside palaces or small sanctuaries as at Mycenae or Asine. On the other hand, frescoes, especially those of Pylos (Lang 1969), paint processions of men and women with offerings who are certainly going to the Pylian sanctuaries which have not yet been found. Must we believe that the sanctuaries mentioned in the tablets were so architecturally simple that they did not leave any archaeological traces? Or has bad luck kept us from finding one so far? In any case, if the scribes took the trouble to give the names of the sanctuaries in inventories of offerings to gods and goddesses whose very names were used to form the name of their sanctuary, the sanctuaries too must have been well defined. Otherwise we would have to assume that each one of the gods with a sanctuary of his own could receive offerings elsewhere than in his cult-place. The problem remains unsolved.

In the same tablet **Tn** 316 there appears *po-ti-ni-ja* (*potnia*), 'Lady' or 'Mistress', a divine designation often used in the Linear B texts. Four times, at Pylos, it is used alone. Sometimes it is said of a goddess, sometimes, in parallel with *wa-na-ka*, 'king' it must be used for the queen (Gérard-Rousseau 1968: 188; the occurrences in texts are: Knossos, **Gg** 702:2; **M** 729:2; **Oa** 7374:2; **V** 52:1; **W** 444; Pylos, **An** 1281:1,9; **Cc** 665; **Fn** 187:8; **Fr** 1206; **Fr** 1225:1; **Fr** 1231:1; **Fr** 1235:2; **Fr** 1236; **Tn** 316:3; **Un** 219:7; **Vn** 48:3; Mycenae, **Oi** 701:2; **Oi** 704:1). The Hittite *Ishassara*, with the same meaning, is also sometimes used for a goddess, sometimes for a mere human (Ehelolf 1936: 184–6; Laroche 1947: 67). This use is exactly comparable to what is found among other ancient civilized peoples; in Sumerian, GAŠAN is so used; in Akkadian *Beltum* (Mullo-Weir 1934: 54–55; Tallquist 1938: 57) and in Hurrian *Allai* or *Allani* (Laroche 1947: 44 and 1948: 113–136: von Brandenstein 1940: 109–110). Perhaps the reverse process occurred in the case of the Hattian title *Katahha*, 'queen' which was used as a divine designation (Laroche 1947: 28, 104).

In all other instances *po-ti-ni-ja* is qualified by a genitive placed in front, as in *da-pu-ri-to-jo po-ti-ni-ja*, 'Lady of the Labyrinth' (**KN Gg** 702; Gérard-Rousseau 1968: 56–8), or by an adjective following it, as in *po-ti-ni-ja i-qe-ja*, 'Lady with/of the horse (or chariot)' (**PY An** 1281:1). This latter name deserves study, not only because it refers to the horse or an artefact directly connected with it, but because what may be an actual representation of the goddess whom the text mentions has been found, of much the same date as the Pylos tablets, and it shows strong oriental influence. This is a little statuette of the twelfth or thirteenth century B.C., from a grave in the Attic Mesogeia, which shows the 'crescent-shaped' deity seated on a horse. It is the oldest representation in the Greek world of a goddess associated with a horse (Levi 1951; the statuette is now in the Stathatos Collection in the Athens National Museum). We may also note that in 1957 tablet **PY An** 1281 was found in the large room of the north-east wing of the palace of Pylos, close to an inside court where an altar and a small chapel were found (Blegen and Lang 1958: 175–91). This makes me believe that the 'Lady with the Horse' was the divine protector of at least one part of the palace (on the special connections between horses and Neleids, see below C. Sourvinou-Inwood, p. 218). We may consider as a possible Anatolian parallel the Hittite goddess *Askasepa(s)*, 'genius of the *aska-*', i.e. 'of the door' or 'front room' (Laroche 1947: 67), who is also associated with horses.

These examples show how our picture of Mycenaean religion will be filled out by study of the Linear B texts and by comparisons with Anatolia. I should mention also the divine throne, the *haruspex* and the numerous denominations of cult-attendants among the Hittites as other possible points of similarity. It will be clear that we should have much to discover by comparison of the two Bronze Age civilizations which flourished on opposite sides of the Aegean, influencing each other in many ways.

References

BENNETT, E. L. 1958. *The Olive Oil Tablets of Pylos. Text of Inscriptions Found 1955.* (*Minos; Suppl.* 2). Salamanca.

BLEGEN, C. W. and LANG, M. 1958. 'The Palace of Nestor excavations of 1957.' *AJA*, 62: 175–91.

EHELOLF, H. 1936. 'Hethitisch-akkadische Wortgleichungen.' *ZA*, N.F., 9: 184–6.

FARNELL, L. R. 1907. *The Cults of the Greek States III.* Oxford.

GERARD-ROUSSEAU, M. 1968. *Les mentions religieuses dans les tablettes mycéniennes* (*Inc Graec.* 29), Rome.

GOETZE, A. 1938. *The Hittite Ritual of Tunnawi.* New Haven.

GÜTERBOCK, H. G. 1961. 'Hittite mythology'; in S. N. Kramer, *Mythologies of the Ancient World* (New York): 141–179.

LANG, M. 1969. *The Palace of Nestor at Pylos in Western Messenia. Vol. II: The Frescoes.* Princeton.

LAROCHE, E. 1947. *Recherches sur les noms des dieux en hittite.* Paris.

——. 1948. 'Teššub, Ḫebat et leur cour.' *JCS*, 2: 113–36.

——. 1960. 'Koubaba, déesse anatolienne et le problème des origines de Cybèlé'; in *Éléments orientaux dans la religion grecque ancienne* (Paris): 113–28 (*Travaux du centre d'études supérieures spécialisé d'histoire des religions, Strasbourg*).

——. 1963. 'Le dieu anatolien Šarruma.' *Syria*, 40: 277–302.

——. 1965. 'Textes hittites en transcription: mythologie anatolienne.' *RHA*, 23: 61–178.

LEVI, D. E. 1951. 'La dea Micenea a cavallo'; in *Studies Presented to D. M. Robinson* (ed. G. E. Mylonas, Saint Louis, Mo.): 108–25.

MULLO-WEIR, C. 1934. *A Lexicon of Akkadian Prayers.* Oxford.

PALMER, L. R. 1963. *The Interpretation of Mycenaean Greek Texts.* Oxford.

RAPP, A. 1886. 'Kybele'; in W. H. Roscher, *Ausführliches Lexicon der Griechischen und Römischen Mythologie*, II/I (Leipzig): cols. 1638–72.

TALLQVIST, K. 1938. *Akkadische Götterepitheta.* Helsinki.

VON BRANDENSTEIN, C. G. 1940. 'Zum churrischen Lexicon.' *ZA*, N.F., 12: 83–115.

WILL, E. 1960. 'Aspects du culte et de la légende de la Grande Mère dans le monde grec'; in *Éléments orientaux dans la religion grecque ancienne*: 95–111.

5

Archaeology of the Late Bronze Age and the Early Iron Age

Bronze Age Greece and the Balkans: problems of migrations

JAN BOUZEK

Charles University, Prague

THERE was always some degree of contact between Greece and the Balkans during the Aegean Bronze Age, but only occasionally was it more than casual and very rarely of such a character that migrations of populations between the Aegean area proper and the Balkans can be posited.

For example, the relations between the Baden culture and the Poliochni *azzuro* phase are very close (Bouzek 1966: 243; Neustupný 1968: 25–6). Some degree of population movement from south to north seems to be one of the most plausible explanations (cf., however, Renfrew 1969).

Greek 'Corded Ware' is closely related to Rumanian and Bessarabian 'Corded' pottery (i.e. Kurgan IV; Gimbutas 1970), not to the classical Central European Corded Ware. Its dating in Greece is however, not completely certain. It was found in an EH III context at Eutresis, but by Milojčić at Argissa in his Early Macedonian I levels, according to his preliminary reports (Milojčić 1959: 51, fig. 21; his final publication is still awaited). Some scholars are inclined to connect the 'Corded Ware' in Greece with the late EH II destructions, but no samples of this ware have been found, as yet, either at Lerna or in destruction levels at other contemporary sites. The hypothesis that it was the Greeks who arrived with Minyan pottery does not account for the presence of Greeks in the Greek hinterland and in Epirus later, and probably also in the MBA. Besides this, the spread of Minyan ware looks rather as if it were no more than the diffusion of a new fashion and a technological innovation; it does not

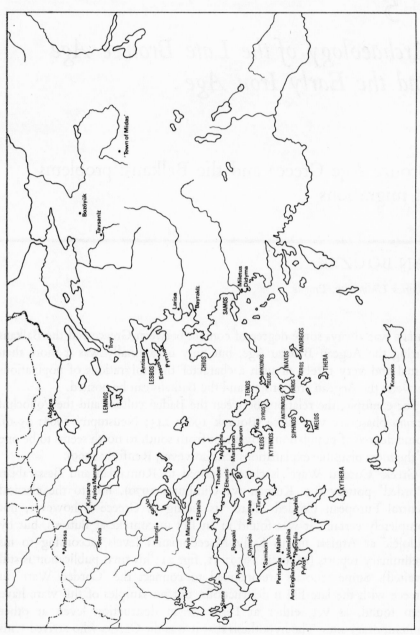

Map 4. The Aegean and western Anatolia in the Middle and Late Bronze Age, showing principal sites

correspond to the usual archaeological pattern of a migration (cf. Howell pp. 76, 87). I cannot find any exact parallels for the 'European' vases from Lerna and Kirrha (Caskey 1966: 11), even if their models might originate in the north, perhaps in an area similar to the one which provided the models of the Greek 'Corded Ware'.

Some of the shapes of Middle Bronze Age European pottery seem to reflect southern (Aegean, Anatolian) Middle Bronze Age models, but this very general resemblance can probably be connected with the many other objects that link Bronze Age A2(–3) cultures in the northern Balkans (especially Transylvania) with Anatolia and the Aegean. We may mention here the Transylvanian types of the Karo A family of swords, the bone objects with spiral decoration, similar artistic motifs on bronzes and pottery, four-spoked wheels, imitations of metal vessels, the 'ivy leaf' motif etc. These objects find Greek parallels in MH (MM) III and Late Helladic (LM) I–II, and they are closest in the Shaft Grave period. Some of the Anatolian parallels to these elements (imitations of metal vessels) are dated as early as the early second millenium B.C., while others (bone carvings etc.) are later than their Greek relatives (Bouzek 1966; Gimbutas 1965: 56–70; Mellaart 1968). Transylvania, rich in copper and gold, was during this period certainly in contact with the south and south-east, whereas Bohemia with its tin ores was almost unaffected by these influences (*contra* Mellaart 1968: 193). The southern connections of Transylvania probably resulted simply from trade or metal-prospecting, or both, and a large-scale migration need not be assumed. Some raw material could have been imported from Transylvania, but only a few southern pieces can be presumed to have had a northern origin. An example is the group of ear-rings (*Noppenringe*) from Mycenae Shaft Grave AIV, once supposed by Evans to have been brought into Greece as the dowry of a barbarian princess. The closest parallels, as far as I know, are those from the Tufalau hoard in Transylvania (Bouzek 1966: 254–5). The 'Hungarian' axe in the Schliemann Troy collection is also very likely of Balkan origin (Dörpfeld 1902: 405, fig. 404; Schmidt 1902: 267, Nr. 6768).

In Late Helladic II, the area of contacts becomes narrower. Sandars type swords and contemporary Mycenaean spear-heads are known from Bulgaria and Yugoslav Macedonia, but hardly any are known north of the Danube (Sandars 1961: 119–20; Alexandrescu 1966: 119–21). The European swords related to the Mycenaean type D are known only from the western part of central Europe and from Denmark (Randsborg 1967: 20–25; the Drnovo sword is much later and does not belong to this group), while amber came to Greece most probably via England and southern France, not through central Europe. It seems, then, that in central Europe only a group of spear-heads reflects Mycenaean models (Bouzek 1966: 250–1).

The situation changes rapidly in LH mB or, to be more exact, in its later part. The Sprockhoff flange-hilted na swords are distributed from southern Sweden and Norway throughout central Europe (east of the Rhone and west of the Vistula and Prut) to Greece and Cyprus (Fig. 15.1), the lanceolate (*geflammte*) spear-head from central Europe through Italy and the Balkans to Greece and Cyprus, and the violin-bow fibula (Fig. 15.2) together with certain articles of protective armour, in approximately the same area, though some of the finds lie further to the north. Helmet, shield, corselet and greaves were all originally inspired by Mycenaean armour, but were then developed in Europe and reintroduced into Greece. The final forms of these objects, as with the swords, spear-heads and fibulae, are probably of north-western Balkan origin. Other Aegean metal objects of northern origin or inspiration are less important: the knives point mostly to the northern Balkans, Peschiera daggers to north Italy and the Balkans, the winged axe-mould from Mycenae to Italy. Gold spirals, rings and small ornaments find resemblances in many parts of Europe. The only really close parallel in the way of wire ornaments, which is also restricted in its spatial distribution, is that between the Tiryns gold wheel with its 'woven' gold wire and the east Bohemian gold 'figures-of-eight' (Bouzek 1968).

Prehistoric pottery usually has a much more limited distribution than bronze objects and only a few of the vessel types from Late Mycenaean Greece are paralleled in the north (Fig. 15.3). The Macedonian 'Lausitz' ware is best paralleled in the north-west Balkan Urnfields (sometimes called Middle Danubian), the Attic (Cretan and Rhodian) Protogeometric incised ware in the central Balkans and partly also in the Late Apennine pottery of central Italy. The Trojan Knobbed Ware (one sherd of which has been identified also in Mycenae; Hood 1967) shows resemblances to certain local wares in eastern Rumania and north-east Bulgaria, while some early vessels from Vergina, decorated with rows of incised strokes, are related to Late Bronze Age vessels from central Bulgaria. The Cephalenian and Ithacan hand-made wares seem to be an off-shoot of the Illyrian pottery distributed in Albania and southern Bosnia. Other forms are not paralleled in the north, or consist of plain vessels that have analogies both in Italy and in the Balkans (Bouzek 1969: 41–45). The schematic distribution map (Fig. 15.3) shows clearly that only the Macedonian Lausitz ware finds resemblances north of the central Balkans.

In contrast to the LH mB–C bronze objects of northern origin, the distribution of the new LH mC–Submycenaean bronze types is much more limited; the bow fibulae (Fig. 15.4) and certain types of long pins are not paralleled north of Italy and the western Balkans; their distribution is 'Adriatic' i.e. along the shores of the Adriatic sea; Hungary and Rumania are also outside this territory. Other metal objects seem to confirm this conclusion.

To sum up: only the EH II–III and LH IIIB–C changes can be possibly explained as evidence of migration from the north. There is as yet no general study of the pattern in the archaeological record which is created by migration of population. The preliminary results indicate that it differs from what general observers have usually expected, but support the view that there were some migrations in the period in question (Bouzek 1968).

The archaeological evidence does not enable us to place the Dorians far north of Greece. If they were simply pastoralists, as the historical tradition records, they would hardly have been able to capture and destroy Mycenaean towns and fortresses. The violent destructions and the spread of new metal and pottery types could mean that European tribes from the Balkans (some of them from the north-western Balkans) attacked Mycenaean Greece in the thirteenth century B.C. and after several attempts destroyed its citadels, towns, and country settlements. During these wars, the Mycenaeans were forced to adopt the more effective barbarian armour and were also influenced by other objects of European origin, but this does not mean that the barbarians colonized the land that they had devastated; they probably amassed their booty and went further east to Anatolia, where the Hittite empire fell soon after Troy, while further east still Syrian cities came to an end.

Only after the Mycenaean power had been broken could the Dorians enter the depopulated country (in the late twelfth century B.C.) and—after many further wars—establish themselves as rulers in most parts of the Greek mainland. The 'Return of the Herakleidai' was already the beginning of the Dark Age, accompanied by many local wars and by the absence of any central power.

The downfall of Mycenaean Greece was a time of great prosperity in Europe. It cannot be excluded that a climatic change altered the balance of power between the civilized states of the Mediterranean and the barbarians from Europe (cf. Bouzek 1970: 81–8, 101–4, 199–203; Desborough 1964).

References

ALEXANDRESCU, D. 1966. 'Die Bronzeschwerter in Rumänien.' *Dacia*, 10: 117–90.

BOUZEK, J. 1966. 'The Aegean and Central Europe: an introduction to the study of cultural interrelations 1600–1300 B.C.' *Památky archeologické*, 57: 242–76.

——. 1968. 'The Aegean, Balkans and Central Europe 1700–700 B.C.' (dissertation, University of Prague; to be published in *Studies in Mediterranean Archaeology*, Lund).

——. 1969. 'The beginnings of the Protogeometric Pottery and the "Dorian Ware".' *Opuscula Atheniensia*, 9: 41–57.

——. 1970. *Homerisches Griechenland*. Prague.

174 *Jan Bouzek*

CASKEY, J. L. 1966. 'Greece and the Aegean islands in the Middle Bronze Age.' *CAH* (rev. ed.) Vol. II, Chap. IVa/Fasc. 45.

DESBOROUGH, V. R. d'A. 1964. *The Last Mycenaeans and their Successors*. Oxford.

DÖRPFELD, W. 1902. *Troja und Ilion*. Athens.

GIMBUTAS, M. 1965. *Bronze Age Cultures in Central and Eastern Europe*. The Hague.

——. 1970. 'Evidence of the Indo-European (Kurgan IV) culture in the Aegean, Ionian, Adriatic and East Mediterranean areas at *c*. 2600–2300 B.C.' *Indo-European and Indo-Europeans*: 158–79.

HOOD, M. S. F. 1967. 'Buckelkeramik at Mycenae.' *Europa: Festschrift E. Grumach*. (ed. W. C. Brice, Berlin): 120–31.

MELLAART, J. 1968. 'Anatolian trade with Europe and Anatolian geography and cultural provinces in the Late Bronze Age.' *AnatSt*, 18: 187–202.

MILOJČIĆ, V. 1960. 'Ergebnisse der deutschen Ausgrabungen in Thessalien 1953–58.' *Jahrbuch RGZM Mainz*, 6: 1–56.

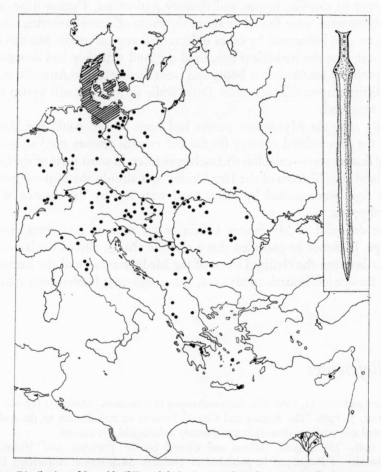

Fig. 15.1. Distribution of Sprockhoff IIa and derivative swords in the eastern Mediterranean

1. ● True Sprockhoff IIa swords.
2. ○ Late and derivative Sprockhoff swords.

NEUSTUPNÝ, E. 1968. 'Absolute chronology of the Neolithic and Aeneolithic periods in Central and South-Eastern Europe.' *Slovenská Archeologia*, 15: 19–60.

RANDSBORG, K. 1967. ' "Aegean" bronzes in a grave in Jutland.' *ActaA*, 38: 1–27.

RENFREW, A. C. 1969. 'Die Ausgrabungen in Photolivos und die Badener Kultur'; in *Nitra Baden Symposium* (1969).

SANDARS, N. 1961. 'The first Aegean swords and their ancestry.' *AJA*, 65: 17–29.

SCHMIDT, H. 1902. *Heinrich Schliemann's Sammlung trojanischer Alterhümer*. Berlin.

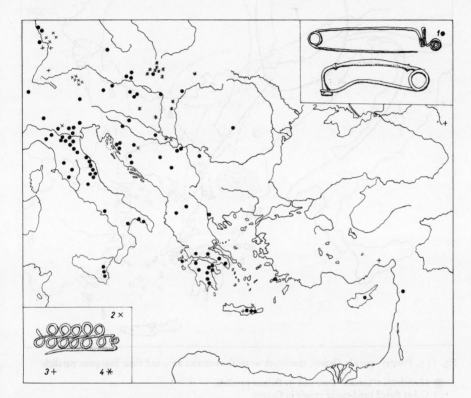

Fig. 15.2. Distribution of the violin-bow fibula in the Aegean region and the central Balkans: (1) variant with flat ended shield bow; (2) variant with bow coiled in 'figure of eight'; (3) variant with 'waved' bow; (4) the 'posamenterie' fibula

1. ● Variant with flat ended shield bow.
2. × Variant with bow coiled in 'figures of eight'.
3. + Variant with 'waved' bow.
4. ✳ 'Posamenterie' fibulae.

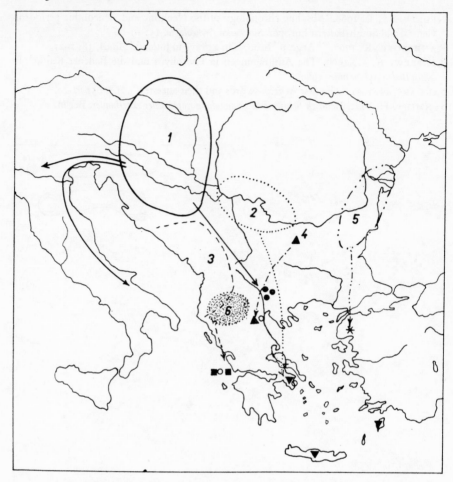

Fig. 15.3. Pottery types in Greece, thirteenth to tenth centuries B.C., and their European parallels

1. ● Macedonian 'Lausitz' ware and its Balkan parallels.
   ○ Other fluted hand-made vessels in Greece.
2. ▼ 'Attic' incised Protogeometric pottery with its Cretan and Rhodian parallels and the Balkan Žuto Brdo—Dubovac—Cîrna—Gîrla Mare wares.
3. ■ Pottery of the Illyrian culture area and the area of its influence in the Ionian islands.
4. ▲ Devetaki cave and similar incised pottery at Vergina.
5. ✳ Trojan Knobbed Ware and its parallels.
6. ⦂⦂⦂ Area of the Bobousti and related wares.
7. + LH IIIC hand-made cups (Lefkandhi).

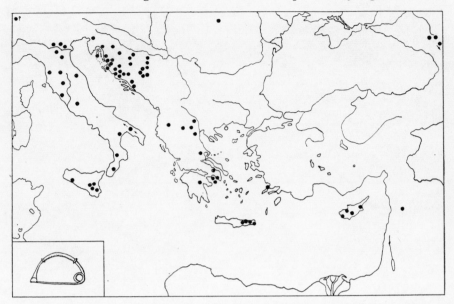

Fig. 15.4. Distribution of the bow fibula with 'knobs' in the Aegean region and the central Balkans

Grey Trojan ware in Cyprus and northern Syria

H.-G. BUCHHOLZ

Archäologisches Institut, Universität Giessen

AT the beginning of this article I wish to acknowledge with gratitude the friendly collaboration of Professor C. F. A. Schaeffer, and the valuable opportunity which I enjoyed of taking part in his excavation of Ras Shamra in 1961 and 1963.

Investigating Bronze Age migrations in the Aegean region involves examining the usefulness of archaeological evidence in historical research. This is made clear by the partly contradictory contributions to this volume of J. Bouzek, J. D. Evans, M. Garašanin, N. G. L. Hammond, M. S. F. Hood, R. J. Howell and P. M. Warren. It seems necessary to find criteria which make it possible to identify ethnic groups by pottery associated with them. If they can be identified in this way, geographical displacement of pottery groups may imply displacement of the peoples or tribes who produced them. However, F. J. Tritsch's warning against equating pottery styles with racial entities (see below p. 236) should be kept in mind, as well as M. Garašanin's reminder about the dangers of confusing different kinds of migration, "the slow reclamation and colonization of new territory, the sudden irruption of lower cultures among higher ones, the gradual mingling of peoples".

It is conceivable also, and it has in fact often happened, that pottery has moved from one region to another as objects of trade, or as containers used in trade, without this meaning that those who produced it moved also. Further, there have also been instances of 'cultural contact', shown by form, material, kind of burning, colour or painting of vases, without this being evidence for 'migrations' or 'trading' at all. The historical importance of 'influence' and 'contact' must not be over-estimated. At any rate, the historical interpretation of any 'congeries' of archaeological material should be examined *ab initio* in every case (cf. Adams 1968; Trigger 1968).

We shall not consider here the significance of metallurgical products,

which A. M. Snodgrass has discussed (see below pp. 209–13), but only that
of ceramics. G. Kossinna inaugurated the 'Siedlungsarchäologische Methode'
(correlation of archaeological entities with geographical areas; Kossinna
1936), and he already treated 'Corded Ware' as strong evidence for
migrations of 'Northerners' into south-eastern Europe. He was followed by
S. Fuchs in his *Die griechischen Fundgruppen der frühen Bronzeseit und ihre
auswärtigen Beziehungen* (Fuchs 1937; cf. Bittel 1945: 35–6). From such
arguments and counter-arguments it has become increasingly clear that
typical features of each relevant ware must be looked for, which are not to
be found elsewhere. J. Bouzek and M. S. F. Hood have cited intrusive
corded ware as evidence of Balkan influence in Greece (see above, p. 169
and pp. 59–61), but this has been challenged by M. Garašanin (see above,
p. 124). One has to take corded ware, even if showing characteristic
features, as a warning example when pottery is brought into discussion of
historical problems.

In the sense indicated above, much has been written in the last decade
about the historical interpretation of 'Grey Ware'. Now, R. J. Howell
regards the Grey Minyan ware of Greece as a product of local evolution in
EH III, under the influence of Balkan proto-types (see above, p. 87). But it
is well known that J. Mellaart, J. Driehaus and F. Schachermeyr have tried
to prove that the origin of this ware was in north-western Anatolia
(Mellaart 1955, Driehaus 1957: 93–101: Schachermeyr 1962: 346–7; cf.
Buchholz 1965: 572; Mellaart 1958: 15–17). These scholars have connected
'Minyan' with the products of the strong and long-lasting 'Grey-Ware
tradition' of that cultural area. Involved in their hypothesis was the question
of language: the problem of the coming of a Greek-speaking population
into Greece (Beattie 1962; Crossland 1967: 18, 29; Dunbabin 1957: 65–6).
The association of 'Grey Ware' with postulated Greek-speaking ethnic
elements is the subject of my discussion in so far as 'Polished Grey Ware' in
fact shows typical features not to be confused with those of anything else. It
does indeed appear to have been restricted to specific cultural areas within
the Aegean region at certain times. But if Archaic Grey Bucchero from
Etruria (see Dohrn 1969) is taken into consideration, its distribution can be
regarded as one more argument for close relation between the Etruscans, a
non-Greek-speaking people, and north-western Anatolia. The main reason
for not pressing this argument is that black bucchero and painted fabrics are
much commoner in Etruria than grey wares.

W. Lamb defined the area where 'Polished Grey Ware' flourished as the
Aeolic lands of Classical times and called it 'Grey Lesbian bucchero' (Lamb
1932: 136–7; Cook 1960: 338, 347). Indeed, on Lesbos there was such a
strong tradition of the ware that even Mycenaean *kylikes* were imitated in
grey polished clay (see Pl. 25C, from Antissa; Lamb 1931: 170, 178 pl. 28/2).
Archaic plain copies of metal *phialai* are reported in Lesbian bucchero also

(Boardman 1967: 136 fig. 84, 473–4). Further, Corinthian *oinokhoai* were imitated in this technique at Troy (Blegen, Boulder, Caskey and Rawson 1958: 265 No. 36 and No. 722, pl. 292, 317/27). Grey ware flourished in the region of north-western Anatolia and Lesbos from the Early Bronze Age onwards; cf. for example, thin hand-made sherds, mouse-grey, metallic in appearance, from Bozöyük (in the Akademisches Kunstmuseum, Bonn; unpublished) and similar sherds from J. Boehlau's excavations at Pyrrha in Lesbos (now in the Archaeological Institute of the University of Göttingen; publication by H.-G. Buchholz forthcoming). Wheel-made examples are known from Archaic, Classical and even Hellenistic times (Ziegenaus and De Luca 1968: 100, Nos. 12, 13; 114, Nos. 88, 89; 119, Nos. 124, 125; 124, Nos. 154, 155; pls. 35, 39, 40, 64). J. Schäfer mentioned "Grey polished Aeolic pottery" of different periods from the 'Town of Midas', Larisa, Bayraklı-Smyrna, Gordion, Didyma and Alişar Hüyük (Naumann and Tuchelt 1964: 55 no. 56; Schäfer 1968: 13, 23; Bouzek 1969b: 109, 121). Plain and relief-decorated Archaic grey ware is also known from Miletus (Kleiner 1966: pls. 20, 26; Weickert 1960: pl. 56).

The classification and dating of such fabrics may need more attention. There is, for example, fine grey ware of Early Minoan II date from eastern Crete (Branigan 1970: 29–30). Interesting also are J. L. Caskey's observations on the classification of the ceramics of Troy: "The grey ware of Schmidt's Nos. 3174–3175 . . . looked to me like the archaic 'Lesbian' bucchero of Troy VIII rather than any fabric of the Early Bronze Age" (Caskey 1964: 66 note 17; Schmidt 1902). An unpublished fragment of a North Aegean-Aeolian *karkhesion* of fourth-century B.C. manufacture from Abdera may demonstrate grey ware traditions in that area of Hellas even after Classical times (Pl. 27B; in a German private collection)[1]. *Karkhesion*, apparently a pre-Greek word, meant in the Aeolic dialect a drinking vessel similar to the *kantharos* (for contradictory identifications of the shape after *Athenaeus* XI, 480–1 and 741, see Brommer 1967: 546 and Langlotz 1969: 382). Sappho from Eresos praises *karkhesia* as precious possessions of the gods (Love 1964).

Thus, if grey ware is to be found outside the Aeolid, it seems to provide evidence for connections with that area. (P. Themelis has recently informed me that some grey bucchero has now been found in Protogeometric context at Lefkandhi in Euboea; for Aeolic grey ware at Athens see Kübler, 1970: pl. 128). This must be recognized if one observes the almost total lack of any grey ware over large areas of the eastern Mediterranean (on this question and on the distribution of Lesbian bucchero see Boardman 1964: 54, 71, 73, 106, 141). Besides what Boardman has mentioned, there is the profiled, everted rim of a large late Classical vessel with incised decoration of egg-and-dart pattern on the outer level and of rope pattern on the bevelled slope (Fig. 16.1). This piece of grey clay with a dark grey slip surely comes

Fig. 16.1. Section of a grey vase fragment in the Museum of the American University in Beirut (see also Plate 27A)

from a north-eastern Aegean workshop. (It came to the Museum of the American University in Beirūt, Accession No. 6098, from the Ford Collection; most objects in this collection came from Sidon in the southern Lebanon[2]; see also Pl. 27A.)

Grey ware is rare in the eastern Mediterranean. D. H. French has assembled, with full references, information about what was found at Minet el Beida, Ras Shamra, Tell abu Hawam and Tell ed Duweir up to 1969 (French 1969: 69–70, 90, fig. 24). I have noted the following additional occurrences:

1. A *krater* with incised wavy lines was found by P. Dhikaios in a tomb at Pyla-Vergi (Pl. 25D; Dhikaios 1969: pl. 234/4 called by him 'Grey Minyan')[3]. This vase was clearly an import into Cyprus. It can be identified by its form, decoration, material and colour as being of late Troy VI or early Troy VII origin. The pot has been put together from many sherds, which are not quite homogeneous in colour. It varies from dark brownish-grey to light mouse-grey; on the rim are incised wavy lines. This item of pottery gives for the first time an indication of connections, whatever they may have been, between north-western Anatolia and Cyprus during the transitional period Troy VI/VII. The context of the burial in the tomb at Pyla (north-east of Larnaka) is LH IIIB.

2. There are more of these extremely rare grey sherds with incised wavy lines from Enkomi in Cyprus, Level IIIA. P. Dhikaios calls these also "Grey Minyan ware" but classifies them as north-west Anatolian (Dhikaios 1969a: 258, 1969b: pl. 68/21).

3. J. Bouzek has kindly informed me that he saw grey ware of the type under discussion in the National Museum at Damascus; it was excavated at Tell Qasr in Syria by A. Bounni[4].

4. Among thousands of sherds found in the southern quarters of Ras Shamra-Ugarit only one relevant item had been observed by 1963; it is a fragment of a typical light grey Troy VI/VII vessel (Fig. 16.2, Pl. 25A); Find-

No. *Ras Shamra* 1963, West 349, minus 2·00 m.; now in the stores of the Ibn
Hani Excavation House). The fragment is 13 cm. long, 8·2 cm. high and
1–1·2 cm. thick. Its curve indicates that it belonged to a rather large pot of an
open *krater* type (see Fig. 16.3 for the reconstruction). It is of fine, well fired
mouse-grey clay with very little mica; both outside and inside have a thick,
shiny slip of the same clay. The inside confirms that the vessel must have
been of a very open-mouthed form. On the outside surface there are bands
of wavy lines impressed while the slip was still wet, each band divided from
the next by vertical parallel lines. The instrument used for this decoration had
four teeth and was drawn in a regular and elegant manner over the surface,
not as on certain unpublished sherds from Troy (Pl. 26, A, C, D[5], but much
as in the case of fragment No. 3357 of Schliemann's collection, which derived

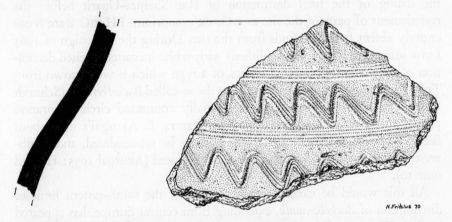

Fig. 16.2. Grey Troy VI/VII sherd with wavy lines, from Ras Shamra, in the reserve collection of the
Ibn Hani Excavation House (scale 1:2; see also Plate 25A)

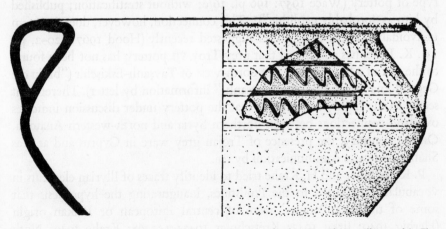

Fig. 16.3. Reconstruction of a Troy VI/VII vessel from the sherd at Ras Shamra illustrated in Fig.
16.2 (see also Plate 25A)

from Troy vɪ/vɪɪ (Pl. 26ʙ; Schmidt 1902: 162–3, No. 3357; it survived the 1939–45 war; see von Müller and Nagel 1964)[6].

5. In the same excavation area of Ras Shamra, where No. 4 was found, there came to light another grey sherd, which is much darker, covered with a slip on the inside and the outside. There is a shallowly impressed, clumsy wavy line on its surface (Find No. *Ras Shamra* 1961, Abschnitt 51, minus 1·80 m.; now in the store of the Ibn Hani Excavation House). This fragment, also part of an open-mouthed pot in view of the covering of slip in the interior, does not appear to me to resemble any pottery found at Troy. It seems to be a totally isolated imitation of Trojan ware in Ugarit (Pl. 25ʙ).

We cannot decide definitely whether No. 4 is of late Troy vɪ, or early Troy vɪɪ, date. Determination of its date would be of great importance for the dating of the final destruction of Ras Shamra-Ugarit before the resettlement of parts of the site as a Greek emporium. LH ɪɪɪC ware is not entirely absent from the finds from the site. During the campaign of 1963 I saw some sherds (not yet published) with white incrusted, incised decoration of tangentially connected circles, of a type which is well known from Troy vɪɪ, where it belongs technically to the so-called *Buckelkeramik* (Schmidt 1902: 177 Nos. 3625–3629). If tangentially connected circle decoration proves to have been observed at Ras Shamra, E. Akurgal's note about *Buckelkeramik* in northern Syria will have to be reconsidered, and northwest Anatolian penetration there may be indicated (Akurgal 1955: 113 and note 10).

All this would be exciting, since until now the south-eastern limit of distribution of *Buckelkeramik*, extending from central Europe, has appeared to lie in Thrace and the Troad, even if some hand-made grey sherds from Mycenae might be taken into consideration as being possibly related to this type of pottery (Wace 1957: 196 pl. 36/e; without stratification; published by him as "probably neolithic")[7]. This connection, however, does not seem unavoidable, as M. S. F. Hood suggested recently (Hood 1967: 120–2, pl. 13). K. Bittel has confirmed that grey Troy vɪɪ pottery has not been found to the east of a line running just north-west of Tavşanlı-Eskişehir ("bis in die Gegend knapp vor Eskişehir-Tavşanlı;" information by letter). Therefore it seems to me highly improbable that the pottery under discussion indicates overland connections between northern Syria and north-western Anatolia. On the contrary, the presence of Trojan grey ware in Cyprus and at Ras Shamra indicates communication by sea.

P. Kretschmer and H. Krahe tried to identify traces of Illyrian elements in vocabulary attributed to the Philistines, inaugurating the hypothesis that some of the 'Sea Peoples' were of central European or Balkan origin (Herbig 1940; Jirku 1943; Kretschmer 1943: 152–68; Krahe 1949; Noth 1966: 41). So far, archaeological evidence which might support this view has been lacking (but see Kimmig 1964). Even now, I believe, the archaeological evidence which has been discussed in this article does not offer clear proof of the participation of Illyrian tribes in the sea-raids of the Philistines, or even of participation of north-western Anatolians in them.

But we have learned from some far-travelled pots and sherds that during the second half of the thirteenth century B.C. and the beginning of the twelfth sea-faring in the eastern Mediterranean was not confined to the southern part of the Aegean region but also reached its northern part. In examining the usefulness of equating pots and peoples, even negative evidence is of some value, as was shown long ago by E. Wahle in his paper 'Zur ethnischen Deutung frühgeschichtlicher Kulturprovinzen' (1941)[8].

Notes

1. I thank Professor P. R. Francke of the University of Saarbrucken for permission to publish this fragment.

2. I thank Miss Helga Seeden of the Museum of the American University of Beirut for her helpful information about this fragment and the Director of the Museum for permission to publish it.

3. I thank Professor P. Dhikaios for full information and a photograph of the *krater* which he reported: 'Pyla (Cyprus).' *Fasti Archaeologici* (1954) 132-3, Dr. V. Karageorgis gave me the opportunity to study the pot, which is now in Larnaka Museum, in the autumn of 1970.

4. I have not been able to obtain further information about this pottery directly. E. Akurgal has confirmed J. Bouzek's observation about it: ". . . in Syrien sah ich Fragmente von grauer Keramik, die den Bruchstücken aus Larisa und Troja VI sehr ähnlich sind". (Letter of 20 June 1970.)

5. I thank Dr. W. Nagel for identifying these sherds in the reserve of the Museum für Vor- und Frühgeschichte in Berlin and for providing me with photographs of them.

6. Dr. Nagel has kindly provided the following further information about Schliemann's Collection. At the beginning of the War part of it was removed for safety to Silesia and Oderbruch, and the objects in this were reported to have been brought back to East Berlin with some losses, in the 1960s. Other objects were in the 'Gropius Building' in Berlin when it was hit by bombs in 1945. A very small number of these objects was rediscovered in the ruins of the building in 1947-8 and brought first to the 'Museum für Völkerkunde' and later transferred to the 'Museum für Vor- und Frühgeschichte' in West Berlin.

7. I would not attempt to classify these sherds without having seen them myself; but even comparisons with Italic material of the twelfth to tenth centuries B.C. should be taken into account: see Peroni 1963: 365-6, fig. 1/58, 373-4, fig. 4/475.

8. I thank Professor W. A. von Brunn for his help in preparing the figures in this article,

Mr. H. Fritzius of the Institut für Vorgeschichte of the University of Giessen for executing the drawing reproduced as Fig. 16.2, and Mrs. K. Vischer in Berlin for that reproduced as Fig. 16.3, based on Troy VIIa proto-types (see Blegen 1958: pls. 239–8, 249, 287).

References

ADAMS, W. Y. 1968. 'Invasion, diffusion, evolution?' *Antiquity*, 42: 194–215.

AKURGAL, E. 1955. *Phrygische Kunst*. Ankara.

BEATTIE, A. J. 1962. 'Aegean languages of the Heroic Age'; in A. J. B. Wace and F. H. Stubbings, *A Companion to Homer* (London): 311–24.

BITTEL, K. 1950. *Grundzüge der Vor- und Frühgeschichte Kleinasiens* (2nd ed.) Tübingen.

BLEGEN, C. W. 1937. *Prosymna; the Helladic Settlement Preceding the Argive Heraeum*. Cambridge.

——. 1958. *Troy IV*. Princeton.

BOARDMAN, J. 1964. *The Greeks Overseas*. Harmondsworth.

——. 1967. *Excavations in Chios 1952–55: Greek Emporio*. London.

——. 1968. 'A Chian phiale mesomphalos from Marion.' *Report of the Department of Antiquities of Cyprus*, 1968: 12–15.

BOUZEK, J. 1969a. 'The beginnings of the Protogeometric pottery and the "Dorian Ware".' *Opuscula Atheniensia*, 9: 41–57.

——. 1969b. *Homerisches Griechenland*. Prague.

BRANIGAN, K. 1970. *The Foundations of Palatial Crete*. London.

BROMMER, F. 1967. 'Kylix.' *JdI/AA*, 82(1967): 546.

BUCHHOLZ, H.-G. 1965. Review of H. Schliemann, *Ithaka, der Peloponnes und Troja; Mykenae* (1869, 1878; reprints Darmstadt, 1963, 1964; ed. E. Meyer). *Gymnasium*, 72: 569–73.

CASKEY, J. L. 1964. 'Chalandriani in Syros'; in *Essays in Memory of Karl Lehmann* (*Marsyas: Studies in the History of Art*; Suppl. 1; Inst. of Fine Arts, New York University; ed. L. C. Sandler): 63–9.

COOK, R. M. 1960. *Greek Painted Pottery*. London.

CROSSLAND, R. A. 1967. 'Immigrants from the North.' *CAH* (rev. ed.), II, Chap XXVII/Fasc. 60.

DHIKAIOS, P. 1969a. *Excavations at Enkomi: 1948–58*, I. Mainz.

——. 1969b. *Excavations at Enkomi: 1948–58*, IIIa. Mainz.

DOHRN, T. 1969. 'Stamnoi und Kratere aus grauem Ton, Nachahmungen von Metallgefässen (Città Castellana)'; in W. Helbig and H. Speier, *Führer durch die öffentlichen Sammlungen klassischer Altertümer in Rom*, III (rev. ed., Tübingen): 701, Nr. 2791.

DRIEHAUS, J. 1957. 'Prähistorische Siedlungsfunde in der unteren Kaikosebene und an den Golf von Çandarlı.' *IstMitt*, 7: 76–101.

DUNBABIN, T. J. 1957. *The Greeks and their Eastern Neighbours*. London.

FRENCH, D. H. 1969. 'Prehistoric sites in north-west Anatolia II. The Balıkesir and Akhisar-Manisa regions.' *AnotSt*, 19: 41–98.

FUCHS, S. 1937. *Die griechischen Fundgruppen der frühen Bronzezeit und ihre auswärtigen Beziehungen*. Berlin.

HERBIG, R. 1940. 'Philister und Dorer.' *JdI*, 55: 58–89.

HOOD, M. S. F. 1967. 'Buckelkeramik at Mycenae?' *Europa: Festschrift für Erst Grumach* (Berlin, ed. W. C. Brice): 120–31.

JIRKU, A. 1942. 'Zur illyrischen Herkunft der Philister.' *WZKM*, 49: 13–14.

KIMMIG, W. 1964. 'Seevölkerbewegung und Urnenfelderkiltur'; in R. von Uslar and K. J. Narr, *Studien aus Alteuropa* I (*Beihefte der BonnJbb.* 10/1; Cologne): 220–83.

KLEINER, G. 1966. *Alt-Milet* (*Sb. J. W. Goethe Univ.* 4/i; 1965/1), Frankfurt am Main.

KOSSINNA, G. 1936. *Ursprung und Verbreitung der Germanen in vor- und frühgeschichtlicher Zeit* (3rd ed.) Leipzig.

KRAHE, H. 1949. *Die Indogermanisierung Griechenlands und Italiens.* Heidelberg.

KRETSCHMER, P. 1943. 'Die vorgriechischen Sprach- und Volksschichten (Fortsetzung), *Glotta*, 30: 84–218.

KÜBLER, K. 1970. *Kerameikos* VI. Berlin.

LAMB, W. 1931. 'Antissa.' *BSA*, 31: 166–78.

——. 1932a. 'Antissa.' *BSA*, 32: 40–67.

——. 1932b. 'Grey wares from Lesbos.' *JHS*, 52: 1–12.

LANGLOTZ, E. 1969. 'Beobachtungen in Phokaia.' *JdI/AA*, 84(1969): 377–86.

LOVE, I. C. 1964. 'Kantharos or karchesion?' *Essays in Memory of Karl Lehmann*: 204–22.

MELLAART, J. 1955. 'Some prehistoric sites in north-western Anatolia.' *IstMitt.* 6: 53–88.

——. 1958. 'The end of the Early Bronze Age in Anatolia and the Aegean.' *AJA*, 62: 9–33.

NAUMANN, R. and TUCHELT, K. 'Die Ausgrabung im Südwesten des Tempels von Didyma 1962.' *IstMitt*, 13/14: 15–62.

NOTH, M. 1966. *Geschichte Israels* (6th ed.). Göttingen.

PERONI, R. 1963. 'Dati di scavo del sepolcreto di Pianello di Genga.' *JdI/AA*, 78 (1963): 361–403).

SCHACHERMEYR, F. 1962. 'Forschungsbericht über die Ausgrabungen und Neufunde zur ägäischen Frühzeit 1957–60.' *JdI/AA*, 77 (1962): 104–382.

SCHÄFER, J. 1968. *Hellenistisches Keramik aus Pergamon.* Berlin.

SCHMIDT, H. 1902. *Heinrich Schliemann's Sammlung trojanischer Alterthümer.* Berlin.

TRIGGER, B. G. 1968. *Beyond history: the methods of prehistory* (*Studies in Anthropological Method*). New York.

VON MÜLLER, A. and NAGEL, W. 1964. 'Ausstellungen und Bestande im Museum für Vor- und Frühgeschichte Berlin.' *Berliner Jahrbuch für Vor- und Frühgeschichte*, 4: 225–8.

WACE, A. J. B. 1957. 'Mycenae 1939–56. 1957: Part I. Neolithic Mycenae.' *BSA*, 52: 195–6.

WAHLE, E. 1941. '*Zur ethnischen Deutung frühgeschichtlicher Kulturprovinzen.*' *SBHeidelberger Akad. d. Wissenschaften, Phil.-Hist. Kl.* 2. 1940/41.

WEICKERT, C. and HOMMEL, P. 1960. 'Die Ausgrabung beim Athena-Tempel in Milet 1957; Vorbemerkungen. Der Abschnitt östlich des Tempels.' *IstMitt*, 9/10: 1–3, 31–62.

ZIEGENAUS, O. and DE LUCA, G. 1968. *Das Asklepieion. Altertümer von Pergamon* XI/1. Berlin.

Grave circles in Albania and Macedonia

N. G. L. HAMMOND

University of Bristol

THE Great Tumulus at Pazhok in central Albania stands over two grave circles some 11 m. and 21 m. in diameter, set concentrically one within the other (Pl. 28; Islami and Ceka 1964: 95–7). The earlier circle was made with orthostatic slabs, and its tumulus of earth was covered on top with a layer of stones, so that it was sealed off from the upper tumulus which belonged to the outer circle of large white stones. One burial in the upper tumulus is dated by a two-zoned cylindrical cup of the Vaphio type and by a bronze sword to LH I or IIA. The inner tumulus contained daggers, spear-heads and tweezers dated to the eighteenth century B.C. by the excavators. Some burials may be earlier than this. The central burials of the inner tumuli (two double tumuli were excavated) were in round or rectangular pits, dug into virgin ground and lined with cobbles. A double tumulus has been excavated at Vodhinë in southern Albania (Prendi 1956). There the inner grave circle of unworked stones measured 13 m. in diameter, and the central burial was covered by a cairn of stones (Pl. 29). A later burial in a slab-lined cist-tomb, which was set on the cairn, was of Middle Helladic date. At Vajzë four large tumuli, 18 to 24 m. in diameter, contained weapons of Middle Helladic and Middle Minoan date (Prendi 1957). Other tumuli have been excavated in the Mati valley; the reports are very brief but the illustrations show weapons again of Middle Helladic and Middle Minoan types.

The tumuli at Pazhok, Vajzë and Vodhinë are far inland; situated beside rivers, they are close to main routes used by the inland traveller. Those of the Mati valley are on a route which leads from the coast to the interior (Islami, Ceka, Prendi and Anamali 1955: 137; Islami and Ceka 1964: 101–5; Hammond 1967a: 328–31, 341). The excavators thought the arrangement of the tumuli in small groups reflected a tribal organization in which the chieftains and their families were buried with weapons, jewellery and pottery and sometimes with a sacrificial feast in the tumulus. Pairs of tumuli were in contemporary use at Pazhok (the double tumuli) and at Vajzë (two pairs). These tumuli are large; they overflow the grave circles and run generally between 20 and 40 m. in diameter. They are or were some 3 to 5 m. high, being shield-shaped. The secondary graves are shaft-graves in the sense that they were sunk into the soil of the tumulus.

In western Macedonia there are two examples of such burials. The lowering of the waters of Lake Ostrovo has revealed a grave circle of orthostatic slabs, 11·50 m. in diameter, near Arnissa (Cook and Boardman 1953: 159). As cist-graves were noted both inside and outside the circle, it was evidently a double tumulus, like those at Pazhok and Vodhinë. It is presumably also of Middle Helladic date. The other is a circular pit at Servia which is dug into the debris of the Early Neolithic settlement there (Pl. 30A. Heurtley 1939: 54–6, figs. 50–2). It is lined with cobbles. There was evidently a roof over the mortuary chamber and a layer of wood ash above the roof had remains of a funerary feast. A secondary burial was made above this layer in what was evidently a tumulus of soil. Both burials had obsidian blades, waisted pebble-axes and stone celts. The older burial had some red material, perhaps ochre. The pottery in the secondary burial belongs to Servia IIb (Heurtley 1939: pots Nos. 76 and 91), that is late in the Macedonian Late Neolithic Age which, in my opinion, overlaps with part of Early Helladic in Greece. It is possible that the older burial should be dated to the start of Servia IIb.

Thus in Albania and western Macedonia we have tumulus-burials which are to be placed within the time span of EH and MH. These areas are particularly suitable for hunting and for pastoral life, especially for the transhumance of sheep. The lakes too are rich in fish. The prosperity of a large site by Lake Malik was due to these natural resources. In addition, the imported objects which have been found at Malik show that from Neolithic times onwards a considerable trade between the Aegean and the Adriatic Sea passed from Thessaly via Servia up the Haliacmon Valley, crossed the Balkan range to Malik and descended through central Albania to the Adriatic coast (Islami and Ceka 1964: 91–5; Prendi 1966: 272–80).

The users of tumulus-burial were certainly members of a Kurgan group, which expanded from southern Russia into Central Europe c. 2500 B.C.: the Kurgan IV Group which Professor Gimbutas has discussed. (If the earlier burial at Servia is to be dated, following Heurtley, to the start of Servia IIa, then it is due to an earlier wave of Kurgan people; that is of the Kurgan III phase in Gimbutas's terminology.) The most likely route for them into our area is from the upper Vardar valley into the Ochrid basin and Pelagonia. Some features of the Kurgan peoples' culture may be noted in addition to tumulus-burial: ochre perhaps at Servia; Corded Ware (*Schnurkeramik*) at Gajtan near Scodra (probably Late Neolithic A to EBA: Rebani 1966: 44, fig. 2/dh), at Kastritsa near Ioannina (EBA/MH; Hammond 1951: 177, fig.

2; 1967a: 309, fig. 7/1), at Aphiona in Corcyra (LNA/EBA; Bulle 1934: 178 fig. 7, 188) and at Agios Mamas and Kritsana in Chalcidice (EBA; Heurtley: 1939: 83 and fig. 46a). A new kind of pottery at Malik IIb resembles the silver pots and vases of the Kurgan peoples, and there is an influx of perforated stone hammer-axes in the top layer of Malik IIIA (Prendi 1966: 260–2; Gimbutas 1956: Pls. 10, 11/1, 12/2 and 5, 18). Malik IIb began early in the Macedonian Bronze Age and the top layer of Malik IIIA corresponds approximately to EH III. Lastly the Kurgan people had horses. The earliest evidence of the horse in the western Balkans is a figurine in Pelagonia at Porodin, the typical site of a culture which had a long life in the Neolithic Age and ended towards the end of the Macedonian Late Neolithic Age, that is early in EH (Grbić 1960: 54 and pl. XXXII/6). Horse-bones were reported by Heurtley in Central Macedonia in the EBA and MBA of Macedonia (Heurtley 1939: 88, 93).

It is generally believed that the Kurgan peoples spoke languages of the Indo-European family (Gimbutas 1963: Crossland 1967: 40–4) and here we have the first conclusive evidence of their appearance in the south-western Balkans. In this area it is to be expected that in the Early Helladic period they spoke a language which was ancestral to either Illyrian or to Greek. Let us now turn to the south for evidence of their expansion in that direction.

Tumuli with grave circles were excavated by Dörpfeld in Leucas. The earliest are dated by Helladic sauce-boats to EH II; the circles consist of a pair in contemporary use which are the largest in Leucas, R 1 and R 26, measuring 9·30 and 9·60 m. in diameter, and one somewhat later, R 16 (Dörpfeld 1927: 233–6, 244–7). They differ from the tumulus-burials of inland Albania in several respects and particularly in that the corpse was usually placed in a *pithos* within the mortuary chamber (Pl. 30c). But there is no doubt that these tumulus-burials are also in the Kurgan tradition, and their users evidently came to Leucas by sea from the eastern Adriatic coast, with which the Mati valley area was in close touch. Thus from EH II onwards we may distinguish two groups of Kurgan peoples: one sea-borne in the Ionian Gulf and identifiable at Leucas; the other inland, straddling the central Balkan range from western Macedonia to central and southern Albania.

A considerable number of tumulus-burials of Middle Helladic date have been found in Greece. In many cases the reports are provisional, but they fall mainly into two groups which show affinities respectively with the Leucas group and with the inland group.

Those which seem to have derived from the Leucas group are at Same in Cephallenia (Dontas 1964: 317); at Samikon in north-western Peloponnese (Hood 1956: 17; Yalouris 1965); at Peristeria and Papoulia, near Pylos in Messenia (Hood 1955: 11, fig. 7) and at Aphidna in Attica (Wide 1896). The Aphidna tumulus is especially interesting in that *pithoi* were used in the earliest burials and twin-vessels for cult purposes were found, as in

Leucas. Professor Marinatos has reported what is probably a double tumulus at Marathon (close to Aphidna), which has similarities in its paving-stones and covering of slabs with R 16 and other tumuli of Leucas (Marinatos 1970: 68, figs. 7–9). It is likely that the tumuli at Aphidna and Marathon are memorials of the first Kurgan peoples to reach Attica; they came probably by sea from the Ionian Gulf.

The members of the other group which seem to have derived from the inland group of Albania and western Macedonia are as follows: at the end of EH II one at Lerna in Argolis in the form of a large tumulus, apparently a cenotaph until in the MH period when a shaft-grave was sunk into it (Caskey 1956: 165, and fig. 3); in the MH period three at Pylos in Elis (Themelis 1965: 216), one in a less regular form at Malthi in Messenia (Valmin 1938: 188–207), one at Kea in Ceos, as reported by Professor Caskey in a lecture at Princeton; and a pair of tumuli called Grave Circle B and Grave Circle A at Mycenae, which were in contemporary use for some time around the transition from MH to LH I. (Hammond 1967b: 83–91). A number of shaft-grave burials of MH date have been reported by Marinatos at Kephalovryson near Volimidhia in Messenia and they were evidently covered by a tumulus in their original state (Marinatos 1964: 92–3). The distribution of tumuli with grave-circles of orthostatic slabs is particularly interesting, as it leads us back to Ostrovo and Pazhok, both far inland. Moreover at Mycenae in the fourteenth century, when a monumental circle was made to commemorate the founders, evidently of the late MH period, a grave circle of orthostatic slabs was constructed. Then when tholos tombs had come into use, the tumulus and its grave circle survived as the visible elements above the tholos tomb. It is clear that there was continuity of rulers at Mycenae from the later half of the MH period to the middle of the fourteenth century. The instances of pa: s of tumuli in contemporary use at Pazhok, Vajzë, Leucas and Mycenae are also of interest.

The Kurgan founders whom the rulers of Mycenae commemorated as their ancestors are likely to have introduced the Greek language there. For it was to serve this language that the Linear B script was devised. Members of the group which came from inland Albania and western Macedonia are likely to have migrated overland and to have brought the horse and the chariot with them.

There are two other tumuli which were excavated long ago. One at Ayia Marina near Chaeronea, some 20 m. in diameter, contained two burials, remains of a funerary feast and a layer of ash, while a black zoomorphic vase with white filling is like one at Servia (Sotiriadhis 1905: 120–9). This tumulus is of the Macedonian Late Neolithic period. The other which is at Elateia had a cairn of stones over the one burial, as at Vodhinë, and a funerary feast of an ox, as at Pazhok; this tumulus is of MH date. These two cases suggest that one route of penetration overland came via eastern central

Greece. The suggestion is supported by the occurrence of slab-lined cist-tombs with particular objects in northern Greece at this time, especially at Tsangli and at Sesklo in northern Thessaly. Thus at Tsangli there are close links with Malik, Porodin, Pazhok, Vodhinë and Servia in pottery, in incised stamps on pot-bases, in clay *phalli*, zoomorphic vases, altar-tables and figurines of humans and animals. At Sesklo there are links with Mati, Pazhok, and Leucas in bronze tweezers, one-edged bronze knives with a snout, and hair-rings of gold wire in sets of three.

In short, if our inferences from the tumulus-burials are correct, some Kurgan peoples reached places in the territory of south-western Macedonia, central and southern Albania and Leucas around the middle of the third millennium. From there two streams entered Greece, mainly in the MH period, one by sea and the other by land. The Indo-European language which they spoke was the ancestor not of Illyrian but of Greek, and within this 'Ur-Greek' it is probable that the seeds of the Ionic dialect were carried into Attica and the Peloponnese and the seeds of the Aeolic dialect into Thessaly and farther south.

The reservoir from which the Greek-speaking peoples came south was not drained by the emigrations of the MH period. Indeed tumulus-burial was practised in central and southern Albania until the end of the Bronze Age at least. There are indications of one reason for the emigration southwards in the MH period. The Macedonian Bronze Age was marked by two invading cultures which spread progressively westwards. One brought anchor-shaped hooks of clay into eastern central Macedonia, and the other brought an early type of Minyan pottery into north-eastern Macedonia. They may be called respectively the 'Paeonian' culture and the Bubanj-Hum culture, and the evidence shows that they spread into western Macedonia until they met in Pelagonia. The pincer-movement of these two cultures set up an emigration of peoples southwards from the Haliacmon valley into Thessaly and south-westwards from Pelagonia and Lyncus into Albania and Epirus. It seems likely that these pressures set the main waves of Greek-speaking peoples on their way southwards in the Middle Helladic period (Garašanin 1958: 123: Srejović 1963: 14–15).

Something very similar happened at the end of the Bronze Age. When Heurtley discovered the traces of Lausitz invaders on the eastern bank of the Vardar river in central Macedonia, he was able to date their arrival by Mycenaean pottery of the Granary class and by a violin-bow fibula to within LH IIIC, *c*. 1150 B.C. But the relationship between the invasion and the so-called Dorian invasion of *c*. 1120 B.C. was not clear, because no one saw evidence of any invasion of Greece from central Macedonia. Recent discoveries have given us a new insight into the Lausitz invasion. Cist-tombs excavated near Prilep and others excavated by the Crna Reka, both in Pelagonia, have produced large arching fibulae, spiral-ended finger-rings, and hand-made pottery of a distinctive kind. Similar objects have been found in central Epirus at Elaphotopos (Vokotopoulou 1969: 179–91) and at Kalbaki (Dhakari 1956: 116, fig. 2) in cist-tombs, and the date of the last is firmly fixed at the transition from LH IIIB to LH IIIC, i.e. *c.* 1180 B.C. The Lausitz type of fluted pottery has been found also at Gajtan and in the Mati valley. It seems that the Lausitz invasion was on a much greater scale than has been supposed. It passed through Pelagonia into Albania and influenced central Epirus in the period 1200–1150 B.C. and central Macedonia later still, from 1150 B.C. onwards. It was this pressure which set the so-called Dorian invasion in motion southwards from Epirus. We see now the impetus we need at the time we need and in the place we need.

The confirmation we need is supplied by a preliminary report from Mycenae. Lord William Taylor found in 1964 "three cist-tombs cut into the last Mycenaean remains" inside the citadel of Mycenae. They were presumably burials of a people who had conquered Mycenae *c.* 1120 B.C. The cist-tombs included *inter alia* three arching fibulae of the Prilep type; an open-ended finger-ring with spiral ends as in early Lausitz examples; two long bronze pins with small mushroom tops and small swellings as at Vajzë in Albania; and hand-made pottery which has analogies in Pelagonia. It looks as if the leaders of those who destroyed Mycenae at the end of the Bronze Age came from Epirus and were themselves influenced by the Lausitz invasion of the twelfth century B.C.

References

BULLE, H. 1934. 'Ausgrabungen bei Aphiona auf Korfu.' *AthMitt*, 59: 147–224.

CASKEY, J. L. 1956. 'Excavations at Lerna, 1955.' *Hesperia*, 25: 147–73.

COOK, J. M. and BOARDMAN, J. 1953. 'Archaeology in Greece, 1953.' *ArchRep.* 1953/*JHS*, 75: 142–69.

CROSSLAND, R. A. 1967. 'Immigrants from the North.' *CAH* (rev. ed.) I, Chap. XXVII/Fasc. 60.

DESBOROUGH V. R. D'A. 1965. 'The Greek mainland *c.* 1150–1000 B.C.' *ProcPS*, 31: 213–28.

DHAKARI, S. I. 1956. 'Proïstorikoi taphoi para to Kalbaki-Ioannion.' *ArchEph*, 1956: 115–53.

DÖRPFELD, W. 1927. *Alt-Ithaka*. Munich.

GARAŠANIN, M. 1958. 'Neolithikum und Bronzezeit in Serbien und Makedonien.' *RGKomm*, 39: 1–130.

GIMBUTAS, M. 1956. *The Prehistory of Eastern Europe, Part I*. Cambridge, Mass.

——. 1963. 'The Indo-Europeans: archaeological problems.' *American Anthropologist*, 65: 815–36.

GRBIĆ, M., MAČKIĆ, P., NAD, S., SIMOSKA, D. and STALIO, B. 1960. *Porodin: kasno-neolitsk naselje na tumbi kod Bitolja*. Bitolj.

HAMMOND, N. G. L. 1967a. *Epirus*. Oxford.

——. 1967b. 'Tumulus-burial in Albania, the grave circles of Mycenae, and the Indo-Europeans.' *BSA*, 62: 77–105.

HEURTLEY, W. A. 1932. 'Excavations at Sérvia in western Macedonia.' *Antiquaries Journal*, 12: 227–38.

——. 1939. *Prehistoric Macedonia*. Cambridge.

HOOD, M. S. F. 1955. 'Archaeology in Greece.' *ArchRep*, 1954 (*JHS*, 75): 3–19.

——. 1956. 'Archaeology in Greece.' *ArchRep*, 1955 (*JHS*, 76): 3–35.

ISLAMI S. and CEKA, H. 1964. 'Nouvelles données sur l'antiquité Illyrienneen Albanie.' *StudAlb*, 1964: 91–137.

ISLAMI, S., CEKA, H., PRENDI, F. and ANAMALI, S. 1955. 'Zbulime të kulturës ilire në luginën e Matit./Les vestiges de civilisation illyrienne venus à jour à Mati.' *BUSS*, 1955/1: 101–49.

MAČKIĆ, P., SIMOSKA, D. and TRBUHOVIĆ, V. 1960. 'Ranohalstatska nekropola na lokalitetu Saraj u Brodu.' *Starinar*, N.S., 11: 189–208.

MARINATOS, SP. 1966. 'Anaskaphai en Pylo.' *Praktika*, 1964: 78–95.

——. 1970. 'From the silent earth.' *AthAA*, 3: 61–8.

PRENDI, F. 1956. 'Mbi rezultatet e gërmimeve ne fshatin Vodhinë, te rrethit te Gjinokastres.' *BUSS*, 1956: 180–8.

——. 1957. 'Tumat në fushën e fshatit Vajzë.' *BUSS*, 1957/2: 76–111.

——. 1966. 'La civilisation préhistorique de Maliq.' *StudAlb*, 1966: 255–80.

REBANI, B. 1966. 'La céramique illyrienne de la cité de Gajtan.' *Studime Historike*, 1966: 44–90.

SOTIRIADHIS, G. 1905. 'Untersuchungen in Boiotien und Phokis.' *AthMitt*, 30: 113–40.

SREJOVIĆ, D. 1963. 'Versuch einer historische Wertung der Vinča-Gruppe.' *Archaeologia Iugoslavica*, 4: 5–17.

STAEHLIN, F. 1906. 'Zur Landeskunde des Phthiotis.' *AthMitt*, 31: 1–37.

THEMELIS, P. G. 1965. 'Dokimastiki anaskaphi eis tin Eleiakein Pylon.' *Deltion*, 20: Khron.: 215–18.

TSOUNTAS, Ch. 1908. *Ai proistorikai akropoleis Dhiminion kai Sesklou* (The Prehistoric Citadels of Dimini and Sesklo). Athens.

VALMIN, M. N. 1938. *The Swedish Messenian Expedition*. Lund.

VOKOTOPOULOU, Y. P. 1969. 'Neoi kivotoskhimoi taphoi tis YE IIIV-G periodhou eks Ipeirou.' *ArchEph*, 1969: 179–209.

WACE, A. B. and THOMPSON, M. S. 1912. *Prehistoric Thessaly*. Cambridge.

WIDE, S. 1896. 'Aphidna in Nordattika.' *AthMitt*, 21: 385–409.

YALOURIS, N. 1965. 'Mykenaïkos tymbos Samikou.' *Deltion*, 20. Khron.: 6–40.

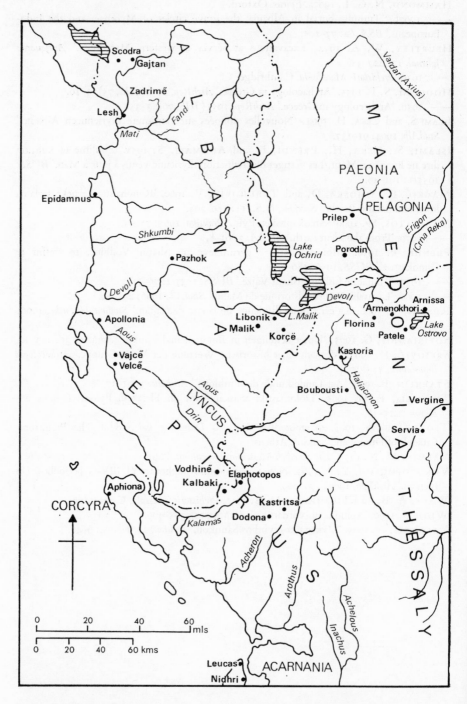

Fig. 17.1. Albania, Epirus and western Macedonia (after Hammond 1967b: fig. 1)
(Note: Lake Malik has now been drained and the course of the river marked as 'Devoll' has been changed, east of that lake.)

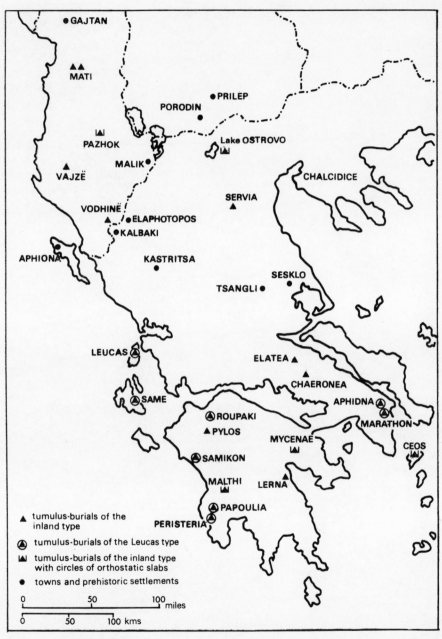

Fig. 17.2. Distribution of Bronze Age tumulus-burials in Albania, southern Yugoslavia and Greece.

Fig. 12a. Distribution of Bronze Age tumulus-graves in Albania, southern Yugoslavia and Greece.

Plate 1. Ayia Irini, Keos. 1969.
Jugs in red-brown and black burnished ware. Early Bronze Age, later phases.

Plate 2. Ayia Irini, Keos. 1969.
Walls of Houses. Early Bronze Age.

CASKEY

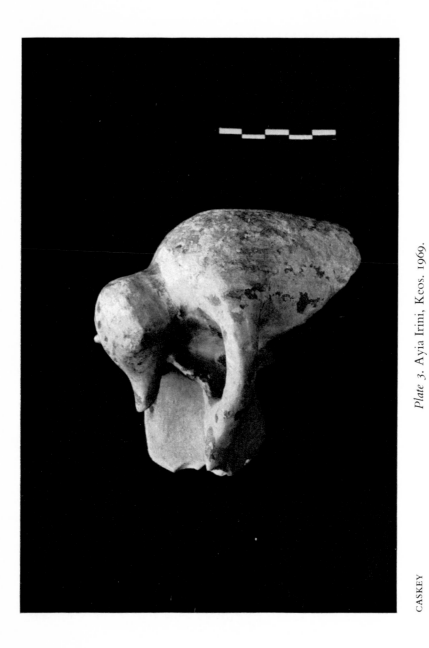

CASKEY

Plate 3. Ayia Irini, Keos. 1969.

Fragment of theriomorphic vessel. Early Bronze Age, period of the sauceboats (EH II/EC II).

Plate 4. EH I pottery sherds from Kastraki, Kythera. Scale 1:2.

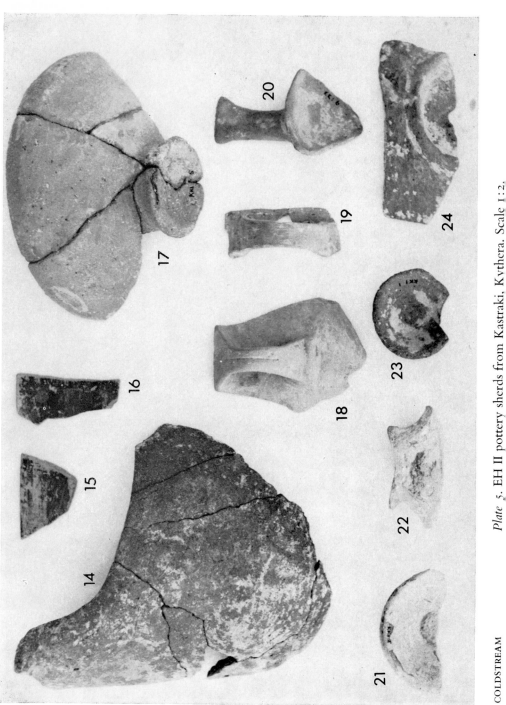

COLDSTREAM

Plate 5. EH II pottery sherds from Kastraki, Kythera. Scale 1:2.

COLDSTREAM   *Plate 6.* EM II–MMIA pottery sherds from Kastri, Kythera. Scale 1:2.

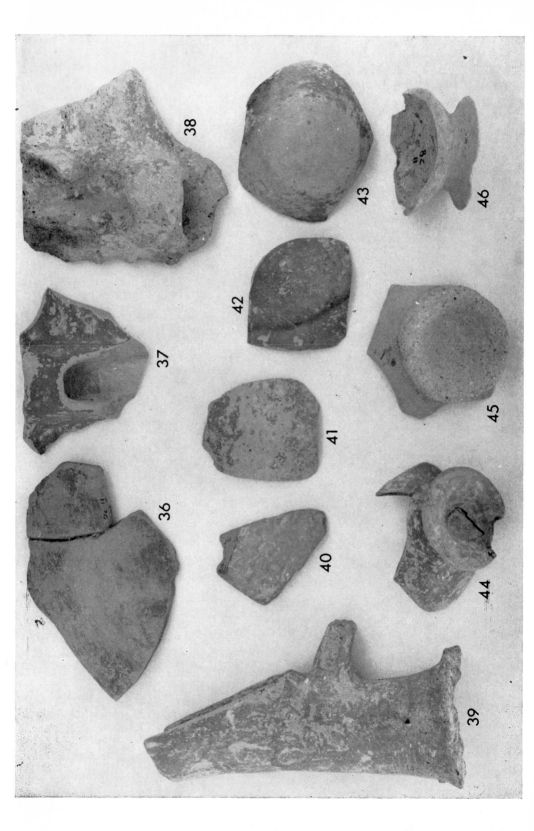

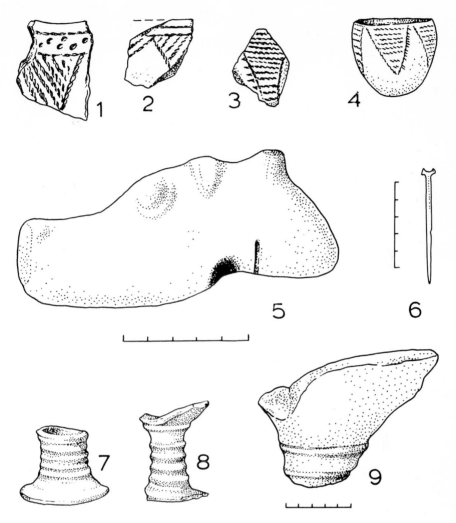

Plate 8. 1–3, corded ware from Eutresis (after Goldman 1931: 123, fig. 169, 1–3).
4, vase from Berezhnovka (after Gimbutas 1956: pl. 13 A 1).
5, stone horse-head sceptre from Fedeleșeni (after Nestor 1932: 45, pl. 2.2).
6, bone pin from Lerna (after Caskey 1956: pl. 47 b).
7–8, Minyan ringed stems from Eutresis (after Goldman 1931: 137, fig. 183, 5, 10).
9, ringed stem from Cucuteni (after H. Schmidt 1924: 351, fig. 1).
Scale in centimetres.

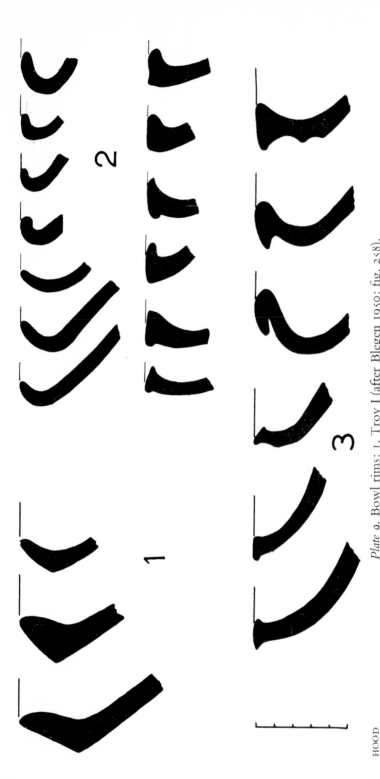

Plate 9. Bowl rims: 1, Troy I (after Blegen 1950: fig. 258).
2, Macedonian Early Bronze Age from Kritsana (after Heurtley 1939: 166, fig. 36).
3, Troy IV–V (after Blegen 1951: pls. 180.1; 254.1; 257.2; 251.11, 12, 15).
Scale in centimetres.

HOOD

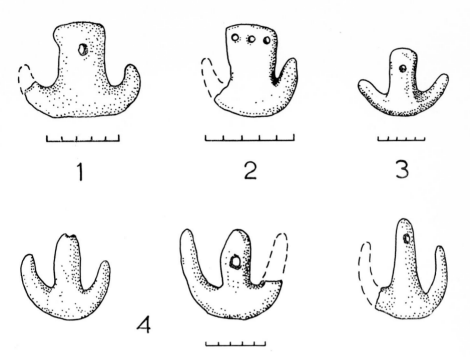

Plate 10. Anchor ornaments: 1, Eutresis (after Goldman 1931: fig. 269.1).
2, Lerna (after Caskey 1956: pl. 47.1).
3, Servia (after Heurtley 1939: 203, fig. 67 f).
4, Thessaly (after Milojčić 1956: 151 fig. 8).
Scale in centimetres.

Plate 11. Clay flasks: 1 and 2, Lerna (after Caskey 1957: pl. 40 d, f).
3, Vinča (after Milojčić 1949b: 281, fig. 7.11).
Scale in centimetres.

Plate 12. Marathon, 1970.
Tumulus I showing the exterior and the interior stone circles.

Plate 13. Marathon, 1970.
Tumulus I, the inner stone circle and the horse's grave.

MARINATOS

Plate 14. Marathon, 1970. Part of the horse's skeleton during the excavation.

Plate 15. Marathon, 1970. Tumulus I, tomb 2. A small shaft-grave which contained traces of a contracted corpse and eleven MH vases.

MARINATOS

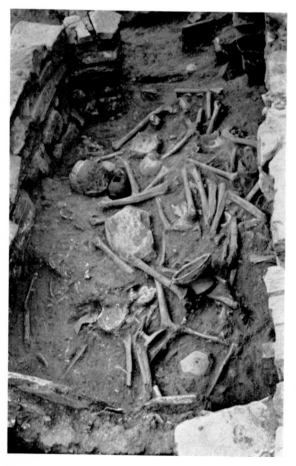

Plate 16. Marathon, 1970. Tumulus II. The only tomb in the centre of the tumulus, in the form of an apsidal house.

Plate 17. Marathon, 1970. Tumulus IV. One of the burial compartments with several burials exclusively of the Mycenaean period.

MARINATOS

A

B

Plate 18. Mediana I pottery from Mediana (Brzi Brod near Niš). National Museum of Yugoslavia, Belgrade.

A, no. 4941.   B, no number

GARASANIN

A

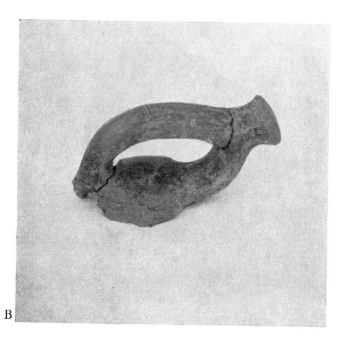

B

Plate 19. Mediana I pottery from Mediana. National
Museum of Yugoslavia, Belgrade.
A, no. 5219. Scale 1:1.
B, no. 5151. Scale 1:2.

GARAŠANIN

A

B

Plate 20. Mediana II pottery from Mediana. National
Museum of Yugoslavia, Belgrade.
A, no. 5158. Scale just under 1 :2.
B, no. 5304. Scale just over 1 : 1.

GARAŠANIN

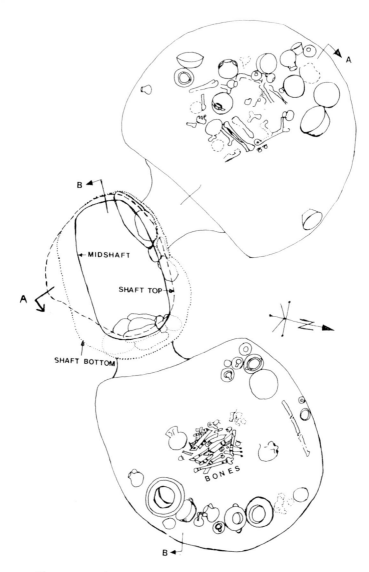

MIDSHAFT

SHAFT TOP

A

SHAFT BOTTOM

BONES

B

Plate 21. A, Plan of Tomb A 76 from Bâb edh-Dhrâ cemetery, on the eastern side of the Dead Sea; *c.* 3200–3100 B.C. (after Lapp 1968a: 16, fig. 4).

GIMBUTAS

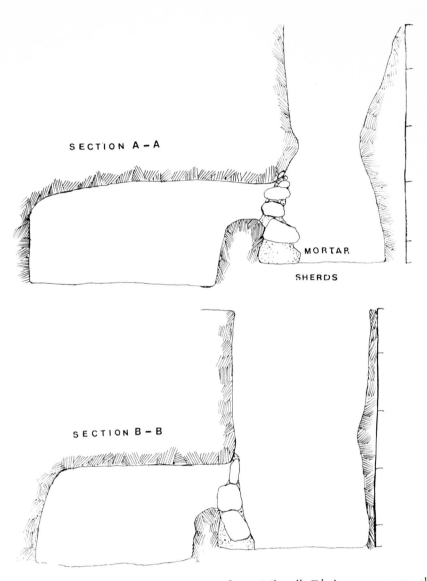

SECTION A – A

MORTAR

SHERDS

SECTION B – B

Plate 21B. Sections of Tomb A76 from Bâb edh-Dhrâ cemetery on the
eastern side of the Dead Sea; c. 3200–3100 B.C. (after Lapp 1968a: 17, fig.5).

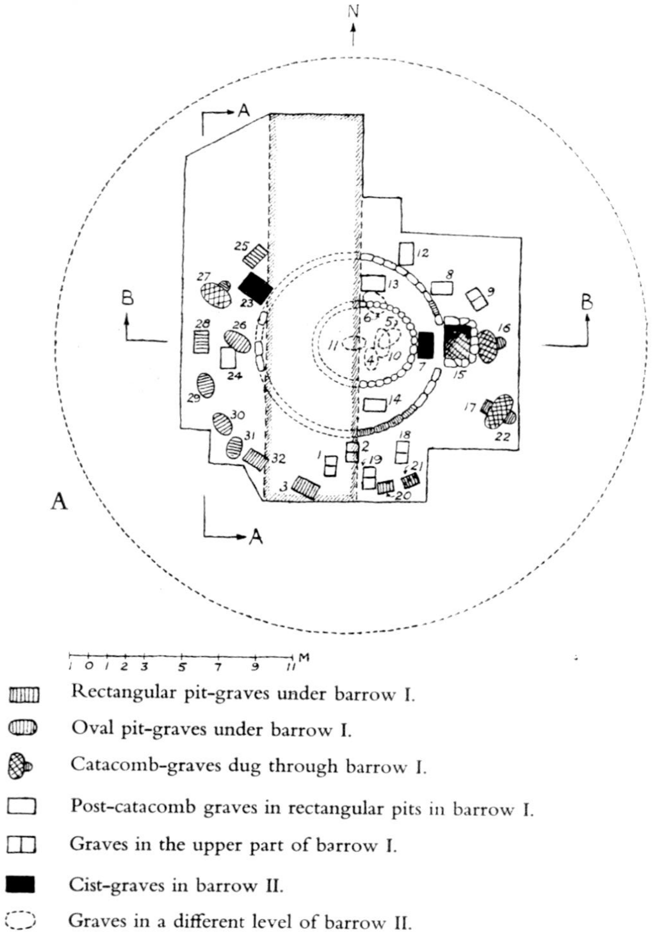

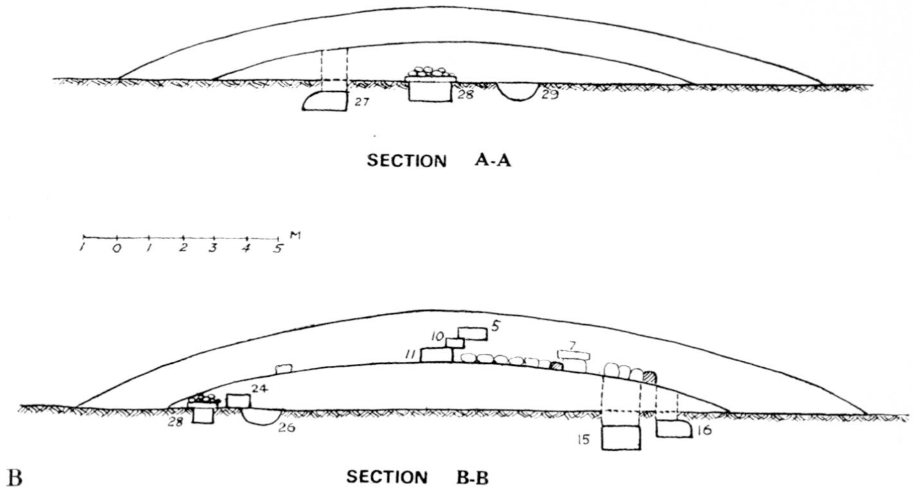

SECTION A-A

B

SECTION B-B

Plate 22. Kurgan in Odessa.
A, Plan and B, Cross-sections (after Gimbutas 1956: 86–87, figs. 47–48).

GIMBUTAS

A

▦ Rectangular pit-graves under barrow I.

◖ Oval pit-graves under barrow I.

🔶 Catacomb-graves dug through barrow I.

▢ Post-catacomb graves in rectangular pits in barrow I.

⊟ Graves in the upper part of barrow I.

■ Cist-graves in barrow II.

○ Graves in a different level of barrow II.

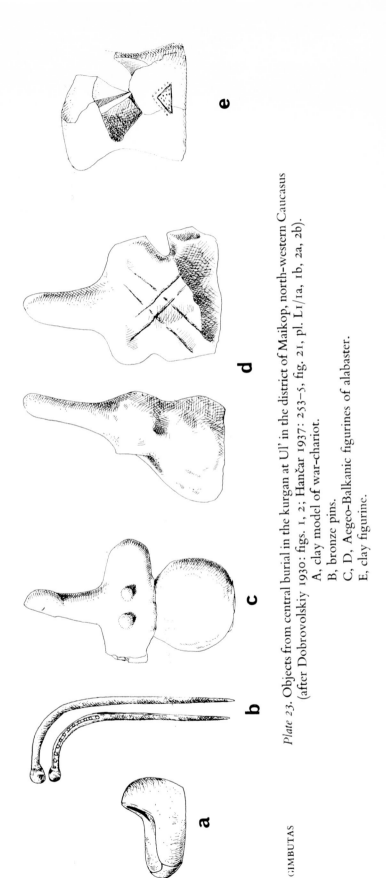

Plate 23. Objects from central burial in the kurgan at Ul' in the district of Maikop, north-western Caucasus (after Dobrovolskiy 1930: figs. 1, 2; Hančar 1937: 253–5, fig. 21, pl. L1/1a, 1b, 2a, 2b).

A, clay model of war–chariot.
B, bronze pins.
C, D, Aegeo–Balkanic figurines of alabaster.
E, clay figurine.

GIMBUTAS

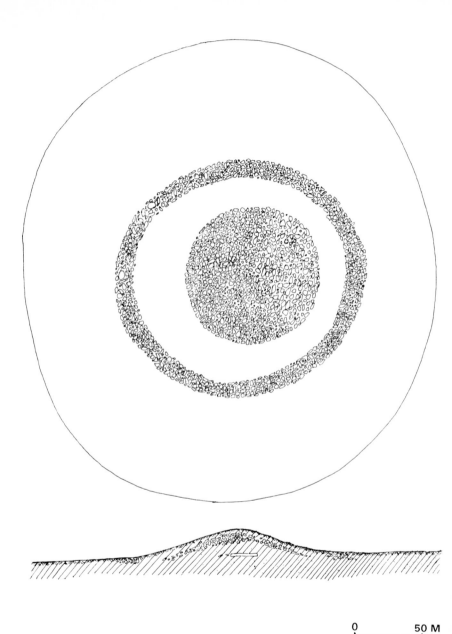

Plate 24. Kurgan with stone cairn in the middle covering a grave and a stone ring. Novyi Arshti, near Bamut, north-eastern Caucasus; of Tsarskaya period, *c.* 2200 B.C.

GIMBUTAS

Plate 25. A, grey Troy VI/VII sherd from Ras Shamra, Syria (RS 1963); in the magazines of Ibn Hani Excavation House. See p. 183, figs. 16.2, 16.3 Sherd measures 12.8 cm by 8.2 cm.

B, local imitation of Troy VI/VII ware from Ras Shamra, Syria (RS 1961); in the magazines of Ibn Hani Excavation House. Length 7.2 cm.

C, local imitation in grey polished clay of a Mycenaean kylix, from Antissa, Lesbos.

D, Troy VI/VII krater from a tomb near Pyla-Vergi in Cyprus. Diameter 29 cm; height 25 cm.

A

B

C

D

Plate 26. A–D, grey sherds with engraved wavy lines, from Troy; Schliemann's collection, Berlin-Charlottenburg, Museum für Vor-und Frügeschichte; A, C and D are unpublished and unidentified; B, no. 3357, Troy VI/VII. Scale 1 :2.

BUCHHOLZ

A

B

Plate 27. A, rim of a grey late classical vessel with incised decoration, said to be from Sidon; Beirut, Museum of the American University, inv. no. 6098; see p. 182, fig. 16. 1. Length 10.5 cm. B, bottom of a grey karkhesion with medallion in relief from Abdera; Saarbrücken, private collection. Greatest diameter 7.6 cm.

BUCHHOLZ

Plate 28. Double tumulus at Pazhok.

Plate 29. Inner tumulus at Pazhok with a circular pit in the centre, shingle of white stones over the tumulus and ring of darker orthostats. Piece of outer tumulus ring beyond.

HAMMOND

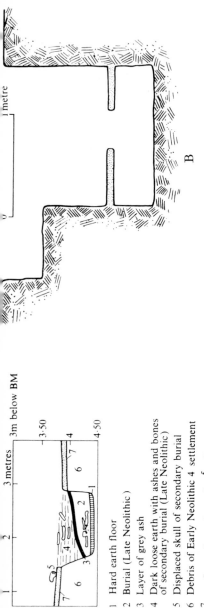

3m below **BM**

3 metres

3·50

4·50

1 Hard earth floor
2 Burial (Late Neolithic)
3 Layer of grey ash
4 Dark loose earth with ashes and bones
   of secondary burial (Late Neolithic)
5 Displaced skull of secondary burial
6 Debris of Early Neolithic 4 settlement
7   ,,   ,,   5   ,,

A

1 metre

B

TUMULUS

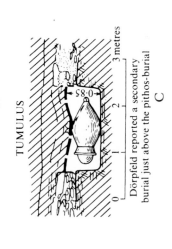

0   1   2   3 metres

Dörpfeld reported a secondary
burial just above the pithos-burial

C

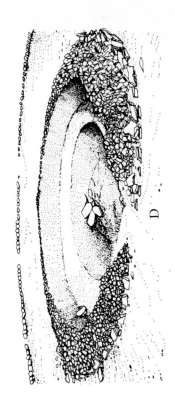

D

Plate 30. A, Circular burial-pit and two burials at Servia.
B, Circular burial-pit without remains at Vergina.
C, Tumulus and mortuary chamber at Nidhri in Leucas.
D, Double tumulus and circular burial-pit at Pazhok (after N. G. L. Hammond, *Macedonia* (in press)).

HAMMOND

Plate 31. Thera. Part of a fresco showing children boxing.

MARINATOS

Plate 32. Thera. Part of a fresco showing oryx-antelopes.

MARINATOS

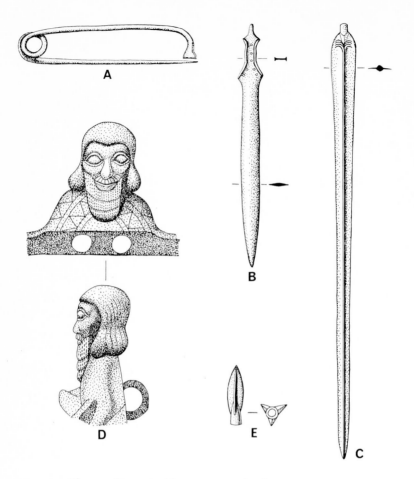

Plate 33. 'Intrusive' bronze types in the Aegean area.
A, violin-bow fibula (Mycenae). Scale 1:2.
B, flange-hilted cut-and-thrust sword (*Griffzungenschwert*) (Siteia region, Crete). Scale 1:8.
C, Minoan rapier (Karo's type A) (Arkalokhori, Crete). Scale 1:8.
D, 'Siren'-attachment from cauldron (Olympia). Scale 1:2.
E, 'Scythian' arrowhead (Athens). Scale 1:2.

SNODGRASS

Ethnic problems raised by recent discoveries on Thera

Sp. MARINATOS

Directorate of Antiquities of Greece, Athens

THERA is revealing to us a town of the richest period of the Aegean Bronze Age. The whole character of the town, which lies buried under a thick layer of volcanic ashes, is highly interesting. The town was abandoned hastily, and so everything but the most precious movable objects lies *in situ*. No skeletal remains have been found, so the inhabitants apparently had time to escape. Art and architecture are Cycladic in character but with a strong Minoan influence and much pottery was imported from Crete. Only the ethnic questions raised by some of the latest finds in my excavations of the town will be discussed in this paper, as they seem especially relevant to the theme of this Colloquium.

The frescoes are exceptionally interesting finds. Among them there is one of a man's head about half natural size (maximum length from top of the head to chin: 0·10 cm; *Frontispiece*). The anthropological features differ from anything we know in the field of Minoan and Mycenaean art, and so the person represented became known as 'The African' (Marinatos 1969a: 54, pl. B/3, 4; 1969: 374). He is distinguished by extremely thick lips, pug nose, a 'notched' eye-brow, short wavy hair. Two blue ribbon-like objects project from the hair and could be plumes. Lastly, a huge circular ear-ring hangs from his ear. In Egyptian art, these last two ornaments are peculiar to Nubians. But the Theran fresco clearly does not show a Nubian, and the figure's skin colour is red, as is the rule for men in Minoan-Mycenaean paintings. Semitic people, on the other hand, are not represented with ear-rings and feathers in Egyptian works of art. The Theran personage might be called a kind of Bedouin, but I preferred the general term 'African'.

The ethnic problem is not restricted to him. One of the two graceful children who appear to be boxing is again wearing a large ear-ring and both have blue wigs (perhaps of lapis lazuli) which are well known from Egyptian and Near Eastern literary texts and works of art (Pl. 31, Marinatos 1967: 1–2). Furthermore, we should mention that two further frescoes depict a herd of East African blue monkeys (*Cercopithecus Callitrichus*) and a herd of East African antelopes (*Oryx Beissa*; Pl. 32).

Thus, a racial problem emerges from the Thera excavations. To begin with, the artist must have known the African or Syrian desert animals well. They had been truly studied and their habits are so vividly rendered. They are not depicted according to a mere artistic tradition, as for instance the lion, at all times. On the other hand, it is problematic whether monkeys and antelopes, presumably from the early quaternary geological period before the sinking of the Aegean region, could have survived on a tiny volcanic island such as Thera. It is more probable that such animals were brought there by people coming from Africa or Syria. We know indeed from many works of art, Egyptian, Assyrian and others, that monkeys and antelopes travelled with groups of emigrants or were presented as gifts and tribute.

The Aegean prehistorian should always correlate his conclusions with 'mythology', that is to say with proto-historic tradition. In the case of Thera, tradition seems to fit well with the results of the excavations. There are two separate traditions about the earliest inhabitants of Thera. The first is concerned with what we term prehistory. It reports that Kadmos, when in search of Europa, and before he reached Thebes, came to Thera, whose name was then Kalliste. A number of his men remained there, under the leadership of one of his relatives, Membliaros (Hdt. IV, 147; Paus. III, i, 7). The second tradition is concerned with historical times. According to it, the Spartan Theras, son of Autesion, colonized the island and gave his own name to it. This tradition is well known, as it is further connected with the colonization of Cyrene in Africa. It is, however, interesting that Theras is in some way connected with the former mythological tradition, as he is descended from Theban ancestors. He was *genos Kadmeios* and he went not as a conqueror, but as a friend welcome to his relatives in Thera (*es tous suggeneas*; Hdt. IV, 147).

We cannot as yet suggest definite dates. All antiquities unearthed at Thera show that the town was buried about 1520 to 1500 B.C. under the ashes of the tremendous volcanic explosion that took place then. The 'African' fresco should be assigned for preference to the turbulent Hyksos period with which some scholars have connected the legend of Danaos and Aigyptos. According to Herodotus, only eight generations separated Theras from Membliaros. Moreover, no tomb of the Greek period at Thera could be much earlier than 700 B.C. and there is no Protogeometric phase at Thera (Cook 1960: 107; Huxley 1962: 105 fn. 99). In view of this, Membliaros might be dated to the very end of the Mycenean era or even to the Protogeometric period. But this is not compatible with his Theban ancestry and with the early date of the Kadmos legend as a whole. It would be premature to discuss this chronological problem further at present. It is enough to say that some eastern ethnic element seems to have been present on Thera as early as the sixteenth century B.C.

References

COOK, R. M. 1960. *Greek Painted Pottery*. London.

DESBOROUGH, V. R. D'A. 1952. *Protogeometric Pottery*. Oxford.

HUXLEY, G. L. 1962. *Early Sparta*. London.

MARINATOS, SP. 1967. *Kleidung, Haar- und Barttracht* (*Archaeologia Homerica* I, A-B; ed. F. Matz and H.-G. Buchholz). Göttingen.

——. 1969a. *Excavations at Thera II* (*Bibliothiki tis en Athinais Arkhaiologikis Etaireias*, 64; second fascicule).

——. 1969b. 'An African in Thera?' *AthAA*, 2: 374–5.

The identification of the 'Sea Peoples'

ALESSANDRA NIBBI

Oxford

IT may be relevant to the theme of this Colloquium to point out that the attacks on Egypt at the end of the Bronze Age in the Aegean should not be thought of as a migration. The Egyptian records considered as a whole do not suggest a migration, in the sense of a movement of a large number of people intending to settle in a new area, but only attacks on Egypt. We know that western Asiatic princes normally took their wives and families with them when they went south to Egypt periodically with their tribute.

The passages from Egyptian texts which are so often quoted to prove an invasion of Egypt and western Asia by the so-called 'Sea Peoples' have not been properly understood because they have been studied out of context and certain expressions like those for 'foreign countries' and 'isles' have been misunderstood precisely for that reason. The conclusion that the 'Sea Peoples' came from the sea and had previously been unknown to Egypt was reached soon after the relevant texts were discovered and before they could be seen in perspective in the context of the whole Egyptian literature of their period as we can see them today.

From the time of Merenptah (1236–1223 B.C.) we have four inscriptions that give an account of the attacks of peoples from the northern lands against Egypt (Kitchen, 1968; 2–24, Nos. 2, 3, 4, 5). Only one of these peoples, the *Ekwesh*, are referred to in these texts as being 'of the sea'. The Karnak inscription, which is the longest and most detailed of the four, tells us that the attackers were allied with the Libyans, that they possessed a very large number of metal objects including swords and knives, that they had cattle, goats, horses and leather tents and that they travelled with their families. All this is consistent with Asiatic practice. The records from both Karnak and Athribis tell us that all the attackers except the Libyans were circumcised.

A strong indication that they were Semitic comes from the 'Hymn of

Victory' (also called the 'Merenptah' or 'Israel Stele'), which tells us: 'The princes are prostrate, saying: "Shalam!" Not one raises his head among the Nine Bows.' (Pritchard 1955; 376). The use of the Semitic word *shalam* or *salam* in the Egyptian text with reference to men of the 'Nine Bows' (the allied attackers of Egypt's frontier) emphasizes this, as well as the fact that later inscriptions accompany labelled portraits of TWRWS, SHERDEN and SHEKELESH all of whom are bearded (Pritchard 1954: 4, fig. 9, 250).

Explicit statements that these attackers of Egypt's frontier were Asiatics occur in many inscriptions from the time of Ramesses III. One example is the passage where the god Amun-Re says to the Pharaoh: 'Thou hast taken captive him who violates thy frontier. My sword was with thee, over-throwing for thee the lands. Thou hast cut off the heads of the Asiatics'; to which Ramesses replies after the usual preliminaries: 'Thy sword is mine as a shield, that I may slay the plains and hill-countries which violate my frontier . . . the Peleset, the Denyen and the Shekelesh' (Edgerton and Wilson 1936: 46).

The Pharaoh states clearly that he has defeated these people *on their own territories*, which he has subsequently added to his own. He has also destroyed their towns and their trees (Edgerton and Wilson 1936: 54–57). Moreover, on a number of occasions they are shown speaking of *Baal*, spelt out in full in the earlier Egyptian inscriptions because he was a foreign god.

One of the difficulties about the so-called 'Sea Peoples' was their association with the 'Great Green' and the 'Isles'. While it would be agreed by many, if not all, Egyptologists today that the term 'isle' is often used for an inland area in ancient Egyptian (a definite example of the use occurring in the story of Sinuhe) there is no clear agreement about the meaning of the term 'Great Green', which is all too often translated by 'sea', even when this meaning does not make sense of the context. An example of this can be found when the weapons of the 'Sea Peoples' are said to be falling in the sea immediately *after* their ships have been recorded as having entered the Nile mouths (Edgerton and Wilson 1936: 41). 'Great Green' should be taken primarily to mean inland, fresh water, productive of vegetation, as its basic determinative, the papyrus stem (meaning 'green') suggests.

The reason for such an unprecedented attack on Egypt's frontier by western Asiatic states may have been the treaty concluded between Egypt and the Hittites in 1283 B.C. The text of this treaty suggests that it had been intended both as an offensive and defensive measure against western Asia. It may well be that during the fifty years that followed, leading up to the first attack on Egypt, the oppressed states felt that they had nothing to lose and everything to gain in an extreme effort to get back their independence.

The implications of the identification of these peoples as Western Asiatics will be far-reaching. We know that such people were traders who travelled far with their merchandise, often on foot, in the latter part of the second millennium B.C. We know too of their early skill in metal-working. Ferdinand Hoefer (1852: 65) suggested long ago that *Melqarth*, the god of the city of Tyre, came to be worshipped by the Greeks under the name *Herakles*, or was identified with Herakles by them, as a result of the trading activity of his protégés (Hoefer derives the name *Herakles* from Semitic *ha-rokel*, 'pedlar', from the root *r-g-l* or *r-k-l*, which occurs in Hebrew and in Arabic). The god Herakles may be an important clue when we consider cultural influences on the Greek mainland during the Late Bronze Age and in determining the identity of the *Herakleidai*, his 'sons and grandsons' (*Iliad* 2, 666).

References

BARNETT, R. D. 1969. 'The Sea Peoples.' *CAH* (rev ed.) II, Chap. XXVIII/Fasc. 68.
BREASTED, J. H. 1906. *Ancient Records of Egypt*. Chicago.
EDGERTON, W. F. and WILSON, J. A. 1936. *Historical Records of Ramesses*, III. Chicago.
HELCK, W. 1962. *Die Beziehungen Ägyptens zu Vorderasien im 3. und 2. Jahrtausend v. Chr.* Wiesbaden.
HOEFER, M. E. 1852. *Chaldée, Assyrie, Médie, Babylonie*. Paris.
KITCHEN, K. A. 1968. *Ramesside Inscriptions* IV/1. Oxford.
PRITCHARD, J. B. 1954. *The Ancient Near East in Pictures Relating to the Old Testament*. Princeton.
——. 1955. *Ancient Near Eastern Texts Relating to the Old Testament*. Princeton.

Discussion

R. D. BARNETT: The difficulties of identifying the ethnic names mentioned in the Egyptian texts which Dr. Nibbi has referred to must not be under-estimated, and in general it is risky to base identifications and theories on mere similarities between names recorded in texts in different languages. Contrary to Dr. Nibbi's statement, the general opinion among Egyptologists is that the 'Great Green' normally means the Mediterranean in Egyptian texts and that it is unlikely that it was ever used in referring to an inland area. While there is no doubt that Greeks identified Melqarth with Herakles very early it is most improbable that the name *Herakles* represents a borrowing of *ha-rokel*, for the following reasons: the assumed transference of the Semitic article *ha-* with a noun borrowed into Greek seems to be unparalleled; *rokel* would most naturally have been adopted by Greeks as *Rokelos*, not as *Herakles*; there is no evidence whatever that

Melqarth was ever imagined as a pedlar, merchant or patron of merchants, or that he had the epithet *ha-rokel*.

M. S. DROWER: A number of points in Dr. Nibbi's paper call for comment. First, the Egyptians of the reigns of Merneptah and Ramesses III distinguished the peoples whom they called 'northerners' regularly and without difficulty from the peoples of Western Asia, the inhabitants of Syria, Palestine and Sinai, to whom they gave the names *Aamu*, *Fenkhu*, Canaanites, Hurrians, people of *Retenu*, people of *Djahy*. Such Asiatics are also distinguished pictorially in all periods by their dress and accoutrements from the other traditional enemies of the Egyptians, the Libyans and the Nubians. All are included among 'the Nine Bows'. The 'Sea Peoples' were recognized to be different both from the two latter and from Asiatics, and their novelty is stressed by implication in the inscriptions. In Egyptian reliefs beards are characteristic not only of Semites but also of the linguistically non-Semitic Mitannians, the peoples of Punt, the Aegean and Libya, and occasionally of Nubians; i.e. of almost anyone who was not an Egyptian or a Hittite. Some of the prisoners in the Medinet Habu reliefs have short square beards, different from the typical long pointed or heavy bushy beards of Asiatics. Others are beardless.

The Semitic word *sala(a)m* had apparently been borrowed into Egyptian by the time of the XIXth Dynasty; the *Meshwesh* (Libyans) use it in addressing Ramesses III (Helck 1962: 570–1, No. 225; Burkhardt, M. 1909: Nos. 866–70). The Asiatic storm- and war-god Baal was adopted into the Egyptian royal cult in the nineteenth dynasty (Helck 1962: 482–4, 503–5); both Seti I and Ramesses II are described as 'terrifying like Baal' in battle against the Hittites, and at Medinet Habu, Ramesses III rages like Baal against both Libyans and Asiatics (Edgerton and Wilson, 1936, *passim*) and Amon-Reʿ calls him 'my son, Baal in wrath'.

On the use of the 'Great Green' and 'the isles', cf. W. Erichsen (1933): "I made for thee ships with bowmen equipped with their weapons upon the Great Green . . . in order to transport the goods of the land of Djahy (Phoenicia) and of the countries of the ends of the earth to thy great treasuries."; also Pritchard 1954: 260. It should further be noted that in the story of the Shipwrecked Sailor, the Great Green must be the Red Sea or Indian Ocean, and that the "Keftiu and the Isle in the midst of the Great Green" in Theban tombs of the eighteenth dynasty wear Minoan-Mycenaean dress.

R. A. CROSSLAND: The paper and discussion of it have shown that accepted identifications of peoples mentioned as invaders in Egyptian texts of the end of the first millennium, whom we refer to as the 'Sea Peoples', may need reconsideration. The Egyptian evidence about these peoples is clearly of the first importance for the history of the Aegean Late Bronze

Age, in view of the strong indications that it was migrating peoples who caused the evident disturbance and destruction which took place in Anatolia and in the south-eastern Aegean, at least, c.1200–1100 B.C., and of the theory that their migrations were part of a more extensive series of ethnic movements which originated in the Balkans north of Greece or in central Europe. These events and the Egyptian and other documentary evidence relevant to them need to be discussed in detail at a future meeting.

References

BURCKHARDT, M. 1909. *Die altkanaanäische Fremdwörter und Eigennamen im Ägyptischen* Berlin.

ERICHSEN, W. 1933. *Papyrus Harris* I (*Bibliotheca Aegyptiaca* 5). Brussels.

Metal-work as evidence for immigration in the Late Bronze Age

A. M. SNODGRASS

University of Edinburgh

THE great wave of destruction and abandonment of Mycenaean sites at or near the end of the Late Helladic IIIB period is one of the inescapable landmarks of the Aegean Late Bronze Age. For the past twenty years and more, however, many scholars have also seen it as something else: as the occasion of a mass-immigration and permanent settlement in Greece of non-Mycenaean peoples.

The prime basis for this conclusion is the occurrence of new metal types in Greece at this time; it is true that much other evidence has been adduced as well, but this supporting evidence is not, on its own, decisive. There is first of all the mere fact of the destructions; but these (like other destructions in prehistory) in themselves betray nothing about the agency behind them; still less do they imply anything about the subsequent settlement of the destroyers in Greece. Thus Miss N. K. Sandars, in her review-article on V. R. Desborough's work (Desborough 1964), proposed attributing these destructions to raiders who afterwards withdrew (Sandars 1964: 259). Next, there is the fortification-wall built at this period at the Isthmus of Corinth: we must now accept this as a northward-facing wall which ran right across the isthmus, in the light of O. Broneer's latest investigations (Broneer 1966 and 1968). But the wall in itself does not imply a threat from beyond the Mycenaean world, rather than from, say, central Greece. Again, we have the undoubtedly significant coincidence of this epoch with the activities of the land and sea raiders recorded in Egyptian and Hittite documents; but these texts scarcely suggest that this agency lay behind the Aegean destructions, and they give no hint of permanent settlement by the raiders in Greece.

When we examine the other archaeological evidence from the Aegean, we find that the testimony of architecture, of funerary practices, of grave goods, and above all of pottery, so far from giving any suggestion of the arrival of a non-Mycenaean population, presents an almost uniform picture of the post-destruction period, the earlier part of Late Helladic IIIC, as a survival of its predecessor. It is the new metal types, and they alone, which form the corner-stone of the case for mass-migration. Most of the scholars who incline to accept that this occurred regard it as immigration, or perhaps merely infiltration, from the north. It is unnecessary here to review the voluminous literature on this question, beyond acknowledging the influence of V. Milojčić's initial paper (Milojčić 1949), and beyond citing one or two important recent authorities, such as Professor M. Gimbutas (Gimbutas 1965: especially 339), and the late Professor E. Grumach who harnessed this evidence to the radical theory that the first coming of the Greek-speakers of any kind took place at this time, and that their point of departure was the western Danube basin (Grumach 1969: 50).

Let us therefore scrutinize these metal types (they are all bronzes) more closely, and see how far they justify the inference of immigration and permanent settlement from their regions of origin. None is more important than the *violin-bow fibula* (Pl. 33A; for good recent discussions, see Desborough 1964: 54–8; Gimbutas 1965: 113–16), and to its case we may apply certain particular arguments. Those who cite this type as evidence for migration of Central European peoples southwards into Greece seem to me to be positing an odd historical coincidence. For all authorities agree that the violin-bow fibula makes its first appearances, whether in the proto-Urnfield phase of central Europe, in the Terremare of northern Italy, or in the Aegean of LH IIIB–C, at roughly the same time. It is not any clear indication of temporal priority in the north that leads most people to ascribe a northern origin to the type, so much as the association of the fibula with thicker clothing and therefore with a cooler climate. Thus, on the 'migration' hypothesis, it follows that the invention of the violin-bow fibula in one of these three areas must have been followed by a strangely swift *diaspora* of its wearers to the other two regions. This would have to be coincidental, since the fibula could hardly be causally linked to a migration. But if, on the other hand, we ascribe the diffusion of the fibula to its own merits, however humble, as a form of dress-fastening, then the element of coincidence disappears: it spread swiftly because it was a good idea.

The factor of climatic change in Europe in the thirteenth and twelfth centuries B.C. has also been introduced into this problem; but I do not think that it alters the arguments. The fibula and its associated costume may well have been first adopted in the middle Danube region because the climate had become cooler and wetter there; and it seems to have got relatively cooler and wetter in the Aegean area too, although in neither case are the climatological data precise in terms of date (Frenzel 1966: 113, 118). This change was no doubt a contributory cause for the adoption and retention of the fibula in Greece. But this argument is not easily combined with the hypothesis of a southward migration, unless one supposes that the climate in Greece, for some centuries after 1200 B.C., was colder and wetter than that of Czechoslovakia and Hungary hitherto; for fibulae of this type and its successors were commonly worn in Greece right down to the seventh century B.C.

If we turn from fibulae to weapons, and especially to that weapon whose chronology, diffusion and significance seem to have much in common with those of the violin-bow fibula, namely the *Griffzungenschwert* (flange-hilted cut-and-thrust sword; Pl. 33B), then the case changes. First, the degree of coincidence involved in a hypothesis of southward migration is slighter: for the development of a new weapon might serve as a spur to an armed migration, or at least ensure its successful outcome, and so a causal connection could exist. Once again, it is true that the *Griffzungenschwert* was an important new development whose very wide diffusion began soon after its perfection (Cowen 1966). In this situation, I can only say that I again find it a more attractive hypothesis to believe that the qualities of the sword itself, appreciable as they are, were responsible for its wide distribution, rather than the mass-migration of its bearers.

There is a further argument, relevant to both these bronze types, which there is not time to develop here, but which I regard as of great significance for this problem: namely, that these intrusive bronzes are now attested in Mycenaean graves of pure LH IIIB date, and were thus demonstrably used by Mycenaeans before the horizon of the great destructions.

I now wish to cite briefly one or two cases of new metal types and practices from other periods in the Aegean, which seem to me further to weaken the hypothesis of migration if based on intrusive metal-work.

First, there were few steps in Greek metallurgy more important than the introduction of the full-length sword to the Greek mainland. It appears in the two circles of shaft-graves at Mycenae; here, from my own calculations based on the available publications (Karo 1930; Mylonas 1957: 128–75; Sandars 1961), out of 56 traceable swords from these graves, at least 41 are of a long type of rapier (Pl. 33C; Karo's type A) which most scholars agree to be of Minoan derivation. Yet few today would claim that the shaft-grave rulers, or the inhabitants of other parts of the Greek mainland who soon adopted this sword, were Cretan immigrants.

Secondly, and conversely, an era for which almost all scholars agree in accepting a wave of immigration and permanent settlement in Greece is Early Helladic III and the early part of Middle Helladic. Yet how far is this belief founded on innovations in metallurgy? I suspect that not only is the answer 'Not at all', but that on the contrary the new era was marked by something of a metallurgical recession (Vermeule 1964: 75).

Next, by overstepping the chronological limits of this colloquium it is possible to attain greater certainty. A major innovation in Greek metal-work of a later period, around 700 B.C., was the adoption of the Oriental type of bronze tripod-stand with separate cauldron. This ousted, almost totally, the old Geometric Greek type of one-piece tripod cauldron, and became a characteristic article of domestic and sacral metal-work in seventh-century Greece. A common variety had siren-attachments round its rim (Pl. 33D), and a recent authority has shown that out of 49 such attachments known from Greece, 37 are of actual Oriental workmanship and only 12 are Greek adaptations (Herrmann 1966: 30–2, 57–8 as against 91–2, 102). Yet mass-immigration of Orientals into Greece at this date is out of the question, and even the theory of immigrant craftsmen is hotly debated.

Later still, in the seventh, sixth and fifth centuries B.C., Greece whole-heartedly adopted a new type of arrow-head, the tiny socketed bronze form, usually of roughly triangular outline, and this is overall by far the common-est type on Greek sites of these periods (Pl. 33E; Snodgrass 1964: 148–54). It had been devised by the Cimmerians or Scyths and partly diffused, it is true, by their warlike migrations in western Asia. But we have no evidence that a Cimmerian or Scyth ever discharged a bow in anger on the soil of mainland Greece or the islands, at least until the later sixth century B.C.

Although I wish to confine my arguments to the Aegean area, and indeed largely to the Greek mainland proper, I suspect that supporting evidence could be adduced from Etruria, either from the sudden increase in the range and quantity of fibulae in the graves at Quattro Fontanili, Veii, about 800 B.C. (Close-Brooks 1968: 323–9), or from the more general and massive influx of foreign metal-work in Etruscan graves about a century later; for a major immigration into Etruria at either time is coming to appear increas-ingly unlikely.

In these later instances, there is historical evidence which helps to provide an ultimate barrier to any hypothesis of mass-immigration. For the Aegean Late Bronze Age such evidence is largely absent, though not entirely so. The later cases provide archaeological evidence of other kinds, from pottery and other materials, and from continuity of settlements and cemeteries, which I think would have been on its own a strong deterrent to such a hypothesis. Archaeological evidence of this kind is present in the Aegean Late Bronze Age, for all the violence of the destructions around 1200 B.C., and it is at least arguable that its collective weight is greater than that of the new 'northern' bronzes. I have concentrated on those types which make their appearance in the era of the great destructions, but it should be observed that hypotheses of foreign immigration have been founded, at least in part, not only on the later series of bronzes which appear in Mycenaean graves from the late twelfth century onwards (the so-called 'second wave'; e.g. Desborough 1964: 70–2), but also on the introduction of practical iron-working to Greece in the eleventh and tenth centuries (e.g. Kimmig 1964: 241–4).

My own belief is that the civilization of the Aegean in the Late Bronze Age (and probably in the other periods referred to in the list of examples above) was a culture too sophisticated in its organization, with trade-contacts that were too long-standing and widespread, and perhaps with a degree of specialization in labour that was too high, for us to be able to base hypotheses of foreign immigration on the appearance of new metal types in its area, in a way that is the common and undoubtedly justified practice with some other prehistoric cultures. I would finally stress that I am arguing not against the incidence of violence and turmoil in the Aegean of *c.* 1200 B.C., since that is self-evident; nor against the presence of individual foreigners, whether as traders, pirates or mercenary soldiers, from central Europe and elsewhere, since this too seems extremely likely; but against assumption of the mass-immigration and permanent settlement of non-Mycenaeans in Greece, when this theory depends to any considerable degree on the appearance of new metal types and practices there.

References

BRONEER, O. 1966. 'The Cyclopean wall at the Isthmus of Corinth and its bearing on Late Bronze Age chronology.' *Hesperia*, 35: 346–62.

——. 1968. 'The Cyclopean wall at the Isthmus of Corinth and its bearing on Late Bronze Age chronology: Addendum.' *Hesperia*, 37: 25–35.

CLOSE-BROOKS, J. 1968. 'Considerazioni sulla cronologia delle facies arcaiche dell'-Etruria.' *StEtr*, 35: 323–9.

COWEN, J. D. 1966. 'The origins of the flange-hilted sword of bronze in Continental Europe.' *ProcPS*, 32: 262–312.

DESBOROUGH, V. R. D'A 1964. *The last Mycenaeans and their Successors*. Oxford.

FRENZEL, B. 1966. 'The Atlantic/Sub-Boreal transition.' *World Climate from 8000 to 0 BC.* (Royal Meteorological Society): 99–123.

GIMBUTAS, M. 1965. *Bronze Age Cultures in Central and Eastern Europe*. The Hague.

GRUMACH, E. 1969. *The Coming of the Greeks* (reprinted from *Bulletin of the John Rylands Library*, 51, 1 and 2). Manchester.

HERRMANN, H. V. 1966. 'Die Kessel der orientalisierenden Zeit, I.' *Olympische Forschungen*, 6. Berlin.

KARO, G. 1930. *Die Schachtgraber von Mykenai*. Munich.

KIMMIG, W. 1964. 'Seevölkerbewegung und Urnenfelderkultur'; in R. von Uslar and K. J. Narr, *Studien aus Alteuropa* I (*Beihefte der BonnJbb*, 10/1; Cologne): 220–83.

MILOJČIĆ, V. 1949. 'Die dorische Wanderung im lichte der vorgeschichtlichen Funde.' *JdI/AA*, 63/64 (1948/49) *Beiblatt*: 11–30.

MYLONAS, G. 1957. *Ancient Mycenae*. London.

SANDARS, N. K. 1961. 'The First Aegean swords and their ancestry.' *AJA*, 65: 17–29.

——. 1964. 'The Last Mycenaeans and the European Late Bronze Age.' *Antiquity*, 38: 258–62.

SNODGRASS, A. M. 1964. *Early Greek Armour and Weapons*. Edinburgh.

VERMEULE, E. T. 1964. *Greece in the Bronze Age*. Chicago.

Discussion

JAN BOUZEK: The fibula is a development of the European pin, not of Mycenaean buttons, and therefore could hardly have originated in Mycenaean Greece, where buttons were used only exceptionally. The distribution of many metal objects over a vast area of Europe and the eastern Mediterranean between the thirteenth and twelfth centuries B.C. is a unique event which has no parallel throughout the whole of the rest of the Bronze Age and the early Iron Age. Unlike the later diffusion of metal types, which was never so wide or so homogeneous, that of the late thirteenth century and the early twelfth is contemporaneous with the large-scale downfall of a complete culture; cities were destroyed and only partially rebuilt in much impoverished style, arts and crafts declined, writing and fine *objets d'art* disappeared, population decreased; at the same time many new elements were introduced in pottery and probably also in architecture (oval houses; and cf. hut models from Crete). Most historically attested migrations have left considerably less archaeological evidence of such kinds.

Movements of populations in Attica at the end of the Mycenaean period

CHRISTIANE SOURVINOU-INWOOD

St. Hugh's College, Oxford

ONE of the main claims of the Athenians was that their city had been a refuge for all Greeks in times of trouble (Thucydides I, ii, 6). Archaeological evidence has shown this to be true, at least for the period immediately following the destructions of the end of the Late Helladic IIIB. (The desertion of other areas of the Greek mainland contrasts with the flourishing condition of eastern Attica in LH IIIC; Hope-Simpson 1965; map; Desborough 1964; *passim*; Ålin 1962; *passim*). The purpose of this short paper is to suggest some probable patterns of movements of refugees in Attica in the transition from LH IIIB to IIIC.

Many people are supposed to have moved in that region in this period, but in the short space that we have available here we will mainly be concerned with the movement of refugees from Pylos, and the implications of these movements. That Pylians moved into Attica was a tradition deeply rooted in the memory of the Greeks (Herodotus v, 65, 146; Demon, *FGrH* 327, frag. 1; Hellanicus, *FGrH* frag. 125; Pherecydes, *FGrH* frag. 155; Pausanias II, xviii, 7, VII, ii, 1–2, IX, v, 16; Strabo XIV, 633) and it is not in contradiction with the archaeological evidence. We are interested in tracing their itinerary in that region.

Imports to the Pylos region, let alone tradition, show that its people were able sailors and traders (on the Homeric Catalogue of ships and traditions about the Minyans and their connections with the Pylians cf. Nilsson 1932: 139–43: Marinatos 1968: 293: Hope-Simpson and Lazenby 1970: 173–5). As the catastrophe which put an end to the palace at Ano Englianos seems to have come by land (Desborough 1964: 223–4), the Pylian fleet must have survived; its existence is indicated by the *o-ka* tablets (Mühlestein 1956) and the Tragana *pyxis* (Kourouniotis 1914: 107–10, figs. 13–15). And it is reasonable to suppose that the Pylians fled by sea, in their fleet, and that their main concern was to find good harbours in a new homeland which would allow them to continue their trading activities. The eastern coast of Attica offered the possibility of trading with the central and southern Aegean, an area untouched by the great catastrophe, and with the eastern Mediterranean areas (Desborough 1964: 227–8, 230, 238). It is established that this eastern coast received an influx of refugees at this time of transition from IIIB to IIIC (Desborough 1964: 115; Hope-Simpson 1965: map). It is interesting to observe that four out of the seven IIIC sites discovered on it are concentrated in a small area near Brauron, where later tradition knows Neleids, Peisistratus and his family, living in the deme of Philaïdai (Herod. v, 165; Diogenes Laertius I, 53; Plato, *Hipparchus*, 228b; Plutarch, *Solon*, x, 2; Hope-Simpson 1965: 364, 366–8, map). These sites are Brauron, Ligori, Kopreza, Perati. On the basis of the large number of objects showing intense contacts with the Levant (including Cyprus), Egypt, Anatolia and the islands of the Aegean, the excavator of Perati affirms that this cemetery reflects a very important settlement of sea-farers and traders (Yakovidhis 1964: 87–90). It starts in the transition from IIIB to IIIC. So we have a cemetery of traders and sea-farers in the area where Neleid families are established in later times, starting when one would expect the Neleids and the Pylians in general to arrive in Attica. It seems only reasonable to connect Perati with the Pylian refugees. There are some links between the pottery of Perati and the pottery of Pylos, but as the similarities are in common shapes and decoration, this evidence cannot be conclusive (cf. shape 65c of Pylos; Blegen and Rawson 1966: fig. 39/i; also the pot from Perati; *Praktika* 1953: 100 fig. 12, Blegen and Rawson 1966: fig. 353; and *Praktika* 1958: pl. 24a/509; shape 48a, Blegen and Rawson 1966: fig. 371 and *Praktika* 1959: pl. 9/720).

According to one tradition the first stop of the Neleid Melanthos in Attica was Eleusis (Demon, *FGrH*, 327 A.; the other traditions do not mention specific places). That this Pylian family had some sort of connection with Eleusis seems to be a genuine memory, since we are informed by another, independent, tradition that when the Neleids migrated to Anatolia they held the priesthood of the Eleusinian Demeter (Strabo XIV, 633). We should consequently suppose that the Pylians, on their arrival in Attica, divided themselves into two groups, one of which went to the Brauron-Porto Rafti area, and the other to Eleusis, which has a reasonably good and well-protected harbour. However, they did not stay in Eleusis for long. In the tradition Melanthos becomes king of Athens (Herodotus v, 65; Pausanias II, xviii, 7; see Toepffer 1894: 2672–5 for more references). In archaeology it seems that there is a break in IIIC1 and some sort of desertion (the IIIC material from Eleusis is not published; Desborough 1964: 115; Hope-Simpson 1965: 110). Where did these people go, then? To Athens, some of them, according to the Melanthos-Kodros tradition. I suggest that this movement is reflected in the Kerameikos cemetery. But this we shall discuss below. It is obvious that this hypothesis implies the acceptance of Desborough's suggestion (Desborough 1964: 20) that the sub-Mycenaean Kerameikos is contemporary with the late IIIC of some other areas. I accept this, but I have reservations as far as the IIIC phase in the Argolid is concerned. Our evidence about a possible increase of population in Athens at the beginning of the sub-Mycenaean period is very sparse indeed, and we should not in any case suppose a shift of very large numbers of people from Eleusis to the city. Where did the rest of these people go, then? A logical refuge for people running away from Eleusis would be the neighbouring island of Salamis, especially if the refugees were sea-farers. And it is highly suggestive that at approximately the time of the Eleusinian break a very important cemetery of cist-tombs starts to be used on Salamis, on the coast just opposite Eleusis, the cemetery of the Arsenal (Hope-Simpson 1965: 111, map, Eleusis no. 386, Arsenal on Salamis no. 387; Ålin 1962: 114; Wide 1910; Styrenius 1962; cist-tombs in the Arsenal cemetery perhaps show the arrival of newcomers, but the area seems to have been inhabited before; Hope-Simpson and Lazenby 1970: 59). The bulk of the pottery is sub-Mycenaean, an early sub-Mycenaean directly linked (stylistically) with IIIC (Kraiker 1939: 134); according to Furumark and Styrenius a number of pieces are purely IIIC (Furumark 1941: 77; Styrenius 1962: 121–3; Styrenius there assigns a false-necked jar, No. 3614, and an *amphoriskos*, No. 3632, to IIIC). What is more important, Mylonas seems to suggest that there are parallels between the unpublished material from his excavations at Eleusis and the Salaminian pottery (Mylonas 1936: 426, fn. 2). Under these circumstances, the conjecture that some people moved to Salamis and established themselves in the Arsenal area at some stage in IIIC 1 seems reasonable. Tradition can perhaps be of some help. It tells of a certain Skiros, a seer from Eleusis, who is supposed to have instituted the cult of Athena Skiras in Athens. And there is another Skiros, connected with Salamis, who in one tradition is supposed to have established a settlement there (Photius, *Lexicon*, s.v. *Skiros*; Paus. I, xxxvi, 4; Harpocration, s.v. *Skiron*; Suidas, s.v. *Skiron*; Plut., *Theseus*, XVII, 6; Hesychius, s.v. *Skiras Athena*). Since it was ably argued long ago that these two persons are the result of the splitting of one original figure (Schmidt 1927), because the cult of Athena Skiras which the Eleusinian Skiros is supposed to have instituted is clearly a Salaminian cult (Robert 1885: 349–51. Ferguson 1938: 15–17), we have a memory of people from Eleusis establishing a settlement on Salamis, a memory which supports our previous hypothesis.

The period of use of the cemetery of the Arsenal covers the Early sub-Mycenaean phase; there are some Middle sub-Mycenaean tombs as well (Styrenius 1962: 121–3; 1967: 39). To the question of what happened to these people afterwards, tradition answers: they migrated to Athens and the eastern coast of Attica. Philaios, son or grandson of Aias, or Philaios and Eurysakes, sons of Aias, are supposed in some traditions to have conceded the island of Salamis to the Athenians and, in all traditions, to have migrated to Attica where they—or he—acquired Athenian citizenship (Her. VI, 35; Pherecydes, *FGrH*, 3 F 2; Paus I, XXXV,1; Scholia Pindar Nemean Odes II, 19, Boeckh; Stephanus Byzantinus, *s.v. Philaïdes*; Plut., *Solon*, x, 2; Harpocration, *s.v. Eurysakeion*). The tradition which mentions both of them gives more details: Eurysakes went to Melite and Philaios to Brauron, where he became the eponym of the deme of the Philaïdai (Plut., *Solon*, x, 2). So it suggests that the second movement from Salamis followed a pattern similar to that which we suggested for the movements of the Pylians when they first arrived in Attica. We supposed that part, perhaps the most important part, of the population which moved from Eleusis to Salamis and from Salamis to Athens and the eastern coast were Pylians, and tradition seems to support this. Philaios is said to have been the son of Aias and Lysidike. It seems to me that the genealogy connecting him to Aias is false, a later construction which, as many scholars have suggested, aimed at associating the alleged donor of Salamis with the most famous hero of that island (Ferguson 1938: 16). And indeed this genealogy cannot stand up to the most superficial test: from the sixth century back to Aias only thirteen generations are given, which puts the Mycenaean hero at the end of the tenth century instead of the end of the thirteenth. We are then left with Philaios himself; Eurysakes, who, as has been suggested, seems to be a later construction based on the *eurù sákos* of Aias (Ferguson, 1938: 17); and Lysidike. Philaios is a Pylian name occurring in **PY Un** 249.1. Lysidike, his mother, is the daughter of the Lapith Koronas; there are some indications of Pylian connections for her too. There is another Lysidike, wife of the Neleid Boros and mother of Penthilos (Hellanicus, *FGrH*, I F 125) and this can hardly be a coincidence, given the close connections between Lapiths and Neleids (cf., e.g , Homer, *Iliad* I, 163–70; Lapiths and Neleids seem to coincide in the same localities very frequently). Koroneia, the only place-name in Attica named after her father Koronas (Steph. Byz. *s.v. Koroneia*) or indeed after any Lapith if we dismiss as one is tempted to do the dubious Perithoidai; Fontenrose 1937: 268, *s.v. Peirithoos*), is less than a mile away from Perati. Furthermore, G. Thompson states that the ancestral emblem displayed on the shields of the Neleid Peisistratids, a horse, and that of the Philaides, the hindquarters of a horse, are connected, and that the second has its origin in the first (Thompson 1954: 121).

We are now concerned with the implications of these patterns of movements, their reflection in the archaeological evidence. The cemetery of Perati reflects a clearly Mycenaean way of life (Desborough 1964: 115). Chamber tombs are the normal grave-type and the grave-offerings are typically Mycenaean. There are, however, some cist-tombs and some of the so-called 'non-Mycenaean' sub-Mycenaean features, for example a few fibulae. These seem to be late in date, supporting Desborough's theory of the contemporaneity of the later part of Perati with Kerameikos and Salamis (Desborough 1964:20, 116). One cannot exclude that these features may reflect a second wave of the Pylian movement to the east coast after the end of early sub-Mycenaean, at some stage in the middle sub-Mycenaean.

From the patterns traced above it is possible to distinguish an intriguing relation between the legendary movements of Pylians from Eleusis after the break in IIICI and the appearance of cist-tombs in Attica. The refugees go to Athens and Salamis (at least this is a reasonable suggestion) and shortly afterwards we have the sub-Mycenaean cemeteries of cist-tombs in Kerameikos and on Salamis. The origin of this grave-type is controversial. Desborough thinks that it comes from the North (Desborough 1964: 37–8), but until the presence of this type of cist-tomb is well established in the northern regions (and for the moment Sandar's statement that it is very rare north of Pindus is still valid; Sandars 1964: 261) one is rather inclined to believe in Deshayes' and Styrenius' theory of a revival of the MH cist-tombs (Deshayes 1966: 241–3; Styrenius 1962: 121; 1967: 161–2), especially since new archaeological finds make clear that this grave-type survived much more widely than was previously believed during the Mycenaean period (Deshayes 1966: 241; the two groups of cist-tombs recently discovered by J. P. Vokotopoulou in Epirus in a LH IIIB/C context cannot support the theory of a northern origin of the grave-type, as the excavator herself states; they are not sufficiently northern in characteristics and are under Mycenaean influence; Vokotopoulou 1969: 206).

We have already observed that tradition and archaeological evidence indicate that people who left Eleusis in IIICI appear in those places in which cist-tombs appear. This is highly suggestive, given the fact that Eleusis is the one and only site in Greece where cist-tombs are the normal grave-type and chamber-tombs the exception in the LH period (Desborough 1964: 114; Mylonas 1932: 40–1; 1961: 33). When one sees that the sites in Attica which show sub-Mycenaean cist-tombs are those at places for which an influx of people has been postulated from the very locality which preserved this grave-type throughout the whole LH period (i.e. Eleusis) one is tempted to connect the two things. I suggest that this relation (*a*) is a further element in favour of the patterns of movement traced above and (*b*) allows the conjecture that early sub-Mycenaean cist-tombs in Attica are dependent on Eleusis. The low expense which the construction of a cist-tomb requires, as compared with that of a chamber-tomb, could explain the general acceptance of this grave-type in a time of relative poverty.

As for the grave-offerings such as fibulae and long dress-pins, I think that Deshayes has shown convincingly that they need not be of northern origin at all (Deshayes 1966: 205–8, 243; Muscarella 1964: 35). He has also suggested that the sub-Mycenaean culture developed in the Argolid and expanded from there, and Styrenius has supported this suggestion (Deshayes 1966: 195, 247, 251; Styrenius 1967: 163). There is not enough evidence, I think, to speak of movements of Argives to Attica, as Styrenius does; but some sort of 'culture exchanges' between the Argolid and Attica, and even an influence of the Argive sub-Mycenaean in Attica, cannot be excluded. This is perhaps reflected in the tradition which makes the Kypselids of the north-east Peloponnese relatives of the Salaminian Philaids through the Lapiths, a genuine memory one would think, since Kypselos' ancestor Melas bears a name connected with the Neleid presence in Attica (cf. also Melanthos, Melainai, Dionysos Melanaigis; see Herod. v, 92, vi, 198; Paus. ii, iv. 4, v, xviii, 2).

It has been argued that anthropological study of the Kerameikos skulls and skeletons shows the presence of people with northern racial characteristics, and that this is in agreement with the linguistic evidence suggesting the presence of Doric elements in Attic-Ionic, which must have infiltrated the dialect before the Ionic migration (Desborough 1964: 40, 245; Chadwick 1956: 38–40). The anthropological evidence is somewhat puzzling for the non-specialist. The two scholars who have published relatively extensive studies of the available skeletal material from Attica have come to different conclusions. J. L. Angel concludes that the material of sub-Mycenaean date from Attica indicates the arrival of newcomers, probably from the North. He has studied for the sub-Mycenaean period and the early Protogeometric nineteen skulls and twelve skeletons from Kerameikos, two skulls from Salamis and a skeleton (of Protogeometric date) from the Agora. The two individuals from Salamis are classed as 'Basic White' (a type considered to have been frequent in Greece since the Neolithic; cf. Angel 1945: 285–6, 291–4); so his conclusions would appear to be based on the Protogeometric skeletons from the Agora and the Kerameikos material (Angel 1945: 300, 322–4; it seems to be generally accepted that no important influx of population into Attica occurred within the Protogeometric period; thus the material of Protogeometric date may be considered relevant to the comparison in which we are interested). The Kerameikos material had been studied and published by E. Breitinger six years before Angel's article. Breitinger's conclusions were that 'pure northern' elements are extremely sporadic in the material; mixed physical types with some 'northern' features are somewhat less rare (Breitinger 1939: 253). Breitinger seems to identify the 'northern' elements with the 'Greeks' and the others with 'pre-Greeks' who absorbed them. One can hardly regard the anthropological evidence as conclusive.

As for the linguistic evidence, the alleged presence of Doric elements in Attic is no more than an implication of the Porzig-Risch theory of the origin of the dialects of Greek (Porzig 1954: 147–50; Risch 1955: 61–70;

1959: 125–27). If one accepts this theory one has to explain some features of Attic, which do not correspond to those of Arcado-Cyprian, as results of Doric influence. But as the theory itself still remains to be proved, it follows that linguistics cannot provide us with any independent evidence relevant to our problem.

In these circumstances, I believe that there is nothing which proves or even suggests in a plausible way a connection of the Attic cist-tombs with northern newcomers. My own suggestion, based on the population-movements reconstructed above, is that appearance of this grave-type in Attica is the result of a revival dependent on Eleusis. A cultural influence from the Argolid would then be important, but not determining[1].

Notes

1. I thank Professor Anna Morpurgo-Davies for her advice and help in preparing the published form of this article and Dr. J. K. Davies for help in putting its text into English.

References

ÅLIN, P. 1962. *Das Ende der mykenischen Fundstätte aus dem griechischen Festland*. Lund.

ANGEL, J. L. 1945. 'Skeletal material from Attica.' *Hesperia*, 14: 279–363.

BLEGEN, C. W. and RAWSON, M. 1966. *The Palace of Nestor at Pylos in Western Messenia*, I. Cincinnati.

BREITINGER, E. 1939. 'Die Skelette aus den submykenischen Gräbern'; in H. Kraiker, *Kerameikos* I: *Beitrag*. Berlin.

CHADWICK, J. 1956. 'The Greek dialects and Greek pre-history.' *Greece and Rome*, N.S., 3: 38–50.

DESBOROUGH, V. R. d'A. 1964. *The last Mycenaeans and their Successors*. Cambridge.

DESHAYES, J. 1966. *Argos: les fouilles de Deiras*. Paris.

FERGUSON, W. 1938. 'The Salaminioi of Heptopylai Sounion.' *Hesperia*, 7: 1–74.

FONTENROSE, J. E. 1937. 'Peirithous.' *RE*(I). 19: 114–40.

FURUMARK, A. 1941. *The Chronology of Mycenaean Pottery*. Stockholm.

GIOVANINI, A. 1969. *Étude historique sur les origines du Catalogue des Vaisseaux*. Berne.

HAMMOND, N. G. L. 1967. *Epirus*. Oxford.

HOPE-SIMPSON, R. 1965. *A gazetteer and atlas of Mycenaean sites*. London.

—— and LAZENBY, J. F. 1970. *The Catalogue of Ships in Homer's Iliad*. Oxford.

KOURONIOTIS, K. 1914. 'Pylou messiniakis tholotos taphos.' *ArchEph*, 1914: 99–117.

KRAIKER, 1939. *Kerameikos* I. Berlin.

MARINATOS, SP. 1967. 'Anaskaphai en Pylo.' *Praktika*, 1965: 102–20.

——. 1968. 'Mycenaean culture within the frame of Mediterranean anthropology.' *AttiICIM* (I): 277–94.

MÜHLESTEIN, H. 1956. *Die o-ka Tafeln von Pylos. Ein mykenischer Schiffskatalog*. Basel.

MUSCARELLA, O. W. 1964. 'Ancient safety pins: their function and significance.' *Expedition*, 6: 35–40.

MYLONAS, G. 1936. 'Eleusiniaka.' *AJA*, 40: 415–31.

——. 1961. *Eleusis and the Eleusinian Mysteries*. Princeton.

——. 1962. *Proïstoriki Elefsis*. Athens.

NILSSON, M. 1932. *The Mycenaean Origins of Greek Mythology*. Cambridge,

PORZIG, W. 1954. 'Sprachgeographische Untersuchungen zu den griechischen Dialekten.' *IF*, 61: 147–69.

RISCH, E. 1955. 'Die Gliederung der griechischen Dialekte in neuer Sicht.' *MH*, 12: 61–76.

——. 1959. 'Frühgeschichte der griechischen Sprache.' *MH*, 16: 215–77.

ROBERT, C. 1885. 'Athena Skiras und die Skirophoren.' *Hermes*, 20: 349–79.

SANDARS, N. K. 1964. 'The last Mycenaeans and the European Late Bronze Age.' *Antiquity*, 38:

SCHMIDT, J. 1927. 'Skiros.' *RE*(2). 3/1: 547–9.

SMITH, W. 1854. *Dictionary of Greek and Roman Geography*, I. London.

STYRENIUS, C. G. 1962 'The vases from the sub-Mycenaean cemetery on Salamis.' *Opuscula Atheniensia*, 4: 103–23.

——. 1967. *Sub-Mycenaean Studies*. Lund.

THOMPSON, G. 1954. *The Prehistoric Aegean*. London.

TOEPFFER, J. 1894. 'Apaturia.' *RE*(1). 1/2: 2672–80.

VOKOTOPOULOU, Y. P. 1969. 'Neoi kivotoskhimoi taphoi tis YE III V-G periodhou eks Ipeirou.' *ArchEph*, 1969: 179–209.

WIDE, S. 1910. 'Gräberfunde aus Salamis.' *AthMitt*, 35: 17–36.

YAKOVIDHIS, S. 1956. 'Anaskaphai mykenaïkon taphon Peratis.' *Praktika*, 1953: 88–102.

——. 1964. 'Mykenaïkoi taphoi Peratis.' *Deltion*, 19. *Khron.*: 87–95.

——. 1965a. 'Anaskaphai mykenaïkon taphon Peratis.' *Praktika*, 1958: 18–26.

——. 1965b. 'Anaskaphi mykenaïkon taphon Peratis.' *Praktika*, 1959: 12–7.

Discussion

M. MILLER: If we apply the term 'tradition' to any statement about a god or a hero made in any source from Homer to Eustathius, we must distinguish between at least the following kinds: (1) Probably the greater half of the total mass of statements that one called 'traditions' originate in ancient learning: they are generalizations, speculations, constructions, historiographic and chronographic and sociological and theological doctrines. Under this heading we must include all dates, many genealogies, most sequences of, and even within, dynasties; all such constructions as that which brought together the foundation legends of the various Ionian cities into the 'Ionian Migration'; and we must not forget that the intellectual problems of a semi-orthodox polytheistic theology are formidable, and were not neglected: to this we owe such statements as that Orthia 'is' Artemis. (2) Of the remainder, most are poetic in origin. We must remember that when a poet is planning an *Iliad* or an *Argonautika*, he is assembling a cast, not mobilizing an army or a crew. The laws of poetry are not those of history. (3) We cannot therefore expect a residue of more than about 5–10 per cent of the total mass of the statements surviving in traditions to be pre-literary, and the statements in it (where identifiable) appear to be religious or legal, or for entertainment. The legal statements include legal fictions, perfectly proper in their own field, but unhistorical. The religious statements may be made either with piety about one's own religion, or with horror at other people's. Entertainment includes such examples as Theseus doing his James Bond act along the road from Troizen to Athens. In brief, genuine pre-literary statements are never historically intended, though we may sometimes be able to extract historical matter from them. Theseus went by land from Troizen to Athens: all the commentators since Pausanias remark that people normally went by sea, and that in fact the Skironian road was only made passable by Hadrian. If the archaeologists can tell us when the seas were closed (even in home waters) to the Mycenaeans, then we have a starting point for the genesis of this cycle of entertainment stories. And if the archaeological answer is twelfth century B.C., then in view of (1) above, we must accept that the poetic dating of Theseus before the Trojan War is poetic only. Finally, if we suppose that some statement is pre-literary in origin, it must be an inherent part of this supposition to explain when and how the statement was taken into literature, and by what genre; and its pedigree up to the moment of reaching our sources must be determined.

M. W. M. POPE: Since in the few days of this archaeologico-linguistic colloquium we have heard the Greeks being brought into Greece from every direction save the south and in every post-mesolithic millennium B.C. except the first, one conclusion emerges with tremendous clarity: neither archaeology nor linguistics can tell us anything for certain about the movements of people. This is not really very surprising. In so far as they deal with movement at all, the one discipline deals with the spread of techniques, the other with the spread of languages. But there does exist a discipline which deals, *inter alia*, with the spread of human populations, and that is medical genetics. It has already solved problems from Iceland to the Cape of Good Hope, and its methods are improving all the time. I am not sure whether genetic surveys that make any significant contribution to our subject of 'Bronze Age migrations in the Aegean region' have yet been undertaken—presumably not, or we should have heard about them; but what I am sure of is that genetic surveys in the areas that interest us will be taken in the near future, and that as historians we should be alive to the existence of a tool of enquiry which may prove to be as powerful in its own way as radiocarbon dating or as palaeo-botany are in theirs. Moreover the usefulness of the surveys is likely to be greater the more the historical problems for which they may help to provide answers can be defined in advance.

References

GIBLETT, E. R. 1969. *Genetic markers in human blood.* Oxford.

KATTAMIS, C. A. KYRIAZAKOU, M., KHAIDAS, S. 1969. 'Favism: clinical and biochemical data.' *Journal of Medical Genetics,* 6: 34–41.

KATTAMIS, C. A., KHAIDAS, A. and KHAIDAS, S. 1969. 'G6PD deficiency and favism in the Island of Rhodes (Greece).' *Journal of Medical Genetics,* 6: 286–91.

MOURANT, A. E. 1954. *The distribution of the human blood groups.* London.

POULIANOS, A. N. 1968. *E proelefsi ton Ellinon.* Athens.

RACE, R. R. and SANGER, R. 1968. *Blood groups in man* (5th ed.) London.

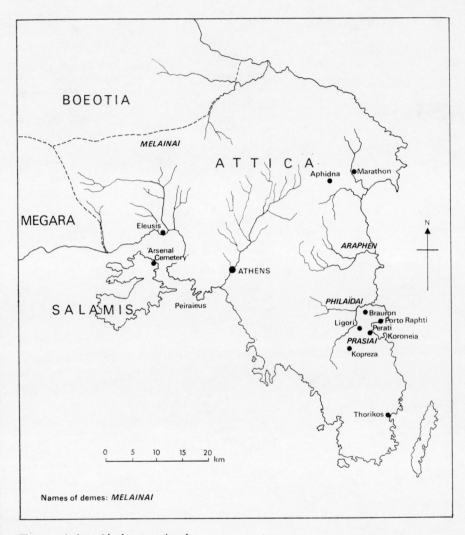

BOEOTIA

MELAINAI

A T T I C A

Aphidna

Marathon

MEGARA

Eleusis

Arsenal
Cemetery

ARAPHEN

ATHENS

N

SALAMIS

Peiraieus

PHILAÏDAI

Brauron

Porto Raphti

Ligori

Perati

Koroneia

PRASIAI

Kopreza

Thorikos

0   5   10   15   20
                    km

Names of demes: *MELAINAI*

Fig. 21.1. Attica, with places mentioned

Messenia and the catastrophe at the end of Late Helladic IIIB

IMRE TEGYEY

University of Debrecen

THE catastrophe at the end of the Bronze Age in Messenia presents an interesting problem for archaeology, for several reasons. The soil of Messenia has given us the largest archive of Bronze Age documents so far found in Greece and its territory provides the clearest case of a Late Bronze Age region where there are no signs of recovery after the decline at the end of Late Helladic IIIB. As a result of various Greek and American excavations and explorations we have a thorough knowledge both of the palace at Ano Englianos itself and of the whole district which we may believe to have been ruled by Nestor.

If the question of the cultural decline of Messenia needs to be raised again after P. Ålin's survey and V. Desborough's fundamental work (Ålin 1962; Desborough 1964, 1969; Desborough and Hammond 1964) this is due on the one hand to new Greek excavations (Marinatos 1961; Yalouris 1968), on the other to the final report of the University of Minnesota Messenia Expedition (McDonald and Hope-Simpson 1961; 1964; 1969).

The nature of the cultural evolution of Greece in Late Helladic III is indicated by the uniformity of the style of pottery in use; it was a time of peaceful development and security. The influence of Mycenae could presumably be felt all over Greece. At the end of this period there are many signs of disturbance; for example the devastation of the houses of the Lower Town in Mycenae and signs of preparation there against an expected attack. The period closed with a series of widespread acts of destruction in mainland Greece as a result of which many settlements and citadels were abandoned, especially throughout the Peloponnese, the inhabitants taking refuge in adjacent territories, while others escaped to eastern Attica. Some territories never recovered from this catastrophe; in others, above all at Mycenae itself and later in Attica, there are clear signs of recovery. The final disaster, which brought the Mycenaean Age to an end, came at the close of the Late Helladic IIIC period when, about 1150 B.C., Mycenae was destroyed.

Messenia is one of the territories which was devastated and depopulated by the first attack at the end of LH IIIB and in which there was no recovery in the subsequent period. The number of habitation sites diminished substantially. What peculiarity in the cultural evolution of Messenia might have been responsible for this sudden break? Our interest is concentrated on the relation between the palace at Ano Englianos and the inhabited countryside of Messenia in the transitional period from LH IIIB to LH IIIC and in possible habitation of it in sub-Mycenaean times.

The palace fell victim to an attack when Late Helladic IIIB pottery was going out of use but had not yet been superseded by IIIC. (Blegen and Rawson 1966: 419–22). Among about seven thousand pots found in it only ten are indisputedly of the IIIC period. These are all *krater* bowls (Blegen and Rawson 1966: 421, pls. 385–6, Shape 60). Blegen assigns six vessels of four other types to LH IIIC too (Blegen and Rawson 1966: pls. 375–6, Shape 52; pls. 387–8, Shape 63; pls. 389–94, Shape 65; pl. 396, Shape 68). It is more difficult to determine the sequence of events in provincial areas of the Pylian state. If we take the evidence of Linear B tablets into account, we cannot avoid the conclusion that those areas, towns or hamlets whose names occur on a list which was completed in the very last year of the existence of the palace were still intact like the palace itself at that time and still in contact with its bureaucracy. Although the identifications of the towns listed on the clay tablets are hypothetical, it is obvious that the provincial areas as a whole were not devastated before the catastrophe which destroyed the stronghold of Nestor (Palmer 1953: 10–13; 1963: 147–63). This fact points to a sudden attack on the Pylian Kingdom. It is unfortunate indeed that Mouriatadha north of the palace has not yielded any pottery that could help in a more detailed stratigraphic analysis. A clear contrast exists, however, in that there are no signs of burning there (Marinatos 1966: 201–6; Desborough 1964: 93–4; McDonald and Hope-Simpson 1969: 133, No. 22A).

The situation in particular areas under Nestor's rule is as follows. The northernmost district in the southern part of Elis embodying the small centres of the Alpheios valley and its vicinity was heavily populated in the Late Bronze Age. The most important settlements of the IIIB period were at Agios Andhreas and Agios Georgios, where a Late Helladic house has recently been excavated (McDonald and Hope-Simpson 1961: 224, 227; 1969: 128–9, Nos. 1, 12; Yalouris 1968: 178). Next comes the area round Olympia where excavations on the site of the new museum unearthed a Mycenaean cemetery which yielded thirteen chamber-tombs with LH IIIB vases, jewellery and objects of metal (McDonald and Hope-Simpson 1969:

128–9, No. 8A; Yalouris 1968: 176–7); near the village of Kladheos another cemetery was opened also with LH IIIB pottery (McDonald and Hope-Simpson 1969: 129, No. 9B; Yalouris 1968: 178–80). The finds of the settlement near Agios Ilias (Makrisia) are to be put in the LH IIIB period (McDonald and Hope-Simpson 1961: 258, fn. 16; 1968: 126–7). With regard to survivals in the next period we have very modest results so far. Some individual finds were found in Agios Andhreas, Agios Georgios and Agios Ilias (McDonald and Hope-Simpson 1961: 251–2). There is better evidence from Diasela since the contents of three chamber-tombs there are mainly LH IIIB–C (McDonald and Hope-Simpson 1961: 258, fn. 16). Now we can add an excavation at the south-eastern edge of Platanos village in an area called Tombrino where three pillaged chamber-tombs were excavated (the vases in them belong to LH IIIB–C; McDonald and Hope-Simpson 1969: 128, No. 7A: Yalouris 1968: 177) and another north of the Kladheos village on the right bank of the Kladheos river (Tripis) where ten chamber-tombs yielded a great many LH IIIA–C vases and objects of bronze, gold and ivory (McDonald and Hope-Simpson 1969: 129 No. 9C; Yalouris 1968: 177).

The few centres known in the area between the rivers Alpheios and Kyparissia have not yielded any material which indicates occupation after LH IIIB (McDonald and Hope-Simpson 1969: 130–2, Nos. 19, 20). The publication of the excavation of a tumulus at Samikon carried out by Yalouris must be considered a new result (Yalouris 1965). This burial site was in use during a long period from MH times to LH IIIB. Among the settlements near the river Kyparissia and in neighbouring areas the one at Malthi is very well known from the Swedish excavation. There is some evidence that there it survived into LH IIIC and even into sub-Mycenaean times. On a hill called Kongilion or Kastro, surface exploration showed traces of an oval enclosure that can be regarded as prehistoric on the basis of the pottery found. Some of this belonged to LH III so the site was probably an important stronghold, resembling Malthi in its history and other features (McDonald and Hope-Simpson 1969: 141–2, No. 28A). A new find has been made near Krebeni (Kato Melpia). Among the fragments of pottery found one or two are LH IIIC (McDonald and Hope-Simpson 1969: 143, No. 31).

In the immediate vicinity of the palace at Ano Englianos the finds at Iklaina and Tragana are well known; the tholos-tomb at the latter site clearly indicates LH IIIC occupation (McDonald and Hope-Simpson 1961: 239–41: 1969: 149, No. 52). New evidence came from the excavation at Volimidhia where Marinatos excavated about thirty chamber-tombs which were in use from Middle Helladic to Late Helladic IIIB times (Orlandhos and Marinatos

1964, 1965). The most important site among the settlements along the coast of the Messenian Gulf is Kaphirio where some sub-Mycenaean sherds were found and in the occupation of the site continued in the Protogeometric period (McDonald and Hope-Simpson 1969: 152–3, No. 76). Nikhoria (near Rizomilo) was of strategic importance and a large settlement was found there also with signs of continuous occupation lasting from Middle Helladic to Geometric times; the cemetery belonging to this site showed sub-Mycenaean and Protogeometric burials and Mycenaean chamber- and tholos-tombs (McDonald and Hope-Simpson 1969: 156, No. 76). A new issue here is raised by Khorimis' excavation of a tomb where a transitional phase between the Bronze and Iron Age and also a ruined Mycenaean tholos, were observed (Khorimis 1968: 209). In the upper part of the Pamisos valley Thouria (Ellinika) was one of the most impressive Mycenaean centres of the whole area. From the major settlement of the Bronze Age some deep bowls with duller than average paint could be LH IIIC (McDonald and Hope-Simpson 1969: 158, No. 78).

At the end of this short survey we may point out that our picture of destruction at the end of LH IIIB has not changed fundamentally. It seems that areas relatively remote from the palace at Ano Englianos, like the Alpheios district or the littoral of the Messenian Gulf, have yielded more evidence of LH IIIC and sub-Mycenaean than other parts of the Bronze Age state of Pylos.

There has been much speculation about the causes of the catastrophe that brought the Mycenaean period to an end at the transition from LH IIIB–C. Theories have been advanced about invaders coming from the North, and there is evidence also for a piratical raid from the sea. The *stasis* mentioned by Thucydides (1, 12) is also worth considering, as a possible cause, although it seems improbable that the depopulation of this area was the consequence of internal disturbances alone.

There have been many interpretations of Linear B tablets along the same lines: it has been emphasized more than once that the tablets indicate preparations against an attack, although archaeological observations show no signs of such preparation in the palace itself; the walls were not fortified and the storerooms were full of vessels (Tritsch 1958; Palmer 1963: 116–20; Deroy 1968: Schmitt-Brandt 1968). It seems more profitable to explain these events as a natural result of the history of Messenia in the Late Mycenaean Age. The concentration of the local resources of the region and its development of the highly centralized state bureaucracy attested by the Linear B tablets were a quick evolutionary process, lasting perhaps less than a century. The power developed during so short a period could be maintained only with the help of a strongly concentrated bureaucracy. If we compare the Linear B tablets of Pylos with those of Knossos, they show some peculiarities. Although there is much conformity in language, style and even in economic life in the case of the palaces at the two places, the organization of the palace at Ano Englianos is somewhat different from that of the Cretan residences. The bureaucratic system in Pylos was too strictly organized and thus did not allow any self-reliance to the provincial settlements. The effect of an attack on this state from abroad was devastating, for with the destruction of the central palace the local settlements could not offer any resistance to invaders[1].

Note

1. Between the acceptance of his paper for the programme of the Colloquium and the Colloquium itself Dr. Tegyey was invited to contribute an extended version of it to *Acta Classica* 6 (University of Debrecen). The editors thank him and the editors of *Acta Classica* for agreeing to the publication of this shorter version here.

References

ÅLIN, P. 1962. *Das Ende der mykenischen Fundstätte auf dem griechischen Festland.* Lund.

BLEGEN, C. W. and RAWSON, M. 1966. *The Palace of Nestor at Pylos in Western Messenia,* I. Cincinnati.

DEROY, L. 1968. *Les leveurs d'impôts dans le royaume mycénien de Pylos.* (*IncGraec.* 24). Rome.

DESBOROUGH, V. R. d'A. 1964. *The Last Mycenaeans and their Successors.* Cambridge.

——. 1968. 'History and archaeology of the last century of the Mycenaean Age.' *AttiICIM* (3): 1073–90.

—— and HAMMOND, N. G. L. 1964. 'The end of the Mycenaean civilization and the Dark Age.' *CAH* (rev. ed.) II, Chap. XXXVI/Fasc. 13.

KHORIMIS, A. 1968. 'Tholotos taphos eis Karpophoran Messinias.' *AthAA,* 1: 205–9.

MCDONALD, W. A. and HOPE-SIMPSON, R. 1961. 'Prehistoric habitation in southwestern Peloponnese.' *AJA,* 65: 221–60.

——. 1964. 'Further exploration in southwestern Peloponnese: 1962–63.' *AJA,* 68: 229–45.

——. 1969. 'Further explorations in southwestern Peloponnese: 1964–68.' *AJA,* 73: 124–77.

MARINATOS, SP. 1961. 'Die Messenischen Grabungen und das Problem des homerischen Pylos.' *Anzeiger Österreich. Akad. Wiss.* 1961: 235–49.

——. 1966. 'Anaskaphai Pylou.' *Praktika,* 1960: 195–209.

ORLANDHOS, A. K. and MARINATOS, SP. 1965. 'Pylos.' *Ergon,* 1964: 77–90.

——. 1966. 'Pylos.' *Ergon,* 1965: 76–92.

PALMER, L. R. 1956. 'Notes on the personnel of the O-KA tablets (Pylos 1952).' *Eranos,* 54: 1–13.

——. 1963. *The Interpretation of Mycenaean Greek Texts.* Oxford.

SCHMITT-BRANDT, R. 1968. 'Die Oka-Tafeln in neuer Sicht.' *Studi Micenei ed Egeo-Anatolici,* 7 (*IncGraec,* 28): 69–96.

TRITSCH, F. J. 1958. 'The women of Pylos.' *Minoica* (ed. E. Grumach): 406–10.

YALOURIS, N. 1965. 'Mykenaikos tymbos Samikou.' *Deltion,* 20: 6–40.

——. 1968. 'Trouvailles mycéniennes et prémycéniennes de la région du sanctuaire d'Olympie.' *AttiICIM* (1): 176–82.

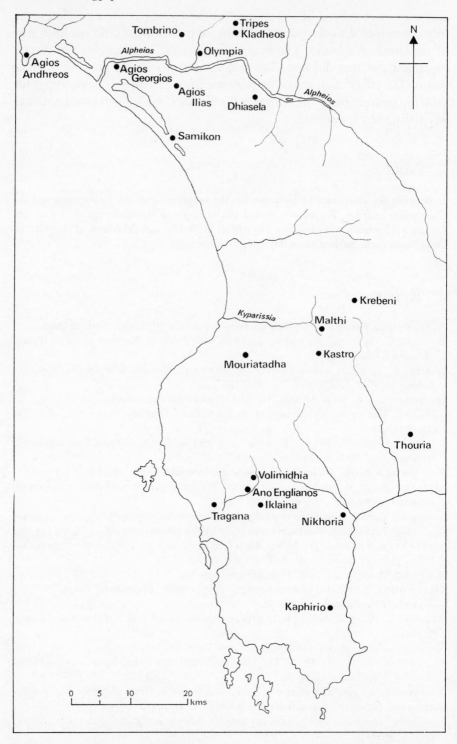

Fig. 22.1. The south-western Peloponnese, with sites mentioned (based on McDonald and Hope-Simpson 1969: Illustration 2)

The 'Sackers of Cities' and the 'movement of populations'

F. J. TRITSCH

University of Birmingham

THE centre of Greece was never really Athens, nor Sparta, nor any state of the mainland. The real centre of Greece was the Aegean. Communication by sea was both more characteristic and more natural than movement by land. In this respect Greece is very different from most of the other countries in Europe.

Gilbert Murray pointed this out long ago in *The Rise of the Greek Epic* (1934: 52), when he spoke of the 'Greek Dark Ages', the age of migration. As he says, when people moved by land, they took most of their belongings with them, and that was an arduous process in Greece, over rocks and mountains. When they moved by sea, possessions had to be very precious before they could be allowed space in those comparatively small boats. But the journey was less cumbersome and less fraught with difficulties. Indeed, as we know from Greek tradition, most migrations went by sea.

Gilbert Murray continues in his evocative style:

"In the earlier migrations of the Dark Age a tribe or a group of people took to the sea when driven by the fear of death. That was not time to think of women or herds. You might desire greatly to take your young wife with you—or your old wife, for that matter; but you would scarcely dare to make such a proposal to the hungry fighters about you. You might wish to take your little boy. But would the rest of us, think you, choose to be encumbered with another consumer of bread, who could never help in a fight, who might delay us in charging or flying, might cry from the pain of hunger or fatigue and betray us all? No, leave him on the beach, and come! Put some mark on him. Probably some one will make him a slave and then, with good luck, you may some day knock up against him and pay his ransom.

When we are off on the sea, what are the prospects before us? We have some provisions, though no water. Instead, we take guides who know where there are springs near the seashore in diverse islands and unfrequented promontories. We can move by night and hide in caves during the day. The guide probably knows places where cattle may, with some risk, be raided. Better still, he knows of some villages that have been lately attacked by pirates and where the men are still weak with their wounds. Not all their flocks have been killed. We might as well take the rest. If we stay at sea, we die of thirst ... piracy on the high seas will not keep us alive. In the good old days ... pirates could live like princes. But the business has been spoiled. There are too many men like ourselves, and too few ships with anything on them to steal. If we go back to our old homes, the enemies have by this time got our women as slaves, and will either kill us or sell us in foreign countries. Is there anywhere an island to seize? A waterless rock will be of no use. Can we seize some inhabited island? Alone we are too weak. But what if we are combined with some other outlaws? There are some outcast Carians in like plight with ourselves. In our normal life we would not touch a Carian. Their weapons are no gentleman's weapons. Their voices make one sick. And their hair! But what does it matter now? ... And with them are some Leleges, who worship birds. Some unknown savages from the eastern side ..., answering to babyish names like Atta and Tatta and Dunda. And, good omen, some of our old enemies from near home, whom we were always fighting with and had learned to hate in our cradles. A pleasure to meet them again! One can understand their speech. We swear an oath that makes us brothers. We cut one another's arms, pour the blood into a bowl and drink some all round. We swear by our gods; to make things pleasanter, we swear by one another's gods, as far as we can make out their outlandish names. And then forth to attack our island.

After due fighting it is ours. The men who held it yesterday, are slain. Some few have got away in boats, and some day come back to worry us; but not just yet, not for a good long time. There is water to drink; there is bread and curded milk and onions. There is flesh of sheep or goats. There is wine or, at the worst, some coarser liquor of honey or grain, which will at least intoxicate. One needs that, after such a day ... No more thirst, no more hunger, no more of the cramped galley benches, no more terror of the wind or sea. The dead men are lying all about us. We will fling them into the sea tomorrow. The women are suitably tied up and guarded. The old one who kept shrieking curses has been spiked with a lance and tossed over the cliff. The wailing and sobbing of the rest will stop in a day or two; if it torments you, you can easily move a few paces out of the sound. If it still rings in your ears, drink two more cups and you will not mind it. The stars are above us, and the protecting sea round us, we have got water and food and roofs over our heads. And we wrought it all by our own wisdom and courage and the manifest help of Zeus and Apollo. What good men we are, and valiant and pious; and our gods . . . what short work they make of other men's gods!"

Gilbert Murray goes on to say: "There is no trait in the above suggested narrative that is not drawn from a real case" (1934: 53–5). And indeed he is right. This is the world which conforms to the Greek tradition of the Heroic Age. It is the way of life evoked by the Homeric epics. And it is the state of affairs in the world of the Aegean area as hinted at in some documents from the Hittite capital at Boğazköy and from the city of Ugarit during the thirteenth century B.C., the period of the end of the Mycenaean Koine (Murray 1934: 47, 51).

Small groups of people consisting mainly of chieftains with their bands of followers appear at various places. At others we find small groups driven from their homes and seeking new ones. It is not usually an army that comes to invade, in fact, only on very rare occasions do we hear of one. Almost in every case we find small bands of chiefs and adventurers going forth in the Aegean region to carve out for themselves a new home, or little principalities, or lives of romance. Often they were invited in as allies or as mercenaries, more often they were not. They had among them a special title of honour: *ptoliporthos*, 'Sacker of Cities'. It represented the height of romantic glory! In the Homeric epics and still in Aeschylus it was a man's chief claim to public honours. The greatest thing was to be a sacker of cities. This was the title that gave him honour and fame. In the Homeric epics not only the great heroes like Achilles bear this title. It is also claimed for the chieftains of the generation before the War of Troy, for Oileus, Otrynteus, Heracles; and Nestor claims it himself for the time of his youth. Indeed, the goddess Athena herself bears the title 'Sacker of Cities' in the Homeric epics, and she bears it with grace. But what does it really mean?

The *Iliad* makes it fairly clear. One does not sack a city in order to increase one's power or political influence, or to capture its trade and commerce. The real purpose is to capture booty, silver, gold and bronze, horses and cattle or sheep, but especially: women! Again and again the phrase occurs in the epics of the fight for 'the city and the women'. And when Achilles tells Odysseus of the twenty-three cities he has sacked, he only mentions *keimelia* and *gynaikes*, treasures and women. Of these he is proud, they give him his claim to fame, to fame which is the only part of life that survives death. And he particularly mentions the beauty of the women he has captured.

Here we may find a clue to the significance of this special title of honour 'Sacker of Cities'. The greater the booty captured, the more gold and silver and bronze, the more beautiful the women obtained in this way, the greater was the fame. It ensured the bearer a large band of followers and a loyalty beyond the bounds of law and order. The effect was cumulative. The greater the fame, the larger the band of followers grew, and thus the greater the enterprise that could be attempted. It is in this way that we find a new class of men like *condottieri* emerging with their following, groups of adventurers, as well as groups of people driven from their homes and seeking new ones. Yet each time the groups are comparatively small. The historical documents from Boğazköy and Ugarit tell a similar story when they speak of the Aegean region. One of the last letters sent from the city of Ugarit tells of seven enemy ships that have sacked several towns on the coast and may return any day. This gives an indication of the size of those bands led by the 'Sackers of Cities'. (Sommer 1932: 2–240; Schaeffer 1968: 87, No. 24 RS 20. 238, 697–8).

Bearing in mind such a state of affairs we should, I think, be more careful when we speak of 'movements of populations' or of tribes migrating about in general. Such terms are rather misleading, for they suggest a situation similar to that of our own early Middle Ages. I think we are misled by this analogy. Superficial similarities can be found, no doubt, but the fundamental issues were entirely different, cause and effect were not the same, and the technical possibilities were not at all similar. Altogether, communications were quite different in the times of the Roman Empire from what they had been in the Bronze Age, the density of the population was very different too, and then there was the Christian Church which stood for continuity. We cannot simply use a false analogy when we are seeking the historical truth.

Nor do we find in the archaeological remains any evidence at all for large-scale migrations or extensive movements of populations, either during the Late Bronze Age or in the ensuing centuries of dark ages. What we do find are comparatively small groups of people moving about, not even large enough to be tribes. The characteristics that they transmit from one place to another (special tomb-types or grave-goods, pottery styles or weapons) are certainly not sufficient for us to speak of ethnic characteristics. In any case, deriving ethnic names from pottery styles is one of the most deplorable habits in archaeology. We cheerfully speak of 'the Minyans' when we only mean a population that uses pottery which we call 'Minyan', although the Greeks themselves never mention the 'Minyans' as a tribe or as a people. We might as well speak of the 'Red-Figure' people in Classical Greece, or the 'Black-Figure' people spreading all over Greece.

The very significant changes that occur and spread all over Greece at the end of the Bronze Age in no way indicate a movement of large population groups. Linguistic criteria cannot be used in this respect, for linguistic affinities do not prove ethnic affinities. Nor can we use the drastic changes in architectural techniques and in tomb construction. For if we used such kinds of criteria, we could then equally well speak of the invasion of Europe later by 'the Baroque People' of Italy and Spain, or even of 'the Perpendicular People' invading and migrating into Cambridge.

Let us look at the question from another angle. The famous Achaean expedition to Troy, even if we take the Homeric catalogue at its face value, was surely not a migration of tribes or a movement of populations. The same applies to the allies of Troy. Both armies were composed of contingents and auxiliary troops. The same is true of the Hittite army at Kadesh, with its contingents of Dardanians, Arzawans, Carians and Lycians. And I believe this also applies to the army and fleet of the so-called 'Sea Peoples', except that once they landed and assembled in Amurru, they were followed by large numbers of people driven from their homes by famine and drought.

In Greece we hear of the 'Dorian Invasion'. But our source is mainly Herodotus whose information is rather one-sided. We cannot find any archaeological evidence for it. Thucydides does not speak of it but only mentions a return of the Heraclids. It is only the spread of Doric dialects over most of the Peloponnesus that has given such credence to the story in Herodotus which he himself admits came from Sparta where it was put forward to justify the Spartans' claim to supremacy over the Peloponnesus. But there is no need to postulate a large-scale Dorian migration in order to explain the spread of the Doric dialects. The spread of a language as a vernacular over a wide area does not always operate in this way. There were no invasions of the Aramaeans as a people, no 'Aramaean Migrations', when Aramaic gradually became the lingua franca of southern Asia Minor and of the Assyrian Empire in the ninth and eighth centuries, nor later when it became the administrative language in the Persian Empire. And as a counterpart I may quote a correlative phenomenon in the Near East during the second millennium. Those tiresome *Habiru* who acted as organized groups and as sackers of cities in Palestine according to the Amarna Letters, were of mixed ethnic affinities, with Hurrian, Amorite and Indo-European elements, joined up into bands, threatening cities or hiring themselves out to them. Their language was no indication of their ethnic origin. Nor did they cause the spread of any particular language or dialect. I suppose one of our main mistakes is to imagine that people were always monolingual, and this is a terrible mistake with far-reaching consequences.

The real problem, the real question we have to tackle, would seem to me to lie in another direction. What was it that caused this universal unrest at the end of the Bronze Age, what caused the breakdown of government, what made so many people want to move from their homes, want to acquire possessions by loot and plunder, rather than by tribute and trade? It is the same situation nearly everywhere; not a picture of vast movements of populations and tribal migrations, as some very fondly imagine, but a picture of genuine unrest everywhere, of a breakdown of established order and of a change in moral values, of new beliefs and new aspirations. It seems to me like putting the cart before the horse if we say that this change or breakdown was caused by the so-called Aegean Migrations. The latter were the effect and not the cause.

The end of the Mycenaeans and of the Hittites is still shrouded in darkness. When a vacuum occurs, quite naturally other people move in. But what created the vacuum? What made social ties, cultural habits, and moral values change to their opposites? In *Ugaritica*, Vol. V, Professor Claude Schaeffer recently postulated not merely a series of catastrophic earthquakes in fairly rapid succession but also, on the basis of his evidence at Ugarit, very severe climatic changes causing lack of water supply and widespread famine (Schaeffer 1968: 761–8). The evidence he gives is very persuasive and he may well be right. But, whatever we do, whatever we suggest or conclude, let us not mix up causes and effects.

The crucial historical question that really requires an answer, is not whether there was an ethnic migration or any significant change in population, or how many people moved or how many languages changed, here and there, but what caused these changes, how did the Mycenaean and the Hittite civilizations break down, what made the people change their cultural beliefs and moral values, and what caused their disbelief in any permanent order. In fact, what causes any civilization to break down?

References

MICKNAT, G. 1954. *Studien zur Kriegsgefangenschaft* (Akad. d. Wiss. Mainz, Abh. Geistes-sozialwiss. 11).
MURRAY, G. 1934. *The Rise of the Greek Epic* (4th ed.). Oxford.
SCHAEFFER, C. F. A., NOUGAYROL, J. and others. 1968. *Ugaritica V*. Paris.
SOMMER, F. 1932. *Die Aḫḫijavā-Urkunden* (AbhBAW N. F., 6). Munich.

Discussion

M. S. F. HOOD: The German invasions of the Roman Empire, as Professor Tritsch says, are probably not a good parallel for what may have happened in Greece at the end of the Bronze Age. The Germans were Christians, like the inhabitants of the Empire, and they were normally organized in large armies. A more useful analogy perhaps is the Slav penetration of Greece from the end of the sixth century A.D. onwards. The

Slavs were much more barbarous, still pagan in religion, and originally at any rate they do not appear to have been organized in large armies but as separate bands. The so-called *Chronicle of Monemvasia* (Lemerle 1963) which now seems to be accepted as giving a reasonably authentic picture of the Slav invasion of the Peloponnese, describes how those of the native Byzantine population who had escaped massacre fled before the incoming Slavs, some to the mountains, others to the strong Gibraltar-like peninsula of Monemvasia, or to islands like Aegina, others again farther afield to south Italy and Sicily. It is interesting to note in connection with the problem of the 'Dorian Invasion' at the end of the Bronze Age that no trace of the Slavs themselves had been recognized in Greece apart from the devastation that it could be assumed they had caused until a few years ago, when a cemetery of their inurned cremations was found by chance on the site of the new museum at Olympia, although references in Byzantine authors, supplemented by the massive legacy of Slav place-names still surviving in the south of Greece, made it quite clear that the Slav occupation was on a massive scale (see Hood 1966; and below 315.).

References

HOOD, M. S. F. 1966. 'An aspect of the Slav invasions of Greece in the early Byzantine period.' *Acta Musei Nationalis Pragae*, 20, 1/2: 165–71.

LEMERLE, P. 1963. 'La chronique improprement dite de Monemvasie: le contexte historique et légendaire.' *Rév. des études byzantines*, 21: 5–49.

PART THREE

Linguistic Problems

Map 5. Dialects of ancient Greek; approximate distribution of dialects, assigned to the groups usually reconstructed *c.* 800 B.C.

1

General linguistic problems of the prehistoric Aegean, south-eastern Europe and Anatolia

The arrival of the Greeks in Greece: the linguistic evidence

V. I. GEORGIEV

Academy of Sciences of the Republic of Bulgaria, Sofia

1. *The linguistic evidence*

The Greeks were not 'autochthonous' in the Aegean region. They realized this clearly themselves. Herodotus (II, 56) tells us that the *Pelasgoi* were the primitive population of Greece and Thucydides (I, iii, I) states the same opinion. Ancient tradition is thus in agreement with the fact that there are many place-names in Greece which cannot be explained as names belonging to the Greek language. Where did the Greeks come from? Thirty years or so ago the general opinion was that they came from central Europe, and this view is still held by some even today (Milewski 1948: map 30; Brandenstein 1954: 9; Chadwick 1964: 14). It has no real basis of proof, and is in fact a atavistic survival from the formerly dominant theory, now almost completely abandoned, that the original homeland of the Indo-Europeans was in northern Germany and certain adjacent regions. It is unnecessary to re-emphasize here the great importance of toponymic studies for determining changes of population in any region. There is no indication in toponymy that the proto-Greeks were ever present in central Europe, in the Pontic region, in any region of the northern Balkans, in Thrace or in north-western Anatolia (*pace* Mellaart 1958).

As for the question of the 'arrival of the Greeks', a study by two

American scholars has continually been cited as the definitive solution. This is the article by the linguist J. B. Haley and the well-known archaeologist C. W. Blegen entitled: 'The coming of the Greeks. 1. The geographical distribution of pre-Greek place-names. 2. The geographical distribution of prehistoric remains in Greece' (Haley and Blegen 1928). Haley assembled place-names of supposed 'pre-Hellenic' origin according to A. Fick's studies (Fick 1905) and drew up a map of the location of a 'pre-Indo-European' population in pre-Hellenic Greece. On the basis of this map, Blegen then tried to determine the diffusion and special features of a 'pre-Indo-European culture' in Greece.

This study illustrates excellently how the syntheses of historians and ethnologists depend on linguistic hypotheses. However, this article was ill-founded. Fick's study was based on the theory which P. Kretschmer had put forward in his *Einleitung in die Geschichte der griechischen Sprache* (1896). But Haley had failed to note that important new evidence had led Kretschmer to change his theory radically later (Kretschmer 1925). While Haley and Blegen based their conclusions on Kretschmer's earlier theory, that the place-names formed with the suffixes -*nth*- (or -*nd*-) and -*s(s)*- were of pre-Indo-European origin, Kretschmer had meanwhile identified several of them as Indo-European. Moreover, recent studies have shown that many place-names which were formerly stated to be pre-Indo-European are in fact of Greek origin (see below).

F. Schachermeyr has recently published maps of the distribution of place-names in -*nth*-/-*nd*- and -*s(s)*- on the basis of which he traces the expansion of a 'pre-Indo-European' culture in the Balkan peninsula, Anatolia and Italy (Schachermeyr 1954; 1955: 242–3, 246–7, 264; 1967). The value of his conclusion depends on the validity of the linguistic data on which it is based, and his handling of toponymic material shows inadequate understanding of the rules which should govern its use. If one identifies as pre-Hellenic a place-name in Greece in -*s(s)*- or -*nth*-, this is because, in the one case, intervocalic $*$-*s*- or $*$-*sy*- was lost according to regular phonetic development in Greek, while in the other Greek -*nth*- cannot derive from the IE suffix $*$-*nt*-. But these features of phonetic development in Greek are not characteristic of e.g. Hittite or Luwian, Thracian, Macedonian or Illyrian; in these languages IE intervocalic $*$-*s*- or $*$-*sy*- is not lost and the IE suffix $*$-*nt*- is treated according to the phonetic laws of each language, as the following examples show.

In his maps Schachermeyr gives the name of the city *Edessa* as pre-IE. Its IE etymology is in fact evident. The city is famous for its springs and streams; hence its modern Bulgarian name *Voden*, 'watery'. *Edessa* comes regularly from $*$*wed-es-ya*, 'watery', a derivative of $*$*wedos*, 'water' (neuter -*es*- stem; cf. Gk. *hudos*, 'water'; -*ss*- regularly $< *$-*sy*-).

Salmydessos in eastern Thrace, cited as pre-IE, comes from $*$*salm-udes-yo-s*, '(city of) salt water'; the city is situated on the Black Sea coast near a salt lake; *salm-* corresponds to Gk. *halmē*, 'sea-water, brine', < **salma;* and **-udes-* to Gk. *hudos;* in Thracian **-sy-* > *-ss-*.

The place-name *Oinoanda* in south-western Anatolia, cited as pre-IE, is in fact the partly Hellenized form of the Hittite or Luwian city-name *Wiyanawanda*, derived from Hitt. *wiyana-*, 'wine', with the suffix *-wand(a)-*, < **-we/ont-*, and corresponding exactly to Gk. *Oinous* (gen. *-ountos*) from **woyno-wont-*, 'rich in wine', or 'vines' (**-nt-* is normally represented by *-nd-* in Hittite and Luwian). Names like *Argyruntum, Avendum* in the western part of the Balkan peninsula, or *Hydruntum, Tiliaventus* in Italy are stated to be pre-IE because of their suffix *-nt-*. But this suffix is very common in all IE languages and is clearly of IE origin. It is found frequently in place-names of Greek origin e.g. *Anthemous, Halous, Opous, Phegous, Strouthous* (all with stems in *-ount-*). Similarly, the Acarnanian place-name *Koronta* which Schachermeyr cites is really a dialectal Greek form from **koro-(w)e/ont-a* (n. pl.) derived from *koros* (m), 'excrement' (**-eo-* > Attic *-ou-*, Doric *ō*).

Many other place-names in Greece which Schachermeyr explains as pre-IE are also of Greek origin. First, names in which *-s(s)-* alternates with *-tt-* are Greek. The alternation *-s(s)-/-tt-* is phonetically regular in Greek and results from different treatments of the sequences **-ky-*, **-khy-*, **-ty-*, **-thy-*. In general, the variants in *-tt-* are characteristic of Attic, Boeotian and Cretan and are confined to particular phonetic contexts in other dialects. Those in *-s(s)-* are normal in other dialects. If one sets up a pre-Hellenic suffix *-s(s)-*, related to the Hittite and Luwian suffix *-ss-*, one cannot explain the alternation *-s(s)-/-tt-*; pre-Hellenic **-s(s)-* could have been represented by *-s(s)-* in Greek, but not by *-tt-*.

All the place-names in Greece formed with *-s(s)-/-tt-* can be explained satisfactorily as Greek formations, as derivatives of stems in *-k-*, *-t-* or *-th-* made with the IE suffix *-(i)yo-*; for example:

Kēttos, name of an Attic deme, < **kēk-yo-s*; derived from Gk. *kēx* (gen. *kēkos*), 'diver, gull'; so, 'place of sea-birds'.

Sphēttos, name of an Attic deme, < **sphēk-yo-s*; derived from Gk. *sphēx* (gen. *sphēkos*), 'wasp'; so 'place of wasps'.

Hermattos, place-name in Aetolia, < **hermak-yo-s*; derived from Gk. *hermax* gen. *hermakos*), 'reef'.

Hymēttos or *Hymēssos*, name of a mountain near Athens, < **humat-yo-s*; derived from Gk. *huma* (gen. *hymat-yo-s*) 'rain'; so 'rain-mountain' (cf. *Regensberg*). The name reflects the characteristic of the mountain. It is well known in Athens that if clouds gather round Mnt. Hymettos the city will have rain. *Hymēttos*, with *-ētt-* instead of *-att-*, probably shows false Atticization; or else **-aty-* > *-ett-*; cf. *Lykabattos*.

Lykabattos, Lykabēttos or *Lykabēssos*, name of a precipitous hill at Athens < **lukabant-yo-s;* derived from Gk. *lukabas* (gen. *lukabantos*), 'year'; so 'mountain of the year', in the sense of *Jahresberg* in German. In southern Germany and Switzerland this name has been given to mountains where the sun appears early over the summit in spring. It is known at Athens that in spring the sun rises over the summit of Lykabettos. The original form of the name appears to be *Lykabattos,* with *-att-* < **-anty-;* or perhaps **-anty-* > *-ātt-* > *-ētt-* with 'compensatory lengthening' (cf. Attic *kreittōn* < **kret-yōn, melitoutta* < **melit-ontyə*)

However, the place-names in which *-s(s)-* alternates with *-tt-* are not the only ones whose Greek origin is obvious. Others among the place-names in *-s(s)-* in Greece which have been supposed to be pre-IE are equally of Greek origin; for example:

Bolis(s)os, with *-s(s)-* < **-ty-;* derived from *boliton,* 'cattle-dung'
Eres(s)os, with *-s(s)-* < **-ty-;* derived from *eretēs,* 'rower'

Another formation is represented by the place-names made with the suffix *-as(s)a-, -ēs(s)a-,* < **-a-went-y;* these are also of Greek origin, for example:

Tiassa (-os), spring and river of Laconia; < **stiā-wessa,* derived from *stiā,* 'small pebble' (**st-* > *t-* in Laconian); *Pagasai,* port in Thessaly; < **pag-āwessa,* 'rocky (late)', derived from *pagos, m.,* 'rock, mountain, hill, hillock.'

There are also place-names containing the sequence *-nth-* which are of Greek origin; e.g. *Akanthos,* which Schachermeyr regards as pre-IE, is identical with the Greek work *akanthos, m.,* 'acanthus, spiny plant', cf. also *akantha, f.,* 'thorn, prickle, thistle', a compound of *ak-,* 'sharp, pointed', and *anthos,* 'flower'. *Olynthos* in Chalcidice is the same word as Gk. *olynthos,* 'late fig which rarely ripens'. We have here a Greek colony named after the tree *olunthos.* Even if the basic adjective was of pre-Hellenic origin, the place-name is Greek, a word in the vocabulary of Greek, used as an appellative. If this is so, we have a case similar to those of place-names such as *Église, Pierre* in French-speaking countries or *Kirchen* in German. These are words of Greek origin, but the place-names themselves are French and German, because the words are part of the vocabularies of French and German respectively. The place-names *Trikorynthos* and *Probalinthos* are also of Greek origin. They are often written with *-nth-,* but their original forms are well attested: *Trikorythos,* cf. *korus* (gen. *koruthos*), 'helmet'; and *Probalithos* from **probato-lithos,* with haplology; *-nth-* was written in these names in place of *-th-* under the influence of the place-names in *-nthos.*

II. *The pre-Hellenic and proto-Hellenic regions*
Certain place-names of Greek origin must thus be removed from the maps drawn up by Schachermeyr. However, there is no doubt that many place-names in Greece and the Aegean islands are pre-Hellenic, though not pre-Indo-European; for example: *Arakynthos, Amnisos, Benkasos, Berekynthos, Erymanthos, Kephis(s)os, Korinthos, Knossos, Kynthos, Labyrinthos, Laris(s)a, Pamisos, Parnas(s)os, Pyranthos, Pyrasos, Tiryns (-ynthos), Tylis(s)os, Zakynthos.* If one amends the distribution-maps of pre-Hellenic place-names in this way one can identify the primitive homeland of the Greeks.

The pre-Hellenic place-names formed with -*nth*- and -*s(s)*- occur in the Peloponnese, in central Greece, in Crete and in most of the Aegean islands, but they are entirely absent north of a line formed by the rivers Achelous and Peneius. The great mountain-range of Pindus forms a real barrier between peoples there. The region north of this line, which comprises Epirus as far as *Aulōn*, in the north (including Paravaia, Tymphaea, Athamania, Dolopia, Amphilochia and Acarnania), western and northern Thessaly (Hestiaeotis, Perrhaebia, Tripolis) and Pieria, i.e. approximately the whole of northern and north-western Greece, is characterized by the following features.

1. *Absence of pre-Hellenic place-names.* Names of the types which we have been considering north of the line of the Achelous and the Peneius on the maps referred to are: *Sabylinthos* and *Salynthios*; these are not true place-names but names of persons, probably of Thracian origin. *Phauttos*, in north-eastern Thessaly is a false form used in place of *Phaistos* (Georgiev 1961a: 15, 40; on *Agassa* and *Tyrissa* in Macedonia see Georgiev 1961a: 43–4).

All the principal names north of the line are of archaic Greek origin; for example:

Ēpeiros = *ēpeiros*, 'mainland'
Khaonia, Khaones, derived from *Khaōn* = **khaw-ōn*, 'place with gulfs' or 'chasms'; cf. *khaos*, 'empty space, yawning aperture, chasm, abyss'; *kha-sk-o*, 'open (intrans.), yawn'
Kammania, Kammanoi, from **kamna* < **(skap-ma*, 'pit, ditch', from *skap-to*, 'to dig'
Arktānes, from *arktos*, 'bear'
Oresteia, Orestai, from *oros, n.*, 'mountain'
Pāloeis, from Doric *pālos* = Attic *pēlos*, 'mud, mire'
Kōkytos = *kōkutos*, 'lamentation' (originally 'noise')
Akherōn, cf. Lith. *azeras*, Russ. *ozero*, 'lake', from **ag'hero-*
Keraunia orē, from *keraunos*, 'thunderbolt'
Lynkos, Lynkaiē, from *lunx* (gen. *lunkos*), 'lynx'

Olympos = **o-lumpos*, 'breaking, debris'; cf. skr. *lumpáti*, 'break, shatter'

Pindos, from **k'windo-*, 'white'; cf. skr. *śvindate*, 'shine'

Onkhesmos; Aeolic = Attic *An-khēsmos*; cf. *ana-kheo*, 'overflow, drain into (intrans.)', *ana-khoē*, 'volcanic eruption'

Euroia = *euroia*, 'easy' or 'abundant course (of a river)'

Boukhetos = *bous*, 'ox, cow', + *okhetos*, 'water-channel, brook, canal'

Kharadra, Kharadros = *kharadra, kharadros*, 'torrent-bed, ravine'

Drys = *drus*, 'oak'

Thessalia, Thessaloi (Thess. *Petthalos*, Boeot. *Phettalos*, Attic *Thettalos;* cf. *thessasthai* (aor.), 'desire';

Lēthaios (e = i) = *Lithaios*, from *lithos*, 'stone'

Dolikhē from *dolikhos*, 'long'

Thus in the region defined just above, roughly northern and north-western Greece, one finds only archaic Greek place-names. Consequently, this is the proto-Hellenic area, the early homeland of the Greeks where they lived before they invaded central and southern Greece. Since Greek place-names are very dense in that region and they have a very archaic appearance, one may suppose that the proto-Greeks were settled in it during many centuries and even millennia.

III. Proto-Aeolic and proto-Ionic in the Mycenaean texts

Research on the Mycenaean (Linear B) texts has established that there are traces of two dialects in Mycenaean Greek (Georgiev 1956: 183–8; 1961b; 1964; 1966: 122–4; Bartonek 1966; Risch 1966; 1968). The most important proof is the double representation of IE sonants in Mycenaean Greek by *o* and *a* or sequences containing them; examples are:

pe-mo and *pe-ma* = Attic *sperma*, 'seed, grain' $(o/a < n̥)$

a-re-po-zo-o and *a-re-pa-zo-o* = *aleipho/a-zoos*, 'unguent-boiler'; $(o/a < n̥)$; cf. Attic *aleiphar*, 'oil' $(-ar < r̥)$

E-ro-pa-ke-ta = *eloph-āgetas*, *e-ro-pa-ke-u* = *eloph-āgeus*, beside *e-ra-po ri-me-ne* = *Elaphōn limenei* (dat.); cf. Attic *elaphos*, 'deer' $(a < n̥)$

a-mo, 'wheel' (dat. plur. *a-mo-si*): Attic *harma*, 'chariot' (dat. plur. *harmasi*), beside *e-ka-ma-pi* = *ekhma-phi* (inst. plur.) from *ekhma*, 'barrier, obstacle' $(o/a < n̥)$

a-no-wo-to = Attic *an-ouatos*, 'without ears' $(o/a < n̥)$ beside *apeasa*, 'absent' (fem.; $a < n$)

to-pe-za = Attic *trapeza* 'table (with four legs)', beside *ka-po* = Attic *karpos*, 'fruit' $(o(r)/ra/ar < r̥)$

wo-ro-ne-ja cf. Attic *arneios*, 'of lamb' (< **wr̥n-*) beside *ra-pe-te* = *raptēr*, 'repairer, tailor', *e-ra-pe-me-na* = Attic *erramene*, 'sewn' (< **wr̥p-*)

e-ne-wo = Attic *ennea* $(o/a < n̥)$ beside *e-ne-ka*, 'on account of' (< **semwekn̥t*)

qe-to-ro-po-pi = $k^w etro$-$po(p)phi$, cf. Attic *tetrapous*, 'four-legged' ($<$
$\star k^w etr$-) beside *pa-we-a* = Attic *phārē* (plur. of *phāros*, *n.*) 'pieces of cloth'
($< \star bh\dot{r}w$-*es*-).

Since it has been established that this double treatment of IE sonants is not
an isolated phenomenon in Mycenaean Greek, but paralleled by others
(Georgiev 1964: 127–30), the most natural conclusion about the dialectal
character of the Mycenaean Greek documents is that 'Mycenaean' represents
a standard language formed by a mixture of proto-Aeolic and proto-Ionic;
i.e., the first Greek *koine*. These data from Mycenaean that we have just
discussed have confirmed the essential part of Kretschmer's theory: that in
the Peloponnese proto-Aeolic was superimposed on a proto-Ionic stratum;
and that the Greeks came into Greece in three waves: first the Ionians, then
the Aeolians and finally the Dorians. The attempts of Porzig and Risch to
substitute other reconstructions for this have failed; the data themselves
have now led them to withdraw their suggestions (Georgiev 1970).
The principal difference between Kretschmer's ideas and mine is that he
supposed that the proto-Greeks came from central Europe, while I have
demonstrated that their 'homeland' lay in northern and north-western
Greece. While Kretschmer defined the place-names in *-nth-* and *-s(s)-* as
pre-Indo-European, and later as partly proto-Indo-European, I have shown
that they belonged to a particular Indo-European language.

IV. *Correlation of linguistic data with archaeological and historical*

If one sets the linguistic evidence and conclusions from it besides those of
archaeology and history, one may sketch in the following outline of the
history of the Aegean from the Neolithic period to the end of the
Mycenaean.

1. During the Neolithic period central and southern Greece, Crete and most
of the Aegean islands were inhabited mainly by the population that formed
and used the pre-Hellenic place-names in *-nth-* and *-s(s)-*. These names of
places, rivers and mountains constitute the most ancient toponymic stratum
in Greece. Since the *Pelasgoi* were the pre-Hellenic population of the
Aegean according to Greek tradition, one may term this stratum 'Pelasgian'.
Thus we are justified in concluding that the Pelasgians, i.e. the pre-Hellenic
population of Greece, were living in central and southern Greece from a
very early period, at least from the times when the tribes of that region
began to lead a settled life, i.e. at least from the Early Neolithic period.
Before that, the population was very sparse and lived a nomadic existence.
Towards the end of the nineteenth century the place-names just mentioned
were stated to be pre-Indo-European and this remained the accepted
opinion for some time. But recent research has shown that they belonged to

a specific IE language whose closest cognates are the Hittite-Luwian group on the one hand and Thracian on the other. In accordance with the phonetic rules established specifically for this 'Pelasgian' language, one may give etymologies for some of the most ancient place-names of Greece, for example (Georgiev 1966a: 107–19, 206–21):

Amnisos, river and city in Crete; cf. Lat. *amnis*, 'river'

Erymanthos, Myc. *o-ru-ma-to* = *orumanthos*; cf. *Uruwantas* in Hittite toponymy; H. Hitt and Luwian *ura-*, 'great', skt. *uru-*, 'wide' (suffix -$^*w/me/ont$-)

Korinthos, the name of the city situated near a mountain; < $^*g^w\mathring{i}ri\text{-}went$-; cf. *kuriwanda-*, a mountain in south-western Anatolia; skt. *giri-*, 'mountain', Alb. *gur*, 'rock', < $^*g^w\mathring{i}ri$-

Panisos, river in Thessaly; cf. Gothic *fani*, 'mud', < $^*po\text{-}ni$-

Tiryns (-*ynthos*; with -*ei*- written as -*i*-) < $^*ders\text{-}\d{n}t$- = Attic-Ionic *deiras* (-*ados*) cf. 'rock, high ground', (Cret. *Dēras*, skt. *dṛsat*, f. 'rock, large stone'

2. According to many archaeologists emigrants from Anatolia who brought with them knowledge of metallurgy established themselves in the Cyclades and in trading stations on the coasts of mainland Greece at the beginning of Early Helladic I (±2750–2450 B.C.) and during Early Helladic II (±2450–2200 B.C.). At the same time (±2400–2200 B.C.) another group of these emigrants settled in Crete, introducing the civilization of Early Minoan II (Rachet 1969: 146). The earliest toponymic in western Anatolia consists of place-names in -*nd*- and -*s*(*s*)- which are of Hittite-Luwian origin. The colonists just mentioned, who exercised a certain influence on the pre-Hellenic population of Greece and Crete and were probably assimilated by it, were thus of Hittite-Luwian origin.

3. The position regarding Crete is clear. The archaeologists recognize two distinct ethnic groups or strata there in pre-Hellenic periods: the population of the Neolithic period (±6000–2600 B.C.) and that of the Minoan (from ±2600 B.C. onwards; Platon 1966: 123–5). The existence of two such groups is in accordance with information in the *Odyssey* (XIX, 172–7) which distinguishes two pre-Hellenic peoples in Crete, *Eteokrētes* and *Pelasgoi*. The origin and provenance of the two ethnic groups mentioned can be determined by means of linguistic evidence. Throughout Crete one finds the same stratum of pre-Hellenic place-names as was characteristic of pre-Hellenic Greece; e.g. *Amnisos, Benkasos, Berekynthos, Knossos, Labyrinthos, Laris(s)a*. These are names of 'Pelasgic' origin. Consequently the population of Crete in the Neolithic period (±6000–2600 B.C.) was Pelasgian. Successive waves of Pelasgian tribes must have moved into Crete from southern Greece.

According to many archaeologists eastern and central Crete received immigrants from south-western Anatolia during the Minoan period (about 2600 B.C.). Eastern Crete, exposed to Anatolian influences, appears to have played a vital role in the initial development of Minoan civilization (Tulard 1962: 19). In the third and second millennium B.C. western and south-western Anatolia was inhabited by a Hittite-Luwian population whose direct descendants were the Lycians, the Carians and the Lydians. According to Greek tradition Crete was inhabited in pre-Hellenic times by a people called the *Termilai*, ancestors of the people of the same name who lived in Lycia in Classical times and whose inscriptions are in a language of Luwian origin. The second pre-Hellenic people of Crete, the *Eteokrētes* of the Odyssey, whom we call 'Minoans', were thus *Termilai*, men of Luwian origin. This is confirmed by the toponymy of eastern and central Crete where we find place-names like *Karnesso(polis)*, *Kytaion*, *Minōa*, *Myrin(n)a* which can be explained as Hittite-Luwian.

4. During the Neolithic period and Early Helladic I and II, i.e. until nearly the end of the third millennium, the Greeks, as shown above, were settled in the part of northern Greece that lies north of the line of the rivers Achelous and Peneius, approximately Epirus, western Thessaly and northern Pieria. Archaeological research has now shown that the people who introduced the EH III culture (±2150–2000/1950 B.C.) were distinct from those who had developed the culture that preceded it. On the other hand, it is now emphasized that there was a continuous cultural development in Greece from the end of EH until the LH period (Rachet 1969: 144–8, 196–200; Caskey 1964: 18–20, 37–8;). We have seen that the three principal dialects of Greek, Ionic, Aeolic and Doric, were in existence before the time of the Mycenaean texts. One may even suppose that the initial tendencies towards the differentiation of these dialects began during the last period in which Common Greek was in use in the Greek 'homeland' in northern Greece. A. Meillet wrote in 1943: "A migration of peoples does not take place as a single movement. Groups detach themselves one after the other, and there are successive invasions until the territory under attack is occupied" (Meillet 1943: 76; English translation). Naturally, we know nothing definite about the successive early movements in the complex process of Greek immigration into Greece, but at least we have a few facts about the Dorian invasion and some vague indications of how that of the Aeolians took place.

Now on the basis of the archaeological evidence and linguistic deductions we may suppose that groups or tribes of proto-Greeks began to invade central Greece and the Peloponnese towards the end of the third millennium. These were the proto-Ionians, the first wave of invaders. A tributary of the R. Peneius in northern Thessaly is called *Iōn* (gen. *Iōnos*; Strabo VII, 327). this name *Iōn* may be explained as **iā-wōn*, 'noisy', from *iā*, 'noise, cry' (on the formation see Schwyzer 1939: 521). The name *Iōnes*, = Homeric *Iāones*, has the same origin. So one may conclude that the proto-Ionians were once settled near the river *Iōn*.

During the first half of the second millennium B.C. the proto-Greeks already occupied almost the whole of Greece. They were distributed as follows: the proto-Dorians in north-western Greece; the proto-Aeolians in the north-east and part of the centre of Greece (Thessaly, Phocis, north-western Boeotia, Locris, Aetolia and southern Acarnania); the proto-Ionians in Attica, most of Boeotia, Euboea and the Peloponnese. Towards the end of the Middle Helladic period (MH III, ± 1700–1550 B.C.) and at the beginning of the Late Helladic (LH I, ±1550–1500 B.C.), so within the period which is termed 'Mycenaean', archaeology notes substantial changes: new ceramic techniques, increase of wealth, use of cemeteries with collective tombs, tholos-tombs and chamber-tombs (Rachet 1969: 196). Granted that Mycenaean Greek contains proto-Aeolic and proto-Ionic elements, one may associate these changes with the arrival of the proto-Aeolians, the second wave of Greeks to enter southern Greece.

5. So, towards the middle of the second millennium, proto-Aeolians, probably Achaeans from Achaea Phthiotis (southern Thessaly) occupied the Peloponnese, or at least the greater part of it, superimposing themselves on the proto-Ionian stratum. As a result there developed between the sixteenth or fifteenth century and the thirteenth, in the Mycenaean period, the first form of standard Greek, formed by admixture of proto-Aeolic and proto-Ionic. This was the Mycenaean *koine*, spoken in the Peloponnese, in part of Crete (at Knossos) and no doubt in other centres of Mycenaean civilization. Nevertheless, this *koine* did not extend to northern and central Greece: proto-Doric continued in use in north-western Greece, proto-Aeolic in its north-eastern parts, and proto-Ionic in Attic, Euboea and even in some places in the Peloponnese.

6. The Dorian invasion, which was not a legend, as is now often said, but a fact of history, was the third wave of migration which broke over the central western part of Greece and over the whole of its southern parts (Desborough and Hammond 1964: 3–7, 22–35). It took place towards the end of Late Helladic III (±1230–1100 B.C.) and at the beginning of the sub-Mycenaean period, i.e. *c.* 1200–1100 B.C. In destroying Mycenaean civilization it also put an end to the use of the Mycenaean *koine*. The last relics of this were the Arcado-Cyprian dialects, which we know after they had been affected by Doric, and the Homeric dialect, preserved by the *aoidoi* (bards) (Kirk 1964: 4–6) but partly ionicized and later atticized (Georgiev: 1961b: 10; 1964: 131–3).

References

BARTONĚK, A. 1966. 'Mycenaean koine reconsidered.' *Cambridge Colloquium on Mycenaean Studies* (ed. L. R. Palmer and J. Chadwick): 95–103.

BRANDENSTEIN, W. 1954. *Griechische Sprachwissenschaft*, I. Berlin.

CASKEY, J. L. 1964. 'Greece, Crete and the Aegean islands in the Early Bronze Age.' *CAH* (rev. ed.) I, Chap. XXVIa/Fasc. 24.

CHADWICK, J. 1963. 'The prehistory of the Greek language.' *CAH* (rev. ed.) II, Chap. XXXIX/Fasc. 15.

DESBOROUGH, V. R. D'A. and HAMMOND, N. G. L. 1962. 'The end of Mycenaean civilization and the Dark Age.' *CAH* (rev. ed) II, Chap. XXXVI/Fasc. 13.

FICK, A. 1905. *Vorgriechische Ortsnamen als Quelle fur die Vorgeschichte Griechenlands*. Göttingen.

GEORGIEV, V. I. 1956. 'La koine créto-mycénienne'; *Études mycéniennes* (ed. M. Lejeune, Paris).

——. 1961a. *La toponymie ancienne de la péninsule balkanique et la thèse mediteranéenne*. Sofia.

——. 1961b. 'Das Problem der homerischen Sprache im Lichte der kretisch-mykenischen Texte.' *Minoica und Homer* (ed. V. I. Georgiev and J. Hirmscher; Berlin): 10–6.

——. 1964. Mycenaean among the other Greek dialects.' *Mycenaean Studies* (ed. E. L. Bennett): 125–39.

——. 1966a. *Introduzione alla storia delle lingue indeuropee* (*IncGraec*. 9). Rome.

——. 1966b. 'Mycénien et homérique: le problème du digamma.' *Cambridge Colloquium on Mycenaean Studies*: 104–24.

——. 1969. 'La stratification principale des toponymes en Grèce ancienne.' *Proceedings of the 9th International Congress of Onomastic Sciences* (Louvain, 1966: ed. J. M. Dodgson and A. D. Mills; *Onoma*, 13, 14; London): 227–35.

——. 1970. 'Le traitment des sonantes voyelles indo-européennes et le problème du caractère de la langue mycénienne.' (Proceedings of the Salamanca Colloquium on Mycenaean studies, 1970.)

HALEY, J. B. and BLEGEN, C. W. 1928. 'The coming of the Greeks. 1. The geographical distribution of pre-Greek place-names. 2. The geographical distribution of prehistoric remains in Greece.' *AJA*, 32: 141–54.

KIRK, G. S. 1964. 'The Homeric poems as history.' *CAH* (rev. ed.) II, Chap XXXIX(b)/Fasc. 22.

KRETSCHMER, P. 1896. *Einleitung in die Geschichte der griechischen Sprache*. Göttingen.

——. 1925. 'Das *nt*-Suffix.' *Glotta*, 14: 84–106.

MEILLET, A. 1943. *Aperçu d'une histoire de la lanque grecque*. Paris

MELLAART, J. 1958. 'The end of the Early Bronze Age in Anatolia and the Aegean.' *AJA*, 62: 9–33.

MILEWSKI, T. 1948. *Zarys jezykoznowstwa ogólnego*, II/2. Lublin-Krakow.

PLATON, N. 1966. *Crète*. London.

RACHET, G. 1969. *Archéologie de la Grèce préhistorique*. Paris.

RISCH, E. 1966. 'Les différences dialectales dans le mycénien.' *Cambridge Colloquium on Mycenaean Studies*: 150–7.

——. 1968. 'Dialectal classification of Mycenaean: conclusions.' *Studia Mycenaea* (ed. A. Bartoněk; Brno): 207–10.

SCHACHERMEYR, F. 1954. 'Prähistorische Kulturen Griechenlands. Die ältesten Kulturen Griechenlands.' *RE* (2). 22/2: 1350–1548.

——. 1955. *Die ältesten Kulturen Griechenlands*. Stuttgart.

——. 1967. *Agäis und Orient*. Vienna.
SCHWYZER, E. 1939. *Griechische Grammatik*, I. Munich.
TULARD, J. 1962. *Histoire de la Crète*. Paris.

Discussion

JOHN CHADWICK: My friend Professor Georgiev has given one of his usual masterly surveys of his own views; but I fear that he has perhaps not indicated to some members of his audience that these represent not a general consensus among linguists, but a personal approach of his own. I take the opportunity of applying a correction, confident that my views are shared by other linguists, at least in part. Professor Georgiev apparently thinks that I hold the view that the Greeks came to Greece from central Europe. In what I have written, the attentive reader will in fact discover that I quote this old view in order to criticize it (Chadwick 1965: 1968; 1969a). My own opinion, advanced with due caution, but firmly held, is that the question 'Where did the Greeks come from?' is meaningless. We can only begin to speak of Greeks after the formation of the Greek language as a recognizably distinct branch of Indo-European; and I gave reasons for believing that this process took place inside Greece during the first half of the second millennium B.C. I agree with Professor Georgiev's strictures on the method applied by F. Schachermeyr, but not for the same reasons. Professor Georgiev believes in the existence of one or more Indo-European idioms which are not preserved in any texts, but may (in his opinion) be reconstructed from the place-names and loan-words that they contributed to Greek. How risky such a procedure is may be tested by applying it to situations where the underlying language is known: we might for instance try to reconstruct the basic phonology of Hindu from Anglo-Indian loan-words. I once amused myself and others by proving that the pre-Columbian language of North America was an Indo-European idiom, on the basis of etymologies of American loan-words in English. This method has been justly and devastatingly criticized by D. A. Hester (Hester 1965; 1966; 1967). I am not willing to accept a single one of Professor Georgiev's Indo-European etymologies of place-names, because in no case can we independently determine the meaning of the name. I agree that there are many non-Greek and therefore pre-Greek names in Greece; but I do not share his confidence that they are absent from north-west Greece. It is a tempting theory that some of the variations in Mycenaean spelling are due to the presence of two slightly differentiated dialects, though some of Professor Georgiev's examples are certainly wrong, and others are at least doubtful. The etymologies given for *heneka* and *rhaptō* are false; and that for *trapeza* is, to my mind, suspect. There is no warrant for the idea that Mycenaean is a mixture of proto-Aeolian and proto-Ionic; some linguists now reject the whole idea of a proto-Ionic existing in the Mycenaean era, and Professor Georgiev is a little optimistic if he thinks E. Risch (I cannot speak for W. Porzig) is now ready to renounce his theory. It follows from this that the sketch of the linguistic history of the Greek peninsula offered by Professor Georgiev is erroneous in most of its details. Those who wish to see a rival view should consult my chapter 'The prehistory of the Greek language' in *Cambridge Ancient History*, (rev. ed.; vol. II, xxxix/Fasc. 15) and my article 'Greek and Pre-Greek' (Chadwick 1965; 1969b). These may bring home to those who are not specialists in linguistic work that the study of place-names and loan-words is rather more complicated than they may have thought; and that the certain facts are few. The only certain historical conclusions to be drawn for Greece from linguistic evidence of this type are these: at least one language was spoken there before Greek; Greek is the product of the engrafting of an IE idiom on non-Greek stock; Greek was already spoken in Greece in the Mycenaean age; finally, the distribution of the Greek dialects within Greece was radically changed by the events that followed the collapse of the Mycenaean civilization.

IVAN PUDIĆ: The following comments should be made on Professor Georgiev's etymologies of Greek and pre-Hellenic place-names and explanations of their meanings.

1. He gives the impression that all pre-Hellenic place-names in the Aegean can be explained simply and easily as IE material. The original form and the IE stem are reconstructed and set up as things certain and established. Such procedure is temptingly reminiscent of the long-since abandoned 'Illyrian theory'. In my opinion, we are in fact dealing, in those place-names, with very old forms of words, no longer always certain and unambiguous, whose meanings cannot be deduced so long as we know no independent words of the languages to which they belonged, with which we might compare them.

2. The suffixes which are adduced occur quite frequently in non-Indo-European languages, e.g. in Basque and in some languages of the Caucasus.

3. Our conceptions of 'Indo-European' and 'the Indo-Europeans' are, fundamentally, still those of German romanticism. On the basis of them, linguists, archaeologists and historians have produced varied theories about the language and the people who spoke it. So we may speak of K. Brugmann's 'Indo-European', A. Meillet's, F. Specht's, and so on.

4. It has become fairly clear in the last twenty or so years that the individual (historical) IE languages became autonomous and unitary idioms

only in late periods, just before their earliest attestation. This is accepted as certain and proved for Germanic, and the same assumption should be made about other IE languages or groups. That means that it was in Greece itself (essentially) that Greek became a distinct and homogeneous language, though naturally it inherited the old 'Indo-European' elements which were common to all IE dialects. Thus, the individual IE languages did not evolve out of a unitary language, nor did they appear in the areas of their currency in historical times as developed entities. It was rather the case that groups of dialects were introduced into those areas and first came to full developement as languages in them.

References

CHADWICK, J. 1963. 'The prehistory of the Greek language.' *CAH* (rev. ed.) Vol. II, Chap. XXXIX/Fasc. 15.

——. 1969a. 'Aegean history 1500–1200 B.C.' *Studii Clasice*, 11: 7–18.

——. 1969b. 'Greek and Pre-Greek.' *TPhS*, 1969: 80–98.

HESTER, D. A. 1964. ' "Pelasgian"—a new Indo-European Language?' *Lingua*, 13: 335–84.

——. 1966. 'A reply to Professor Georgiev's "Was stellt die Pelasgentheorie dar?" *Lingua*, 16: 274–8.

——. 1967. 'Methods of identifying loan-word strata in Greek (a reply to Merlingen).' *Lingua*, 18: 168–78.

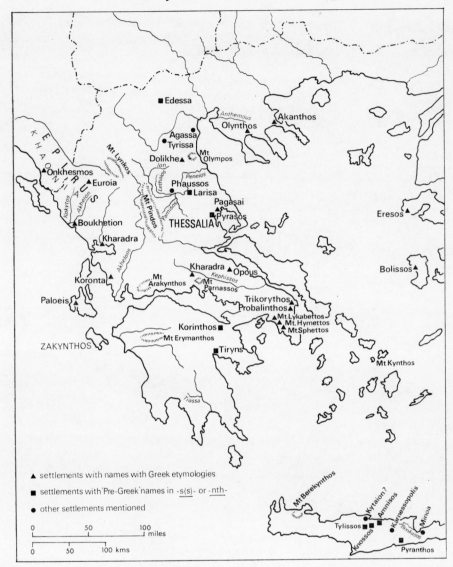

Fig. 24.1. Greece and the Aegean islands: early place-names

Indo-European mythology in the Bronze Age

IVAN PUDIĆ
University of Belgrade

1. *The main features of Indo-European belief*

The greatest god of Greeks, Illyrians, Macedonians, Romans, Germans and Indians was the same, a god of the light: *Zeus, Deipatyros, Ziu, Diespater, Tyr, Dyaus*; cf. also *dŭždĭ-bogŭ* < **dus-diu-*, 'bad weather' (Vassmer 1953: 357, *s.v. dozhd*'); *Tin-daridai*, 'sons of Zeus'; Etruscan *Tin, Tinia*. The principal characteristics of this god were the following. He was associated with the concept of light, and this concept of heavenly and divine light was linked with the idea of authority; this is the reason why *pətēr, 'father', is continually attached to his name. Zeus is the 'father of the family' who looks after the household and has authority over its members. This role is characteristic of the patriarchal society which prevailed among all Indo-European peoples. The cult of the hearth, personified in the Roman *Vesta* and Greek *Hestia*, was regularly connected with this patriarchal family organization. Zeus as 'pater familias' was elevated in belief to the position of tribal forefather not only of gods but also of men: in Greek, *patēr andrōn te theōn te*. The Indo-Europeans had no 'mother-goddess' who stood above men and other deities. 'Heaven' for them was essentially the place of storms and other such meteorological phenomena. For this reason their Storm-god (the Greek *Zeus*) lives on a mountain: the highest mountain; and as Storm-god with his throne on its summit he is the high god and King of the Gods. The others wait on him as subjects. The Greek personification of the upper heavens, where the light is clearer than in heaven nearer to the earth, was *Aithēr*.

II. *Mythological elements common to Greeks, Illyrians, and Macedonians*

1. Kadmos, founder of Thebes, and Harmonie, daughter of Ares and Aphrodite, had several children, of whom one was named *Illyrios*. When their children were smitten with madness, Kadmos and Harmonie died and were

changed into snakes. Their tombs were shown on the Epirote-Illyrian border. The Illyrians were 'snake-men', associated with chthonic deities, such as Poseidon-Messapios. In Epirus Kadmos, snakes, Illyrians and 'eel-men' were connected. The Thracian kings called themselves 'sons of Hermes'. The Greek name for one Illyrian tribe was *Enhelānes*, 'eel-men'; cf. Lat. *enocilis* (gloss) = *anguilla*, Venetic *Enoclia* (personal names).

2. *Semele*, the name of Kadmos' daughter, may be identified with Phrygian *zemelo/zemlya*. Semele bore *Dionysos* to Zeus and he entrusted him to Ino to rear and bring up. Dionysos is an Illyrian and Thracian deity. The Paeonians called him *Dyalos*, cf. Gothic *dwals*, 'foolish', Gk. *thuō, thuiō*, 'to be possessed, demented'. The tomb of *Oibalos*, the first ruler of Sparta, was situated near the temple of Zeus, *Zeus genethlios*. The name *Oibalos* may be compared with Gk. *oiphalos*, 'parent, "genius", phallus'. *Oibalos* is to be connected also with Gk. *Oipholēs*; the correspondence of *b* and *ph* in the two names is parallel to that of *d* and *th* in *Dyalos: Thyales*. This last equation points to the basic feature of the cult of Dionysos: its connection with frenzy. The priestesses of Dionysos were *Thyades* or *Mainades* (Gk. *mainomai*, 'be demented'). Semele too, after apotheosis, was named *Thyonē*.

3. Venetic *Reitia* is connected with Laconian *Orthia* (identical with Artemis). The cults of Dionysos and Orthia (Reitia) have features in common. They are connected through Dionysos' madness. When Alopēkos and Atrabakos found the picture of Orthia, they were afflicted with madness. Orestes too went mad, after killing his mother.

4. Dionysos is also the god of wine. Ptolemy knows a river *Oineos potamou* (gen.) in Liburnia. This name is reminiscent of the name of the Aetolian god *Oineus*, a descendant of Orestes. Stephanus Byzantinus recounts how Orestes, driven by madness, came with his sister Harmonie among the Macedonian *Orestai*.

5. The world of Dionysos is above all a world of women. He was brought up by women, he was accompanied by them everywhere, and they were his first victims. Venetic *Reitia* and *Orthia* are women's deities. *Artemis Korythalia* was worshipped in the *tithēnidia*, 'festival of the wet-nurses'. *Dionysos'* nurse Ino was revered in Rome as *Mater-Matuta*. She too was striken by Dionysos' madness and threw herself into the sea. Dionysos is called *Orthos* in one passage. Finally, Artemis and her Roman counterpart Diana are the protectors of escaped slaves.

6. The origins of Greek drama should be looked for among the pre-hellenic peoples of Greece. Phallus-cult was typical of their religion.

III. *Ancient Macedonian mythology*

The following equations and connections of Macedonian cult-names, ethnika, and other names are of interest. *Agrotera*, attested in inscriptions in Macedonia, was a cult-epithet of Artemis. The *Airopes* are described as a 'clan in Macedonia and the tribe of the founder of Troizen', which is concerned with the legend of the Peloponnesian origin of the Macedonians; *Airopēs* was one of the three brothers who founded the ruling house of the *Argeadai*. The *Arantisin- Erinysi* are identified with the *Eumenides*. *Alkidēmos* was a cult-epithet of Athene of Pela, meaning 'Protector of the People'. The seventh month of the Macedonian calendar was called *Artemisios* in honour of Artemis (Orthia). *Daisios*, the name of ninth month, was formed from *dais* (gen. *daitos*), 'rest, feast, festival', and was sacred to Dionysos. A cult-title of Herakles was *Propatōr*. Many of these names show linguistic connections between Macedonian and Greek, as well as equivalence of Greek and Macedonian deities and legendary heroes.

References

BORGEAUD, W. 1943. *Les Illyriens en Grèce et en Italie*. Geneva.
ČAJKANOVIĆ, V. 1941. *O srpskom vrhovnom bogu*. Belgrade.
DEVOTO, G. 1961. *Origini indeuropee*. Florence.
GRIMAL, P. 1958. *Dictionnaire de la mythologie grecque et romaine*. Paris.
KALLIRIS, J. N. 1954. *Les anciens Macédoniens*, I. Athens.
VASMER, M. 1953. *Russiches Etymologisches Wörterbuch*, I. Heidelberg.

Problems in the general correlation of archaeological and linguistic strata in prehistoric Greece: the model of autochthonous origin

COLIN RENFREW

University of Sheffield

I. *The problem*

The problem of the origin of the Greek language arises from consideration of linguistic data, and in investigating it archaeological evidence is secondary, although it may perhaps contribute towards a solution. The position adopted here arises in the first instance, however, from a consideration of the archaeological data, and specifically from the failure to find plausible material evidence for a cultural intrusion into Greece during the Bronze Age which might be correlated with 'the coming of the Greeks'. As J. D. Evans has said, with reference to the Aegean: "It is a most striking fact that, setting aside the linguistic and traditional evidence, there is little or nothing in the archaeology which demands that we look outside the natural limits of the region for explanations of change" (résumé of paper to the Colloquium: 2).

The point of the present paper is to show that a long chronology for the linguistic changes under consideration may correlate better with the archaeological record than a short one. The time-scale generally adopted for the differentiation and evolution of the Greek language from its 'proto-Indo-European' precursor seems too short. Over the past few decades the decipherment of newly discovered documents has revealed Hittite, Mycenaean Greek and proto-Indic as languages already well differentiated by the middle of the second millennium B.C. And Mycenaean Greek contains words still basic in demotic Greek today, which are not found in Hittite or proto-Indic. No sophisticated appeal to glottochronology is needed to see that when three and a half millennia separate Mycenaean from modern demotic Greek (*dhimotiki*), a comparable period is at least conceivable for the differentiation of the early Indo-European languages from their hypothetical 'proto-Indo-European' predecessors. In any case several essentially philological points seem to be widely agreed by those studying the early origins of the Greek language. It is well to begin with these.

1. The earliest reliable information from historical sources and Greek alphabetic inscriptions indicates that the Greek language was in use over most of the Aegean region by the eighth and seventh centuries B.C.

2. M. Ventris's decipherment of the Minoan Linear B script has established that an early form of Greek was written at a number of Mycenaean sites in Greece and at Knossos in Crete in the second half of the second millennium B.C. This decipherment is at present not universally accepted (cf. Levin 1964; Grumach 1969: 22–6). But the question whether the tablets are or are not written in Greek is so basic as to determine the direction of any further hypothesis or research. Here the decipherment is accepted as showing that the Greek language (in whatever form) was already spoken in southern Greece during the Late Bronze Age. The alternative (that Greek was not then spoken in the Aegean) no doubt remains possible: if it be accepted, however, the remainder of this discussion is invalidated.

3. The Greek language belongs to the Indo-European language-family. The distribution of speakers of IE languages in early Greek times (the earlier first millennium B.C.) is approximately known. It centres upon Europe, with some outliers in Anatolia (where, in the central region, Hittite had previously been a contemporary of Mycenaean Greek) and in more eastern lands. At that time there were in Europe probably only a few localized groups who did not speak some IE language. Certainly by Classical times the distribution of non-IE languages in Europe is very limited.

4. Evidence for early linguistic forms can be preserved in place-names. In Greece the names with -s(s)- and -nth- suffixes have attracted special interest.

II. *Correlation between language and the material record*

It is well established through studies of change in historic times that the language spoken in a given area may change in the course of a couple of centuries, without significant alteration in the material culture. (The term 'culture' is used throughout in its specialized archaeological sense.) Again it is documented that the material culture in a given region may undergo considerable change without significant change in language. On the other hand, when a major transfer of population between two regions occurs, it is often accompanied in the receiving area by both linguistic and a cultural change. As regards the prehistory of Europe, and specifically that of Greece, two polar positions might be maintained:

1. Significant changes in population are likely to have been accompanied by changes in language and in material culture. Consequently discontinuities and changes in material culture may be taken as likely indicators of linguistic change. Moreover, when the material evidence indicates strong influence, and possibly migration, from an outside area, linguistic influences from this area may be assumed.

2. In practice linguistic changes and also changes in material culture have complex origins. Only rarely is there a population shift of such magnitude that it can be confidently designated the 'cause' of such changes, when they occur together. It is vain, therefore, to expect any close correlation between changes in the archaeological and linguistic records. Prehistoric archaeology is not likely to throw much light on the origins of the Greeks or of the Indo-Europeans.

In my own view there is much to recommend the second of these positions. Certainly the mechanisms of population transfer are generally likely to have been complex. And only a rather sophisticated model for the diffusion of innovations or of population, of the kind investigated by Hägerstrand (1967), is likely to do justice to the reality. Unfortunately, however, we rarely have data sufficiently detailed to permit the application of such a model to the prehistoric past, so that the first position, despite its over-simplifications, is taken as the basis for discussion here.

III. *The model of the remote homeland*
The question of the 'coming of the Greeks' must be considered in relation to the more general one of IE origins. It is widely believed that the present distribution of the IE languages in Europe is the result of migrations and folk movements during the Bronze Age. The location of the original point of dispersal of the first IE speakers, the 'homeland', is a matter for discussion: many workers believe it to have been in the regions north of the Black Sea. Such a view makes it inevitable that we view the first IE speakers in Greece, and *a fortiori* the first Greek speakers, as arriving during (or at the end of) the Bronze Age. Their 'arrival' has been set at every possible or supposed discontinuity in the archaeological record: at the end of the Bronze Age (a possibility open now only to those who reject the Ventris decipherment), at the beginning of the Mycenaean period, at the beginning of the Middle Bronze Age, or at the onset of the Early Helladic III period, as recently re-defined by J. L. Caskey (1960). Approaches to the problem have been fundamentally influenced by the important paper of J. B. Haley and C. W. Blegen, 'The coming of the Greeks' (1928). In it Haley produced, on the basis of A. Fick's *Die vorgriechische Ortsnamen*, a map of 'pre-Greek' place-names, of which the most numerous were those with -*nth*- or -*ss*- suffixes. Haley suggested that these were "transferred" from Asia Minor. Blegen

regarded them as "a legacy from pre-Greek times" and considered their distribution in relation to the archaeological data. He wrote of "a pre-Greek linguistic family occupying in force Crete, the Cyclades, the southern and eastern Peloponnese and central Greece, with offshoots extending beyond to the north, north-west and west into the adjoining provinces" (Haley and Blegen 1928: 148). He stressed the "divergence of culture" between the mainland and Crete in the Middle and Late Bronze Ages and the (then) absence of Neolithic finds from the Cyclades. This led naturally to the view that the place-names could be correlated with the archaeological finds of the Early Bronze Age. Indeed Blegen and Wace had already concluded that the Early Minoan, Early Cycladic and Early Helladic civilizations "are all branches of one great parent stock which pursued parallel but more or less independent courses" (1918: 180).

In this way it was concluded that the linguistic stratum represented by the 'pre-Greek' place-names could be correlated with the archaeological finds of the Early Bronze Age. This view is now very widely held. Indeed many writers feel that the best explanation of the evidence available is to postulate a migration from Anatolia at the onset of the EBA, with the accompanying spread of these place-names, and a further influx (of uncertain origin) at the end of the Early Helladic II period bringing with it the Greek language itself.

IV. *Objections to the remote homeland theory*

The most obvious objection to this theory, as applied to the languages of Europe in general, is that there is no transformation in the archaeological record of the European Bronze Age on a sufficiently wide geographical basis to account for their distribution. Beaker people, Kurgan people and Urnfield people have all had their advocates, and there are interesting arguments favouring each as disseminators of early IE languages. But it must be conceded that there is no single group of features, found throughout Europe, which can without further reasoning be taken as a correlate of the postulated language spread. This is not perhaps surprising; but it does mean that the first principle enunciated in II above cannot be followed directly. The archaeological and linguistic evidence do not stand independently: they have to be used to support each other, with the ensuing risk of circularity.

As applied to Greek, the theory is unsatisfactory since it offers no suggestion as to where the Greek language developed, if not in Greece. Nor does the archaeological record give proof of any major influx of people from outside the Aegean at the appropriate time, especially since R. J. Howell has at last exorcised the spectre of a 'Minyan' invasion (see above, pp. 94–5).

For the earlier period, the situation in Greece is even more disappointing. Blegen's original conclusion rested on three basic notions, each of which can now be challenged.

1. The distribution of -*nth*- and -*ss*- in place-names is wider than Haley, following Fick, indicated. As well as occurring in Greece and Anatolia, they are apparently common also in Italy, and fairly frequent in the Balkans. F. Schachermeyr (1954: 1502) has given new maps of their distributions, of which Fig. 26.1 is a compounded simplification. (The cogent criticisms of Professor V. I. Georgiev, see above, pp. 244–6, should however be noted.) Both these suffixes have a far larger distribution than could possibly be linked with Blegen's independent branches of "one great stock" which he felt could be recognized in the Aegean region. On this ground alone the argument now seems doubtful.

2. The homogeneity of the Early Bronze Age cultures which Blegen indicated, and interpreted as reflecting some ethnic unity, is now seen to be of a different kind. Many similarities do undoubtedly exist between the different areas of the southern Aegean in the later part of the EBA; indeed it has been possible to write of an "international spirit" at this time; of a "cultural continuum" (Renfrew 1969) in the areas which Blegen singled out. But the similarities observed are seen to be of a special kind, many of them related to the growth of metallurgy and of trade.

Each region of the Aegean in EB 2 period (the time of the greatest apparent similarity) has its own individuality, which can be traced in each back to EB 1. And the similarities at that time are few: Early Minoan 1 in Crete has few resemblances to the Grotta-Pelos culture of the Cyclades; this is different in many ways from Early Helladic 1, which is in turn quite distinct from the Troy 1 culture. The distribution of Kum Tepe 1b bowls does indeed link the Cyclades and north-western Anatolia in the preceding period, but it has no relevance to Crete.

The elements of continuity from Neolithic to EBA in each region are much stronger than was formerly realized. In the eastern Aegean the Emborio sequence now shows an apparently undisturbed evolution from Neolithic to Early Bronze Age of the Troy 1 type. In the Cyclades the Neolithic Saliagos culture now provides a proto-type at least for the schematic figurines of the EB Grotta-Pelos culture; and in mainland Greece Early Helladic 1 is not strikingly different from its Late Neolithic predecessors. The case for an unbroken transition from the Neolithic to the Early Bronze Age in Crete has been argued elsewhere (Renfrew 1964), and while this matter is still open to argument, there as elsewhere in the Aegean the EB 1 culture undoubtedly has more affinities with its Neolithic predecessor than with its contemporaries in the other areas of the region. Dr. French, in his doctoral dissertation, has carefully considered the question of immigration from Anatolia, on the basis of a thorough examination of relevant Anatolian and Aegean finds and concludes: "Early Helladic, Early Cycladic (and Early Minoan) did not have a common origin, and such an origin

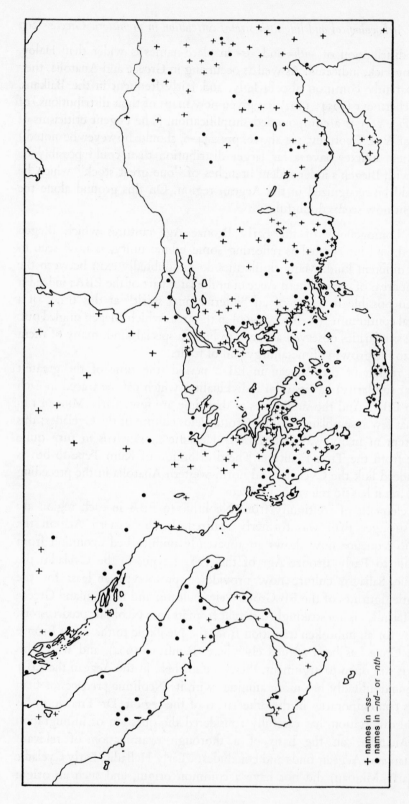

+ names in -ss-
● names in -nd- or -nth-

Fig. 26.1. Distribution of place-names with -ss- suffixes and with -nth- suffixes in Anatolia, the Aegean, the Balkans and Italy (based on Schachermeyr 1954: Maps 3–7)

should not be sought in south-western or even western Anatolia. The theory of a single, combined migration which introduced a common culture from south-western Anatolia into the Aegean cannot on present evidence be accepted" (1968: 167).

3. Neolithic finds are now known from the Cyclades (Evans and Renfrew 1968), and indeed there are indications of Neolithic occupation from six islands, Antiparos, Mykonos, Melos, Kea, Naxos and Amorgos. Obsidian was being fetched from Melos to mainland Greece before 6000 B.C. The absence of a Cycladic Neolithic, which was one of Blegen's key points, can no longer be accepted.

Thus the arguments for the correlation of the 'pre-Greek' place-names with the Early Bronze Age cultures can no longer be maintained. Moreover there are difficulties in a correlation between the Early Helladic III culture and the first Greek speakers. The most important is simply that no 'homeland' for this cultural assemblage has been suggested. The Anatolian affinities of some of the finds from Manika in Euboea have long been recognized, and French has indicated that the earliest remains at Lefkandhi may be seen as the result of contact with the EB 3 culture of north-western Anatolia. But this does not hold for the assemblage of Lerna IV. My own feeling is that further research in the Peloponnese, in Boeotia and in Phocis may well reveal a local evolution for this early Helladic III material. But in any case it can hardly be used as evidence for the immigration of the Greeks when no suggestion has been made as to where, outside of Greece, it may itself have originated.

Subsequent to this time there is considerable continuity. The 'Minyan' (or Middle Helladic) culture is now seen as a direct development from the Early Helladic III culture, and the continuity of the 'Minyan'—Mycenaean transition is very clearly seen in the finds of Grave Circle B at Mycenae. The archaeological record does not seem to support the notion of any later immigration.

V. *The model of indigenous development*

Writing on this subject some years ago (Renfrew 1964: 141) I concluded: "It may be that the Greeks did not come from anywhere, that in the words of Sir John Myres they were 'ever in process of becoming'." It now seems worthwhile to make this hypothesis in more concrete form.

In recent years prehistoric archaeologists have been moving away from migrationist and diffusionist models and turning rather to a consideration of culture process; consideration of the way in which cultures change through the operation of local factors, which themselves require analysis. At a time when one is attempting to view the developments of Aegean prehistory in such terms, and regarding critically claims for significant outside contact, it seems worthwhile to take an analogous standpoint for the Greek language.

The theory here propounded involves three principal postulates.

1. The Greek language developed in Greece from an earlier language which formed part of an IE linguistic continuum extending through much of Europe for some considerable time prior to the Aegean Late Bronze Age.

2. This early IE language was already spoken in Greece before the onset of the Bronze Age.

3. The so-called 'pre-Greek' place-names of the Aegean should not be regarded as belonging to an earlier and unrelated language which was replaced by Greek through a transfer of population or other factors. On the contrary, it is suggested that they belonged, in Greece, to this postulated language, which was directly ancestral to Greek, and that they are preserved (as place-names) like fossils, from an earlier stage in the evolution of the language.

Naturally it may not be possible to interpret in this way all those Aegean place-names which cannot be explained as Greek. Some may have an earlier origin; others will be loan-words from various languages in contact with this early IE language from early times.

Looking soberly at the archaeological record for Europe as a whole, there seems to be one single event in the entire Neolithic period which can be seen to have occurred on a pan-European basis and which conceivably might be linked with a migration of people: its beginning. There is probably no other time when the rate of growth of population changed so dramatically as at the onset of the Neolithic. And the introduction to Europe of domestic plants, and probably animals, native to the Near East, occurred at this time. (Other explanations than that of a migration of people are possible, and are briefly considered in a later section). We may therefore make a fourth, more tentative postulate.

4. The IE languages or dialects, ancestral to those of later Europe, were brought to Europe by the first farmers, arriving from Anatolia with their new subsistence pattern, and spread by their descendants along the north coast of the Mediterranean, up the Danube to central and northern Europe, and eastwards, along the lands north of the Black Sea to central Russia. Enabled by their new subsistence technique to support a much higher population density than their hunter-fisher predecessors in the same area, they effectively assimilated or replaced that population, or at least replaced its languages with their own.

The considerable homogeneity of the First Neolithic of south-eastern Europe has been noted by several authors: proto-Sesklo, Karanovo-Kremikovci, Starčevo and Criş share many common traits, some of them

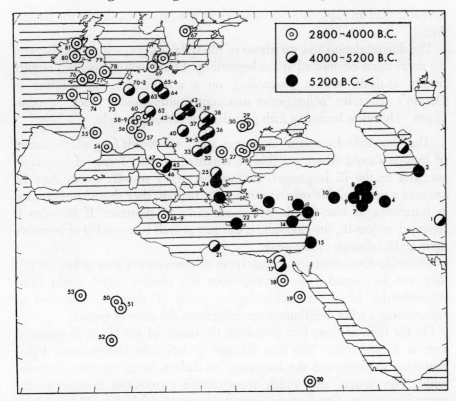

Fig. 26.2. The spread of farming economy to Europe. The map indicates the earliest sites of farming settlements, as determined by radiocarbon analysis up to 1965, in the various territories for which results have been published. Dates are in radiocarbon years on the 5568 half-life (after Clark 1965: 46)

passed on to the *Linearbandkeramik* farmers of central Europe, and others to the 'Impressed Ware' farmers of the First Neolithic of the western Mediterranean. The diffusion of the farming economy from the Near East via Anatolia to the Aegean and so west, north-west and north across Europe has been graphically shown in a map by Professor J. G. D. Clark (Fig. 26.2) based upon radiocarbon dates. In terms of the model here proposed the map might also be taken to illustrate the introduction to Europe, and the spread there, of languages and dialects ancestral to the IE languages of Europe; languages and dialects spoken in central and western Anatolia in Neolithic times, in the seventh millennium B.C.

Of course this new framework does not itself explain the variations seen in the historical IE languages, or the affinities and isoglosses between them. And the distribution of the IE languages of Asia still requires explanation, possibly on the basis of migrations. But I suggest that this model of an early and rapid distribution of Indo-European speakers, which can be correlated with a major economic and population change in Europe, is today more plausible than an explosive expansion from the Pripet marshes in the Bronze Age.

The differentiation and variations of the IE languages, within and beyond the continuum established at the beginning of the Neolithic period, require further analysis, always proceeding on a modification of William of Occam's principle: 'Migrationes non sunt multiplicandae praeter necessitatum.' This view leads to a fifth postulate, or rather principle.

5. The 'non-Indo-European' languages and fossil words (e.g. place-names) of Europe should where possible be regarded as relict forms of languages ancestral to the IE languages. Failing this many non-IE words may be assigned a pre-neolithic origin; more often perhaps they should be regarded as intrusions, as loan-words within an early IE substrate. If Etruscan is regarded as non-IE, for example, it can just as well be regarded as intrusive upon an IE substrate as *vice versa*.

The wide distribution of certain types of place-names seen in Fig. 26.1, if they can be regarded as homogeneous (cf. Hester: 1957) could most conveniently, from the archaeological point of view, be regarded as representing a relict distribution resulting from the early IE spread.

On the basis of these five postulates the origin of the Greek language is seen in a new light. The first farmers to arrive in Greece were Indo-European speakers, and the languages or dialects from western Anatolia, which they spoke, and which were carried throughout Europe by the expansion of these first farmers, were the ancestors of the later IE languages. Crete was settled, possibly from south-western Anatolia, by rather different people, as its Early Neolithic culture shows. Their language, the immediate predecessor of Minoan, was none the less closely related to that of sixth millennium Greece, and presumably also to the other proto-Indo-European languages and dialects.

The Greek language will then have been one of several IE languages evolving in the Balkan peninsula, some of which have perhaps left no trace whatever. Its adoption in Crete must be regarded as due to Mycenaean conquest, or at least strong Mycenaean influence. Here we are in general agreement with Chadwick (1963: 17) although not with his chronology, when he writes: "The old theory of the irruption into Greece of three or more waves of Greek speakers is unnecessary, and the facts can be better explained by setting the genesis of the Greek language inside Greece. . . ." Small localized movements of people, which, unlike the large-scale, unidirectional migrations here eschewed, must have been taking place all the time, will have ensured the relative homogeneity of the Greek spoken in the Aegean by the Late Bronze Age. The 'Dorian invasion' is to be viewed as at the most another of these small, localized movements without any consequences wider than a small modification in dialect distribution. More probably the legend of the 'Invasion' refers to the activities of a few chieftains with small bands of followers rather than to numerically significant population movements, and as Tritsch has argued (see above, p.237), to attach much linguistic significance to early Greek accounts of the deeds and travels of 'heroes' would not be wise.

VI. *Further problems*

In proposing that the Greek language developed locally, in Greece, over a long period, it has been necessary to suggest that there was a population of Indo-European speaking peoples in Greece, and indeed most of Europe, already in the Neolithic period. This may involve several new difficulties and problems, but at least it permits us to escape the stranglehold of the IE 'homeland' theory. Some further points arise.

1. The preceding sections of this paper were written and presented to the Colloquium before I became acquainted with the work of Professor V. I. Georgiev and had the pleasure of discussing these problems with him. He has, on several occasions, suggested that P. Kretschmer's version of the 'homeland' theory is an unsatisfactory one, and that the evidence of place-names indicates an early IE-speaking population throughout much of Europe. He points out that west of the Rhine (and east of the Don) non-IE place-names, and especially river-names do indeed occur. It would be easy to modify the theory proposed above, of a Neolithic spread of IE languages in Europe, to account for this. This original spread of IE languages through the Aegean and Balkans, up the Danube (by the agency of the Danubian 1 culture) and in the western Mediterranean (by the 'Impressed Ware' Neolithic) need not have embraced western and northern Europe, areas where there is good evidence for a flourishing mesolithic population. We could postulate that the inhabitants of the areas which soon adopted what has been termed a 'Western Neolithic' culture, did not at this time adopt the new languages. They kept, perhaps, in both language and culture, more of their own original character than was general elsewhere. Is it indeed mere coincidence that collective burial under long mounds or in built chamber-graves emerged in Europe precisely (and exclusively) in these areas?

2. The model here outlined for the expansion of an IE farming population through most of Europe is undeniably crude. It is, in this simple form, as blithely migrationist as the one which it is designed to replace. The defect is not, however, inherent in the model, but arises from over-simplification in its presentation. As the research into Neolithic origins becomes more sophisticated, we may reasonably expect that the local elements in the cultural development of Europe will become clearer, and the imported ones fewer. The population increase must ultimately be ascribed to the new subsistence economy rather than to the arrival of immigrants from the south-east. It

may be that the economic transformation came about through the acquisition of the domestic plants and animals without significant transfer of population. In this case the genetic composition of the increasing population would be little changed.

But the irreducible minimum which did migrate was the new spectrum of domesticates, especially wheat and barley. The genetic composition of these plants (and probably also of the sheep and goats, although animals may in any case have been less important than plants) was determined initially in the Near East. With these new plants must have come a constellation of farming skills; sowing, reaping, parching and milling, together with ancillary artefact types, such as the parching oven. Even if we allow for no population transfer between regions (surely an extreme position in view of the Danubian expansion) there was still a major cultural change stimulated from outside. It is with this change, and with the considerable population increase, that the model seeks to link the spread of proto-IE languages. If more sophisticated mechanisms for language adoption are preferred to the simple notion of migration, this is an acceptable modification. The only claim here made is that at this time, *and at this time only* in post-Pleistocene Europe, have we a really basic and widespread cultural and economic change. If a pan-European language shift is sought, there is no more plausible opportunity in the archaeological record.

3. The model here proposed, despite its greater time-depth, could still be stigmatized as a 'homeland model'. For it does imply that, at the outset, before the seventh millennium B.C., proto-IE languages were not spoken in Europe, but were spoken in central and western Anatolia. The only escape from this position, which will not be argued in detail here, would be to lengthen the chronology still further and suggest that languages or dialects ancestral to the early IE languages were already spoken in Europe in palaeolithic times. We might even find archaeological units with which to correlate the language group: the Gravettian perhaps, or the Aurignacian? But for an archaeologist these are rather frivolous questions. They do however invite an answer from the speculative linguist. If, moving backward in time, we can situate early IE-speakers in their homeland by 3000 B.C. or 7000 B.C., what sort of language do we imagine their ancestors to have spoken in 30,000 B.C.? There can be no certain answer, but this need not necessarily make the question a foolish one. Should we not, perhaps, be thinking in terms of greater time depth even than the Neolithic diffusion model here proposed?

4. The simple model of a Neolithic diffusion of proto-IE languages over much of Europe does not deny that the linguistic situation perhaps then and certainly later was a very complicated one. Further population movements and other processes will have ensured this. On the linguistic side special

explanations are required to account for the existence of language sub-groups within the general IE grouping, such as the Celtic language-group. And on the archaeological side we have major changes such as the termination of the south-eastern European Chalcolithic, of which Marija Gimbutas has written (Gimbutas 1965: 491), or the spread of the Beaker 'culture' (Sangmeister 1964 cf. Piggott 1965: 100). Some of these may be needed to explain the linguistic variations seen, and may perhaps underlie some of the uniformities of belief and mythology for which some IE languages and cultures give evidence. The work of Bosch Gimpera, Hencken and Gimbutas, among others, has already contributed here, and more is needed if the mythological and social data are to be reconciled with the new and longer chronology.

5. The model proposed here is hypothetical, like all other work in this field. Indeed all discussion of the distribution of languages in Europe before the second millennium B.C. seems doomed to remain hypothetical in the absence of direct linguistic evidence. Without data by which a theory can effectively be tested, one is forced to fall back upon other criteria, among which the most important is that of simplicity. Of course the decipherment of the Minoan Linear A script may one day bring new information; it will be no surprise if the language turns out to be Indo-European. Meanwhile the model here proposed can at least offer an alternative to the curious theory of a sudden expansion from a homeland near the Pripet marshes, an expansion for which no plausible economic or social explanation has ever been given.

References

CASKEY, J. L. 1960 'The Early Helladic period in the Argolid.' *Hesperia*, 29: 285.

CHADWICK, J. 1963. 'The prehistory of the Greek language.' *CAH* (rev. ed.) II, Chap. XXXIX/Fasc. 15.

CLARK, J. G. D. 1965. 'Radiocarbon dating and the spread of farming economy.' *Antiquity*, 39: 45–8.

EVANS, J. D. and RENFREW, A. C. 1968. *Excavations at Saliagos near Antiparos*. London.

FRENCH, D. H. 1968. 'Anatolia and the Aegean in the third millennium B.C.' (University of Cambridge, doctoral dissertation; unpublished).

GIMBUTAS, M. 1965. 'Neolithic and Chalcolithic cultures in eastern Europe'; in R. W. Ehrich (ed.) *Chronologies*: 459–502.

GRUMACH, E. 1969. 'The coming of the Greeks.' *Bulletin of the John Rylands Library*, 51/1 and 51/2 (also published as separatum).

HÄGERSTRAND, T. 1967. *Innovation Diffusion as a Spatial Process*. Chicago.

HALEY, J. B. and BLEGEN, C. W. 1928. 'The coming of the Greeks.' *AJA*, 32: 141–54.

HESTER, D. H. 1957. 'The pre-Greek place-names in Greece and Asia Minor.' *RHA*, 15: 61.

LEVIN, S. 1964. *The Linear B Decipherment Controversy Re-examined*. Albany, N.Y.

PIGGOTT, S. 1965. *Ancient Europe*. Edinburgh.

RENFREW, A. C. 1964. 'Crete and the Cyclades before Rhadamanthus' *KritKhron*, 18: 107–41.

———. 1969. 'Cycladic metallurgy and the Aegean Early Bronze Age.' *AJA*, 71: 1–20.

SANGMEISTER, E. 1964. 'Die Datierung des Rückstroms der Glockenbecher und ihre Auswirkung auf die Chronologie der Kupferzeit in Portugal.' *Palaeohistoria*, 12: 395–403.

SCHACHERMEYR, F. 1954. 'Prähistorische Kulturen Griechenlands.' *RE* (2). 22/2: 1350–1548.

WACE A. J. and BLEGEN, C. W. 1918. 'The pre-Mycenaean pottery of the Mainland.' *BSA*, 22: 175–189.

Discussion

R. A. CROSSLAND: Dr. Renfrew's paper offers a valuable challenge to views which many linguists hold about the probable development of the IE language-family, and it should incite all linguists who are interested in prehistory to consider and define what they think can be deduced from linguistic evidence about prehistoric events. It would not be appropriate to discuss at length here the general questions of method which he has raised (see below, p. 331). The following comments are concerned with particular points.

1. Certain linguistic data tell strongly against the deduction that the original IE language-continuum lay in Anatolia, even if migration out of it is thought to have begun as early as the seventh millennium B.C. There seems to be no evidence for the scale and kind of exchange of vocabulary between Indo-European and proto-Semitic (or early Semitic languages) and/ or Sumerian which one would not expect to have occurred if IE was in use in an area close to Syria, northern Mesopotamia and the Iranian plateau for several millennia during the Neolithic periods. Supposed Sumerian or Semitic borrowings into (common) IE are few and show inexact correspondences, and most of them are words for objects or commodities which might have been transmitted by long-distance trade (for the linguist in this connection it is immaterial in which direction copper, for example, passed along the trade-routes; Crossland 1957: 36; Dayton 1970: 62). The fairly numerous Semitic (mainly Akkadian) loan-words in Hittite need not have begun to be borrowed before the second quarter of the second millennium. The argument is not affected by the slight possibility (it is no more, on present evidence) that proto-IE and proto-(Hamito-)Semitic were, remotely, genetically related; their vocabularies, as reconstructed, look quite different. Similarities in vocabulary between IE and Uralic are more impress-

ive (Collinder 1955: 128–41). Secondly, the Boğazkale cuneiform corpus includes texts written in a non-IE language, Hattic, which was clearly no longer spoken at Hattusas when most of the Hittite texts were written (in the fourteenth and thirteenth centuries) but which evidently was in use there in the sixteenth. Much indicates that Hattic was spoken over at least a large part of central Anatolia, including Hattusas, before (IE) Hittite came into use there; most of the texts in it are mythological, or rituals; several deities prominent in the Hittite pantheon have Hattic names; special features of Hittite, viewed as an IE language, can be convincingly attributed to Hattic influence; and the Hittites called the language, not their own, '[language] of Hatti', referring to it by an adjective based on the name *Hatti*-which they used of their own territory in historical times and would appear to have adopted from a preceding, Hattic-speaking population. The 'economical' conclusion is that Hittite was a late arrival in central Anatolia (Goetze 1955: 45–7; Kammenhuber 1969; Laroche 1947). On the other hand a question is begged if Hittite and eastern IE languages are classed as 'outliers' as in II. 3. The actual distribution of IE languages *c.* 500 B.C. can hardly be said to 'centre on Europe' spatially. If one argues from distribution at that time, dispersal from an area to the east of Europe should certainly be regarded as a possibility. Very few 'Indo-European comparativists' now propose the area of the Pripet marshes as the 'IE homeland'. And if a non-IE stratum is to be identified in place-names in Europe west of the Rhine, this is perfectly compatible with a conclusion that IE speech was introduced into western Europe about 2000 B.C. or even later, since place-names there are recorded only from *c.* 500 B.C. onwards.

2. Apropos V. 3, it may be worth pointing out that if a linguist calls one language the '(direct) ancestor' of another, he will imply that the later language inherited its essential morphological-grammatical and phonic systems (structures) from the earlier. As a generalization, one may say that when populations speaking different languages amalgamate, one of them, essentially, adopts the language of the other; i.e. the language which is eventually spoken by the population which results from the amalgamation will be found to have retained, essentially, the grammatical (i.e. from here on 'morphological and other grammatical') and phonic systems of either one or the other of the two antecedent languages. It is recognized that, within the limits of this generalization, the systems of the language which 'dominates' or essentially 'survives' may be much modified under the influence of those of the language which is 'superseded', and it appears that the vocabulary of a language which is 'superseded' is often largely retained and incorporated into that of the language which is considered to have 'superseded' it by the criteria which have just been indicated; also that, from a different point of view, any language may be considered to have many

'ancestors': all the languages which have contributed to its systems and vocabulary during its development, as if to the gene-pool of a population. But anything approaching a 50/50 mix in grammatical and phonic systems, when populations speaking different languages amalgamate, seems extremely rare. Consequently the linguist will understand Dr. Renfrew's 'language directly ancestral to Greek' as meaning essentially what he means by 'proto-Greek': a dialect of IE which developed through a 'pre-Greek' phase into Greek, retaining from IE, developing and passing on to Greek the phonic and main grammatical systems which characterize it, without their undergoing radical modification under the influence of another language. 'Fossils', in Dr. Renfrew's paragraph, would seem to imply what the linguist would define as functionally restricted categories of words; i.e. groups of words characterized by a common feature, usually a formant, which has ceased to be used in forming words of any other kind in the phase ('diachronic dialect') of a language under consideration; an example in modern English is -*dom*, which is now used 'productively' only in forming literary or jocular words of the type of *Hippie-dom. Such restriction, resulting in formally marked categories with very specialized function, is quite a common phenomenon. Sometimes such a category will have become totally unproductive; i.e. its distinguishing feature may be felt as a characteristic of e.g. place-names, or perhaps place-names of a particular kind, but no new ones are formed on its pattern. The process of specialization which results in such categories does not appear to be one which tends to take a longer time than most other linguistic changes. Consequently, the presence of such 'fossils' in a language does not imply that it had had an exceptionally long period of development free from adstrate influence in the area in which it is first known in historical times; it can in any case hardly indicate to us whether a language had been in use in its 'historical habitat' for just a few centuries or for several millennia. The survival in a particular category of words, in a given phase of a language, of a phonic feature which has become 'asystemic' in it (i.e. in conflict with normal speech habits) would seem to be very rare. A theoretical example would be the retention in place-names in English (in areas where it was not affected by a Gaelic substrate as in parts of Scotland) of the phoneme [χ] (German -*ch* in *Dach*) from Old English. Categories of words which have become functionally isolated and exceptional in formation in a language do not tend to escape the effects of phonetic changes in it. Even categories borrowed from another language which are phonically 'asystemic' when adopted tend to be assimilated quickly to native phonetic patterns (cf. the replacement of [ʒ] by [dʒ] in vernacular pronunciation of *garage* in English). The only case in which a phoneme or sound-sequence which has ceased to occur in the normal vocabulary of a language is likely to be retained in a particular category of words in it is that in which an earlier 'diachronic dialect' of the language has been kept in use alongside the current vernacular, e.g. for literary or religious purposes, and the traditional conventions of pronouncing it have been very carefully maintained. Such preservation must be unusual in non-literate societies. Regarding *-nth* (/-nt^h-/) and *-ss-*/*-tt-* in place-names in Greek, the sequence *-nth-* does appear to be 'asystemic' in Greek, and so the words or formants which contain it might well have been adopted into Greek from another language. *-ss-*, with its dialectal variant *-tt-*, is more problematic. The same alternative sequences constitute or occur in formants which appear to be IE (*e.g.* *-ss-*/*-tt-* in verbs like *tassō*/*tattō*, probably < *-k^y-; cf. Lat. *facio*). Within the context of Greek itself they might reasonably be regarded as inherited from proto-Greek. But it is difficult to regard the occurrence of names in *-ass^o-* (-^{o}š-š^o- in cuneiform) in south-western to south central Anatolia as fortuitous. Since there is no evidence for use of (proto-)Greek in Anatolia before *c.* 1000 B.C. (except perhaps in isolated Mycenaean settlements after *c.* 1425/1400 B.C.) the two explanations of the distribution of the *-ss-* names which are worth considering are that which concludes that they were spread westwards from Anatolia by migrants; and the assumption that a formant ancestral to Anatolian *-ss-* and Greek *-ss-*/*-tt-* was inherited both by pre-Luwian and pre-Greek and underwent largely parallel devlopment independently in both. The significance of the occurrence of place-names in *-ss-* in Italy and Spain is even more difficult to assess. On the decipherment of the 'Minoan Linear B' script see now Heubeck 1970; Lejeune 1966.

References

COLLINDER, B. 1955. *Fenno-Ugric Vocabulary*. Stockholm.

CROSSLAND, R. A. 1957. 'Indo-European origins: the linguistic evidence.' *Past and Present*, 12: 16–46; 13: 88.

DAYTON, J. E. 1970. 'The problem of tin in the Ancient World.' *World Archaeology*, 3: 49–70.

GOETZE, A. 1957. *Kleinasien* (2nd ed.). Munich.

HEUBECK, A. 1970. Review of J. Eckschmitt, *Die Kontroverse um Linear B*; *BiOr*, 27: 253–5.

KAMMENHUBER, A. 1969. 'Das Hattische'; in J. Friedrich and others, *Altkleinasiatische Sprachen* (*Handbuch der Orientalistik* II, i/ii, 2; ed. B. Spuler, Leiden): 428–446.

LAROCHE, E. 1947. 'Hattic deities and their epithets.' *JCS*, 1: 83–142.

LEJEUNE, M. 1966. Review of S. Levin, *The Linear B Decipherment Re-examined*: *JHS*, 86: 215–8.

Reflections on linguistic and cultural relations between Anatolia and Dacia in the Bronze Age

ARITON VRACIU

University of Iași

OWING to its geographical position Anatolia has formed an effective natural bridge linking Asia with eastern Europe as far as the Balkans, and with central and western Europe, in many periods, not only in the Bronze Age, *c.* 2300–1100 B.C. There can be no doubt that such favourable conditions of communication promoted cultural, economic and linguistic relations and contact between the ancient peoples of Asia and those of Europe; such contacts were bound to occur and their effects were reciprocal. These are processes which certainly began during the Neolithic period and which archaeologists identify also in the course of the Bronze Age (Berciu 1966: 132, 144, 147–8, 154–7, 164; Condurachi 1966: 14, 16, 18; Kenyon 1961: 17–26, 45–8; 1966: 63–4). In this latter period, according to D. Berciu, the question concerns only the Cernavoda culture, since in general the Bronze Age in Dacia, as is now well known, is clearly local and autochthonous in character. At the same time, the plentiful archaeological material brought to light by recent excavation in Rumania reveals the exceptional progress made during the Bronze Age in the Carpatho-Danubian region, progress comparable in many respects with that in the Mycenaean world, as V. Parvan (1882–1927) first noted and others both historians and archaeologists after him (e.g. Berciu 1966: 141). H. Z. Koşay, V. Dumitrescu, J. Mellaart and V. Mikov have recently discussed the influences which Aegean and Anatolian cultures exerted on south-eastern Europe (Koşay 1971; Dumitrescu 1971; Mellaart 1971; Mikov 1971). But of course theirs is only one point of view and one should not ignore the arguments in favour of the contrary opinions advanced by some linguists, and archaeologists too, who speak of migrations coming from the north or north-west (see Daicoviciu 1960: 34; Daicoviciu 1961: 17; Daicoviciu 1964: 6–8; Russu 1967: 30; Vraciu 1969c: 360–9; Russu 1969: 30; Vraciu 1970g: 83–92; Petrescu-Dîmbovita 1971;

Duridanov 1971; Gindin 1967 and 1969). In this connection I should like to lay stress on A. C. Renfrew's recent interpretation, which observes that on the one hand the flourishing metallurgy of the Balkans during the Bronze Age antedates that which originated in the Aegean basin; while on the other hand the similarities noted by certain writers between the pottery and figurine forms of the Vinča culture and those characteristic of the Early Bronze Age in the Cyclades should be considered fortuitous (Renfrew 1969). In such circumstances, it appears very difficult, even impossible, to accept for Dacia the view that any one archaeological culture influenced the rest (through connection in forms, style etc.). In accepting nevertheless some influences "coming as much from the east as from the west and south" C. Daicoviciu concluded: "In spite of the regional peculiarities, we find none the less a clear cultural unity in the Carpatho-Danubian Bronze Age throughout the territory basic to the Geto-Dacians" (Daicoviciu 1964: 12). It follows that it would be preferable to speak in the cases quoted of *contacts* and not of *influences* proper, although the theory of the latter has gained wide credence, as we have noted already. For the contacts see also P. Detev (1968: 9–48; 1969). The Sheffield Colloquium (see Vraciu 1970c: 593–6) has once again demonstrated the wide divergence of opinion among specialists about the nature of the relations between the Balkans and the Aegeo-Anatolian regions in the Bronze Age. Recent research in the fields of linguistic geography and comparison of the Indo-European languages has led to remarkable conclusions (see most recently Ivănescu 1970: 9–35). All these new or very recent linguistic and archaeological discoveries have obliged scholars to reconsider a great number of questions which have constantly been brought foward and discussed even with some passion. On the strictly linguistic side we might mention, first of all, the question of the nature of the relations between Hittite and the other Indo-European languages and groups, namely Italo-Celtic (Vraciu 1969a), Tocharian, Armenian, Phrygian, Thracian, Dacian, Balto-Slavonic (Vraciu 1970b) etc. The study of problems which are so disputed is naturally of quite special importance for the archaeologist and the linguist, for it is only the combined effort of specialists in their fields that will lead to more acceptable, even definitive, solutions.

In the light of the data now available it will be impossible to accept without reserve E. H. Sturtevant's hypothesis of a period during which Indo-European and proto-Anatolian existed side by side, though proto-Anatolian should not be regarded as an idiom entirely similar to primitive Indo-European. But in spite of all this, the data which languages of the Hittite-Luwian group provide have very great significance for IE historical and comparative linguistics.

It is clear that from the standpoint of their cultural level and degree of historical importance the Hittites stood relatively close to the peoples of the

Aegean region and mainland Greece and the native peoples of the Near East (especially the Hurrians of Syria and Mesopotamia) with whom they established close contacts. Of course, reciprocal relations had already existed since the time of Common Indo-European between 'Proto-Anatolian' and any other IE dialect.

In localizing the first Indo-Europeans in the Carpatho-Danubian regions and in allowing that the formation of Common Indo-European took place during the fifth and fourth millennia B.C. (see, e.g. Hornung 1963: 10), we must suppose that the process of differentiation must have occurred approximately from the third millennium onwards. The Hittites, for example, entered Anatolia at the end of the third millennium B.C.

The rich linguistic material which is now at our disposal and which derives from various groups of IE languages, and strict analysis of our data, allow us to establish and specify much more closely the relations which existed among the IE dialects in the prehistoric and proto-historic periods. In particular it has been shown (e.g. Russu 1967: 151; 1969: 106; 1970: 221) that the phonological system of Dacian (or, really, of Thraco-Dacian) is relatively close to the primitive system of IE. In my opinion this provides a most powerful argument for the autochthony of the tribes which occupied the territory of Rumania in a very early period; in any case at the time when Common IE was formed.

In delimiting the linguistic zones which are properly termed *Thracian* (south of the Danube) and *Dacian* (north of the Danube; see Georgiev 1965a; 1971; Duridanov 1971; Poghirc 1969: 313–365; Crossland 1971; Vraciu 1969b; Vraciu 1970d; 301–314; 1970e: 101–116; 1970g: 489–98; 1971) we shall find some striking similarities and some no less obvious differences between those two languages, and also between them and the other idioms of the Balkan peninsula and the IE languages of Anatolia. Certainly, in contrast to the Anatolian languages (in the first place, in contrast to Hittite, rich in texts), Dacian, Thracian and Illyrian may only be reconstructed in part, and in their phonology. As the Dacian material is very scanty, it does not permit us to identify important points of correspondence with other IE languages or groups; in any case no correspondence similar or even comparable to those which have already been established, for example, for Hittite and (Balto-)Slavonic (Ivanov 1957: 3–28; 1966). While revealing close links with Balto-Slavonic, Dacian does not share the features of special similarity which languages of this group share with Anatolian languages. These linguistic data, which are corroborated by archaeology, have their own special significance.

The etymological analysis of the Dacian linguistic material (glosses, proper names and inscriptions) has made it possible to establish certain facts about the position of Dacian within the IE framework (Russu 1959: 93–100; 1967: 144–57; 1969: 107–12; 1970: 54, 59–60, 62–7; Georgiev

1965a; 1969; Poghirc 1967; Poghirc and others 1969; Reichenkron 1966). Compared with that of primitive IE, the phonic system of Dacian appears as follows (Poghirc 1969: 316): $a(ə) > a$; $é > ie$; $e > e$; $o > a$; $ā > o$; $ē > a > o$; $ō > ö > e$; $ū > ü > i$; $ay > a$; $ey > e$; $aw > a$; $ew > e$; $ņ > a$ $r > ri$; $bh > b$; $dh > d$; $gh > g$; $k' > s$; g', $g'h > z(đ)$; $k^w > k(?p)$; $g^w, g^wh ŗ > g(?b)$. To these traits, which in the present writer's opinion are characteristic for Dacian in general in the Bronze Age, Poghirc (Poghirc and others 1969: 317) adds a few other phonetic changes specific to late Daco-Moesian (of the A.D., third to sixth centuries approximately). The traits in question are as follows: unaccented a (in some positions even $e) > [ə]$ (Rumanian $ă$); $a > o$ (-*dava* > -*dova*; *Pelendova*; *Gildova*; *Patavissa* > *Potaissa*; *Paralisenses* > *Porolisum*; cf. also Poghirc 1967: 25); $é$ followed by a (or $e) > ya$; $ó$ followed by a (or $e) > wa$; the alternation m/b (Poghirc 1963: 97–100); the changes $si > š$; $sr > str$ etc. In comparison with the other ancient languages of the Balkans, Dacian is characterized by phonic features of the type: IE $o >$ Dac. a, Alb. a, Thrac. a, Ill. o/a, Phryg. o, Arm. o, Mac. o, Gk. o; IE $ņ >$ Dac. $a(n?)$, Alb. en/un, Thrac. un, Phryg. un, Arm. an, Mac. a, Gk, $a(n)$; IE $ŗ >$ Dac. ri, Alb. ir/ri (ur), Thrac. ur, Phryg. ur, Arm. ar, Mac. ar, Gk. ar/ra; IE *tenues* $(T) >$ Dac. T, Alb. T, Thrac. TA (*tenues aspiratae*), Ill. T, Phryg. TA, Arm. TA, Mac. T, Gk. T; IE *mediae* $(M) >$ Dac. M, Alb. M, Thrac. T, Ill. T, Arm. T, Mac. M. Gk. M; IE $k' >$ Dac. s, Alb. s $(þ)$, Thrac. s $(þ)$, Ill. k $(s?)$, Phryg. s, Arm. s, Mac. k, Gk. k; IE $k^w >$ Dac. $k(p?)$, Alb. k, Thrac. kh, Ill. k, Phryg. kh, Mac. p, Gk. k^w.

The vocabulary of modern Rumanian contains an appreciable number of elements which are of Dacian origin and so go back to the IE period (Philippide 1928: 694–71; Brâncuş 1963; 1966a; 1966b; 1968; Georgiev 1965a; 1965b; Poghirc 1967; 1968: 174–7; 1969; Rosetti 1968: 264–276; Vraciu 1970d; 1970e; 1970f; 1970h). For a part of these lexical elements which are common to Rumanian and Albanian more or less probable IE etymologies have been established recently. Whatever our opinions may be about the system adopted for reconstructing Dacian, we must nevertheless recognize the archaic character of this language of the Carpatho-Danubian region, which may be compared, even in the Bronze Age, with that of the Anatolian IE languages. Irrefutable proof of this is provided by the fact that many autochtonous words which are frequently used in Rumanian today are derived from IE through the intermediary of Dacian (see especially Russu 1970: 217–19). The lexical elements in question are:

Etymon or root	Rumanian or other word	English translation
*awe-l-	abur(e)	steam, vapour
*are-g-	argea	loom
*gʷōu-, *gʷū-	baligă	dung, manure
*bhel-	baltă	marsh, swamp, pool, moor, lake, pond
*bhereg'-, *bher(e)g'-	barz	grey
*bhas-k-	bască	fleece
*bhre-dh-	brad	fir (*Abies alba*)
*bher-, *bhre-n-	brîu	girdle, belt
*bhreus-	brusture	burdock (*Arctium lappa*)
*bhā(u)-g-, *bhu-ǵ	bunget	thicket. old forest
*bu-z-	buză	lip
*kadh-s-	căciulă	fur cap
*kap-	căpuşă	sheep louse, tick (*Mepophagus ovinus*)
*(s) kep-	căpută	foot, toe-cap, upper leather, vamp (of shoe)
*kat-	cătun	hamlet, parish
*(s)kep-	copac	tree
*kru-k- (?)	(a) cruta	to spare, pardon, forgive
*skeu-r-	(a) curma	to interrupt, break off, cease, put a stop to, break
*kʷerp-	curpen	tendril, stem, switch; *Clematis vitalba*
*kʷer-	cursă	trap, snare, pitfall
*dhe(i)-	daş	lamb
*der-	(a) dărîma	to pull down, demolish, break down, level, crush, overpower
*derew(o)-	fruete	wood, log
*k'er-	dărîmă	small piece, morsel, fragment, scrap
*gherdh-	gard	fence, hedge
*ger-d-	gardină	groove, notch, fluting
*g(h)at-	gata	ready, prepared, prompt
*gʷel-bh-	gălbează	liverwort(s) (*Hepaticae*; *Fascicola hepatica*; *Dicrocelium dentriticum*); sheep pox.
*gʷel-, *gle-m-p-	ghimpe	thorn, prickle, splinter, needle
*gel-, *g(e)le-gh-	ghioagă	maul, club, cudgel
*ghel-, *gh(e)lo-n-	ghionoaie	woodpecker (*Picus*)
*ger-	grapă	harrow
*gh(e)re-s-	gresie	gritty stone, whetstone
*ghrebh-	groapă	pit, hollow, excavation, grave, tomb

Etymon or root	Rumanian or other word	English translation
⋆gʷer-	grumaz	neck, nape
⋆gh(e)re-nd(h)-	grunz	lump, clod
⋆geu-, ⋆geu-s-	guşă	crop, gizzard, maw, goitre, wen, dewlap
⋆mel-, ⋆mela-	mal	lakeside, shore, coast, bank, edge, border
⋆mag'(h)-	mazăre	pea (*Pisum sativum*)
⋆geu-l-	măgură	hill, hillock
⋆mer-	mărat	deplorable, pitiable, poor (*German*: bedauernswert, arm)
⋆mad-, ⋆ma(n)d-	mînz	foal, colt
⋆mē-, ⋆mo-t-	moş	old *or* grey-headed man; forefather, ancestor
⋆nē-(+ pert-?)	năpîrcă	adder, viper (*Pelias berus*)
⋆pes- + ⋆tal-	păstaie	pod
⋆per + re-n-(er-)	pîrîu	brook, rivulet, stream, flood
⋆rendh-	rînză	gizzard
⋆k(e)re-p- (?)	(a) scăpăra	to strike, throw, sparkle
⋆ker-	scrum	ashes
⋆skeubh-	(a) scula	to wake, awake (*intrans.*), raise, call
⋆ster-	sterp	sterile, unfruitful, barren
⋆serp-, (⋆srep-?)	strepede	cheese maggot, hopper (*Piophila casei*)
⋆streng-	strungă	sheepfold, gap between two teeth; gorge, ravine; pass, opening, breach
⋆k'el-	şale	loins, small of back
⋆s(e)w-e-p-	şopîrlă	lizard (*Lacerta*)
⋆teu-, ⋆tw-e-p-	ţap	he-goat
⋆twer-	ţarc	fold, pen
⋆āt(e)r-, ⋆wāt-	vatră	hearth, fireplace, house, dwelling (place), home
⋆wet-	vătui	year-old kid (young goat); leveret
⋆weg'h-	viezure	badger (*Meles taxus* or *vulgaris*)
⋆(s)ker-, ⋆sker-d(h)-	zgardă	dog collar
⋆sker-	zgîra	to scratch, scrape

(On *măgură, pîrîu*, see Georgiev 1965b: 287–8, 288–90; on *scrum*, Albanian *shkrumb* and cognates, see Duridanov 1968: 403–4; on *strungă* see Duridanov 1968: 404–6; on *zgardă* and Alb. *shkardhë*, see Çabej 1958: 133).

Unfortunately, except in the work of a few linguists such as B. P. Hasdeu (1838–1907), G. Reichenkron (1907–66), I. I. Russu, V. I. Georgiev, C. Poghirc and I. Duridanov, very little use has been made of Rumanian evidence in attempting to explain the relations which long existed between the various IE dialects. Now, as we have already noted, Rumanian has in fact preserved up to the present day some words which it inherited from Dacian.

Whilst recognizing that the primitive habitat of the Indo-Europeans is to be sought in the area of south-eastern Europe (Georgiev 1958: 272–4), we must reconsider the problem of the localization of 'proto-Anatolian'. In a recent study (Ivănescu 1970: 31–2) the present writer's attention was drawn to the following statement: "But it is very difficult to specify whether the tribes which spoke the Hittite, Luwian or Palaic languages were living in the Balkan peninsula before their migration to Asia Minor, as many scholars believe. And it is quite as difficult to specify whether the Hittites had moved into Asia Minor by the beginning of the second millennium B.C. I consider, however, that the geographical position of Hittite, Luwian and Palaic in relation to the other IE languages is not too different from the geographical position which the Hittite-Luwian-Palaic dialect held among the other proto-IE dialects; Hittite, and also Luwian and Palaic, remained in the historic period in the neighbourhood of a *centum* language: ancient Greek." Like other linguists today, however, I am of the opinion that the division of the IE languages into *centum* and *satəm* groups is not of such great importance and, further, that this division must be re-examined from a fresh viewpoint. It would be more exact to speak of the co-existence of *centum* and *satəm* elements in individual dialects and to refrain from now on from *ad hoc* explanations (for example, assumption of borrowings between dialects). The traditional *centum-satəm* pattern cannot be reconciled in its entirety with the distribution of dorsal consonants in any single IE idiom. (Consider, for example, ideas put forward about the *centum* or *satəm* character of Illyrian and *centum* features in the Slavonic languages; Gołąb 1969.) The existence of Illyro-Baltic parallels is very significant, for it allows us to define more closely the area of the central IE dialects (Toporov 1964: 52–8; contrast Russu 1969: 108).

In contrast to 'Pelasgian', Hittite, Phrygian, Armenian, Thracian, Germanic and Ossete, Dacian does not show mutation of consonants, thus preserving the primitive IE sound-system relatively unchanged. In Armenian, this mutation is of an older kind that than of Germanic and it took place between the third millennium and the twelfth century B.C. (Dzhaukyan 1967: 330–1). In some of the languages mentioned this phonetic phenomenon was the result of the influence of a pre-Indo-European substratum (Abaev 1949: 76, 110–12, 515–16, 518–25; Gamkrelidze 1961). But in Dacia there is no linguistic trace of peoples that might be identified as pre-Indo-European. Already in the Early Neolithic period the Indo-Europeans were present in the Carpatho-Danubian and Balkan regions.

As for the problem of contact, up to the third millennium proto-Anatolian had contacts with Italo-Celtic (Vraciu 1960a; 1969a), Greek, proto-Slavonic, proto-Baltic (Vraciu 1970b) and perhaps also with proto-Dacian. Later, between the third and the second millennia, proto-Dacian came into closer relation with proto-Slavonic and proto-Baltic. The relatively recent character of its contacts with these dialects explains, among other things, the survival in Dacian and Balto-Slavonic of a number of linguistic features which are specific to them (Vraciu 1959; 1960b; 1965).

It is not out of the question that at the time when the tendency towards mutation of consonants began the (proto-)Hittite-Luwians were settled in the eastern part of the Balkan peninsula. It follows from this that they moved towards Anatolia before the assibilation of the IE velars. (The time in question is in any case the last centuries of the third millennium B.C.; this accords generally speaking with the presence of Indo-Europeans in Greece and the Aegean islands).

As for the expansion of the Illyrians towards the Adriatic coast of the Balkans, it has already been noted (Russu 1969: 30) that it probably represents the last sizeable movement of Indo-Europeans from the north or north-east in pre-classical times, perhaps coming from the territory of present-day Poland. The migrants infiltrated towards the south-west, let us add, by the same route as had the 'proto-Anatolians' previously. In spite of all this a scholar such as Russu (1969: 56) still opposes these theories which maintain that the Illyrians expanded and migrated into Greece, Anatolia and Crete. (For the presence of Indo-European peoples in the Balkans in the period discussed and their reciprocal relations see: Condurachi 1971; Garašanin 1971; Vraciu 1970a-h; 1971).

Since Albanian was closely linked to the Balto-Slavonic language-group (Shirokov 1969: 10) it follows that the question just discussed is of quite special importance for Dacian, in view of the connections which exist between proto-Rumanian and proto-Albanian.

For a definite solution of the question about Bronze Age migrations in the geographical area which is of direct interest to us we need to correlate the linguistic data with the archaeological, a point which has been emphasized by nearly all the contributors to the Sheffield Colloquium (see the papers by R. A. Crossland, J. D. Evans, Sp. Marinatos, A. C. Renfrew, C. Sourvinou-Inwood and V. I. Georgiev, in that order).

During the period of transition from the Neolithic to the Bronze Age one observes in the Carpatho-Danubian region a cultural fusion between the nomads of the steppes and the autochthonous peoples of south-eastern Europe. Near Eastern influence and indeed Aegeo-Anatolian must not be underrated, but they did not play so important a role either in the Bronze

Age or in the preceding periods. In consequence we must allow for successive migrations from the Balkans into Anatolian regions. This is the most likely view. But neither archaeology, nor history, nor linguistics considered in isolation will give us a satisfactory answer to our question. Thus, from an archaeological point of view it is almost impossible to establish the order of the movements of peoples into the Anatolian, Aegean, palaeo-Balkanic and Carpatho-Danubian zones. The same holds good for the migration of the Indo-Europeans (see Renfrew 1969: 1: "absence of clear evidence for IE migration reaching Greece in BA"). As to anthropology, it must be categorically reiterated that it is equally incapable alone of explaining in an acceptable way the facts which we have been discussing, since in the past as in the present 'Indo-Europeans' included quite a variety of physical types.

On the other hand, the problem of the chronology of the differentiation of common Indo-European and that of the migrations of the tribes who spoke different IE dialects; the distinctions that must be made between movements of Indo-Europeans and subsequent displacements, between migrations and infiltrations, and their direction; all these are questions of great importance and ones which researchers should keep constantly in mind.

References

ABAEV, V. I. 1949. *Osetinskiy yazyk i fol'klor*, I. Moscow-Leningrad.

BERCIU, D. 1966. *Zorile istoriei în Carpati şi la Dunăre*. Bucharest.

BRÂNCUŞ, G. 1963. 'Über die einheimeschen lexikalischen Elemente im Rumänischen.' *RESEE*, 1 309–17.

——. 1966a. 'Les éléments autochtones dans le dialecte aroumain.' *RRLing*, 11: 549–65.

——. 1966b. 'Probleme ale reconstructiei elementelor lexicale autohtone în româna comună.' *SCL*, 17: 205–18.

——. 1968. *Relatii lingvistice româno-albaneze. Vocabular autohton comun* (rezumatul tezei de doctorat). Bucharest.

ÇABEJ, EQREM. 1958. 'Rumänische und albanische Wortdeutungen.' *CLing*, 3 (Supliment): 131–4.

CONDURACHI, EM. 1966. *Preface* to the Rumanian translation of V. G. Childe, *Man makes himself (Făurirea civilisatiei)*. Bucharest.

——. 1971. 'L'ethnogenèse des peuples balkaniques: les sources écrites.' *Plovdiv Symposium*: 249–69.

CROSSLAND, R. A. 1971. 'The position in the Indo-European language-family of Thracian and Phrygian and their possible close cognates.' *Plovdiv Symposium*: 225–36.

DAICOVICIU, C. and others. 1960. *Istoria României*, I. *Comuna primitivă. Sclavagismul. Perioada de trecere la feudalism*. Bucharest.

——. 1961. *Din istoria Transilvaniei*, I (reprint). Bucharest.

——. 1964. *Dacia liberă şi Dacia romană/La Dacie libre et la Dacie romaine*. Bucharest.

—— and others. *Istoria . . .* Bucharest.

DETEV, P. 1968. 'Praistoricheskoto selishte pri selo Muldava.' *GP*, 6: 9–48.

——. 1971. 'Données archéoligiques pour la continuité de la culture du tell Razkopanica près du village Manole, département de Plovdiv.' *Plovdiv Symposium*: 93–105.

DUMITRESCU, V. 1971. 'À propos de la plus ancienne culture néolithique de la Roumanie.' *Plovdiv Symposium*: 37–51.

DURIDANOV, I. 1968 'Balkanskii etimologii.' *BE*, 4/5: 401–6.

——. 1969. *Thrakisch-dakische Studien. Erster Teil. Die thrakisch und dakisch-baltischen Sprachbeziehungen (BalkE*, 13/2). Sofia.

——. 1971. 'Die Vorgeschichte Mygdoniens im Lichte der Sprache.' *Plovdiv Symposium*: 199–205.

DZHAUKYAN, G. B. 1967. *Ocherki istorii dopis'mennogo perioda armanyanskogo yazyka*. Erevan.

GAMKRELIDZE, T. V. 1961. 'Peredvizhenie soglasnykh v khettskom (nesitskom) yazyke'; in I. M. D'yakonov (Diakonov) and G. V. Tsereteli (ed.), *Peredniaziatskiy sbornik. Voprosy khettologii i khurritologii* (Moscow): 211–91.

GARAŠANIN, M. V. 1971. 'Nomades des steppes et autochtones dans le Sud-Est européen a l'époque de transition du néolithique à l'âge de bronze.' *Plovdiv Symposium*: 9–14.

GEORGIEV, V. I. 1958. *Issledovaniya po sravmitel'no-istoricheskomu yazykoznaniyu. Rodstvennye otnosheniya indoevropeyskikh yazykov*. Moscow,

——. 1965a. 'Le dace comme subtrat de la langue roumaine.' *RRLing*, 10: 75–80.

——. 1965b. 'L'origine des termes roumains *măgură* et *pîrîu*.' *OR*, 287–90.

——. 1971. 'L'ethnogenèse de la péninsule balkanique d'après les données linguistiques.' *Plovdiv Symposium*: 155–70.

GINDIN, L. A. 1967. *Yazyk drevneyshego naseleniya yuga Balkanskogo poluostrova*. Moscow.

——. 1971. 'Le "pélagique" et la thrace.' *Plovdiv Symposium*: 237–42.

GOŁĄB, Z. 1969. ' "Kentum" elements in Slavic.' *Papers from the Fifth Regional Meeting of the Chicago Linguistic Society*: 330–6.

HORNUNG, B. V. 1963. *Iz predystorii obrazonvaniya obshcheslavyanskogo yazkovogo edinstva*. Moscow.

IVĂNESCU, G. 1970. 'Vérité et erreur dans la recherche des dialectes proto-indoeuropéens.' *Philologica*, 1: 9–35.

IVANOV, V. V. 1957. 'O znachenii khettskogo yazyka dlya sravnitel'no-istoricheskogo issledovaniya slavyanskikh yazykov.' *Voprosy slavanskogo yazykoznaniya*, 2: 3–28.

——. 1966. *Obshcheindoebropeyskaya, praslavyanskaya i anatoliyskaya yazykovye sistemy (sravnitel'no-tipologicheskie ocherki)*. Moscow.

KENYON, K. M. 1961. *Beginning in Archaeology*. (2nd ed.) London.

KOŞAY, H. Z. 1971. 'La culture Aras-Karaz dans la région de l'Euphrate Moyen et l'expansion de cette culture.' *Plovdiv Symposium*: 139–51.

MELLAART, J. 1971. 'Prehistory of Anatolia and its relations with the Balkans.' *Plovdiv Symposium*: 119–37.

MIKOV, V. 1971. 'La Bulgarie à l'âge du bronze.' *Plovdiv Symposium*: 51–61.

PETRESCU-DÎMBOVITA. M. 1971. 'Quelques considérations concernant la fin de l'âge du bronze et le début de Hallstatt dans l'espace carpatho-balkanique.' *Plovdiv Symposium*: 107–17.

PHILIPPIDE A. 1928. *Originea românilor. II. Ce spun limbile română şi albăneza*. Iaşi.

POGHIRC, C. 1963. 'L'alternace *m/mb/b* en thrace et en albanais.' *BalkE*, 6: 97–100.

——. 1967. 'Considérations sur les éléments autochtones de la langue roumaine.' *RRLing*, 12: 19–36.

——. 1968a. *B. P. Hasdeu. Lingvist si filolog*. Bucharest.

——. 1968b. 'Probleme actuale ale etimologiei româneşti.' *LbR*, 17: 15–23.

——. and others. 1969. *Istoria Limbii române*, II. Bucharest.

REICHENKRON, C. 1966. *Das Dakische (rekonstruiert aus dem Rumänischen)*. Heidelberg.

RENFREW, A. C. 1969. 'The Aegean and the Balkans at the close of the Neolithic period. The evidence of Photolivos.' *Nitra Baden Symposium* (in press).

ROSETTI, A. 1968. *Istoria limbii române de la origini pînă în secolul al XVII-lea*. Bucharest.

——. 1969. 'Sur les éléments autochtones du roumain.' *Studia Albanica*, 1: 133–5.

RUSSU, I. I. 1967. *Limba traco-dacilor* (reprint). Bucharest.

——. 1969. *Illirii Istoria—Limba și onomastica-Romanizarea*. Bucharest.

——. 1970 *Elemente autohtone în limba română. Substratul comun româno-albanez*. Bucharest.

SHIROKOV, O. S. 1969 'Indoevropeyskie dialekty i slavyano-germanskie lingvisticheskie svyazi'; in V. V. Martynov (V. U. Martinaw), *Tipologiya i vzaimodeystvie slavyanskikh i germanskikh yazykov* (Minsk): 5–11.

TOPOROV, V. N. 1964. 'Neskol'ko illiriysko-baltiyskikh paralleley iz oblasti toponomastiki'; in V. N. Toporov, *Problemy indoevropeyskogo yazykoznaniya. Ėtyudy po sravnitel'no-istoricheskoi grammatike indoevropeyskikh yazykov* (Moscow): 52–8.

VRACIU, A. 1959. 'Caracterele generale ale limbilor baltice.' *SCStI*, 1–2: 109–30.

——. 1960a. 'Ipoteza unității lingvistice italo-celtice.' *SCStI*, 1: 106–14.

——. 1960b. 'Problema comunității lingvistice balto-slave.' *Romanoslavica*, 4: 87–106.

——. 1965 'Slavia și baltica. Problema vechilor raporturi dintre ele în lumina noilor cercetări.' *Romanoslavica*, 12: 283–97.

——. 1969a. 'Unele considerații asupra raporturilor dintre limbile italice și celtice.' *AUI*, 15: 1–15.

——. 1969b. Review of I. I. Russu, *Limba traco-dacilor (Bucharest; 1967)*; *CLing*, 14: 360–9.

——. 1970a. 'Asupra raporturilor dintre greacă și limbile indo-europene din Asia Mică.' *SCȘtB*: 315–21.

——. 1970b. 'Asupra raporturilor dintre hitită și alte limbi indo-europene.' *AUI*, 16: 9–34.

——. 1970c. 'Colocviul international de lingvistică și arheologie de la Sheffield.' *SCL*, 21: 593–6.

——. 1970d. 'Considerații asupra substratului daco-moesian al limbii române.' *SCȘtB*: 301–14.

——. 1970e. 'Precizări in legătură cu elementele autohtone ale limbii române.' *LbR*, 19: 101–16.

——. 1970f. *Problema elementului autohton în limba română*. (Tribuna Școlii Argesene; Pitești): 42–8.

——. 1970g. Review of I. I. Russu, *Illirii. Istoria-Limba și onomastica-Romanizarea* (Bucharest, 1969). *SCL*, 21: 83–92.

——. 1970h. Review of Rosetti and others, *Istoria limbii române*, II (Bucharest, 1969). *LbR*, 19: 489–98.

——. 1971. 'Sur le caractère autochtone des populations anciennes de la Dacie.' *Plovdiv Symposium*: 179–92.

ZLATKOVSKAYA, T. D. AND MELYUKOVA, A. I. 1969. *Drevnie frakiytsy v Severnom Prichernomoriye*. Moscow.

2

The dialectology and prehistoric development of Greek

Greek and general dialectology

N. E. COLLINGE

University College, University of Toronto

THE prehistory of the Mediterranean and Aegean regions in the Bronze Age has always been a treacherous marsh. Of late there has been more floundering than usual, as several seeming solidities have proved false. A golden thread of certainty along a safe path is not to be had; possibly some warning barriers, erected by sad experience, may seem, if brazen, yet salutary. Some of the linguistic sloughs may be fenced off, especially in one sector (ancient Greek dialects) where documentary evidence beckons from the farther side and texts are thought to reflect divisions and movements of a fairly homogeneous, and fairly locatable, body of people.

Academic follies have here led many astray; yet perhaps only five errors deserve the rank of 'deadly sin'. Of these the first is to confuse a dialect with a language, and the second—not always extricable from the first—is to equate dialects and dialect-groups.

Whereas a dialect and a language both represent an aggregate of individual competences of speech, the former comprises idiolects which are different from one another only in non-operational features. That is, the speakers of one dialect do not use items and mechanisms which are appreciably distinct from each others'. A language, however, may have its idiolects tied in so many bundles, the bundles differing in (and owing their recognition to) appreciably distinct items and processes of sound and form organization. North-western English people are like one another but different from southern British speakers in (for instance) not having a separate phoneme /ŋ/ but only [ŋ] as one member of the class of sounds which realize the phoneme /n/[1]. Between bundles the 'tolerance' level tends to move lower; if mutual unintelligibility is reached in more and more parts of more and more utterances there comes a point at which the bundles have to be reclassified as members of different languages. This result may be evolutionary, which is why I cannot understand Frisian (for a startling example of such non-communication between Greeks cf. Allen, 1968: vii); it may equally, especially in 'morbid' linguistics, stem from an inadequate analysis in the first place. One can set two dialects apart on the grounds that each has peculiar operational features (which may be unusual reflexes of a common inheritance: so Winter 1966: 201, speaks of dialects as "variants of one language that are characterized by clustering of divergent developments from several unitary features of the proto-language"). At this point, although a simple count of likenesses has caused one to handle these speech-forms together, it is really optional (in the absence of a standard form or a prestige dialect) whether one calls the aggregate a 'language' at all. 'Basque' is no more than a convenient label for a set of seven co-existing dialects; and Martinet (1954: 7) could ask "to what extent are we entitled to speak of Breton as a language?", there being four traditional dialects and a still more complex reality. The decision is forced (granting that there is a multiplicity of dialects in the first place) by the co-occurrence of few operational barriers between the dialects and many such between them all and any other known body of speech[2]. Then the dialects do compose a language, of which the total operational inventory is their own aggregate, and of which overall inventory they have each a peculiar share. Add the factor of close co-habitation, however interrupted, and the share will differ largely in combinations rather than in preclusions or even omissions. No item need be found in any one given dialect alone; the recipes, not the ingredients, will differ. Then—and this is clearly the Greek case—a language-difference must be stated explicitly and positively (for one cannot characterize Illyrian just by listing the items of Greek which it has not got, any more than one can so describe French as not English); but a dialect-difference can only be properly stated combinatorily and negatively. And yet, with this lesson learnt and one's gaze fixed on unparalleled combinations of features, one does not always avoid the third sin (of inadequate negativity), of which we must speak shortly.

The second deadly sin may appear to refer to an oversubtle and esoteric nuance. In effect, the error can be gross and much misleading, especially if prehistorians and archaeologists come to rely on apparent connectedness of speech-groups. The Greeks themselves sometimes shifted their term *glôssa* to mean the individual (city) dialect, as opposed to *diálektos*, the group (Hainsworth 1967: 70). This was because they started with the groups, expecting monolithic speech-types to correspond to ethnic (and ethic)

divisions of their nation as they saw them, and subsequently found themselves face to face with the truth (e.g. that not all 'Dorians' spoke alike but
used different operational items or distributed them differently). But for us
the split is theoretical and fundamental. A dialect, after all, is a demonstrable
idiom of a number of persons who can be geographically pointed out
exactly, or whose historical existence and locale can be predicted with fair
certainty and detail. A dialect-group, on the contrary, is a scholars' heuristic
fiction. It is a device to summarize certain linkable distributions of important variants within a general speech-area. The 'importance' rests on circular
arguments, presupposing possible groupings; but the *ad hoc* bundling of
variations and the prejudiced weighting of diagnostics do continue to
reduce a mass of town-idioms to a handful of migration-groups. The thing
to remember is that nothing about the groupings is immutable. We speak,
in our convenient way, of 'Arcado-Cyprian', in the face of Arc.
ei ... (*k*)*án* ..., Cypr. *ē* ... *ke* ... We set up 'Aeolic', although Lesbian is
detached and infected, to say the least (Porzig 1954; Risch 1955; Coleman
1963; the last-named suggests that Boeotian has much to do with Doric).
Any alignment can be upset by some test: the shift *-rs-* > *-rr-* slices all
usual groups, being present in Arcadian but (probably) not in Cyprian;
in Attic and West Ionic but not in Central or East Ionic; in Rhodian but
not in Cretan or Coan Doric; in Theran but not in Cyrenean, and so forth.

One can be too simple-minded, too classificatory, not merely in the sense
that some dialects (Elean or Pamphylian, say) are often moving house from
one academic group to another, but in the senses which are illuminated by
Winter's experiment with Armenian (1966). He establishes four pre-
classical dialects, using differences in historical shifts applied to inherited
phenomena (sounds only) but applying a reduction-process by counting
only classes of shifts. No historical path is proved; the opinion that one of
the resulting dialects represents pre-classical Armenian is neither needed nor
safe (as we shall shortly see). More importantly, an increase in diagnostics
(e.g. morphology) and other value scale would lead to other (and
more) dialects; and the inherent minimalizing is really producing not
dialects at all, but crypto-groups. And pseudo-groups are just as easy. If we
bear in mind the curious connection of Argos with many West-Greek-
speaking islands (as the reputed metropolis of Crete, Rhodes, Cos and the
arbitration resort of other islands; cf. *IG* 12.3.1259), we can use the
incidence in these places of lexical indexes (*khrēizō*, 'wish') and phonological
indexes (*-V:n/r/l/s-* as the regular result of *Vn/r/l/s-* before *w*, as in *xēnos*) as
cues to recognize a group. Add the essential testimony of morphology (first
declension plural accusatives in *-ăs*, perfect infinitive in *-kein*, active endings
for the future passive and—though this is in Cyrenean too—an infinitive in
-ĕn in *-éō* verbs), and one brings a novel speech form—call it *Inseldorisch*—
on the historical and even literary scene. And how welcome is that?

The third sin is to be insufficiently negative. It is not enough to delineate a dialect by noting the absence elsewhere of certain co-occurrences. One must first establish groups (preferably considering and discarding other possible, but less suggestive or economic groupings), and do so by accepting absences. Thereafter it is just as essential to assign textual phenomena (and sets of like texts) to groups, by similar elimination. Let us use the clearly preclusive (Greek) features: (a) accusative plural 'us', 'you', marked by zero; (b)-(k)ot- as specialized perfect active participle-stem; (c) first plural verb marker -mes retained. By the group test, A will be set apart from the rest as not having (a), B from CD as not having (b); C from the relict D as not having (c). (In fact, A = Ionic-Attic, B = Aeolic, C = Arcado-Cyprian and D = West Greek.)[3] By the second test a set of texts, let us suppose Arcadian, by not failing to have (a) or (b) is not assignable to Ionic-Attic and Aeolic, respectively, but by failing to have (c) cannot be assigned to West Greek but must belong to the group which remains. Re-arrangement of the shibboleths gives fresh groups and new assignments; all is provisional until trial and application fix the most fruitful, economic and consistent result. And the diagnostics are tested at the same time; one soon learns the practical unreliability in this matter of the shift $-ti(-) > -si(-)$ (which Nagy, 1970, does not entirely cure for the 'Classical' dialects and brings out unhappily clearly in Mycenaean, 140–8; a pity, for it might have borne the brunt of establishing that the 'common Greek' period ended before the time of the tablets, against the indication of the perfect participle (Myc. -wos-, not -wot-) and the comparative adjective (Myc. -os-, not -on- as even in Aeolic) that a period of common Greek innovation persisted after Mycenaean).

We fall into the fourth deadly sin if we forget in what type of dialectology we are engaged. For our Bronze Age (and Classical Greek) periods, we should always bear in mind that our concern is with atomistic evidence in a field of morbid data (for a defence of atomism, consult Ellis 1966: 26). Coleman's belief (1963: 69) that structural pressures operate similarly but independently in the dialects is more important than his plea to relate each item to the structure of its own dialect. It is not just that general trends are realized independently (Coleman 1963: 82; cf. Morpurgo-Davies 1968: 85: "Greek dialects...follow parallel lines...at different times and at different speeds"); the whole concept of structure-pressure is too battered to be of use any longer. 'Push-chain' or 'drag-chain' causation (Martinet's terms) is known not to be reliable. The chain of Greek shifts $\star h > \emptyset \sim \star s > h \sim t(i) > s(i) \sim k^w(i) > t(i)$ is falsified by the way Arcado-Cyprian pushes $k^w i$ through to si (if the occurrence of 'simplified san' in the Arcadian inscriptions permits this interpretation; see Buck 1955: 18) though it has emptied $t(i)$ into $s(i)$, or Aeolic shifts $k^w(i)$ to $t(i)$ (tīma, tís; písures is only Homeric) but keeps $t(i)$ intact, early or late. (And one may read Jones's critique, 1964: 176, of Bartoněk's spirited essays, 1961, in this field[4].)

By adding to Coleman's idea on structural causation his further correct observation (1963: 88) as to how dialects make an equally independent selection of 'same' items (from a like store), we gain some procedural clues. In our search for diagnostics, if we want to separate and to link dialects, first we should look for items which are not the products of presumed structure-pressure; and secondly we will be safer with shifted features than with unchanged reflexes of chosen items. Now if Coleman's own fifty-one diagnostics are winnowed, only nine unpressured shifts emerge in usable form. The tally might be extended by including simple assimilations of the $rs > rr$ type, but these are so general in human speech and so sporadically applied in Greek as to lose critical value. The shift of prefixed *eks-* to *ek-* or *es-*, and the replacement of *Vns* (where *ns* is word-final or secondary medial) by *V:s* or *Vis* or *Vs*, are perfectly sound criteria for grouping and sub-grouping, but may be left aside as we, for the moment, think in terms of the traditional divisions. The shift $\bar{e} > e$ ([ε:]), by the negative procedures outlined above, only establishes 'non-Ionic'. The six remaining shifts lead to these deductions:

absence of -*ti-* > -*si-* splits Aeol., WGk from AC, Ion.
absence of -*eo-* > -*ĕŏ-* splits Aeol., AC from WGk, Ion.
(and absence of > -*ĕŏ-* as result, despite shift, sets Attic apart).
absence of -*mes* > -*men* sets up WGk.
absence of -*toi* > *tai* sets up AC.
absence of $k^{w}o/e > po$ but *te* sets up Aeol.
(as does failure to locate compensatory length in vowels; so *emmi*, *krénnō*, etc.).

It is noteworthy that by this process one has to conclude that Ionic is not to be set apart as a group on any really basic evidence, which may hearten those who put its identity late among Greek dialectal phenomena.

Yet it may be safer to retreat into general negativity again. Evidence from structure has seemed more seductively 'scientific' than atomism. Catford (1957: 107–10), after a fine description of differences of vowel systems in the dialects of Scots English, speaks of eight-vowel systems as separate rarities (one in Bute, one in Ayrshire and neighbouring Lanarkshire), but then sees a nine-vowel area around Glasgow 'sending a spearhead down Clydesdale and Nithsdale into Dumfriesshire and east Kirkcudbrightshire'. Luckily his evidence lets one see that there are two different nine-vowel systems, and Dumfries seems to be rather equatable in this respect with, but cut off from, Berwickshire (cf. his figs. 1 and 3). And the most complex system, that of twelve vowels, as uniform as is the eight-vowel system, occurs in the extreme south-west and north-east of the whole speech-area. Does this argue marginal status in evolution? It may. But Coleman's considerations undermine all the faith one might have, procedurally, in the fact that two dialects have chosen the same number, within a small possible range of operational variation, of vowels from a tiny common store. This is a strong point. Rather weaker is the objection to drawing deductions from gross unlikeness of systems. So King (1969: 32) cites the revelation by Moulton (1960: 176-7) that two dialects of Swiss German, less than fifty miles apart, have each an inventory of eleven vowel phonemes of which only three (or perhaps one) are shared.

Both the metaphors of Catford and the polemics of King (who is tilting especially at the notion of calculating dialect history from the numbers of shared operational items, Weinrich's 'diaphonemes' etc.) lead us into the fifth deadly sin. This is that of confusing (observational and) descriptive adequacy, which is a matter of practical achievement, with explanatory adequacy, which is a test of the theoretical viability of one's view of how forms of communication really work and really change. The transformational approach can handle a dialect difference of, say, inventory and distribution of vowel phonemes (cf. King's fictitious but credible case, 1969: 33-6), by showing how dialect B has one more 'rule' than dialect A (or some simple change in order or generality of rules). But on this peak of success one looks in vain for a rationale. On what grounds an added rule is to be held a certain reflex of a historical change (by argument from the more obvious converse?), or why dialect A must be so regularly seen as the predecessor of dialect B (on which whole area of possibly gross error in dialectology, see Thomas 1967: *passim*, especially 195), on these points no proof is offered. Cues to re-interpretation, yes; proof of certain historical paths, no. And one does well to remember that if the stages intervening between proto-Indo-European and New High German were as theoretical as most of prehistoric Greek, it would be a brilliant man who would see the need for successive revisings of the rules to inject history into the reflex *NHG t* (in *Vater*) < *pIE t* (in *pHter-*), which appears to merit no descriptive notice, let alone explanation.

Where two clearly different stages of one dialect are to be compared (e.g. in internal reconstruction) one may argue that a generative, or any other sophisticated, operational analysis will lay bare the real mutations and give proven precision to history. Unhappily, we tend to be offered a choice of precisions.

A simple example is afforded by the curious third-century change of Boeotian *oi* from the diphthongal value [o^i] to some monophthong which could be written *u*, using the Ionic-based sign which had long since conveyed in Ionic-Attic something no longer *u*-like but not quite *i*-like. If the Boeotian result (like the Ionic-Attic result, from original [u]) was a lip-spread [u] (cf. Russian *ȳ*) we may denote it as [ɨ] and still a back vowel; if lip-rounding alone is retained in what is now otherwise identical with [i] and by this means *pustós* is kept apart from *pistós*, we will write it [ü], a front vowel. A halfway movement, ignoring certain subtleties, will produce the high central vowel [y]. What have we in Boeotian? How does this shift relate to the series of re-arrangements, between the fifth and third centuries B.C., which make Boeotian such a curious predictor of much of modern Greek vocalism (namely [eⁱ] > [iː], [aⁱ] > [ɛː], [ɛ] > [e̩ː]?

The shifts may first be plotted in articulatory-acoustic terms, with reference: (*a*) to a triangular disposition of the simple vowels which is an analogue of organ-positions in the mouth (hence 'front', 'back', 'low', 'high', etc.); and (*b*) to a placing on a frequency-grid of which the parameters are the two lowest significant bands-of-harmonics (formants 1 and 2) in the acoustic composition of vowel sounds. A monophthongization of *ai*, *ei*, *oi*, with a length-feature compensating for the palatal loss, is to be allowed as the prior process in the total shift. Then the battery of shifted values is to be stated most simply and systematically by assigning one general movement of fronting and raising—a drift towards the 'north-west', so to speak—affecting items successively: so

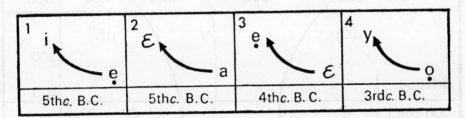

Fig. 28.1. Vowel shift in Boeotian in the fifth, fourth and third centuries B.C.

One might suppose a drift of all vowels towards [i]. This is scarcely likely, and it is even less likely that [o̩] should have arrived there but not [ɛ] or [u] or that there should have been a symmetrical movement upwards and outwards from the centre, which would call for a (non-existent) shifting of [ɔ] and a shift of [a] > [ɛ,ɔ]. These notions, needed to support presumed shifts of [o̩] > [ü], [ɪ] respectively, are clearly inferior to that which has been here supposed. The order of candidates for the result of shifted *oi* must be: first [y], third equal [ü], [ɪ]—in our later terms, C . . . D/E.

Secondly, we may appeal to the transformational generative model, which handles the actual exponents of speech (its 'systematic phonetics') in terms of 'distinctive features'. It does this largely because the Jakobson-Fant-Halle notion, that significantly different sounds are built up of combinations of a few binary features (that is, features which are by definition simply either used or not used), offers a sound-'alphabet' which is universal and which by-passes the concept of phoneme; its adoption is largely ideological, therefore (Jakobson, Fant and Halle 1965). Jakobson's 'Prague School' doctrine is given precision by Fant's spectrographic pictures of speech-sounds in action; and the distinctive features are partly characterized in articulatory-acoustic terms (e.g. *nasal, consonantal, strident*) and partly in terms of spectrographic formant-shapes (e.g. *diffuse, flat, acute*). Let us ignore, for convenience, the features 'tense' (vowel length does not distinguish our examples at any stage), 'nasal' (irrelevant), 'vocalic/consonantal' (otiose) and some recent features applying to consonants ('coronal', 'anterior'). Then we may first visualize the relation of features to vowels by the super-imposition of the two manners of description, plotted by frequency, in Fig. 28.2; thereafter the specification of the vowels involved in these shifts is as given in the matrix which is Fig. 28.3[5].

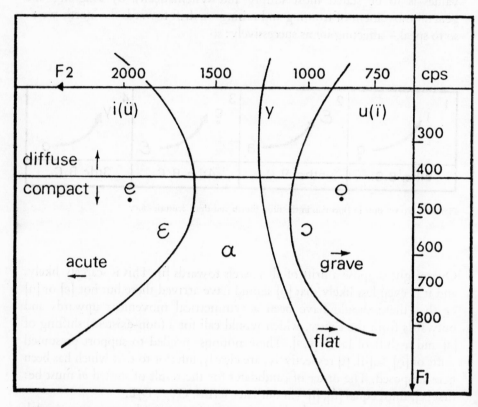

Fig. 28.2. Features of vowels in Boeotian, in the fifth, fourth and third centuries B.C., plotted according to acoustic frequencies

F = formant
cps = cycles per second (the frequencies are typical not absolute)
[y] is allowed to maintain roundness.

	ẹ → i		a → ε		ọ → y		or ü	or ï
flat	—	—	—	—	+	+	+	—
compact	—	—	+	+	—	—	—	—
diffuse	—	+	—	—	—	+	+	+
grave	—	·	—	—	+	—	—	+
acute	+	+	—	+	—	—	+	—
	A		B		C		D	E

Fig. 28.3. Specification of vowels in Boeotian in the fifth, fourth and third centuries B.C.

Two measurements are then possible:

(a): Vowel-shift A involves one specification-change (~ diffuse)
Vowel-shift B involves one specification-change (~ acute)
Vowel-shift E involves two specification-changes (+ flat → − flat; − diffuse → + diffuse)
Vowel-shift C involves two specification-changes (− diffuse → + diffuse; + grave → − grave)
Vowel-shift D involves three specification-changes (− diffuse → + diffuse; + grave → − grave; − acute → + acute)
(*Note*: [ε] > [ẹ] involves one change, ~ compact).

(b): comparison of the total long-vowel system (including ɔ:, u:) for third-century Boeotian, before and after the shift of *oi* and allowing the three possibilities C, D, E, is possible from consideration of Fig. 28.4, and one can then calculate the differences in the overall implicational relationship between the horizontal ranks (of incidence in each feature).

(*Note*: an isolated plus or minus is not counted).

	ẹ	i	a	ε	ɔ	u	ọ	/y	/ü	/ï
flat	—	—	—	—	+	+	+	+	+	—
compact	—	—	+	+	+	—	—	—	—	—
diffuse	—	+	—	—	—	+	—	+	+	+
grave	—	—	—	—	+	+	+	—	—	+
acute	+	+	—	+	—	—	—	—	+	—
							→	C	D	E

Fig. 28.4. Changes in the long-vowel system of Boeotian in the third century B.C.

With [o̹] in the system these implications are true:

$$\begin{array}{rcl}
\text{flat} & \equiv & \text{grave} \\
+\text{flat/grave} & \supset & -\text{acute} \\
+\text{acute} & \supset & -\text{flat/grave} \\
+\text{compact} & \supset & -\text{diffuse} \\
+\text{diffuse} & \supset & -\text{compact}
\end{array}$$

With shift C, flat $\equiv$ grave ceases to be true, yet in its place:

$$\begin{array}{rcl}
+\text{grave} & \supset & +\text{flat} \\
-\text{flat} & \supset & -\text{grave}
\end{array}$$

With shift D, flat $\equiv$ grave again ceases to be true and is replaced as with shift C ($+$flat $\supset$ $+$grave; $-$ flat $\supset$ $-$grave); but the following also cease to be true:

$$\begin{array}{rcl}
+\text{flat} & \supset & -\text{acute} \\
+\text{acute} & \supset & -\text{flat}
\end{array}$$

With shift E, flat $\equiv$ grave is replaced by:

$$\begin{array}{rcl}
+\text{flat} & \supset & +\text{grave} \\
-\text{grave} & \supset & -\text{flat}
\end{array}$$

Taking Figs. 28.3 and 28.4 together we must designate shift C or E as the likeliest retrodiction (of generative grammar), if we seek economy in the revising of rules and the re-ordering of implication; that is, if maintained intelligibility rests on ease of re-structuring in the grammar. The articulatory test's order, C ... D/E, is at variance with the transformationalist tests' preference, C/E ... D. There is no revelation here, and optimistic speculation must be chastised; yet either analysis would present a masterly commendation of a known answer.

Can one end on a note of positivity? Perhaps not, but there may be some progressive force in the negative procedures outlined above. For instance, in theory (although not in the use of particular diagnostics) Cowgill's findings (1966: 95) are unexceptionable. Right or wrong in fact, it is procedurally correct to offer a quadrant of dialect-groups (for pre-classical times) arranged by the criterion that sharing of significant features is absent between the groups diagonally opposed to each other. Perhaps we can tinker with Cowgill's diagram by re-ordering it, so that at least Arcadian and some Aeolic speakers are put in a recognizable geographical relation, thus:

Aeolic	West Greek
Achaean (i.e. Arc-Cypr)	Ionic

Fig. 28.5. Suggested relative spatial positions of Greek dialect-groups at the end of the second millennium B.C.

And that, if crude meaning may be attached at all, puts the early West Greek speakers not so very far from the Troad, after all.

Notes

1. Thus the phonological difference of *sing* from *sin* is, in southern usage, a matter of replacement of the third phoneme, /sin/→/siy/, and for the north-westerner an addition of a fourth phoneme to the sequence, /sin/→/sing/.

2. The same distinctions operate, of course, in other dimensions than the one here under consideration, whence we encounter 'registers', 'styles' and perhaps 'strains' (Stimson's biological term). Any differential phenomenon offered as evidence in dialectology may really be a witness within another dimension; this warning may excuse their being ignored in the rest of the present discussion (see Heger 1969, with references; Stimson 1962).

3. Not all apparent group-members offer examples of the diagnostic forms (but this does not invalidate the forms for this purpose, whereas criteria which produce idiosyncratic results invalidate themselves, whatever their reputation: the 'Doric future' is, if you think about it, useless). And some texts are simply out on a limb, like the Sillyon inscription (Pamphylian), the Andania inscription (Messenian), the Sotaerus inscription (Thessalian).

4. The following symbols have been used in this article in addition to those which are frequent in comparative linguistic studies:
   ∼ means 'related to'
   ≡ means 'always has the same specification as'
   ⊃ means 'necessitates'
   ø means 'zero'

5. The names of features can be defeating. *Compact* (versus *diffuse*) refers to the closeness of formant 1 to the third (and higher) formants—or just to a high F1. It correlates with the articulatory feature of a wide vertical mouth-cavity, so that open (or wide) vowels are compact, close (or narrow) vowels are diffuse. See Jakobson-Fant-Halle, 1965: 27. Recently, the more familiar terms 'round(ed)' and 'back' have been used instead of 'flat' and 'grave'; but the more esoteric names are perhaps preferable here, in a commentary on Halle's kind of historicism.

References

ALLEN, W. S. 1968. *Vox Graeca*. Cambridge.

BARTONĚK, A. 1961. *Vývoj konsonantického systému v řeckých dialektech* (with English translation *Development of the Consonantal System in Ancient Greek Dialects*). Prague.

BIRNBAUM, H. and PUHVEL, J. (editors) 1966. *Ancient Indo-European Dialects*. Berkeley and Los Angeles.

BUCK, C. D. 1955. *The Greek Dialects*. Chicago.

CATFORD, J. C. 1957. 'Vowel-systems of Scots dialects.' *TPhS*, 1957: 107–17.

COLEMAN, R. G. G. 1963. 'The dialect geography of ancient Greece.' *TPhS*, 1963: 58–126.

COWGILL, W. C. 1966: 'Ancient Greek dialectology in the light of Mycenaean'; in Birnbaum and Puhvel, 1966: 77–95.

ELLIS, J. O. 1966. *Towards a General Comparative Linguistics*. The Hague.

HAINSWORTH, J. B. 1967. 'Greek views of Greek dialectology.' *TPhS*, 1967: 62–76.

HEGER, K. 1969. 'Sprache und "Dialekt" als linguistiches und soziolinguistiches Problem.' *Folia Linguistica*, 3: 46–67.

JAKOBSON, R., FANT, C. G. M. and HALLE, M. 1965. *Preliminaries to Speech Analysis* (6th reprint). Englewood Cliffs, N. J.

JONES, D. M. 1964. Review of Bartoněk, 1961: *CR*, N.S., 14: 175–7.

KING, R. D. 1969. *Historical Linguistics and Generative Grammar*. Englewood Cliffs, N.J.

MARTINET, A. 1954. 'Dialect.' *RomPh*, 8: 1–11.

MORPURGO-DAVIES, A. 1968, 'Article and demonstative: a note.' *Glotta*, 46: 77–85,

MOULTON, W. 1960. 'The short vowel systems of northern Switzerland.' *Word*, 16: 155–82.

NAGY, G. 1970. *Greek Dialects and the Transformation of an Indo-European Process*. Cambridge, Mass.

PORZIG, W. 1954. 'Sprachgeographische Untersuchungen zu den griechischen Dialekten.' *IF*, 61: 147–69.

RISCH, E. 1955. 'Die Gliederung der griechischen Dialekte in neuer Sicht.' *MH*, 12: 71–66.

STIMSON, H. 1962. 'Ancient Chinese -*p*, -*t*, -*k* endings in the Peking dialect.' *Lg*, 38: 376–84.

THOMAS, A. R. 1967. 'Generative phonology in dialectology.' *TPhS*, 1967: 179–203.

WINTER, W. 1966. 'Traces of early dialectal diversity in Old Armenian'; in Birnbaum and Puhvel, 1966: 201–11.

The place of the Dorians in the Late Helladic world

ANTONÍN BARTONĚK

University of Brno

THE deciphering of the Linear B script gave us the possibility of a direct insight into the very beginning of the dialectal differentiation of Greek in the second millennium B.C. To be sure, the light which the deciphered texts throw on the dialect situation in Greece at that time is but weak and often only indirect. Nevertheless, the Greek character of the language of the Linear B script is reflected quite clearly in the texts and this Mycenaean language really appears to be a genuine ancient Greek dialect. Its precise dialectal classification is, however, not so well agreed. It is true that during the last twenty years different research workers have tried to determine a number of linguistic features that they regard as typical of Mycenaean Greek. But the interpretation of some of these features is still uncertain, while others hardly reveal anything definite about the dialectal classification of 'Mycenaean' either because we have to deal with evident archaisms or because we lack any other dialect of the Late Helladic period for scientific comparative study; any direct comparison of Mycenaean with the Classical dialects is rather risky, particularly when the less frequent phenomena are concerned, because these dialects are substantially younger. If we put aside the Greek of Homer, which is an artificial language with elements of various dialectal and chronological provenience, the chronological gap between the latest Mycenaean texts (*c.* 1200 B.C.) and the oldest alphabetical texts is nearly five hundred years; and as for the dialects that according to usual recent views are considered to be the nearest relatives of Mycenaean, namely Arcadian and Cyprian, their oldest documented inscriptions are as late as the sixth and seventh centuries B.C. respectively.

Only if we are fully aware of these difficulties may we have some hope of sketching in the characteristic dialectal features of Greek in the Mycenaean period, i.e. the Late Helladic. In my paper to the Mycenaean Colloquium in Salamanca (April 1970) I have tried to determine the level of relevance of the more notable linguistic peculiarities of Mycenaean Greek for the dialectal classification of the language of Linear B script and I have come to the conclusion that of the comparatively large number of various linguistic parallels that have been collected so far as arguments in favour of associating Mycenaean more closely with one or other of the Classical Greek dialects, no more than eight phenomena deserve to be treated seriously from this point of view (Bartoněk 1971).

At the same time a detailed analysis of even these phenomena does not present a sharp enough picture of the possibilities of classification as far as the dialectal character of the language of the Linear B texts is concerned. The only comparatively certain result appears to be a closer connection of Mycenaean with Arcado-Cyprian; their basic linguistic similarities, which to be sure are not all of equal relevance for classification, may be supplemented by a significant indirect argument if we combine the traditional and generally accepted thesis about the original genetic unity of Arcadian and Cyprian with the realization that the Late Helladic precursor of Arcadian was spoken in the territory stretching between the Argolid and Messenia, i.e. between the two important Mycenaean coastal countries and between two of the three most important places where tablets in the Linear B script have been found; and if we further consider that the 'Achaeans', who were colonizing Cyprus during the Late Helladic period, came to this island for the most part directly from the coastal areas of the Peloponnese, then we can hardly question seriously a close connection between the language of Linear B texts and the Late Helladic phase in the development of the Arcadian and Cyprian dialects. Yet complete identity of all these dialects can scarcely be assumed, particularly if we accept the view now meeting with increasing approval, that the Greek of the Linear B texts was in fact either a sort of spoken 'supra-dialect' perhaps originally based on one of the 'Arhaean' sub-dialects (maybe of the Argolid)[1] and possibly betraying traces of other dialectal elements; or else that it was simply an official written language, fixed and rigid, yet displaying some internal linguistic differences, which occasionally became evident (Bartoněk 1966; 1968a; 1968b: 175–81, 189–91).

A close connection of Mycenaean with Arcado-Cyprian presents us of course with the question of what the relation of Mycenaean was to the other Greek dialects of the Late Helladic period; and in particular we must face the problem of how far the distribution of the Greek dialects in the Classical period can be retrospectively projected to the second millennium B.C.

During the last twenty years numerous views have been formulated about Greek dialectal interrelations in the Late Helladic period. They have been widely different, even antagonistic. If precursors of dialects or dialectal groups of the Classical period were declared to be closely akin to

Mycenaean, they were always either proto-Ionic or proto-Aeolic. Mycenaean of the Linear B texts was in principle never associated with proto-Doric. The reason was not only that the arrival of the Dorians is usually connected chronologically with the destruction of the Mycenaean civilization, irrespective of whether the Dorians themselves directly participated in this event or not, but also that linguistic analysis of Linear B texts clearly demonstrates the non-Doric character of the language used in the centres of Mycenaean civilization, as we can see for instance from the safely documented change of the original suffix *-ti(-)* into *-si(-)*, notably in the ending of 3rd person plur. active verbal forms. As for the sporadic instances in the Mycenaean texts which do not show this change, we need not ascribe them to Dorian influence, or to scribes of Dorian origin (Nagy 1968); they may be compared with certain other phenomena of conservative character, such as the considerably later anomaly of Classical Greek *Korinthios* (in conformity with *Korinthos*) compared to Mycenaean *ko-ri-si-jo* (= *Korinsios*; Lejeune 1968).

If we accept this view, however, we have to ask where the Dorians actually lived before the fall of the Mycenaean civilization, and above all whether they resided far enough from the Mycenaean centres to justify us in regarding their arrival in the Peloponnese as a separate migration of Greek-speaking people.

The author of this article can naturally take an attitude to these problems from the linguistic point of view only, and in this light he deduces the following characteristics for the proto-Doric dialectal area *c.* 1200 B.C.: (*a*) a comparatively uniform dialectal basis, by that date not yet greatly differentiated; (*b*) a comparatively close affinity of this dialectal basis to the assumed Late Helladic precursors of the other dialectal groups of the Classical period.

We obviously do not wish to maintain that proto-Doric of the thirteenth century B.C. was necessarily an altogether uniform dialect. We believe, however, that we shall not be far wrong if we assume that the Doric-speaking territory in the north-west of Greece was not extensive and that it was not without contact with the Mycenaean region. If we take into account the prevailing opinion that the later creators of the Mycenaean culture came to Greece about the beginning of the second millennium B.C. and that in the sixteenth century B.C. they were already taking the lead in the development of Aegean civilization, even if perhaps with foreign dynasties as rulers, then it is hard to imagine from the linguistic point of view that the proto-Doric tribes should meanwhile have lived in complete isolation from Mycenaean culture. (Above all, the linguistic data do not support the assumption that the predecessors of the Achaeans and Ionians had come from Anatolia and those of the Dorians and Aeolians directly from the north.) Proto-Doric, as we can reconstruct it for about 1200 B.C. from the rich variety of more than fifteen separate Doric dialects of the

Classical period, was no doubt a dialect readily intelligible to those who lived in the centres of Mycenaean civilization; while the absence of any distinctly different Indo-European admixture practically excludes any hypothesis that proto-Doric was one of a number of distinct IE languages that amalgamated to form Greek by a secondary process of linguistic convergence subsequent to the Dorian migration (Pisani 1955). Peloponnesian Doric appears to be a dialect too stabilized from the systemic point of view to permit this assumption: it displays only a few sporadic substrate traces (mainly of 'Achaean' origin) and does not at all give the impression of being a non-Greek language overlaid with a Doric Greek superstratum.

That even the 'Achaean' substrate as such did not have any considerable effect on the Doric dialects may best be demonstrated by comparing Laconian Doric or Argolic Doric from the valley of the Inachus (i.e. distinctively Doric dialects of the former main areas of the Mycenaean culture) with Arcadian, which rather firmly maintained its 'Achaean' character in mountainous regions of the central Peloponnese.

In this connection, one theory even associates Doric of the Mycenaean period with the contemporary dialect of the Aeolian area and recognizes a close kinship between the two. We have in mind E. Risch's hypothesis, derived from W. Porzig's convincing argumentation, according to which the Late Helladic precursor of the Aeolic dialects had its suffix -ti still unchanged into -si, as we find documented even in the Classical period in Thessalian and Boeotian, while Lesbian was indebted for its -si to the influence of neighbouring Ionia after its colonization (Porzig 1954: 147-50; Risch 1955: 61-76). On the basis of these assumptions Risch divides Late Helladic Greek into North Greek (with -ti in pheronti), which included Doric and Aeolic, and the innovating South Greek (with -si in pheronsi) which would have to comprise both the contemporary proto-Arcado-Cypriot dialects (including Mycenaean) and the entire proto-Ionic dialectal grouping.

Risch's hypothesis has been subjected to criticism from various quarters, but the long-lasting preservation of original -ti in the entire proto-Aeolic sphere appears to the present author to be a much more convincing explanation of the difference between the Boeotian-Thessalian -ti and the innovating Lesbian -si than the older hypothesis which suggests that proto-Aeolic -ti changed into -si far back in the second millennium B.C., after which the -ti- form was restored in European Aeolic territory, after the Aeolian colonization in Anatolia (e.g. even in Thessalian Pelasgiotis, which otherwise was affected by Doric linguistic influence only to a very small extent).

On the other hand, this attribution of Late Helladic Aeolic to the -ti- type of dialects, which is reasonably acceptable, need not imply any closer genetic relation between Aeolic and Doric. The assibilation $ti > si$ is an innovation, and its non-occurrence in Aeolic (which is an archaic feature) does not of necessity imply close dialectal affinity over the entire linguistic area in which it did not occur. It may rather be inferred that this change simply did not progress northward beyond the Gulf of Corinth and beyond Attica, and if Late Helladic Aeolic appears to have been associated with contemporary Doric in this respect, that does not mean much, for we become acquainted with the successors of these two dialects so much later that we are not justified in assuming that no other differences existed between them in the second half of the second millennium B.C.

The existence of a division between the precursors of Aeolic and Doric in the Late Helladic period may actually be indicated by several distinct and rather ancient differences between the Classical Aeolic and Doric dialects (cf. for instance the Doric innovation *dōséō* instead of *dōsō*; or the 'elective' relation between Doric *-mes* and non-Doric *-men*; or the non-Doric, and Central Cretan, innovation *hoi* for original *toi*).

The chronology of these phenomena cannot be precisely fixed, but their geographic extension makes us conclude that the innovations or choices in question were accomplished at the latest shortly before the final disintegration of either the former proto-Doric or the former proto-Aeolic community, which would imply as the *terminus ante quem* in each case the time closely following the destruction of the Mycenaean civilization. At the same time, however, we can hardly assume that all the changes just mentioned were accomplished approximately simultaneously, let us say in the twelfth century B.C., and for this reason it appears more probable that a line of division between proto-Doric and proto-Aeolic may have existed even before the fall of the Mycenaean civilization.

Thus one feels rather inclined to side with Chadwick (1956; 1963), who conceives of Aeolic as a special *-ti-* dialectal unit which began to differentiate already in the Mycenaean period, obviously first in Thessaly. We have to stress, in this connection, that at present the great majority of known documents in the Linear B script are either from the Peloponnese or from Crete, i.e. from the 'Achaean' (or 'proto-Arcado-Cyprian') area, and we do not exclude the possibility that the next finds from Thebes, the ancient rival of Peloponnesian Mycenae, may disclose Linear B tablets in which the suffix *-ti* will appear unchanged, thus documenting the existence of a Mycenaean Greek of Aeolic type. It is unquestionable that Late Helladic Boeotia had a high level of civilization. Greek mythology itself indicates that the cradle of Mycenaean poetry should be associated with Boeotia, with its Kitharion, Helikon, and Parnassos, rather than with the Peloponnese.

A still more distinct line of division existed between proto-Doric and proto-Arcado-Cypriot, or between proto-Doric and that dialect and proto-Ionic. The fact that Ionic seems to have shared some important linguistic features with Doric may be attributed, with Chadwick, mainly to contact between the two dialect-groups in post-Mycenaean times (Chadwick 1956: 42–4).

The conclusion of this discussion may be formulated as follows: the comparatively close affinity of the dialectal basic of Doric to those of the other Greek dialects hardly permits us to locate Dorians too far from the Mycenaean world, but a line of division clearly existed between proto-Doric and any of the Late Helladic precursors of the other main groups of Classical Greek dialects.

To be sure, the arguments presented here express the views of a linguist, who is not in a position to explain in any other way the absence of a greater number of more pronounced differences between the comparatively uniform Doric deduced for the close of the second millennium B.C. and the other dialects of the contemporary Greek world. Thus it rests in fact with the archaeologists to judge to what extent the predecessors of the Dorians may have formed an integral part of the so-called 'Minyan' population of the Middle Helladic period and whether the so-called Dorian invasion was not just a partial and secondary migration southward of one fraction of the proto-Greek population, which had come to the southern part of the Balkan peninsula together with the others, but had then lived for a number of centuries along the north-west border of the Late Helladic world, maintaining some loose contact with the centres of the Late Helladic culture, especially with those of the proto-Aeolic area. From the thirteenth century B.C. these people presumably began to move to the more southerly regions, and while they perhaps did not bring about the catastrophic end of the Mycenaean civilization themselves, they nevertheless emerged as the dominant population in the Peloponnese in the early centuries of the first millennium B.C.

Notes

1. 'Achaean' is used as a comprehensive term, subsuming all dialects of Greek in use within the Peloponnese, and in areas already colonized from it, in the final phase of the Mycenaean period. On the basis of available evidence, it is reasonable to assume that all such dialects were 'closely related' to each other, as against incipiently differentiated groups of dialects of Greek in use in areas to the north. (Use of the term leaves open the question whether 'proto-Ionic' and/or 'proto-Aeolic' dialects or groups of dialects were already substantially differentiated from the dialects of the Peloponnese by that time). An 'Achaean' set of dialects, as defined, must presumably have included the dialect or dialects ancestral to Arcadian and Cyprian, as well as (recorded) 'Mycenaean', of the Linear B tablets; although, as noted, this last may have been a composite or standard dialect, not the vernacular spoken in a particular area.

References

BARTONĚK, A. 1966. 'Mycenaean koine reconsidered.' *Cambridge Colloquium on Mycenaean Studies* (ed. L. R. Palmer and J. Chadwick; Cambridge): 95–103.

——. 1968a. 'Greek dialectology after the decipherment of Linear B.' *Studia Mycenaea* (ed. A. Bartoněk, Brno): 46–51.

—— and others. 1968b. 'Dialectal classification of Mycenaean.' *Studia Mycenaea:* 155–210.

——. 1971. 'Relevance of the Linear B linguistic phenomena for the classification of Mycenaean.' *Salamanca Colloquium.*

CHADWICK, J. 1965. 'The Greek dialects and Greek pre-history.' *Greece and Rome*, N.S., 3: 38–50.

——. 1963. 'The prehistory of the Greek language.' *CAH* (rev. ed.) II, Chap. XXXIX/ Fasc. 15.

LEJEUNE, M. 1968. 'L'assibiliation de *th* devant *i* en mycenien.' *AttiICIM*: 733–43.

NAGY, G. 1968. 'On dialectal anomalies in Pylian texts.' *AttiICIM*: 663–79.

PISANI, V. 1955. 'Die Entzifferung der ägäischen Linear B Schrift und die griechischen Dialekte.' *Rheinisches Museum*, 98: 1–18.

PORZIG, W. 1954. 'Untersuchungen zu den altgriechischen Dialekten.' *IF*, 61: 147–69.

RISCH, E. 1955. 'Die Gliederung der griechischen Dialekten in neuer Sicht.' *MH*, 12: 61–76.

Final Discussion

PART FOUR
Final Discussion

Migration in explanation of culture change

D. J. BLACKMAN: The reaction against excessive recourse to migration theories as an explanation of cultural change is clearly healthy. But I hope it will not go to the other extreme. Knowledge of the *Völkerwanderungen* of the late Roman period in Europe has clearly coloured interpretation of the prehistoric period. But a recognition of this should not make us reject entirely the historical analogues. Study of these can still be valuable, if we are careful to bear in mind differences of cultural development. Concerning historically attested migrations, some obvious points of advantage need to be stressed: we know that they actually happened and in most cases we know something of how they happened. One example must suffice here: the Slav migrations into the Greek peninsula in the late sixth and early seventh centuries A.D. There is clear literary evidence of invasions by large groups. Information on the numbers who settled (rather than simply raided and withdrew) is less precise, but bearing in mind also the clear evidence of toponyms we may accept that the Greek peninsula (except perhaps some parts of the eastern coast and offshore islands) was occupied by Slav settlers. What is particularly significant here is that this migration is scarcely attested by material remains: only by a few traces of destruction, and some cremation burials at Olympia (Hood 1966; Schlager, Blackman and Schäfer 1968). The parallel with the 'Dorian invasion' is striking, especially if we reject any connection between this and the destructions of *c.* 1200 B.C., as I think we should. It seems to be generally and implicitly assumed that significant migration into an area should be traceable archaeologically in signs of destruction or changes in material culture. This seems to me a questionable assumption.

SP. MARINATOS: I take this chance to speak briefly about a question of principle in our studies. I wish to stress the usefulness of conferences like this present one because they provide the scholars of various disciplines with their only opportunity to attack problems from different sides, in collaboration. The past generation was the last one in which one man could speak with considerable authority on a fairly wide range of subjects in the field of the humanities. Today Science has become a spacious palace, in which nobody can possess more than one or two rooms. Such wide-ranging scholars as Mommsen or Wilamowitz or Eduard Meyer or Sir John Myres are not likely to appear again. Let me now consider a single question, that of the origin of the Ionians, taking Professor Georgiev's broadly-treated and stimulating paper as my point of departure. The multiple aspects of this problem, which must be taken into consideration by any scholar who discusses the Ionians, are as follows. The people known as 'Ionians' in Greek tradition appear in different localities of Greece, but, characteristically, these all lie along the coasts. Our people appear as 'Minyans' from Iolkos to Orchomenos, as 'Neleids' along the coasts of the western Peloponnese; they also inhabit some parts of the eastern coasts of the Peloponnese (Kynouria) and the northern coast of the same peninsula, along the Corinthian gulf. There they were specially well organized and their community (*Koinon*) comprised twelve major towns (the *Dodekapolis*) with Helike as its religious centre. They worshipped Poseidon. Possibly they were the creators of the Amphictyony of Kalaureia. The Pylians in particular adored a further god, Hades, a thing for which already Pausanias expressed his admiration (Paus. VI, xiv, 8). No other Greeks had this special cult of the God of Death. This would explain an otherwise unparalleled tradition in the *Iliad*: Dione's statement that Herakles wounded Hades with an arrow when in Pylos (*Iliad* V, 395–7). Scholars usually give the explanation that Pylos means the gates of the Underworld and that the reference is to Herakles' capture of Cerberus. But it is more reasonable to imagine that Hades came to the help of the Pylians when they were defeated by Herakles. I have expressed the opinion that this special tribe of the Minyans came into contact with the Mesopotamian worshippers of Lilith, a goddess of death. Her symbol was the owl and this ominous bird is closely connected with the Minyans: two daughters of Minyas were transformed into owls, while Demeter transformed Askalaphus into a kind of owl, which thereafter had this name. One of the two heads of the Orchomenian contingent in Troy bore this very name: they were Ialmenos and Askalaphos. Next comes the question of migrations. I cannot discuss in detail here the evidence from the epics. It is clear, however, that the Minyan stock of the Pylians, the worshippers of Poseidon, is a chief element in the *Iliad* as well as in the *Odyssey*. It appears that the kernel of the *Odyssey* was originally composed in Pylos, whose neighbours are Ithaca, Kephallenia, Zakynthos, the islands where, it seems, refugees from Pylos found new homes. The Pylian migration to Attica is well known to ancient tradition. The owl of Athena was the Pylian owl of the Neleids. It is clear that the worshippers of Poseidon came into cruel conflict with the indigenous old dynasty of the prehistoric goddess of Attica, Athene. Poseidon killed Erechtheus with a blow of his trident. The hatred remained, until the local dynasty expelled the intruders in the end. This national story may have been represented on the western pediment of the Parthenon. Neileos had to abandon Athens. He took Ionians from Attica and Boeotians to a new home in Asia Minor. In eastern Boeotia, indeed, the tribe involved was called *Aones*, possibly akin to *Iaones*. In Asia Minor a new Dodekapolis was created, and this fact connects the Ionians of the migration with the Ionians of Aigialeia. Mimnermos of Kolophon, on the other hand, around 700 B.C. claims that the Minyans went directly from Pylos to Asia Minor.

All the above facts, which are a solid element in Greek tradition, if taken together, give a vivid picture of what may be called the feverish movement of the Greek tribes during the Mycenaean period. Anyone who approaches the question must take into consideration very many factors, some of which have been mentioned here. If the Ionians were the first Greek tribe to enter Greece, there are several centuries of eclipse before they appear again, and they appear especially as sea-faring people from Iolkos and the men of Argonautic adventure, down to the historical times of Sparta and the colonization of Thera, according to Herodotus. This is why such problems may be profitably examined by several scholars at the same time.

T. G. E. POWELL: With regard to affirmation or denial of prehistoric population movements on archaeological grounds, a major weakness is apparent in current expressions of opinion: a tendency to adopt extreme positions on one side or another, and to draw only on the crudest concepts of what may have been involved whichever view is taken. Hostile strangers from a distance seem to provide the principal model for migration. Sedentary dwellers in village or town, intent on gainful employment, have furnished the opposite ideal. Discussion throughout the Colloquium has revealed some awareness of many other alternatives, especially as illustrated by historically attested examples. It would be out of place to range over the whole field, and here only a few observations are offered on matters particularly relevant to the Colloquium. There has been a general welcome for R. J. Howell's elucidation of Minyan ware as a widespread development of essentially Aegean ceramic tradition. It does not follow, however, that on present showing Minyan was equally acceptable in all households that might have been able to obtain it, much less that all householders who enjoyed the benefits of Early Bronze II prosperity were members of an undifferentiated sedentary population. J. D. Evans has emphasised the vitality, and complexity, of interrelations throughout the Aegean region during his culture-phase, and has spoken of the archaeological evidence for widespread availability of goods and services. As an underlying factor in the promotion of this prosperity sphere, A. C. Renfrew has drawn attention to the advantages of olive and grape cultivation (Prehistoric Society Conference on Prehistoric Greece; London, March 1970). Specialist cultivation of this kind should be indicative of a very stable population. A matter that may go some way to a better understanding of the occurrence of seemingly strange pottery styles in contexts that were both established and prosperous may be raised by asking if it is not probable that different peoples, if only represented by individuals, or families, had brought in, and continued to practise, their own special skills. As each well-placed small urban centre grew, its technical demands would best be met by craftsmen seeking the opportunities that such markets would certainly offer. If, in this, one may take more recent anthropological models (and pre-industrial India should be a fair comparison) it may be expected that craft or other occupational minorities in these larger population units would have preferences in domestic pottery styles, in turn reflective of diverse foods, cooking habits, and rituals attached thereto. Parallel demands for particular shapes and purposes might be expected to have arisen over the whole geographical extent of the economic complex. This matter might be put to the test in excavation of domestic quarters in different streets or parts of a town. Would Minyan ware be present in certain proportions, or entirely absent, according to the nature of the household? In general it would be worthwhile to ascertain if domestic utilitarian and cult appliances varied in relation to the households of copper workers, oil-pressers, or weavers, or indeed any sections of the community. This question will not, however, be resolved by excavation of the store-rooms of a central authority, valuable as their evidence may be on wealth and relative chronology. What may contribute to explaining problems in Early Bronze II may be no help in other situations. It is a solace to find general acceptance for the case that the Dorians had in fact travelled no great distance, but that they had taken opportunity to avail themselves of more attractive lands, long known to them, but previously well defended. This proposition in no way excludes the possibility that small fragments of other more outlandish peoples may in turn have trailed behind in Epirus or Macedonia. Finally, a plea is put forward for less rigid and exclusive archaeological evaluations for or against migrations by bearers of the 'Kurgan Culture'. As yet imponderable matters that may have been of great consequence seldom find mention in treatment of this problem. But drought, cattle wastage, and especially over-exploitation of grazing, with consequent environmental deterioration, must have been recurrent hazards across the Pontic region. 'Destruction levels' at sites in raided territory may indeed witness to the impact of peoples thus up-rooted, but the very poverty of their circumstances should warn against expectation of immediate archaeological testimony. It would seem, judging from some other examples, that it was only after full exploitation of what was there to enjoy in occupied territory that homeland traits emerged, and these perhaps mainly if reinforcements continued to arrive. The Celtic migrations into Italy illustrate this alternative in 'migration-archaeology'.

Archaeology may point to an event such as the pillage and burning of a town, but it is not inevitable that it should also be capable of furnishing the canteen and weapons of the destroyers. Only their grandsons may find need to renew ancestral preferences in durable goods; and they may equally well find it possible to reject them in favour of more sophisticated equipment. In either case, the hard archaeological remains may be expected to reveal compromises. It would appear that strangers, speaking a foreign language, could well intrude upon settled populations a generation or more earlier than archaeology can signal in terms of altered material culture. A layer of ashes represents an event, but, by itself, it elucidates neither the language, nor the home, of the fire-setter.

References

HOOD, M. S. F. 1966. 'An aspect of the Slav invasions of Greece in the early Byzantine period.' *Acta Musei Nationalis Pragae*, 20, 1/2: 165–71.

SCHLAGER, H., BLACKMAN, D. J. and SCHÄFER, J. 1968. 'Der Hafen von Anthedon mit Beiträge zur Topographie und Geschichte der Stadt.' *JdI/AA*, 83 (1968): 21–102.

PART FIVE

Editorial review and discussion

Retrospect and prospects

ANN BIRCHALL and R. A. CROSSLAND

IT was hardly to be expected that the Colloquium would yield 'definitive' or generally accepted solutions to principal current problems of Aegean pre-history. In the past fifteen years the tempo of archaeological research in Aegean countries has been rapid; opportunities for comparing its results with those of work in neighbouring areas have been far greater than before; and on the linguistic side the results of the decipherment of the Linear B texts have had to be assimilated. In these circumstances it is not surprising that new hypotheses and revisions of chronology have made their appearance at a faster rate than for some time previously. The principal result of the Col-loquium has undoubtedly been to show how great differences in interpreta-tion and explanation are at present. But this may be valuable if it has brought out the main points of disagreement and suggested the research that needs to be undertaken if they are to be settled, and the questions of method that may be involved in correlating evidence from different sites and areas and, still more, from different disciplines. This article attempts to assess the results of the Colloquium from that standpoint. We hope that we have presented the views of contributors accurately and kept our own comments and sug-gestions recognizably distinct. Essentially, the first of the two following sec-tions, on the archaeological data and conclusions from it, is by Ann Birchall, the second, on the linguistic material, by R. A. Crossland. Editorial *homonoia* has proved durable enough for us to dispense with footnotes 'reserving individual opinions'.

The archaeological evidence

For the archaeologists contributing to the Colloquium and to its published proceedings in this volume the major theme for discussion has been explana-tion in archaeological terms of the cultural changes which occurred in the Aegean region during the third and second millennia B.C. The title of the Colloquium in fact included the term 'migrations', but it has recently become unfashionable in some quarters to connect cultural changes with changes in population. Indeed there is now a serious division within the archaeological camp: the 'diffusionist' hypothesis, derived ultimately from the creative work of the late Gordon Childe, who found European barbarism 'irradiated' by Oriental civilization, and whose framework of prehistoric European archaeology has stood for over forty years, is now set in direct opposition to a new theory of indigenous cultural creativity and independent development, a theory which some consider to be required by the 'new' chronology of the revised C-14 dates. Nevertheless in our present state of knowledge it would be invidious to describe either viewpoint in any other way than as extreme; the eventual truth is bound to involve some measure of both. As Professor J. D. Evans writes in his introductory paper, it is really a question of emphasis. However, the immediate result of this controversy has been to inject a 'revolutionary mood' into current archaeological thinking, to give recognition to the need for fresh evidence and for critical re-appraisal of the old. This approach characterizes the papers in this volume which discuss the various problems of the Aegean Bronze Age.

For the Early Bronze Age there is a significant amount of new material, resulting particularly from recent excavations in the islands of Crete, Keos and Kythera. Professor J. L. Caskey in his preliminary work on the Early Bronze Age levels at Ayia Irini (Keos) distinguishes two main phases of occupation; the first, characterized by EH II type pottery, offers no evidence of violence or destruction at its close, while the second phase appears to have some West Anatolian affinities (Caskey pp. 30). Continuing work at this site will clearly be of considerable importance in reconstructing the settlement pattern of EH II and EH III. On Kythera an unexpected situation has presented itself; the discovery of an Early Minoan settlement at Kastri in succession to the Early Helladic one at neighbouring Kastraki leads Mr. J. N. Coldstream to conclude that Cretan settlers arrived in Kythera, probably sometime about the mid-third millennium B.C. (see p. 35). Coldstream also points to some evidence for "political tension on the frontier between the EM and EH spheres of influence" (p. 36).

In Crete Evans draws on the results of recent excavations by Mr. M. S. F. Hood, Dr. S. Alexiou, Dr. I. Tzedakis, Dr. P. M. Warren and himself to put beyond doubt the "substantive existence of a fairly long Early Minoan period" (Evans, p. 20). The beginnings of the process which led to the 'Minoanization' of Crete he puts back as early as the Middle Neolithic and he prefers to explain this process in terms of gradually increasing contacts with the central and eastern Aegean rather than by postulating large-scale immigration. This is a point which Dr. Warren takes up at the beginning of his paper; his main concern, however, is to review the archaeological evidence for immigration into Crete from the beginning of the Early Bronze Age to the middle of the second millennium B.C. Whereas he admits a strong case for the arrival of new groups into the island from western Anatolia (p. 42; *pace* Weinberg 1954 and Branigan 1970) at the beginning of the Early Bronze Age, that is about 2800 B.C., he finds no evidence for further immigration until the arrival of the Mycenaeans at Knossos about 1450 B.C. The important areas of discussion centre on: the end of EM II (about 2170 B.C.) with the destructions at Myrtos and Vasiliki; the end of MM IA (about 1900 B.C.) with the building of the first palaces; and the end of MM II (about 1700 B.C.) with the major destructions of the palaces at Knossos, Phaistos and probably Mallia. In each case Warren finds in the succeeding period continuity of feature and evolutionary development. On the other hand, following the reported major destruction throughout the island about 1450 B.C., explained as the direct result of the volcanic catastrophe on Thera-Santorini, the arrival of newcomers—thought to be Mycenaeans—at Knossos is demonstrated by the LM II Palace Style of pottery, the Warrior Graves at Knossos and the Mycenaean, mainland type of spiraliform stone-carving. Warren's interpretation of the archaeological evidence thus leads him to pose a linguistic question: whether the language written with Linear A script (assumed to be a single language) was really Indo-European and not rather a language which had been developing in Crete since the third millennium (p. 45; comments by Mr. Brice, Mr. Pope and Professor Crossland pp. 48–9).

Although there seems to have been little disturbance in Crete in the final centuries of the third millennium B.C., it is a different picture elsewhere in the Aegean region. There is clear evidence of fairly widespread disruption and reorganization then; there were serious upheavals in western Anatolia at the end of EB II (*c.* 2300 B.C.), which were explained as resulting from an invasion from Thrace by Mr. J. Mellaart (1958 and 1964) who thereby facilitated the introduction of the Luwians into south-western Anatolia (see also Mellaart 1965: 50 on 'Luwian' invasions). This view has been discounted, however, both on linguistic and on archaeological grounds (Crossland p. 12, French p. 53). The explanation for the destruction horizon in southern Greece at the end of EH II (when the House of Tiles, Lerna III was burnt) and in central and southern Greece at the end of EH III (with the destructions at Eutresis and Korakou) may be found in movements of people from the north (Hood, p. 59–61) which may be included elements of 'Kurgan' or 'Mound' people originating from the steppes of southern Russia, Indo-Europeans according to Professor Gimbutas (p. 135–6).

Until recently it had been held for some time that there was a definite cultural break between the periods distinguished by archaeologists as Early Bronze Age and Middle Bronze Age, usually dated about 2000–1900 B.C. The appearance of 'Minyan' pottery in central and southern Greece early in the Middle Bronze Age (as then defined) was taken to denote the arrival of a new ethnic element into those areas (Haley and Blegen 1928), which was generally identified as the first wave of Greek-speaking immigrants (but cf.

Palmer 1958: p. 93–7). This view has, however, been seriously challenged in recent years. To borrow Dr. French's succinct phrasing "the 'coming' of the Greeks is a question to be separated from that of the origin of 'Minyan' ware" (p. 53).

Valuable work on 'Minyan' and pseudo-Minyan pottery has been done by Mellaart (1969; cf. 1958) and some contributors to this volume, Professor H.-G. Buchholz, Professor J. M. Cook, Dr. French and Mr. R. J. Howell. Buchholz has mostly noted the appearance of generally similar ware in Cyprus and North Syria. Cook has surface-explored the Troad to locate sites producing second millennium Grey ware. French finds that 'Minyan' pottery, especially the Grey variety, was not developed in north-west Anatolia but in central and southern Greece.

The development of Grey Minyan figures largely in Howell's discussion of the origins of the Middle Helladic culture; largely but not exclusively, for he is careful to include in his analysis all the constituent elements of that culture. He reiterates Caskey's observations (1960) of a marked cultural break between EH II and EH III, of distinct new features in EH III, and of a less abrupt change than had hitherto been supposed between EH III and MH. With the result of Popham and Sackett's excavations at Lefkandhi (1968) adding further support to Caskey's results at Lerna, Howell finds enough evidence to assume a genetic relationship between EH III and MH; he suggests that EH III be thought of as the first manifestation of MH in Greece. He proposes, therefore, the use of the generic term 'Minyan' to cover the period from EH III to MH III; thus, EH III—'Protominyan'; MH I—'Early Minyan'; MH II—'Classical' Minyan; MH III—'Late Minyan'. Although Howell's proposed new terminology is not without its critics (*sic* Caskey, in discussion following p. 99), yet his main conclusions—albeit expressed tentatively—are of fundamental importance: that the break of the beginning of EH III is strong enough to suggest the arrival of new people with new traditions, that 'Protominyan' may have evolved in the Peloponnese whence it spread northwards, and further that 'Minyan' traditions generally can be ultimately traced back to the Baden group of cultures in central Europe and the Balkans (the route being via north-western Greece).

From Howell's paper it is a short step to the Indo-European question and indeed that topic provides the starting-point for Professor Marinatos. In agreement with Schachermeyr (1968), he recognizes 'Proto-Hellenic' elements as early as EH III; thereafter he finds that conditions remained static throughout Middle Helladic until 1700 or 1650 B.C. (pp. 106–10; 1968). The arrival of newcomers before *c.* 1600 he explains in terms of a few well-organized groups of professional warriors, apparently similar ethnically to the pre-existing populations, who settled down and integrated with them as the continuity of culture shows. Marinatos, then, is not one of those scholars who like Palmer (1958; 1961), sees the early Mycenaeans around 1600 B.C.

as the first Greeks, nor one who, like Hampl (1960) and others, sees the first Greeks entering Greece as late as 1200 B.C. For Marinatos the archaeological evidence is such that he accepts only two breaks during the whole development of the Minoan–Mycenaean civilization: the Cretan *diaspora* about 1500 B.C., resulting from the volcanic eruption on Thera, and the Mycenaean *diaspora* about 1200 B.C. Marinatos' paper concludes with further evidence about the first 'Mycenaeans' in Greece and of the continuity of tradition, discussed with reference to the four tumuli of the 'Kurgan' class which he had recently been excavating at Marathon (1970a; 1970b). These burials are Mycenaean and date as late as the fourteenth century B.C.

The volcanic eruption on Thera was clearly an event which could well have interrupted the main lines of cultural development and ethnic movement in much of the Aegean area in the latter end of the sixteenth century B.C. The nature and extent of its effects are only now being assessed and Professor Marinatos' second article (pp. 199–201) gives advance discussion of his discoveries from his first seasons' excavation on the island itself.

In Section 3, two papers deal with the Balkans and the Kurgan peoples. Professor Garašanin's important paper, discussing ethnographic problems of the Bronze Age in the central Balkan peninsula, points to the formation of related local cultural groups in the Middle Bronze Age (equated with periods Reinecke A2 onwards) in the Morava Valley region which are linked with the Balkano-Carpathian complex. Western Serbia, Montenegro and Albania form a distinct cultural entity; although they shared similar foundations in the Early Bronze Age, there was a differentiation later. Garašanin finds that the Bronze Age cultures which he discusses cannot be associated with linguistically-defined groups; 'definitive ethnic differentiation' took place only during the period of transition from the Bronze Age to the Iron Age, at the time of the Aegean migrations or those of the 'Sea Peoples'; nevertheless the Central Balkan peoples had 'undergone Indo-Europeanization' in the transitional period between the Neolithic and Early Bronze Age. Garašanin finds beyond dispute the formation of large, distinct cultural complexes in south-eastern Europe, from the Bronze Age onwards: the south-eastern complex in later Thracian areas; the Western Balkan complex in the later Illyrian zone; and the Balkano-Carpathian complex north of the Balkan massif as far as the Carpathians, to which the culture of the Morava region should be linked; western elements, from the Illyrian area, became dominant in Kosovo and Macedonia only during the Iron Age.

The basic hypothesis of Professor Gimbutas' paper is that the destroyers of third millennium B.C. Mediterranean civilization were Indo-Europeans, 'Kurgan IV' peoples from north and north-east of the Black Sea, whose migrations are placed within the period *c.* 2500–2000 B.C.; they brought destruction to urban civilization in the Aegean and East Mediterranean area about 2300 B.C. This violent destruction is distinguished from an earlier and less violent wave of Indo-European attack, placed in the last quarter of the fourth millennium B.C., and attributed to 'Kurgan III' elements, tribes living west of the Black Sea whose seaborne migrations as far as Palestine are deduced. By her second invasion hypothesis of c. 2300 B.C. Professor Gimbutas only postulates Indo-European movements which are more extensive to the south than have been assumed previously, at least for Anatolia. The earlier, Kurgan III, movements, however, raise the question whether a migration of c. 3200 B.C. can plausibly be identified as Indo-European (see below pp. 130–1, 136). It is reasonable to accept, however, Professor Gimbutas' view that both waves may have contributed immigrants and influences which formed the basis of the population and culture of Greece in Mycenaean times.

In the final archaeological papers, forming Section 5, the recurrent problem of the Late Bronze Age and early Iron Age is again that of 'migration'. Dr. J. Bouzek finds contact between Greece and the Balkans in the Bronze Age casual and migrations between the two areas only rarely indicated. He refers again to the questions of Greek 'Corded Ware' (i.e. 'Kurgan IV'; Gimbutas p. 133, and 1970; cf. Hood pp. 60–1), and of Minyan in EH II–III on the one hand, and to the Aegean metal objects of northern origin or inspiration, characteristic of the later part of LH IIIB, on the other. Indeed Bouzek summarizes that only the EH II–III and LH IIIB–C changes are possibly explicable as evidence of migration from the north; he points to the present lack of a general study of the pattern in the archaeological record which is created by migration of population. As to the Dorians, he does not place their area of origin far north of Greece on present evidence; a possible reconstruction of events in Greece in the thirteenth and twelfth centuries B.C. would bring Dorians into the country (in the late twelfth century) after it had been depopulated and Mycenaean power broken by European tribes from the Balkans, including the north-western Balkans, in the thirteenth century B.C. The downfall of Mycenaean Greece may also have coincided with a climatic change (cf. Snodgrass, p. 210 and discussion p. 214, on the violin-bow fibula).

Professor N. G. L. Hammond's paper describes tumulus-burials in Albania and western Macedonia, which he places in the EH II–MH time-span; he agrees with Gimbutas that the users of the tumulus-burials were people of the 'Kurgan IV' Group which expanded from southern Russia into central Europe c. 2500 B.C. (though the Servia burial might belong to 'Kurgan III'); other features of 'Kurgan' peoples' culture in addition to tumulus-burial are noted. The new finds provide the first conclusive evidence for IE-Kurgan people in the south-west Balkans in EH (see p. 191; cf. Hood, pp. 59–60). Hammond then discusses the evidence for 'Kurgan' expansion southward: the Lefkas tumuli excavated by Dörpfeld, dateable from EH II on, also in the 'Kurgan' tradition; many MH tumulus-burials in

Greece are now known and they may show affinities either with the Lefkas or with the inland group of Albania and western Macedonia. In sum, Hammond finds that 'Kurgan' peoples reached south-west Macedonia, central and southern Albania and Lefkas about 2500 B.C., whence two streams entered Greece, one by sea, the other by land, mainly in Middle Helladic. It seems that they should be seen (linguistically) as proto- or pre-Greek. Hammond ends his paper with new evidence relevant to the 'Lausitz' invasion; the latter is now seen as more important than had hitherto been realized, passing through Pelagonia into Albania and reaching central Epirus in the period 1200–1150 B.C., and central Macedonia *c*. 1150 B.C. Hammond argues strongly that it was this that provided the pressure which set the so-called Dorian invasion in motion southwards from Epirus, and that from Epirus itself may have come the leaders of those who destroyed Mycenae *c*. 1120 B.C.

The remaining papers deal with a variety of individual topics: Dr. Alessandra Nibbi discusses the 'Sea Peoples' (now to be the theme for the 1973 Colloquium in Sheffield); Dr. Snodgrass gives a timely reminder that new metal types and practices in Greece *c*. 1200 B.C. do not make a mass-immigration there of non-Mycenaeans; Mrs. Sourvinou-Inwood suggests some probable patterns of movements of refugees in Attica in LH IIIB-C, rejecting any connection between northern newcomers and Attic cist-tombs; Dr. Tegyev considers the cultural decline in Messenia at the end of LH IIIB; Professor Tritsch, against the theory of large-scale migrations or extensive movements of populations during LBA, paints an evocative picture of the activities of small-scale bands of raiders-cum-pirates whom he sees as the product and not the cause of the breakdown of Mycenaean civilization.

A.B.

The linguistic data

Papers read to the Colloquium make it clear that there is greater difference of opinion at present about the linguistic prehistory of the Aegean region than at any time in the recent past. The controversial questions falls into four groups.

(*a*) What may be deduced from phenomena in languages of historical periods about linguistic change in late prehistoric times, in particular about differentiation of prehistoric languages into dialects and derivative language-families?

(*b*) What does aberrant onomastic material ('asystemic'; see p. 278) in a historical language show about prehistoric linguistic situations and developments in the area in which the language is first attested, and consequentially about other aspects of the area's prehistory?

(*c*) How should we reconstruct the events which produced the early historical distribution of the Indo-European languages?

(*d*) How should the late prehistory of Greek be reconstructed, in particular the course and chronology of its differentiation into its Classical dialects; and what may be deduced from the results about non-linguistic events in Greece and adjacent regions?

1. A key question in work on all these problems is that of the rate at which linguistic changes take place, especially the rate of differentiation of a language into derivatives. It is noteworthy that no contributor has tried to make use of lexicostatistics (glottochronology) in suggesting a date for the differentiation of Indo-European into its primary derivative languages, or for the beginning of the differentiation of Greek into its known dialects. The reliability of lexicostatistics is put in question by cases where calculated pro-portionate change in vocabulary in a language which is still in use today does not correspond with the amount of change that is actually observed if comparisons are made between its current spoken form and texts written in it, or information recorded about it, a few centuries ago (see pp. 8–9; also Rabin 1970). Even if lexicostatistic calculations are thought to be valid in general, special difficulties are involved in attempting them in the case of the IE languages or the dialects of Greek. The IE languages as a whole are known (or first known) from texts of widely different dates, often with limited and specialized vocabulary, in which many of the items that are regarded as 'basic' in lexicostatistic studies are not represented. Most dialects of Greek are known only from inscriptions with specialized content, and where one of them is represented in literary texts also, few if any of those reflect a vernacular form of it of any date; moreover 'Mycenaean' Greek is five or more centuries earlier than any other known ancient Greek dialect. Certainly, lexicostatistic studies attempted so far have been concerned (as is largely inevitable) with processes of language-differentiation which can be observed, more or less effectively, over historical periods of some centuries at the most (e.g. the differentiation of Latin into the Romance languages); or else they make calculations about the duration of a differentiation which occurred in late prehistoric times, like that of the Indo-European family, the beginning of which cannot be dated closely by means of non-linguistic evidence. More-over, most studies of language-differentiation within historical periods have been concerned with languages whose rate of change may well have been abnormal, because they were used in the administration of empires or large states, like Latin, or as traditional literary or religious media (Crossland 1971: 232–3). More reliable indication of average rate of change and differentiation in languages may come from further study of the 'Hamito-Semitic' family (whatever the total range of languages that is to be included in it; see Bynon, T. and Bynon, J. 1970), and from internal comparison of groups of languages which appear to have differentiated within relatively recent times and have no literary tradition, but may be assumed to have begun to differentiate as the result of an ethnic dispersal the date of which is indicated by archaeological evidence (further discussion will be included in a paper

'Factors affecting language change', for the Sheffield Colloquium on 'Explanation of culture change', December, 1971).

Estimation other than by lexicostatistical methods of the time taken by language change depends on analogy, when it is not just crudely impressionistic: i.e. it uses linguistic developments observed in historical periods as 'models' which may suggest the nature of developments that may be assumed to have occurred in prehistoric times. Extrapolation of this kind seems legitimate, provided that the complexity of human linguistic behaviour in historical times is not forgotten. Probable close analogues for prehistoric linguistic developments are unfortunately hard to find in historical periods. Few languages which are spoken today are known also from written sources which extend back over even as much as a thousand years. Arabic, Chinese, Greek and Egyptian with its derivative Coptic have such a history (Chinese material is of limited value for study of language change, since written with an ideographic script). But change in them may have been retarded by their use as literary, liturgical and administrative languages. In some cases in historical times a population does appear to have adopted a new language within two or three generations (it seems reasonable to conclude that this happened in eastern and south-eastern England at the time of the Anglo-Saxon immigration) and some languages certainly have changed much more extensively in the few centuries over which we know them than Arabic has, for example, during a thousand years. Linguists have not yet found it possible to define with useful precision the social circumstances in which one population tends to adopt the language of another, or those in which a language that remains in use will change relatively quickly (cf. Crossland 1971: 233–5). Unless one feels certain for some reason that linguistic change always took place more slowly in pre-urban and early urban societies than it did on the average in those of, say, the Classical and Medieval periods in Europe, then one cannot expect at present to make any close estimate of the time during which the language of an early historical community had previously been in use in the area in which it is first attested.

The matters about which linguistic evidence may give useful guidance would seem to be: (1) the late prehistoric distribution of communities that spoke dialects or languages ancestral to a historical related group; (2) possibly also the processes which produced such distribution; (3) contact between groups that spoke unrelated languages; (4) whether a known language had superseded another relatively recently in an area under study.

Many linguists will feel disquiet about one view expressed in this volume: the suggestion that it is preferable to assume that a language had been in use in the area in which it is first known for an almost indefinite period before its earliest attestation there, unless there is clear non-linguistic evidence for large-scale migration into the area at a particular previous time (cf. Renfrew, p. 265). This approach may seem to have the merit of simplicity and economy in assumptions made to explain linguistic data. But it may offer us an unjustifiably simplified 'model'. Language change has clearly been frequent and complex in some areas in historical times, e.g. in the Balkans in the early Middle Ages. And there certainly are cases in which a new language has been adopted in an area without obvious associated change in material culture. Conversely, there is for example good reason to believe that the Bulgar invaders of Thrace spoke a Turkic or other central Asian language; but scarcely any trace of it survives in Bulgaria, the country which was named after them although otherwise their original language disappeared in it. 'Economy of assumption' in reconstructing the linguistic prehistory of an area may bias choice of explanation in favour of conclusions about stability of populations, and absence of population movements, which go beyond what general observation of linguistic developments in historical periods will indicate as probable.

2. The conclusion that south-eastern Europe was the area of the Indo-European continuum, as presented by Professor V. I. Georgiev and Professor A. Vraciu (see pp. 251-2, 281-3, 287-9) rests largely on deductions from onomastic data: i.e. identification of supposed earlier IE strata in place-names in Greek, from Mycenaean times onwards, and in other historical languages of the region that are known rather later. The existence of these strata is considered to show, for example, that Dacian had a continuous development in the region from before 4000 B.C. until the second century A.D. (or perhaps even later, as a vernacular). At the same time, the absence of identified non-Greek place-names in the earliest repertoires known from the northern parts of Greece itself is held to prove that Greek was in use in those areas from an equally early date (pp. 247-8). These conclusions are clearly important data for Aegean prehistory, if they may be accepted as sound. So the assumptions that they involve should be examined.

An 'onomastic stratum' is essentially a group of names in a historical language which share formal characteristics that are thought to indicate that the names were taken into the language from another. The reason for regarding such a group as borrowed is usually either: (1) that the words in it show features of collocation (sequence or juxtaposition) of phonemes (i.e. the basic contrasting 'sounds' of the language as used by native speakers), mechanism of formation, etc. which are not paralleled in the main part of the language's vocabulary (see p. 278); or (2) that even if the words are not aberrant in any such respect, they share phonology, formants or stems which occur also in a language or languages known outside the area, or occasionally in a stratum or strata of onomastic material which appear to be accretive in it (or them) also. Evidence from historical periods shows that local place-names, particularly names of rivers, mountains and other main natural features, are frequently taken over when a new language is brought into an area and supersedes the one previously in use in it; and similar borrowing presumably took place in prehistoric times. But it is argued, apparently, that the earliest onomastic stratum that can be identified in an area must represent an antecedent language which has been in use in it previously for some two thousand years, if not longer. This, again, may involve a dubious argument from economy. In a sense it makes minimal assumptions: no change of language is posited for the area before the time when the earliest language that is identified as a substrate in its first known documents came into use in it. In reality, the argument involves a considerable and questionable assumption; this is that before that time, in periods for whose linguistic history we do not have even indirect evidence, there was necessarily less replacement of one language by another than we know to have been the case frequently in historical times. Georgiev, in his latest pronouncement on these questions (Georgiev 1971 : 322) has stated that onomastic data are the 'facts' in reconstruction of linguistic prehistory ("Les faits ce sont les toponymes"). This is true only in the sense that place-names in many languages may be grouped into categories some of which are aberrant and characterized by common features. It is a matter of deduction whether the reason why such a category is aberrant in the language in which it is identified is that it had been borrowed from another language; and the date and manner in which it had been borrowed, if it was, are similarly matters for deduction, not 'facts' in themselves. The view which Georgiev advocates implies that the earliest substrate language identified in an area must necessarily have been in use in it for a thousand years or more before the composition of the earliest documents in which it is attested, and it assumes that there was generally greater linguistic stability in prehistoric times, say between *c.* 4000 and 2500–2000 B.C., than there was, on the evidence, in the Near East and southern parts of Europe in the following two millennia.

3. It is worth noting that no contributor appears to reject the minimal conclusions of Indo-European comparative linguistics. It seems to be accepted that the languages classed as 'Indo-European' did develop by a process of originally dialectal differentiation, and that at some time the late prehistoric dialects of Indo-European, or more probably differentiated derivatives of them that may be thought of as 'languages', were disseminated into extensive new regions. Opinions differ considerably about the area in which 'proto-Indo-European' developed and began to differentiate, and about the chronology of its more advanced differentiation and of the introduction of derivative IE languages into areas outside the original 'continuum'. Two views are strongly supported. The first is that Indo-European developed in south-eastern Europe from the fifth millennium B.C. onwards (according to some exponents also in northern Greece or Anatolia or both; French, p. 53; Renfrew, pp. 270–4). On this hypothesis, it seems necessary to postulate extensive and rather rapid migrations of some IE-speaking peoples, e.g. to Iran and northern India, in the

latter half of the second millennium B.C. and the first centuries of the first, after a long previous period of immobility. The second view is that Indo-European developed as the language of peoples of the western Asiatic steppes, and was introduced by migrants ('Kurgan' peoples) first into the western Pontic region (roughly the southern Ukraine) and then by subsequent movements into Anatolia, Greece and the Danubian region (Gimbutas, pp. 129–30, 135–6). Revision of the dates of earlier 'Kurgan' levels in sites in the Ukraine makes it possible to date these movements earlier than was usual five years ago, and the new chronology makes the reconstruction of the supposed 'Kurgan–Indo-European' migration from the steppes feasible from the linguistic standpoint (cf. Crossland 1967: 49–51).

Granted the impossibility, in this Editor's opinion, of dating prehistoric processes of language differentiation at all closely, either of these hypotheses must be considered compatible with the comparative linguistic evidence: i.e., with the pattern of similarities among historical IE languages.

It may be useful to state here the ideas which most 'comparativists' probably share about 'homogeneity' and 'language-status' when they consider prehistoric linguistic reconstructions. First, there seems to be no reason for assuming that prehistoric languages were less regular and consistent as systems of communication than historical languages; few would accept that they were in general more 'fluid' or variable than later idioms, as late even as the fifth millennium B.C. Secondly, it is recognized that any language which was in use, say, c. 3000 B.C. might have been of recent formation. Some languages of that date or earlier, like some in historical times, may have been formed by processes of convergence (in the so-called 'Sprachbund' situation (see Trubetskoy 1939; Pisani 1949; cf. Thieme 1953: 590–610/56–76; Crossland 1957: 30, and corrigendum *Past and Present* 13: 88). Also, it is recognized that 'homogeneity', applied to a language, is a relative term: no language is ever spoken without some variation among groups of those who speak it. But some languages may be regarded as 'homogeneous' for practical purposes, for example if native speakers are not aware of patterns of variant usage among different groups among themselves. In linguistic reconstruction, it seems legitimate to posit an essentially 'homogeneous' or 'unitary' language for area in a late prehistoric period if internal comparison of a group of related historical languages indicates that the 'construct' (the prehistoric language that is being reconstructed as their 'ancestor') had phonic and morphological systems that included no more alternative features or sub-systems than is common in historical languages.

One's choice between the two main current hypotheses about the origin and differentiation of Indo-European, if it is made on the basis of linguistic criteria only, should probably be based on analogies. If we can find likely parallels in historical periods, we should consider which kinds of social and environmental conditions appear to produce the kind of language-differentiation that we deduce for Indo-European. The 'south-east European' hypothesis assumes that Indo-European was spoken for some two thousand years, at least, by sedentary agricultural communities. According to the 'steppe hypothesis' Indo-European was developed and then disseminated by peoples who were nomadic, even if not as fast-moving and wide-ranging as the later Turks and Mongols. Studies of the languages of groups of contemporary non-urban peoples living respectively as nomads and in regions of sedentary agriculture, which showed that one or the other of their ways of life was the more conducive to a pattern of linguistic diversification similar to that observed in the Indo-European language-family, might indicate whether the 'Indo-Europeans' developed their language as nomads, presumably within the steppe zone, or as static agriculturalists (Crossland 1967: 48–52; 1971: 233–4).

To sum up, most of those who are currently working on Aegean pre-history accept that during the Bronze Age there was some extension of the area of IE speech within the Aegean region, if only the introduction of Greek (more precisely, of 'pre-Greek' or 'proto-Greek'; see Crossland 1971: 230 fn. 7) from northern areas of Greece where it was already in use into central areas and the Peloponnese. Many conclude that such an extension was preceded by, or formed the final stage of, introduction of pre-Greek into northern Greece from more northerly parts of the Balkans or from a region further to the east, as part of a wider process of dissemination of prehistoric IE languages. (The idea that (pre-)Greek was introduced into Greece from north-western Anatolia has lost favour recently.) The radically different view is the one that has been propounded by A. C. Renfrew (pp. 270–4) and welcomed provisionally by D. H. French (p. 53): this suggests that the whole of Greece, and probably Crete too, lay within the region in which Indo-European developed, supposedly from at least as early as *c.* 5000–4000 B.C. The characteristics of Greek, considered in isolation and without reference to reconstruction of the differentiation of the IE language-family as a whole, are not seriously in conflict with this suggestion, as far as mainland Greece is concerned. The obstacle to it lies in the groups of place-names which are aberrant in it (especially those in -*nth*-; see above pp. 12, 279) and even these are absent or rare in northern Greece. Apart from them, there is no obvious indication that Greek had been taken over by a population speaking a different language at a time only shortly before its first appearance in the 'Linear B' tablets. There are important objections to the suggestion that either Greek or any other IE language was in use anywhere in Crete before *c.* 1450 B.C. at the earliest, or generally in the island before the eleventh or tenth century. Texts in 'Eteocretan', which have no identifiable or even putative Greek or other IE features, were written in Crete in the fifth century B.C. (Miller 1909; Friedrich 1932: 147–8; Guarducci 1942: 138–41; van Effenterre 1946a, 1946b; Marinatos, 1958); the Odyssey mentions that Crete was polyglot

(XIX, 172–7); and the texts produced by provisional decipherment of 'Minoan Linear A' again show no apparently Greek features and none which are plausibly explained as IE though not Greek (Pope 1964).

The conclusion that Greek was brought into Greece or disseminated over it at some time between *c.* 2300 and 1100 B.C. (to give extreme dates) is compatible either with the reconstruction which puts the 'IE homeland' in south-eastern Europe (Thrace and the Danubian area) or with that which identifies the 'Kurgan' peoples and their predecessors of the western steppes as the original 'Indo-Europeans'. Indication of the date of the dissemination of Greek, or at least of its chronology relative to other linguistic events, might come either from comparative study of the Mycenaean and Classical dialects of Greek (see below) or from an accepted reconstruction of the chronology of the overall pattern of differentiation of the identifiable 'primary derivatives' of Indo-European and the dispersal (if deduced) of the groups who spoke them (such reconstruction is however still controversial; cf. Crossland 1957: 30–5; 1967: 43–6; 1971: 227–30). One must consider it possible that some other IE language was in use in Greece before Greek became current there, unless one has concluded that Greek developed from a dialect of a phase of IE which was earlier than those from which all other known IE languages evolved. (And even on that hypothesis a complex series of migrations might have brought an IE language derived from a later phase of IE into Greece before Greek was introduced there.) But it will hardly be profitable to speculate about the introduction of an IE language into Greece before Greek was in use there unless a substrate has been identified in Greek that has evident IE but non-Greek characteristics. In the absence of this, any conclusion that early pre-Greek immigrants spoke an IE language will rest on the following assumption: that because archaeology indicates for those immigrants cultural traits which were characteristic of other ancient peoples who are known to have spoken an IE language, or traits which derived from a putative Indo-European area of origin, their language also must have been IE. The 'northern' cultural features identified in EH II Lerna (Caskey 1964: 17–20; 1966: 21–3) raise this problem, and at present there seems to be no way of deciding whether the people who appear to have introduced them would have been (1) 'proto-Greeks', (2) people who spoke an IE language other than (pre-)Greek, or (3) members of some community which had adopted 'Kurgan' culture and perhaps leadership while continuing to speak a non-IE language.

This Editor has made clear elsewhere his preference for the view that Indo-European speech developed in the western steppe zone and that dialects of Indo-European were carried westwards and southwards by migrants of 'Kurgan' culture (Crossland 1967: 49–50). The considerations which make it preferable are that the social organization and somewhat predatory, or at least expansionist, life-style of early Indo-European-speaking communities point to antecedents of nomadism and migration rather than of sedentary farming; and secondly that the distribution and isoglossic patterning of the IE languages when first known imply dispersal from the Pontic region, centrally placed within their early historic region of distribution, rather than from south-eastern Europe (Crossland 1967: 45–7; 1971: 229–30). The hypothesis of south-east European origin would seem to involve a problem of dialectology which appears not to have been discussed yet. If it is assumed, as seems necessary on that hypothesis, that Indo-European had a long period of development in the same area, with presumably some dialectal differentiation within it, followed by spread of IE languages to western and northern Europe and Iran, western Central Asia and northern India, perhaps from *c.* 2000 B.C. onwards, one might expect to find the dialect pattern of Indo-European *c.* 2500 B.C. easy to reconstruct, and to be able to associate postulated IE dialects or proto-languages of about that date with archaeologically defined cultures, in many cases in areas where the languages derived from them are first known. Such dialectal patterning and association with defined material cultures do not seem to have been demonstrated.

4. In ancient Greek dialectology, the following questions would seem to be of particular interest for the prehistorian.

(*a*) The first is that of determining whether an essentially homogeneous 'Common Greek' may be reconstructed by comparison of the Classical Greek dialects and 'Mycenaean' (the Greek of the Linear B tablets; see below, p. 341). Such comparison might, instead, yield two or more late prehistoric constructs (reconstructed ancestral idioms) with some alternative systems or features, which might appear to have been contemporaneous prehistoric languages or dialects for which a still earlier 'unitary' ancestory could not be reconstructed convincingly or in adequate detail; or perhaps 'distinct languages' not derived from a common ancestor which were in process of reciprocal assimilation.

(*b*) The second question is the problem of reconstructing the changes by which known Greek dialects developed from 'Common Greek' (if that is reconstructed or convincingly postulated). This involves sub-grouping of the known dialects by acceptable criteria (on the methodological problem see Hoenigswald 1966) followed by deductions from any sub-grouping that is accepted as valid about the processes by which the sub-groups which are set up developed from 'Common Greek', and individual dialects developed in turn. If a convincing pattern of sub-groups has been established, it may be possible to make deductions from it about (1) the degree of contact between prehistoric dialects which were ancestral to some or all of the sub-groups; (2) chronological phases in the process of differentiation; (3) influencing of one known or reconstructed dialect by another as a result of secondary contact, including as special cases essential 'supersession' of one dialect by another (see pp. 277–8) or mixture of dialects presumably as a result of amalgamation of populations that spoke previously differentiated dialects.

At this point it may be useful to consider what is meant by 'Common Greek' and by the statements of some contributors that it came into existence only late and 'on Greek soil' (see Chadwick, pp. 254–5; Pudié, pp. 255–6). A term such as 'Common Greek' normally expresses the concept of the minimal 'construct' ('ancestral idiom') that will explain the shared and variant features of a group of clearly related historical idioms; *aliter*, the concept of the reconstructed language from which those features in the historical idioms may be convincingly derived, even if some incipient dialectal differentiation has to be postulated for it. It will imply a reconstruction which has not been modified in accordance with deductions about still earlier antecedent development in the prehistoric 'ancestor', which might be made in the light of evidence in cognate languages within a more extensive 'family', or on 'glottogonic' grounds (on the basis of theories about how languages generally develop). If the earliest known dialects of Greek are shown not to differ radically, it will be reasonable to conclude that 'Common Greek', as defined, was still an essentially undifferentiated language as late as the end of the MBA. But relative similarity among the historical Greek dialects will not in itself imply that 'Common Greek' came into existence in Greece itself. One should ask what in fact is meant "by the formation of Greek as a recognizably distinct branch of IE" (see Chadwick, p. 254). Greek, an assemblage of dialects which appear to have been mutually intelligible and so a language, may be called a "recognizably distinct branch of IE" on the grounds that it shares principal systems and features with other languages which are classed as IE while at the same time it shows systematic differences from each of them within this context of general similarity. There is no objection to concluding that this pattern of correspondences results from continuous evolution of a single IE dialect, unless all Greek dialects share major features which are absent from other IE languages and are not be explained as derived from semantically equivalent features in such languages, and are consequently thought to be the results of prehistoric contact with one or more non-IE languages. It is neither necessary not legitimate to assume that every IE language, as first known or reconstructed from dialects, had evolved by a process of complex ethnic amalgamations and linguistic contact-situations. If comparison of known historical Greek dialects indicates that all of them developed from a 'Common Greek' which was still essentially homogeneous as late, say, as *c.* 1500 B.C., this will not in itself prove that 'Common Greek' came into existence as a result of the amalgamation of previously distinct idioms shortly before that time; nor will it prove that 'Common Greek' was by then already in use in what was later Greek territory. The only conclusions from internal linguistic evidence which will be valid are that a single essentially homogeneous idiom was immediately ancestral to the known Greek dialects and, possibly, that it was in existence by a certain time in late prehistory. Deductions about *where* it was spoken will come from reconstruction of the history of populations who may be assumed to have spoken it, or, perhaps, from phenomena that indicate linguistic contact with known or reconstructed languages which can be assigned convincingly to defined areas.

If all this is accepted, it follows that a single dialect of IE, which may be termed 'proto-Greek', might well have developed directly into 'Common Greek' through previous 'pre-Greek' phases (see above p. 335) on which substrate and other adstrate influences may have had their effects, but without there having been any major phase of interruption of the process of development, in which a number of IE languages or dialects, or a set of languages both IE and non-IE, influenced each other and 'amalgamated' in the 'Sprachbund' situation (see above p. 334). If so, we may regard the 'formation of the Greek language' as a continuous process which lasted from the time of 'IE unity' into the historical period, and not just as the late process or set of changes which yielded 'Common Greek' as a final 'pre-Greek' phase; and it is reasonable on grounds of economy of assumption to envisage the prehistory of Greek in this way, unless particular features reconstructed for 'Common Greek' indicate for it major differences from what is to be reconstructed for IE on the basis of IE languages and groups other than Greek. In fact, the close similarities between Greek and Indic and Iranian in morphology, and between Greek and Latin in phonology, suggest that it had evolved with relatively little change from IE, or at least from a late phase of IE (Crossland, p. 9; 1967: 46).

Deductions about 'pre-Greek' have to be made in the context of IE comparative linguistics as a whole. It remains to consider what has been contributed by papers published in this volume to Greek dialectology in the strict sense; i.e. to the reconstruction of 'Common Greek' and the course and chronology of its development into known Greek dialects.

We thank Professor N. E. Collinge, first, for a notable discussion of the sub-grouping of the Greek dialects; i.e. of the question whether, in the first place, those of the Classical period may be shown to have developed from a smaller number of well defined and reconstructed 'primary dialects' of 'Common Greek', and if so how these are to be defined (the dialectal position of 'Mycenaean' presents the further problem of a chronological gap). Collinge's study is an attempt to move on from the important conclusions of R. G. G. Coleman (1963: 105–26) and J. B. Hainsworth (1967: 62–3, 76), which rightly stress the uncertainty of many long accepted ideas, and to exploit findings and methods arrived at in recent dialectological study of modern languages in order to arrive at new positive conclusions. Coleman has shown that isoglossic statement of the similarities and differences between Classical Greek dialects points to a much more complex process of differentiation than is implied by the long-accepted system of Doric-West Greek,

Aeolic, Ionic and Arcado-Cyprian groups. Hainsworth suggests that the Greeks' own recognition of Aeolic, Doric and Ionic groups has little value as evidence. Collinge's paper is to be welcomed as notable experimental application of new methods of classification to the ancient Greek dialects. It offers a fair hope that a pattern of sub-groups may be set up for them which may be accepted as soundly based according to the latest theories about dialect development, in spite of the forbidding difficulties of applying them to material in 'dead' languages (Coleman 1964: 58–59; Collinge, pp. 294, 296). The linguist will note in particular his emphasis on the importance of non-occurrence of features as a criterion of dialectal difference, and his cautious judgment on the value of transformational analysis in establishing the chronology of linguistic changes and stages in differentiation (pp. 296, 302). It is interesting that his re-examination of data which have been re-garded as particularly significant criteria in past studies leads him to set up provisionally Aeolic, West Greek, 'Achaean'/Arcado-Cyprian and Ionic groups, though the suggested pattern of late prehistoric contacts be-tween those who spoke the assumed 'proto-dialects' differs from what has generally been assumed (see below p. 341).

Altogether, 'traditional' views about the grouping of the Greek dialects stood up with some success to the vigorous and technically efficient re-investigation to which they were subjected, however much opinions differed about the earlier history of the Greek language (or whatever one prefers to call the process which resulted in 'Common Greek'). All linguist contri-butors appear to agree that 'Common Greek' was at the least already differentiated into a northern 'proto-Doric-West Greek' group of dialects and a southern by the late Mycenaean period. The questions at issue are whether a third, 'proto-Aeolic' dialect or group should also be set up for the same period; and whether the assumed southern dialect or group, whether it included a 'proto-Aeolic' sub-group or not, was by then differentiated in the Peloponnese and Attica and adjacent areas into 'proto-Ionic' and one or more Peloponnese sub-dialects or not. V. I. Georgiev concludes that dis-tinct 'proto-Ionic' and 'proto-Aeolic' dialects should be postulated for the MBA, and that the long held view that there were three major move-ments of Greek-speaking peoples southward into the Peloponnese is valid (Georgiev, pp. 248, 252; *contra*, Chadwick, pp. 254–5). Professor A. Bartoněk argues strongly and effectively for an incipient differentiation of 'northern' and 'southern' dialects or groups by the LBA, but is cautious about further significant differentiation by that time (pp 307–8, 310). His first conclusion is important for the prehistorian to the extent that linguistic evidence suggests that the populations of the northern and north-western parts of Greece (those to the north and west of Thessaly) and those of its central region and the Peloponnese may well have differed in culture in the LBA and have felt themselves ethnically distinct, even though speaking essentially the same language. This makes the idea of a 'Dorian migration' plausible, whatever its importance and exact nature are thought to have been.

Parenthetically, it may be useful to note the need for greater precision in the use and understanding of the terms 'Mycenaean' and 'Achaean' when used in a linguistic sense. When employed as a linguistic term, 'Mycenaean' will best be used only of the language which is known from the total available corpus of Linear B texts in Greek. At present this means the Greek of three Bronze Age centres, Mycenae, Epano-Englianos-Pylos and Knossos, a form of Greek with little or no apparent variation. Unless and until tablets are found from centres in additional areas, it will be potentially misleading to refer to the Greek which is thought to have been spoken in any such area in the LBA as 'Mycenaean', with the implication that it may be assumed to have been essentially the same as that of the known Linear B texts. Neither should it be assumed that all settlements which developed a Mycenaean culture necessarily spoke the dialect of Greek known from LBA Mycenae, Pylos and Knossos, or even used it as a 'koine' beside their own vernaculars.

'Achaean' is also a term which may cause confusion if used in a linguistic sense. According to normal linguistic practice, it ought only to be used either (a) of the dialect of a population of an area or areas known to have been called 'Achaean' (*Akhaia*, etc.) at a time in question; or (b) of the dialect of a people or group who may be distinguished and defined as 'Achaean' by philological and linguistic evidence even though they have not been located geographically. (If we could define Homer's *Akhaioi* in this latter way and attribute a particular dialect known from documents to them, it would be legitimate to call this 'Achaean'.) As things stand, it seems best not to use 'Achaean' as a linguistic term, except as applied to the Classical dialect of Peloponnesian Achaea.

It is encouraging that Bartoněk's main conclusions can apparently be reconciled without difficulty with Collinge's new provisional scheme of Greek dialect-groups. As presented in diagram (p. 303, Fig. 28.5) this may seem not to correspond to the views about the relative spatial positioning of the main groups in the LBA which have been common recently. These might however be left essentially undisturbed if the diagram were rotated 180° on its north-south axis, which would not seem to invalidate it as a statement of isoglossic correspondence between the four groups that Collinge set up (Fig. 31.1). If so, one might suggest as a possible reconstruction, assuming that the correspondences did not result to any considerable extent from post-Mycenaean contact, that in the LBA 'West Greek' was spoken in areas west and north of Thessaly; 'Aeolic' in Thessaly, 'Ionic' mainly in Boeotia, with later extension to Attica, breaking the contact between 'Aeolic' and 'Arcado-Cyprian' (Fig. 31.1; B). 'Aeolic', 'Ionic' and 'Achaean'

A.			B.	
PROTO- AEOLIC	PROTO- WEST GREEK		PROTO- WEST GREEK	PROTO- AEOLIC
PROTO- ARCADO- CYPRIAN ('ACHAEAN')	PROTO- IONIC		PROTO- IONIC	PROTO- ARCADO -CYPRIAN ('ACHAEAN')

Fig. 31.1. Diagram of alternative suggested relative spatial positions of groups of Greek dialects at the end of the second millennium B.C.

(including 'Arcado-Cyprian') could have formed a continuum, which would have corresponded closely to the region of Mycenaean civilization on the Greek mainland and the cultural contact and exchange which it involved.

Alternatively, assuming that four incipiently differentiated dialects were in existence in the LBA, and that they had the relative spatial distribution that Collinge's diagram suggests, one might explain the relative positions of the Aeolic, Ionic and Arcado-Cyprian groups at the beginning of the Classical period by postulating an eastward movement of Aeolic-speakers which had separated Ionic-speakers from Greeks who spoke West Greek-Doric dialects (Fig. 31.1; A). However the view of Risch and Chadwick that Ionic developed, at least as a well differentiated dialect, only after movements of Greek-speaking peoples in the twelfth to tenth centuries will also explain the similarities between Doric and West Greek dialects and

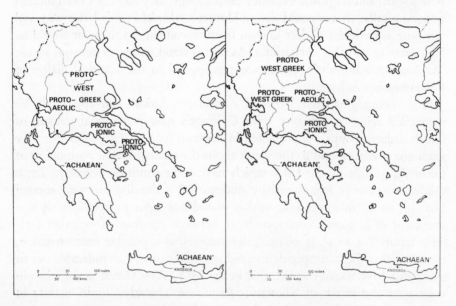

Fig. 31.2. Greece, with alternative suggested positions of groups of Greek dialects at the end of the second millennium B.C.

Ionic adequately in themselves. If Aeolic migration from Thessaly to the Peloponnese, within a South Greek dialect region, before *c.* 1400 or *c.* 1250 B.C. (according to the dating adopted for the Knossos Linear B tablets; see Crossland 1967: 18, fn. 2) were assumed, it would certainly explain Aeolic–Mycenaean–Arcado–Cyprian similarities, within Collinge's scheme.

Conclusions, problems and prospects

It remains to summarize the conclusions which appeared to be generally agreed among members of the Colloquium and to suggest what may be the more important problems in Aegean prehistory in the near future.

1. There seemed to be broad agreement about how and when Greek differentiated into its known dialects, in spite of the fact that the reconstruction of its differentiation involves the important general question of 'subgrouping' (Collinge, pp. 293–5) and although there is much difference of opinion about the earlier history of 'pre-Greek' (see above, pp. 338–9). The consensus of opinion was clearly that 'Common Greek' began to differentiate into the historical Greek dialect-groups relatively late, certainly after *c.* 2000 B.C. and probably later; and that this process began within Greece, at least if the area so referred to is defined broadly. This implies that 'Common Greek' was introduced into 'Greek territory' as a unitary language (see above, p. 334), or alternatively that it developed into one within 'Greek territory' as a result of amalgamation of previously distinct languages and subsequently differentiated into dialects within it. The question whether 'Greek territory' is understood in this connection to include classical Macedonia or western Thrace needs to be considered. No contributor seems to have accepted that a form of Luwian was current in Greece before Greek came into use there, and influenced Greek.

Regardless of different opinions about the deductions that may reasonably be made from onomastic evidence, it is clear that more precise and agreed identification of 'substrata' in Greek or of the effects of other possible prehistoric adstrate influence on it would be valuable. Identification of such linguistic strata or effects is desirable even if linguistic events that they reflect can be dated only very approximately, since they may at least have some value as indications of changes that must have occurred in populations or societies in Greece or adjacent areas at some time in the later Neolithic or the Bronze Age.

Agreed reconstruction of the pattern of the earlier dialectal differentiation of Indo-European itself would naturally be an important advance, as it would indicate the relative spatial position of proto-Greek and other IE dialects and suggest the direction from which pre-Greek was introduced into Greece.

Two general methodological problems became almost trite during discussions: first, the importance of reliable estimation of the duration of linguistic changes, if this can be achieved, which might give absolute chronology for linguistic events; secondly, the need for more understanding of the patterning of correlation between linguistic events, principally change of language in an area and changes within individual languages, and cultural changes, if any general patterns do exist.

2. Some of the important new conclusions suggested by archaeological discoveries and research which were reported do not involve major questions of method in the handling and interpretation of evidence. It seems clear that there were radical cultural changes in Greece at certain times in the Late Neolithic (Evans, pp. 19, 21–3) and that some of them must have been the result of immigration and changes in populations. Evidence was cited for movements into Greece from the Balkans at several times during the Bronze Age also, in particular in the final phases of the EBA (Evans, p. 22; Howell, p. 94); from EH II to MH (Hammond, p. 191); and at the end of the LBA (Hammond, pp. 193–4). On the other hand, some contributors emphasized the general cultural continuity within Greece itself from the beginning of the Middle Helladic to the Late Bronze Age and even into the early Iron Age (Marinatos, pp. 108–10, 112–13). In general, the appearance of Minyan ware in Greece is not now considered to indicate the arrival of a new element in the population early in the second millennium (see above, pp. 325–6).

These conclusions and tendencies do however leave a number of question, requiring an answer. First, the significance of the changes in material cultures particularly in pottery styles, which occurred in Greece c. 2300–1800 B.C. now needs to be determined. Secondly, a new, alternative explanation of the development of Minyan wares and of the increase of the use of them in Greece c. 1900 B.C. is required. In this context, it still seems worth while asking whether southern Thrace (present East Macedonia) should now be considered to have been adequately explored for sites of any kind that may be assigned to a Middle Bronze Age there. D. H. French's article suggests that it may not have been (French, p. 52). The reported association of the appearance of Minyan ware with destructions in central Greece and parts of the Peloponnese needs to be re-investigated.

3. The potential scope of the Colloquium was wide, and so it was natural that some papers raised a question or presented evidence which was not discussed so extensively as the topics which have just been mentioned. The question of contact between Anatolia and the Aegean region is one case in point. Professor Houwink ten Cate has contributed an invaluable presentation and assessment of documentary evidence for the Hittites' activities in western Anatolia c. 1450–1200 B.C. and for possible contacts between them and 'Mycenaeans' (whether these were Greeks as is now generally believed or not). Contact between Anatolia and the Aegean region and Greece and its cultural consequences in the Bronze Age would however repay further study which took in additional aspects. It would be useful if future meetings

set the archaeological evidence for contact across the Aegean in the LBA beside the philological; and the collapse of the Hittite state and its civilization in Anatolia needs to be studied in a broader context which would include events in Greece *c.* 1250–1200 B.C. and the attacks of the 'Sea Peoples' on Egypt. Consideration of cultural changes in Greece *c.* 1400 and *c.* 1250–1100 B.C. will be essential to such a study, and also the question whether much of Greece, or at least the Peloponnese, was evacuated and largely depopulated at the end of the LBA.

4. To turn to earlier periods again, clarification of the wider question of the 'Kurgan' cultures and how far they were spread by migrations would provide a context within which conclusions that northerners or northern cultural features arrived in Greece in the third millennium or at the beginning of the second could be assessed more effectively, and it should give a better chance of determining between V. I. Georgiev's theory about the area of origin of Indo-European movements and that of Marija Gimbutas. However, if we attempt to identify as 'Indo-European' populations or communities as early as *c.* 3000 B.C., we come up against a serious problem of method. The concept of an 'Indo-European language' has a linguistic basis, deductions from linguistic comparison; and different deductions are current about the length of time during which 'Indo-European' must have developed as a unitary language (see above, p. 334) before its dialectal differentiation began, and then the process of dispersal of IE languages which we may reasonably assume for the later centuries of the third millennium and the beginning of the second. It seems reasonable to assume that 'Indo-European' was in existence during the first half of the third millennium, and it may well have had a long history of uninterrupted development as a language before *c.* 3000 B.C. But the possibility that it was formed as the result of admixture or mutual influencing of distinct languages shortly before that time can hardly be excluded, even though no evidence actually indicates that such a development took place (see above, p. 334). Consequently, it would seem best not to refer to any population that is distinguished on archaeological grounds before *c.* 3000 B.C. as 'Indo-European', since one cannot deduce with more than strong probability at the best that it spoke 'Indo-European' (the prehistoric language which may be reconstructed in its main lines by linguistic comparison) at some stage of its evolution, or a derivative language. Even if we think that we can identify archaeologically the people who spoke Indo-European shortly before its first identifiable dispersion, towards the end of the third millennium, and that we can show that this people had been an ethnic entity with a continuous cultural tradition for some centuries before that time, it will still be best to refer to it in the earlier stages of its existence by a name based on the archaeological evidence for it, such as 'Kurgan', rather than by 'Indo-European' or even 'proto-Indo-European'. In the next few years a certain self-discipline in terminology, definition and statement

of concepts may be a particularly important requirement in study of the late prehistory of the Aegean and adjacent regions.

References

BRANIGAN, K. 1970. *The Foundations of Palatial Crete*. London.

BYNON, T. AND BYNON, J. 1970. *Proceedings of the Colloquium on Hamito-Semitic Comparative Linguistics, 1970*. (School of Oriental and African Studies, University of London; in press.)

CASKEY, J. L. 1960. 'The Early Helladic period in the Argolid.' *Hesperia*, 29: 288–303.

——. 1964. 'Greece, Crete and the Aegean Islands in the Early Bronze Age.' *CAH* (rev. ed.) I, Chap. XXVIa/Fasc. 24.

——. 1966. 'Greece and the Aegean Islands in the Middle Bronze Age.' *CAH* (rev. ed.) II, Chap. IVa/Fasc. 45.

COLEMAN, R. G. G. 1963. 'The dialect geography of ancient Greece.' *TPhS*, 1963: 58–126.

CROSSLAND, R. A. 1957. 'Indo-European origins: the linguistic evidence.' *Past and Present* 12: 16–46, 13: 88.

——. 1967. 'Immigrants from the North.' *CAH* (rev. ed.) I, Chap. XXVII Fasc. 60.

——. 1971. 'The position in the Indo-European language-family of Thracian, and Phrygian and their possible close cognates.' *Plovdiv Symposium* (1969): 225–36.

FRIEDRICH, J. 1932. *Kleinasiatische Sprachdenkmäler*. Berlin.

GEORGIEV, V. I. 'L'ethnogénèse des peuples balkaniques: confrontation d'opinions.' *Plovdiv Symposium* (1969): 331–3.

GIMBUTAS, M. 1970. 'Proto-Indo-European culture: the Kurgan culture during the fifth, fourth and third millennia.' *Indo-European and Indo-Europeans*: 158–79.

GUARDUCCI, M. 1942. *Inscriptiones Creticae opera et consilio Friderici Halbherr collectae*. III. Rome.

HAINSWORTH J. B. 1967. 'Greek views of Greek dialectology.' *TPhS*, 1967: 62–76.

HALEY, J. B. AND BLEGEN, C. W. 1928. 'The coming of the Greeks.' *AJA*, 32: 141–54.

HOENIGSWALD, H. M. 1966. 'Criteria for the subgrouping of languages.' In H. Birnbaum and J. Puhvel, *Ancient Indo-European Dialects* (Berkeley and Los Angeles).

HAMPL, F. 1960. 'Die Chronologie der Einwanderung der griechischen Stämme und das Problem der Nationalität der Träger der mykenischen Kultur.' *MH*, 17: 57–86.

MARINATOS, S. 1958. 'Grammaton didaskalia.' *Minoica: Festschrift zum 80. Geburtstag von Johannes Sundwall* (ed. E. Grumach; Berlin, 1958): 226–31.

——. 1968. 'Mycenaean culture within the frame of Mediterranean anthropology and archaeology.' *AttiICIM* (I): 227–94.

——. 1970a. 'From the silent earth.' *AthAA*, 3: 61–8.

——. 1970b. 'Further news from Marathon.' *AthAA*, 3: 153–66.

MELLAART, J. 1958. 'The end of the Early Bronze Age in Anatolia and the Aegean.' *AJA*, 62: 9–33.

——. 1964. 'Anatolia before *c.* 4000 B.C. and *c.* 2300–1750 B.C.' *CAH* (rev. ed.) I, Chap. VII, XI–XIV and XXIV, I–VI/Fasc. 20.

——. 1969. Review of R. A. Crossland, *Immigrants from the North. JHS*, 89: 172–3.

MILLER, J. 1909. 'Eteokretes.' *RE*, VI: 709–10.

PALMER, L. R. 1958. 'Luvian and Linear A.' *TPhS*, 1958: 75–100.

——. 1961. *Mycenaeans and Minoans*. London.

PISANI, V. 1949. 'La question de l'indo-hittite et le concept de parenté linguistique.' *AO*, 17: 251–64.

POPE, M. W. M. 1964. 'Aegean writing and Linear A.' *Studies in Mediterranean Archaeology*, 8.

POPHAM, M. R. AND SACKETT, L. H. 1968. *Excavations at Lefkandhi, Euboea*, 1964–66. London.

RABIN, C. 1970. 'Lexicostatistics and the internal divisions of Semitic.' In T. and J. Bynon (eds.), *Proceedings of the Colloquium on Hamito-Semitic Comparative Linguistics* (London).

SCHACHERMEYR, F. 1968. 'Zum Problem der griechischen Einwanderung.' *AttiICIM*(I): 297–312.

THIEME, P. 1953. *Die Heimat der indogermanischen Gemeinsprache* (*Abh. Geistes- und Sozialwissenschaftlichen Klasse, Akad. der Wiss. und der Literatur*, 11).

TRUBETZKOY, N. S. 1939. 'Gedanken über das Indogermanenproblem.' *Acta Linguistica*, 1: 81–9.

VAN EFFENTERRE, H. 1946a. 'Inscriptions archaïques crétoises.' *BCH*, 1946: 588–606.

——. 1946b. 'Une bilingue crétoise.' *RPh*, 1946: 131–8.

WEINBERG, S. 1954. 'The relative chronology of the Aegean in the Neolithic period and Early Bronze Age.' In R. W. Ehrich (ed.), *Relative Chronologies in Old World Archaeology* (Chicago): 86–107.